Christ The Guru

Christ the Guru

A Vedāntic Key to the Gospels

by

Muni Narayana Prasad

PRINTWORLD

Publishers of Indian Traditions

Cataloging in Publication Data – DK
[Courtesy: D.K. Agencies (P) Ltd. <docinfo@dkagencies.com>]

Narayana Prasad, *Muni,* 1938-
Christ the guru: a Vedāntic key to the Gospels /
by Muni Narayana Prasad.
p. cm.
ISBN: 9788124607503

1. Bible. Gospels – Commentaries. 2. Vedanta. 3. Christianity and other religions. 4. Hinduism – Relations – Christianity. 1. Title

DDC 226 23

ISBN 13: 978-81-246-0750-3
First published in India in 2014

Printed and published by:
D.K. Printworld (P) Ltd.
Regd. Office : *Vedaśrī*, F-395, Sudarshan Park
(Metro Station: Ramesh Nagar), New Delhi - 110 015
Phones : (011) 2545 3975; 2546 6019; *Fax* : (011) 2546 5926
e-mail : indology@dkprintworld.com
Web : www.dkprintworld.com

Preface

It was during childhood that I first became acquainted with the life and ideals of the great modern sage Narayana Guru. By then he was a well-renowned philosopher-poet and social reformer of Kerala (India), my own native place. The Guru wrote his great poems of Advaita Vedānta in classical philosophical language, while his social ideals and activities were unmistakably modern in form. Yet all his diverse activities were firmly grounded in an absolutist vision of Reality. As I grew up, this auspicious familiarity with the modern sage of south India itself kindled a passion within me to study the man and his messages more intimately. Not only that, but the Tao itself seemed to be calling me to live the life of a spiritual aspirant. Then, as if by grace, the chance elements in life conspired to make me a disciple of Nataraja Guru, one of the disciples and wisdom successor of Narayana Guru. It was as a disciple of Nataraja Guru that I was guided into an understanding of the Vedānta philosophy, especially as represented by Narayana Guru.

Even as a fledgling seeker, I had become familiar with the Gospels of Christ and found them to be deeply stirring. But the ocean of philosophical insight hiding within the words and story of Jesus only became accessible to me after I had gone into the depths of Vedānta, especially under the guidance of Nataraja Guru. What was eventually needed then was the opportune time to make such a study. Later in life, the chance finally arose to plumb the depths of wisdom in the Gospels. This happened when our Gurukula began discussing the Gospels during our night classes. We decided to study and appreciate every word of Jesus in the four gospels of the Bible — Matthew, Mark, Luke and John — and also that of Thomas, one of the apocryphal gospels. The current book is the net result of that enjoyment.

My hope is that this attempt at a Gospel commentary in the light of Advaita Vedānta will be found by those who are willing to believe with an open mind in the comparative study of religions, being sure that religion is for man, and not man for religion, that is to say, those seekers of truth who are willing to look beyond the superficial differences of our spiritual traditions until they find the core, unitive principles. Those of such an attitude will undoubtedly become convinced that the essential content of all religions is one. Indeed, it is such persons who will become the true guides for our modern society, which has otherwise already shrunk into a single global village. Such is the aspiration with which this appreciation of the Gospels is presented.

I remember with gratitude all the Gurukula inmates and friends who participated in the long discussions that preceded the writing of our comments here about the words and deeds of Jesus Christ. It was from our night-time discussions that this book was born. My friend and student Ian Jaco of USA has always been with me to clarify certain background factors unknown to me. He also took much pain to carefully go through the entire text to edit it, making it a more readable book. I feel the whole experience was beneficial to both of us. A long-time associate of the Gurukula Dr Peter Oppenheimer of the US also spent a good deal of energy scrutinizing the text, making it ready for publication.

D.K. Printworld has always been willing to publish serious books on spirituality related to the Indian culture. Their service to the cause of wisdom is commendable. By the grace of the Tao all these factors have come together to bring about the publication of this book.

Narayana Gurukula *Muni Narayana Prasad*
Varkala, India
2 March 2014

Contents

Part II
The Gospel According to Mark

Part III
The Gospel According to Luke

Part V
The Gospel of Thomas

Introduction

Of one kind, of one faith, of one God is man.

THIS is the most well-known adage of Narayana Guru. As a great axiom, it touches the Guru's sublime non-dual vision of Reality on the one side and the actualities of human life on the other. Now the words that refer to mankind as "of one kind" or "of one caste" (*oru jāti*) are really just common sense and even modern science confirms it. Yet even the followers of the Guru doubted this idea. But the Guru leaves no room for a debate; humankind is simply one. Building upon this common sense, unitive principle further, we find another statement given by the Guru in his poem *Ātmopadeśa Śatakam* (One Hundered Verses of Self-Instruction). It reads,

> The essential teachings of the various religions are one alone.
>
> — verse 44

In this verse we see that the religions of mankind are also essentially one. Even among the modern folk today, this idea is a difficult one to accept. But the Guru has an unshakable reason for making this striking claim. As we see a few verses later in this same work, the unitive principle implied in these statements is revealed in a final form. Thus,

> Everyone in every way strives always
> To attain happiness.
> This faith is one in all the worlds.
>
> — verse 49

This last verse reveals that the unity of humanity is made evident by an all-underlying urge — the urge to seek the ultimate limit of happiness. Indeed, not only humans, but all beings hold happiness as the underlying drive behind all their thoughts and deeds. In this sense we can see a universal value implicit in the search for happiness itself.

As humans, we often try to attain happiness by making use of our unique gift, the thinking mind. Indeed, all of humanity's diverse ideologies and active plans are aimed just at securing greater happiness. But if we were to think carefully, what would we consider to be the truest or best kind of happiness? That is to say, is there a happiness available to us that amounts to more than the temporary forms of pleasure and security normally pursued by humanity? Is a true and lasting happiness even obtainable? And if there is, then how may it be attained? In India, the Vedānta philosophy has provided an answer for this age-old search for happiness. It is known simply as *paramānanda* (Supreme Happiness). Although a boon to the whole world, this Supreme Happiness is not a kind of social happiness to be attained by everyone at once, as through some group effort. Surely that cannot be possible, rather, it is a personal gain.

If we hope to personally gain this *paramānanda,* then we must carefully consider the nature of this happiness and how it is to be realized. To appreciate this, it would be prudent to take some guidance from those who have already experienced this supreme happiness. In India, such beacons are known as *ṛṣi*s or as *guru*s. Since ancient times they have indicated that supreme happiness is only to be attained by directly realizing our oneness with the total Existence. That is to say, supreme happiness can occur only when we directly perceive that what is ultimately Real in ourselves is that which is ultimately Real in the whole. To elucidate, we may use a well-known analogy in Vedānta, that of the ocean and the wave. Let us for a moment imagine a wave or endless series of waves upon some great ocean that we once visited. Obviously the apparent existence of any such wave upon the ocean would be but a fleeting one, whereas the existence of the ocean itself would be everlasting. But let us, by a stretch, further imagine that such a wave upon the ocean could perceive its own existence. Were it a wise wave, then it would surely perceive that its own existence was something that really belonged to that of the great ocean. And by such wisdom, it would naturally perceive that all the pleasures and pains of its own evanescent existence would not be things merely happening to itself alone, but would really belong to the creativity and experience of the mighty ocean itself. Now we may compare this great ocean to the absolute Reality itself. And each wave upon that ocean to an individual in this world. Just as the wise wave depicted in the analogy, a human who can perceive his or her own existence extending into the existence of the absolute Reality will in this sense be free of both pain and pleasure. Because, as we will see later, this supreme happiness is the very nature of the absolute Reality. Put otherwise, a wise person would see life's everyday experiences of mundane happiness and suffering as but the various facets of the one value or happiness (*ānanda*) content implicit in what ultimately exists. To peacefully and neutrally perceive this *ānanda* content of the absolute

Reality abiding in our everyday experiences would be the experience of *paramānanda*. When this direct awareness dawns, we will then perceive that all of our own actions form but a part of the actions happening in the one Reality. It is this direct perception that liberates us from what originally made us unhappy; that is, a separate sense of self that bears the burden of its own separate actions. Liberated thus, we will then perceive all of life's highs and lows as the creative self-expression of the one all-underlying Reality, called *Ātman* or *Brahman* in Vedānta. It is this unchanging peace which is the highest attainable happiness for a human. But as a goal, this supreme happiness is to be attained on one's own in the here and the now, and never in the hereafter, of which nothing is yet known or knowable.

When the great religions of the world are carefully studied, it becomes obvious that all seek to teach a living wisdom that brings supreme happiness. Seen in this light, it is easy to understand the Guru's words, "The essential teachings of all the religions are one alone" (*pala mata-sāravum ekam*). All religions then aim to help humanity attain happiness, rendering life in the here and now peaceful. As such, the differences existing between religions would then be understood to belong to what is inessential and not universal. Such differences will naturally arise in accordance with the unique historic, geographic and cultural conditions offered by their respective environments. They may be seen in the differing modes and idioms of language employed by the prophets and seers, or in the nature and traditions of the various peoples to whom they addressed their message. The possibilities for such differences are innumerable, and they may well make sense within their own setting. But all such are of a relative nature, being mostly suitable for specific conditions. Keeping these incidental factors aside, the goal of all religions is one alone — the Happiness of Man. It is in this sense also that we may understand the Guru's word, "Of one faith is man".

If we examine the words of wisdom of Jesus with such a broad outlook, then it becomes apparent that what Jesus revealed is none other than the same wisdom or supreme happiness of the Vedānta philosophy. Externally viewed though, these appear as two traditions, each with its own language and beliefs. In the case of Jesus, the language and style belong to a context familiar to the Semitic or Mediterranean culture. In Advaita Vedānta, the language and style belong to a context of the Indian culture. Now through this book, we will attempt to explain the wisdom found in one cultural frame of reference as found in another. That is to say, we will try to elucidate the teachings of Jesus Christ in terms of the characteristics of Advaita Vedānta.

Jesus, as seen in the Gospels, always maintains his position as an enlightened seer (*ṛṣi*). We may also call this the position of a true *guru.* The word *guru* literally means "dispeller of darkness", and only an enlightened seer would have such an authority to enlighten us about the true nature of our life and its goal. In this sense, we see in Jesus a *sad-guru* (genuine *guru*). It is as a *guru* that Jesus reacts to the life situations he naturally comes across. And it is as a *guru* that Jesus positively teaches his disciples and the general public who follow him.

Now we do not claim this to be the only way in which Jesus's words and life may be interpreted. How a Vedāntin would understand each word and deed of Jesus is alone what we attempt to clarify here. Of course, even among Vedāntins, Jesus may be appreciated in various ways. But here we will attempt to demonstrate how Jesus is a Self-Realized *guru par excellence.* And that the purpose of the Gospels is to enlighten those who intended or still intend to follow him to the heavenly place of wisdom where he resides. Jesus did this especially well when ingeniously reacting to the everyday situations in life that arose. From these gospel accounts, we may perceive in his life and words the same absolutist vision that underlies the teachings of Advaita Vedānta. Indeed, attaining *paramānanda,* the ultimate goal of Vedānta, and the coming of the kingdom, described by Jesus, are not two. The essence of this supreme happiness is expressed in the words of Jesus himself when he declares:

I and the Father are one. – John 10.29

We also do not mean to say that putting the comments of this book together will give an overall picture of the philosophy of Vedānta. That is to be found in the Upaniṣads, *Bhagavad-Gītā* and *Brahma-Sūtras.* In modern times, the same could be seen restated in the philosophical poems of Narayana Guru, as well as in the recorded words of Ramakrishna Paramahansa and Ramaṇa Maharṣi. In the lives and words of these modern Indian sages we also see the same peculiar method of teaching resorted to by Jesus. Some of these works mentioned, like certain Upaniṣads, *Bhagavad-Gītā* and *Brahma-Sūtras,* as well as *Vedānta-Sūtras* and *Darśana-Mālā* of Narayana Guru, are highly systematic in their philosophical presentation. But the Gospels do not form such a systematic philosophical treatise. They are rather a narrated, often deeply symbolic, set of records of Jesus's life and words. In this sense, they are closer in literary form to the narrated records of Ramakrishna Paramahansa and Ramaṇa Maharṣi. Although not making for a systematic treatise *per se,* the narration given in the Gospels does shed a clear light upon how we should perceive life's everyday situations from a non-dualistic perspective, and how we should live accordingly. It is precisely this awareness that holds the promise of supreme happiness. We hope this book will help the sincere seeker better understand the Gospels of Christ as such. Our further hope is that this study will help enable those willing enough to understand that the essential teaching of all religions is the same; and that religion is for man, and not the other way around.

We will restrict our comments to the direct teachings of Jesus as found in the four Gospels according to Matthew, Mark, Luke and John. The text we have followed has been the New King James Version of the Holy Bible published by Indian Bible Literature, Chennai, India. There were also other gospels that did not find a place in the Bible. An important one among such is the Gospel According to Thomas, discovered in 1945. We have decided to include this gospel in the present study because of its potent wisdom content. As this gospel is not very well known, the whole of the text is included along with the usual commentary. The method of interpretation for this book was to examine every parable, teaching and event in Jesus's life separately, appreciating each in light of the Vedānta philosophy. Such examinations are grouped into general subjects and presented as individual chapters. Any parable, teaching or event that had been treated prior is not repeated here. To render a study of this book fruitful, it would be most helpful to have a copy of the New Testament of the Bible opened side by side.

Although we term this book a commentary, it would be better called an appreciation, as no explication can unlock all the mystery in Jesus's words and life. Their real meaning must ultimately be perceived intuitively by the seeker.

Part I
The Gospel According to Matthew

1.1

Jesus: The Son of God

THE birth of Jesus is mysterious. Though his mother was Mary the wife of Joseph, his father was not Joseph, but was God. Yet, the Gospel According to Matthew begins with listing the genealogy of Jesus Christ. It begins with saying,

> Abraham begot Isaac, Isaac begot Jacob. — 1.2

and before ending, it says:

> And Jacob begot Joseph the husband of Mary, of whom was born Jesus who is called Christ. — 1.16

If Jesus is not the son of Joseph, who belongs to the genealogical line proper, why is such a long line listed in the Gospel? No one seems to have taken this question seriously.

Biologically considered, as well as logically so, this is an enigma. But, seen from the Vedāntic perspective, it is fully meaningful. Jesus always refers to himself as "the son of man," whereas he is treated by others as "the Son of God." This is an enigma, just as is his genealogy. An enigma is a phenomenon that cannot be logically understood. The birth of Jesus and his genealogy are not the only enigmatic phenomena. The phenomenon of birth and death, the phenomenon of life as a whole, and the apparent world itself are all enigmatic. Where do all these enigmatic phenomena arise from and how? All arise from one ultimate Reality, because of Its own mysterious creative urge, conveniently named *māyā* by Vedāntins. Vedāntins call this Reality *Brahman* or *Ātman,* and religious-minded people call it God. This world is the sum total of all the apparent forms that constantly emerge from and remerge in the very same Reality. Of such countless apparent forms, a human being is one. Jesus too, being such a human being, is an enigmatic phenomenon that appeared in the one Reality or God. He is thus the Son of God, as is a wave a child of ocean.

Though each of us, in this sense, is a son or daughter of God, we live completely oblivious of this truth. For this reason, though we all are really the children of God, in effect we are not so. The case of Jesus is different. He is fully enlightened about being the Son of God.

Revealing to the world that everyone is so, and thus enabling them to reach heaven, the abode of God, was the mission of Jesus. Those who undertake this mission, upon becoming enlightened of being the sons or daughters of God, are called *guru*s. Jesus, thus, was an ideal *guru*. Just as a wave experiences its inseparable oneness with the ocean, a *guru* constantly experiences with full awareness his or her identity with God or *Brahman*. It is this enlightenment that makes a *guru,* the son or daughter of God. Jesus, thus was a Son of God. As the child begotten by Mary, he was the son of man.

Believers consider Jesus as equal to God. Vedāntins also admit that a *Brahman*-knowing *guru* is *Brahman* Itself. Whether called *Brahman* or God, the ultimate Reality is abstract and unmanifest. Such an abstract Reality can never appear among ignorant humans to teach them wisdom or to lead them to the kingdom of God. For doing so, that abstract Reality has to assume the form of a concrete or manifest person and appear among the ignorant as a living *guru*. That means, God has to appear as a son of man. Jesus was such a *guru*. He being so, in principle, is not to be seen by relating him with a biological genealogy, but by relating him with God (*Brahman*). This is the reason why the birth of Jesus, celebrated as Christmas, continues to be an event that exhilarates humans everywhere and will continue to be so forever.

1.2

The Continuator of a Tradition

St Matthew states clearly that events such as the birth of Jesus in Bethlehem; Joseph and Mary, carrying the little child Jesus, and travelling to Egypt; and John the Baptist becoming the harbinger of Jesus, all happened in order to fulfil the words of the bygone prophets. Similar were the events of John baptizing Jesus, the heavens opening before him, the Spirit of God descending like a dove and alighting upon him, and Jesus thus becoming an enlightened *jñānin* (man of wisdom). All these show that Jesus was a continuator of an already existing ancient tradition and yet we also learn how Jesus revised or revaluated many of the traditional belief patterns and concepts.

John the Baptist also belonged to the same tradition, yet he was fully aware of how great the one to follow him was. As Jesus came to Galilee to be baptized by John, he asked Jesus:

> I have need to be baptized by you, and are you coming to me?
>
> — 3.14

John, in terms of his relative clarity of wisdom, was of a quality suitable only to become a disciple of Jesus. But from the point of view of tradition, Jesus has to be necessarily baptized by John and not the other way round respecting the tradition thus, Jesus responded:

> Permit me to be so now, for thus it is fitting for us to fulfil all righteousnesses. — 3.15

It is without disregarding the tradition, but as a continuator of it, that Jesus dares to correct many of the traditional beliefs, behaviour patterns and concepts that had already become almost lifeless, and to revisualize them in the light of the new lively wisdom he attained. Jesus gained the boldness to effect this revisualization of Truth only after being baptized by John and the heavens opened before him and the Spirit of God descended like a dove that alighted upon him. That means, Jesus's attainment of the status of a perfect *jñānin* happened after John became his *guru* at least for the sake of formality which tradition acknowledges.

Two aspects are to be seen implied in Jesus's attainment of wisdom. One is, that the heavens opened before him. The word "heaven" in the Gospels is to be understood as an equivalent to the pure wisdom (*jñāna*) in Vedānta. The first aspect, thus, means the inner secrets of wisdom became revealed to Jesus. The word "God" in the Biblical context is similarly to be understood as equal to the *Brahman* (the Absolute) of Vedānta. Therefore, the Spirit of God descending on Jesus, the other aspect, is to be taken to mean his realization that what is real in him is also the real content of that which ultimately exists, and the dove that alights on him represents the plenitude of the unconditioned and ultimate Peace one feels upon attaining this realization. Jesus thus became a perfect *guru* and it was well acknowledged by John when he saw the Spirit of God descending upon him. In recognition came the words of God:

> This is my beloved son, in whom I am well pleased. — 3.17

It is a well-recognized notion that all the *guru*s and prophets have the blessings of God (*Brahman*). No one can become a *guru* by one's own capability or wilful effort.

1.3

Satan Tempts Jesus

As we study closely the lives of great *gurus* and prophets, we notice a certain stage of penance and spiritual agony in which each had to undergo severe tests to prove their worth, determination and dedication. In the East, such tests are mostly meant to prove one's ability to withstand the temptations of Eros (*māra*) and worldly values. In the Semitic religions it is referred to as the temptations and tricks of Satan. In the Upaniṣads too we see disciples facing severe tests, for example, Naciketas of the *Kaṭha Upaniṣad* and Indra and Virocana of the *Chāndogya Upaniṣad.* It could well be said such occasions in their lives are initiated by God (*Brahman*) Itself.

Jesus was no exception in this respect. At one point he fasted for forty days and nights. It is when extremely hungry that people often give in to temptation. Jesus was in such a state when Satan approached him with a test. It is underscored that he "was led by the Spirit into the wilderness to be tempted by the devil" (4.1). The tempting words of Satan "If you are the Son of God, command that these stones become bread" (4.3) are to be understood as related to the hunger Jesus was feeling then. It is not in his own words, but by quoting the words of the holy scripture, that he faces the temptations of the devil. He says:

> It is written, man shall not live by bread alone, but by every word that proceeds from the mouth of God. — 4.4

Bread or ordinary food, ensures only the bodily well-being of man. But human life is made meaningful by the wisdom man acquires. The ultimate limit of this wisdom is found in the words of God or of *gurus*. For those who feel fully satisfied in life by having enough to eat, wisdom and the higher satisfaction it gives, remain not only inaccessible, but even unknown. On the other hand, for those who are fully convinced that wisdom is of the highest value in life, in addition to experiencing the higher satisfaction of emancipation that wisdom ensures, they do not at all have to worry about their bodily needs like food and clothing. Such needs are taken care of by God or the overall system of life.

The next attempt of the devil to tempt Jesus is also in the name of scriptural passages:

> The devil took him into the holy city, set him on the pinnacle of the temple and said to him, "If you are the Son of God, throw yourself down", for it is written, "He shall give his angels charge concerning you" and "In their hands they shall bear you up, lest you dash your foot against a stone". — 4.6

Jesus faces this test also by quoting yet another scriptural utterance when saying:

> It is written again, "You shall not tempt the Lord your God". — 4.7

God or the ultimate Reality is not to be understood by experimenting or testing but by directly experiencing the presence of God as the essential content of one's own being. No one makes tests to prove one's own existence. God, the all-underlying Reality, is what underlies one's own being also. All the events in life, including that of throwing oneself down from the temple-top, happen or are meant to happen as willed by God, and not as decided by any individual being. An individual, of his own volition, testing such possibilities and capabilities, is in effect testing the capabilities of God.

Again the devil took him up on an exceedingly high mountain, and showed him all the kingdoms of the world and their glory. And he said to him:

> All these things will be given you if you will fall down and worship me. — 4.9

Jesus retorted by quoting another scriptural passage thus:

> Away with you Satan! For it is written, "You shall worship the Lord your God, and Him only you shall serve". — 4.10

Then the devil left him and angels came and ministered to him.

Which value should man strive to attain as of the highest, the abundance of worldly wealth and the comforts of life they afford, or wisdom and the sense of freedom it assures? All the former types of values together, in India, are known as *preyas*, and the latter *śreyas*. Jesus's temptation is very similar to a scene in *Kaṭha Upaniṣad*. There, Yama, the *guru* himself, offers to Naciketas all the pleasures of a royal life, rulership of a large country and many such attractions, and then tells him, "Accept all these, but do not ask this question" (the question was about death and the after life). But Naciketas did not give in. He said, "Let all these be yours, I need only my question answered." Finally Yama had to give in. Only then Yama says, "When *preyas* and *śreyas* were offering themselves before you, you accepted *śreyas* alone. *Guru*s like me are on the look out for disciples like you." And pleased with him, Yama presented Naciketas with a gem-garland that he was wearing himself. The message in the biblical passage, "You shall worship the Lord your God, and him only you will serve" is the same Upaniṣadic call to value *śreyas* over *preyas*.

Though Satan thus tested Jesus by evoking his interests in values ranging from those of a day-to-day character to the noblest one of higher wisdom, he could not be defeated. Ultimately Satan himself was defeated, and had to withdraw. Jesus accomplished this, not by making use of his own abilities and methods, but simply by quoting relevant passages from existing scriptures.

1.4

Jesus Begins to Teach

THOUGH Jesus attained enlightenment in the presence of John the Baptist, the former began to preach only after he heard of the imprisonment of the latter (4.12). This also indicates, as was shown earlier, that the teachings of Jesus were a continuation of an already existing tradition.

His first preaching was:

> Repent, for the kingdom of heaven is at hand. — 4.17

The kingdom of heaven, in the wisdom context, is to be understood as the boundless domain of unconditioned effulgence experience. *Chāndogya Upaniṣad* calls it *svarājya* (the kingdom of the self or one's own real domain). Only upon experientially perceiving this domain one realizes, "I was living completely in ignorance till this moment." One then naturally repents the ignorance one was in so far.

The first two disciples of Jesus were Simon, called Peter, and his brother Andrew. Jesus first met them casting a net into the sea, for they were fishermen (4.18). Jesus told them:

> Follow me, and I will make you fishers of men. — 4.19

They immediately left their nets and followed him (4.20).

Casting nets in the sea is done by men merely to fulfil their basic bodily need of getting food to eat. Such men have their own value notion, but it is confined to the domain of basic physical needs. Sublimating this value concept in order to lead one to the higher levels of wisdom is possible with the guidance of a *guru.* Men of this attainment naturally attract people towards them.

To live interested in seeking food alone and begetting offspring belong to the level of animal instincts. Competition and fighting are also but natural in that value world. When the same men are elevated to the realm of higher wisdom, that wisdom itself makes them friendly. The ultimate limit of such a wisdom is to find one's own inseparable oneness with what ultimately exists. This sense of identity with the total, in actual life, finds expression as the love for everyone, and this unconditional love attracts everyone towards such a person. He thus becomes a fisher of men.

Peter and Andrew, when asked by Jesus, followed him with no hesitation leaving behind their net. The indication is that, attaining wisdom is accomplished only by those who are willing to disregard their livelihood and ordinary worldly interests, just to follow a genuine *guru* (*sad-guru*) in search of wisdom.

1.5

Miracles

THOUGH Jesus went about all Galilee teaching in their synagogues, preaching the gospel of the kingdom, his fame arose throughout Syria mainly as a healer. People brought to him many sick people who were afflicted with various diseases and torments, and those who were demon-possessed, epileptic and paralytic. He healed them. It was this miraculous healing power, rather than what he taught, that attracted ordinary people towards him and inspired multitudes to follow him (4.23-25).

Jesus really was a *guru* who came to this world with the sole mission of leading people to the higher realms of wisdom or to bring down the kingdom of God to this world. But this wisdom-teaching, as we will soon see, and as we do see in the present society, is not appreciated by ordinary people. They easily become attracted by the miraculous healing of their bodily diseases. But the miraculous actions of Jesus are not limited to the domain of such bodily healings alone. The miracle of highest value really is none other than revealing the wisdom secret or the kingdom of God. Viewed thus, the miraculous activities we witness in the life of Jesus could well be seen to represent a graded order of values. Healing diseases and turning water into wine are all miracles that belong to the value world of physical existence. If such miracles are considered as of the lowest order, then at the highest rung is to be seen the greatest miracle of revealing the kingdom of God in a fresh and easily understandable way.

The miracles of the lower grade alone attracted the general public to Jesus. The same trend of attraction continues even now. On the other hand, only a handful of disciples were around him to listen when he performed the miracle of revealing the kingdom of God. Even they were seen struggling to imbibe it.

How could Jesus perform all the miracles described in the Gospels? The entire world, in fact, is a great mystery. The one who knows its secret is also a mystery. Many things such a person does in the normal course of his or her life are seen by those ignorant of that secret as miracles. Jesus's miracles could be viewed in this way.

The miracles could also be seen from another, slightly different, point of view. A *jñānin* (man of wisdom) lives in a higher realm that is his own. Whatever happens in that realm, whatever he does, is quite ordinary and natural for him. But what is ordinary and natural in a *jñānin*'s life is seen by the ignorant as quite unworldly and uncommon and so is treated as a miracle. A *jñānin,* thus, performs no miracle, but an *ajñānin* (an ignorant person) perceives miracles in a *jñānin*'s life.

We come across such miracles all through the life of Jesus. Once when the multitude, attracted by such miracles, gathered around him, he simply walked to the top of a mountain, symbolic of his desire to lead those people to higher wisdom. Mounting a hill is not an easy task. Wisdom is also to be attained only by those who are willing to face and surmount difficulties without complaint, a quality known in India as *titikṣā*. As Jesus reached the top of the mountain, the disciples came to him (5.1). The indication here is that the multitude could not reach the hilltop. There may be a big crowd willing to honour a great *guru*, but only a few will be there to listen to his precious words of wisdom. Jesus taught his disciples that wisdom.

1.6

Sermon on the Mount

JESUS opened his mouth and taught his disciples thus:

> Blessed are the poor in spirit, for theirs is the kingdom of heaven.
> Blessed are those who mourn, for they shall be comforted.
> Blessed are the meek, for they shall inherit the earth.
> Blessed are those who hunger and thirst for righteousness, for they shall be filled.
> Blessed are the merciful, for they shall obtain mercy.
> Blessed are the pure in heart, for they shall see God.
> Blessed are the peacemakers, for they shall be called sons of God.
> Blessed are those who are persecuted for righteousness's sake, for theirs is the kingdom of heaven.
> Blessed are you when they revile and persecute you, and say all kinds of evil against you falsely for my sake.
> Rejoice and be exceedingly glad, for great is your reward in heaven, for so they persecuted the prophets who were before you.
>
> — 5.3-12

Jesus begins his first wisdom-teaching by listing a long line of the "blessed." The list begins with the "poor in spirit," and ends with those who are persecuted for the sake of their *guru*. Who are the poor in spirit? They are the ignorant (*ajñānin*s). They live knowing nothing about themselves and their lives. But the ignorant sitting before Jesus are of a special category. They have taken refuge in Jesus, a perfect *guru* and *jñānin*. These ignorant disciples are well aware that they are ignorant. Those who are ignorant and know that they are so, are fit for being taught by a *guru*. Jesus thus, in effect, says: "You who are knowingly ignorant and humble are blessed, because you are fit for the kingdom of heaven or for attaining wisdom as taught by me." Many are the types of people who yearn for taking refuge in a *guru* (a holy man). Of them, one type is mentioned here as forming the first group of the "blessed", they are the "poor in spirit." *Bhagavad-Gītā* calls such people *jijñāsu*s (those who are in search of wisdom).

Another type of people are those who mourn or suffer a lot (*ārtta*s). They grieve all through their life; they are in search of solace. The solace they expect is not the one that makes their life devoid of all sufferings. Such a relief will be momentary and conditional. Rather, the relief they can get from a *guru* is derived from knowing the nature of life. No one can predict what will happen and what will not happen in life as part of the overall flow of events in the total nature. Such a chance element, in the religious context, is known as God's will. This conviction is what gives lasting solace to those who suffer, and this solace lasts and is unconditional.

Another set of people who are competent to attain wisdom is called here "the meek." They, in the Vedāntic context, are known to be of *sattva-guṇa* (pure and clear modality of nature). Those of this quality are called *sāttvika*s. Having a pure and clear mind, they naturally turn towards wisdom. Their thirst for wisdom is not motivated by any particular end in view; the desire for possessing something also will not have any place in their minds as a motivating force. Such desires are natural more with those who are of *rajo-guṇa* (active nature-modality). Those who yearn for wisdom are not motivated by any particular desire, but for wisdom's own sake. On attaining wisdom they have the full satisfaction of being in possession of everything in all the worlds. In this sense it is said, "they inherit the earth."

Another group of people who are fit for attaining wisdom is of "those who hunger and thirst for righteousness." They, upon feeling that they do not get justice from the society and from the existing laws of the state, begin to think, "What is the meaning of such a life?." If fortunate enough, they get the guidance of a master who can answer this question. It is when we depend on the society and the state to make our life meaningful that we begin to feel we are not getting the justice we deserve. Beyond the domain of man-made laws and customs, there is a realm of God-made laws, the laws that derive from the ultimate Reality or *Brahman.* Those who live depending solely on God constantly experience a sort of contentment that is incomparable. It is not something relative; it knows no hindrance.

Those who have realized God or Truth are merciful naturally. Their mercy would not be the result of any moral instruction from someone else. Rather, it wells up from within oneself as a result of the awareness that we all are the children of one all-merciful God, that all the beings in all the worlds are various fleeting facets that become manifest in the one everlasting ultimate Reality. In the presence of such spontaneously merciful ones, even ferocious creatures often remain friendly.

From those who are aware, "I am poor in spirit" to those who become spontaneously merciful — about all such we could say, they are "pure in heart." Only to such people does the truth become revealed that what appears as the very same "pure heart" is the one ultimate Reality or God. Therefore it is said "they shall see God."

There are those who live by the realization that the ultimate Reality or God is the Substance in their own being. Such people are very few. Still fewer are those who have this realization and are also anxious to make this wisdom their own and find the unconditional peace it results in. These few and their peace reach the hearts of as many people as possible. Such are the "peacemakers" of the world. This peacemaking is quite unlike the peacemaking efforts made by many of today's politicians around the world. While they try to impose peace on others at gunpoint or by economic policies, the peace mentioned here derives its strength from wisdom. Its source is God or the Absolute (*Brahman*). Those who effectively make this peace reach the hearts of those who seek it, and are to be called the "Sons of God." This is a context in which Jesus himself indicates in what sense he is to be considered the "Son of God".

Those who dedicate their lives to ensure this peace and God's justice to themselves, as well as to everyone, may have to endure many persecutions. Such vile actions usually come from people who stand for the very laws created by those who are impure in heart. They prefer to enforce such man-made laws that they think are the best, but really are unmindful of the God-made overall laws of nature. One's wilful ability to suffer such pesecutions without complaints or vengeance is known in Vedānta as *titikṣā*. The harassments such people suffer are merely of a worldly nature. The reward they get for it is the attainment of heaven, that means the transcendental world that pertains to *Brahman* becomes theirs.

Jesus, after giving these initial lessons, forewarns his disciples that people may revile and persecute them, and say all kinds of evil things against them falsely, for his sake. But he asks them in effect, "You find joy in suffering such difficulties, thinking you are the Blessed. The reason is, you are going to attain transcendental wisdom, very rare in this world, as a reward for that." Jesus also brings the disciples' attention to the fact that suffering to find Truth, Godly Justice and Wisdom is nothing new. Even the prophets of the past had to endure such persecutions by those impure in heart.

1.7

Sermon on the Mount (contd.)

JESUS continues,

> You are the salt of the earth, but if the salt loses its flavour, how shall it be seasoned? It is then good for nothing but to be thrown out and trampled under foot by men. — 5.13

Salt not only makes our food tastier, but also helps the body maintain its balance. When its salty flavour is lost, salt is no longer salt. Like this salty flavour are the individuals of the kind mentioned already. They imbibe wisdom's secret from a *guru,* let it seep into the world, and help ensure the internal well-being of humankind. When devoid of this wisdom, men are not to be counted as men at all. If those who have heard the secret of wisdom, remain unmindful of enriching and making well-balanced their own lives and the lives of fellow humans, then they are neither to be counted as *jñānin*s nor as the disciples of a great *guru* or prophet.

Jesus tells his disciples again:

> You are the light of the world. A city that is set on a hill cannot be hidden.
>
> Nor do they light a lamp and put it under a basket, but on a lampstand, and it gives light to all who are in the house.
>
> Let your light so shine before men, that they may see your good works and glorify your father in heaven. — 5.14-16

A *guru* as well as those who become enlightened through his guidance are like burning lamps. They shine by themselves, and they illumine the world around. They do not deliberately do anything to better the world as if out of some sense of obligation. A city built on a hilltop naturally becomes visible to everyone around the hill. Likewise is the way the wisdom of an *jñānin* comes to the attention of the world. A lamp, when lit, is never kept under a basket, it always is placed at a point from where it can shed light to as large an area as possible. Likewise, those to whom the wisdom secret becomes transparent, as taught by a *guru,* also do not hide it as a secret. On the other hand, they show the world the greatness of that wisdom, and how it is beneficial to human life. Here, the analogy of the city on the hill indicates that the grandeur of wisdom becomes spontaneously evident to the world from the life of the enlightened. And the analogy of the lamp indicates that the wisdom of the enlightenend should be left naturally to shine on its own. In order to make the wisdom of the enlightened beneficial to the world, it has to become something spontaneously and directly perceptible to others and so the enlightened must consciously make it visible to the world. It is when these two complementary sides unite together, as if dialectically, that the grandeur of the one Reality (the Father in heaven) becomes realizable as the light of all lights (*jyotiṣām api tad jyotiḥ*). Jesus here wishes such an attainment of enlightenment for his disciples, and for them to shed its light all over the world.

Jesus continues:

> Do not think that I came to destroy the law or the prophets. I did not come to destroy but to fulfil.
>
> For assuredly, I say to you, till heaven and earth pass away, one jot or one title will by no means pass from the law till all is fulfilled.
>
> Whoever therefore breaks one of the least of these commandments, and teaches men so, shall be called least in the kingdom of heaven; but whoever does and teaches them, he shall be called great in the kingdom of heaven.
>
> For I say to you that unless your righteousness exceeds the righteousness of the scribes and Pharisees, you will by no means enter the kingdom of heaven. — 5.17-20

Jesus was born as a Jew, and the people taught by him were also Jews. They lived adhering to the ten commandments and other injunctions of Moses and the prophets true to the letter, without compromise. Among all religionists the world over, there has always existed the tendency to strictly follow the letter of scriptural injunctions, while ignoring their true spirit. Religious practices thus became more and more static, rigid, insipid and lifeless. This trend prevails even now. It was at a stage when this tendency had reached its zenith, touching almost a dead end among the Jews, that Jesus emerged as a formidable force to effect corrections. In those days, the Jewish scribes and Pharisees were among the leaders and representatives of a dead religiosity that needed revitalization.

Jesus first of all declared that his intention was not to completely disregard the religious laws of Judaism and the prophets who formulated them. Though considered inviolable by the Jews, these laws had, by then, become rigid, dogmatic, narrow minded and parochial. The laws thus needed salvaging from this predicament by infusing them with the new life of wisdom. Jesus's intention, therefore, was to bring in a fresh vision of life that is all-inclusive. Within the all-inclusiveness of that wisdom, the existing Jewish laws became insignificant. Put otherwise, the new dynamic and absolutist wisdom taught by Jesus could be considered to engulf within its vastness and openness, the old, static and ritualistic religious notions and practices of Judaism. This cultural process, in *Bhagavad-Gītā* is compared to a small pool getting submerged in a flood of water, and thus becoming of no apparent value, though not rejected. This process of cultural correction is sometimes called "dialectical revaluation" by historians. It is such a revaluation that Jesus accomplished through his life's mission. It is in this context that we should understand and appreciate the words of Jesus: "For I say to you, that unless your righteousness exceeds the righteousness of the scribes and Pharisees, you will by no means enter the kingdom of heaven" (5.20). Already he had made it clear, "Do not think that I came to destroy the law or the prophets. I did not come to destroy but to fulfil" (5.17).

We have already noticed that the biblical notion of the kingdom of heaven signifies higher realms of wisdom. The righteousness or the religious laws that fully agree with that wisdom are always absolutist and unconditioned in nature. All religious practices were originally conceived by the prophets or Masters with this absolutist wisdom as their underlying spirit. Ignoring this spirit and practising the laws in their literal sense is only ritualisitic and conditioned in nature. Absolutist righteousness is eternal and is not just a passing phenomenon. It has a dynamic flow of its own. It is not static. It transcends all limitations of time and clime. Therefore Jesus says: "For assuredly, I say to you, until heaven and earth pass away, one jot or one title will by no means pass from the law until all is fulfilled" (5.18). The rest of the fifth chapter of the Gospel shows some examples of the revaluation effected by Jesus to the already pre-existing religious notions of his time.

1.8

Sermon on the Mount (contd.)
Give Up Worldly Traits

JESUS continues to teach his disciples:

> Take heed that you do not do your charitable deeds before men, to be seen by them. Otherwise you have no reward from your Father in heaven. — 6.1

Doing charitable and pious deeds is considered meritorious in all religions. Such deeds, in the Indian context, are known as *iṣṭāpūrta-karmas*. These are meant to be done as an offering to God, and are to be thus evaluated by God, not by humans. But many forget this basic principle and perform such deeds in order to get the recognition as pious persons of the world. Those who habitually offer their deeds to God, without thinking of convincing people, alone are competent to attain wisdom. Others always remain in the cloggy mire of ignorance simply because of their egoism or uncompromising I-sense. Related to this context are the words, "when you do a charitable deed, do not sound a trumpet before you" (6.2). A similar teaching is:

> . . . when you pray, go into your room, and when you have shut your door, pray to your Father who is in the secret place . . . — 6.6

In short, without giving up your worldly-mindedness, and without cultivating an interiorized vision, you are not going to attain the higher domain of wisdom.

The manner in which one should pray is also clarified by Jesus thus:

> Our Father in heaven, hallowed be your name.
>
> Your kingdom come. Your will be done on earth as it is in heaven.
>
> Give us this day our daily bread.
>
> And forgive us our debts, as we forgive our debtors.
>
> And do not lead us into temptation, but deliver us from the evil one.
> For yours is the kingdom and the power and the glory forever. Amen.
>
> — 6.9-13

Verses 16-23 of chapter 6 give emphasis to the necessity to not become subdued by worldly leanings, and to cultivate the habit of interiorizing one's perception. Concluding this section, Jesus says:

> No one can serve two masters, for either he will hate the one and love the other, or else he will be loyal to the one and despise the other. You cannot serve God and Mammon. — 6.24

The two masters represent the two main value worlds open before man in which he may set his interest. One is that of worldly pleasures and wealth, called *preyas*; and the other is that of *śreyas*, or of the eternal Happiness that comes from realizing what is the ultimate meaning of life. No one can live by giving equal importance to both these value worlds. Of course, there are stories of rare *karma-yogīs* like the ancient king Janaka who was also a perfect *jñānin*. That means, apparently he gave equal place to wisdom and the state affairs in his life. But when his story is closely looked at, it reveals that even when fully involved in the state's affairs as ruler, he was well aware that the state and its administration are all simply part of the self-manifestation of *Brahman*. In other words, he was perceiving only *Brahman* itself in what appears as the state and its affairs.

That Lakṣmī and Sarasvatī do not live together is a well-known adage in India. Lakṣmī, according to Indian mythology, is the goddess of wealth, and Sarasvatī, that of wisdom. The implication is that worldly wealth and wisdom do not flourish in the life of the same person. In the same sense Jesus says, "You cannot serve God and Mammon." According to Jewish tradition, Mammon is the presiding deity of wealth. Wisdom actually is attained only by those who are of determined mind to disregard the world of Mammon, and turn towards the world of God.

Verses 25-34 of chapter 6 shed more light on the inevitability of this discrimination in one's spiritual pursuit. The worldly needs of those who take refuge in God or the ultimate Reality are taken care of by the very same Reality or God. To those seekers who do not yet fully understand this, Jesus says:

> Therefore do not worry about tomorrow . . . — 6.34

1.9

Sermon on the Mount (contd.)
Absolute Morality

To be just in life is one of the desires seen perhaps only among humans. It is this desire that compels us to formulate laws, and to be willing to abide by such laws in life. But how can we decide which act is just and which is unjust? This is a very difficult problem to settle. To settle this problem decisively requires the help of a universal criterion of ethics, a measuring rod by which we can measure every human act and so decide which ones are just and which are not. As long as such a criterion is not available, there is always the possibility that one may judge another wrongly on the strength of the prevailing laws and sense of morality. The one who judges thus could be a person who violates the laws and sense of justice himself. The judgement pronounced by such a person would only be meant to convince the world. Jesus, pointing towards this human tendency not to see one's own faults and yet to see clearly those of others, says:

> And why do you look at the speck in your brother's eye, but do not consider the plank in your own eyes? . . .
>
> First remove the plank from your own eye, and then you will see clearly to remove the speck out of your brother's eye. — 7.3, 5

To "see clearly", in the ultimate sense, means to become fully aware of one's self. The clarity of self-awareness is called *ātma-jñāna* in Vedānta. As long as one lacks self-knowledge, one is tempted to see the shortcomings of others.

What will happen when one attains self-knowledge? No fault will be found in anyone. One will realize then that it is the Reality that has assumed the form of oneself that has also assumed the form of others. One is that Reality in essence; others are also so. Thus one will see oneself in everything. One will then realize, "everything indeed is myself" (*ātmaivedam sarvam*). One then perceives what is good and dear to oneself is good and dear to others also. Judging others, thus, means judging oneself.

Attaining self-knowledge, though very simple, is not an easy job. It is ordinarily not gained by self-effort alone; it requires the loving guidance of a *guru*. Jesus, as a *guru*, stands here before his disciples with his helping hand. Yet all the disciples gathered here may not necessarily be fully competent to imbibe that wisdom. Attaining wisdom requires certain prerequisite qualities on the part of the seeker. Such competence, in Vedānta, is known as *adhikāra*, and one who is competent is known as an *adhikārin*. What a *guru* does initially with a competent disciple is to turn his or her attention, which usually is externally oriented, within oneself. That is what Jesus also does here.

Knowing oneself is a sort of holy knowledge, where the knower becomes the known. Imparting the secret aspects of this wisdom to the incompetent, Jesus forewarns, is like giving what is holy to dogs, and casting pearls before swine. Swine may trample the pearls under their feet, and turn and tear you to pieces (see 7.6). The incompetent disciple, if taught, will trample that wisdom under his feet, and may even attack the *guru* who taught him. Such events are many in history. Jesus was no exception.

A competent disciple is always all ears for the words of wisdom that fall from the mouth of the *guru*. *Bhagavad-Gītā* also says:

> Only one endowed with faithful attention (*śraddhā*) obtains wisdom (*śradhāvān labhate jñānam*). —4.39

Jesus also in the same tone says:

> Ask, and it will be given to you; seek, and you will find; knock, and it will be opened to you. —7.7

A *guru* never teaches ignorance (*ajñāna*) to a seeker who approaches him with an intent on wisdom (*jñāna*). With this in mind, Jesus says:

> What man is among you who, if his son asks for bread, will give him stone? —7.9

All such things are known even to ordinary people. Jesus then says:

> If you then, being evil, know how to give good gifts to your children, how much more will your Father who is in heaven give good things to those who ask Him! —7.11

One knowing oneself and one knowing the Father in heaven, in essence, are not two. In Vedānta self-knowledge (*ātma-jñāna*) is equal to knowing *Brahman* (*brahma-jñāna*). Jesus here clearly shows how life becomes transformed as this non-dual awareness leads one's day-to-day life. He says:

> Therefore, whatever you want men to do to you, do also to them, for this is the Law of the Prophets. —7.12

The words "this is the Law of the Prophets" indicate that this ethical principle is not conditioned by anything and is not at all relative; it is absolute in nature. To judge in the way previously mentioned (7.3), on the other hand, is relative and conditioned in nature. The echo of the unconditioned absolute morality visualized by Jesus here could be heard in the following words of Narayana Guru in modern times:

> Whatever one does for one's own happiness
> Should be conducive to the happiness of others as well.
> — *Ātmopadeśa Śatakam*, verse 24

1.10

Sermon on the Mount (contd.)
Two Kinds of Knowledge

JESUS says:

> Enter by the narrow gate; for wide is the gate and broad is the way that leads to destruction and there are many who go by it.
>
> Because narrow is the gate and difficult is the way which leads to life, and there are few who find it. — 7.13-14

Knowledge is of two kinds. One is obtained by looking externally. We observe and examine the phenomena seen in the world and gain an understanding of these. The world that is to be understood in this manner lies before us as something endless. Knowing the whole of it fully to the end is hardly possible. Our five sense organs exist to help us gain this kind of knowledge. The mental faculties (*antaḥkaraṇa*s) are always there to assist the sense organs. Wide and broad is this path, and entering it is not at all difficult. All we have to do is simply let the sense organs and mental faculties remain open. But such knowledge never gives peace and restfulness in life. And moreover, it very often makes us agitated, conflicted and restless.

There is yet another kind of knowledge. Instead of looking at the external world, one turns one's attention to one's own being and tries to find out the Reality that has assumed one's own appearance, and for that matter, the appearance of the world. To do so is to strive to know the ultimate Reality. No sense organ can help one attain this awareness. It really is an experience in which the knowing mind itself merges in the being of what one finds out to be Real. There is no room in it for the differentiation of the knower and the known, for the knower himself becomes the known. In this sense, very narrow is its gate. The only path to true peace, though difficult, is the interiorized search into oneself with all the sense organs shut out.

Most people actually live in ignorance about even the possibility of such a knowledge, the necessity of it and the path to it. Finding out that path, as well as feeling the necessity of treading it, happens only with the grace of a *guru*. Such chosen ones realize the Reality in the being of themselves as well as the being of the entire world. Such persons are very few in number.

It is only the seeker-disciples who face the problem whether the path they choose to tread has to be an easy and broad one, or the difficult and narrow one. Is it enough that such seekers go to any *guru*? No, they have to find out and approach a true *guru* (*sad-guru*). Who then is a true *guru*? *Guru*s who tread the path that is broad and easy, and organize large gatherings of admirers are plentiful. Such *guru*s have worldly knowledge and a worldly-like knowledge of the self (*ātmā*) also. Their main goal is to become famous and amass money rather than impart the essential content of wisdom to seekers. The way to differentiate such *guru*s from the true ones who teach the core of wisdom and who are not concerned with fame and money, is from the fruits they yield. Jesus says:

> Beware of false prophets, who come to you in sheep's clothing, but inwardly they are ravenous wolves.
>
> You will know them by their fruits. Do men gather grapes from thorn bushes, or figs from thistles?
>
> Even so, every good tree bears good fruit, but a bad tree bears bad fruit.
>
> A good tree cannot bear bad fruit, nor can a bad tree bear good fruit.
>
> Every tree that does not bear good fruit is cut down and thrown into the fire.
>
> Therefore by their fruits you will know them. — 7.15-20

Jesus continues:

> Not everyone who says to me, "Lord, Lord" shall enter the kingdom of heaven, but he who does the will of My Father in heaven.
>
> Many will say to Me in that day, "Lord," have we not prophesied in Your name, cast out demons in Your name, and done many wonders in Your name?"
>
> And then I will declare to them, "I never knew you; depart from Me, you who practise lawlessness!" — 7.21-23

The disciple who approaches a *guru* should also be a true seeker (*sacchiṣya*). He or she should be competent to be taught wisdom and should also be interested in obtaining it. A wilful determination not to back out until one is properly taught by the *guru* and one becomes englightened, should also be in such a seeker. Simply by going before a *guru* and respectfully calling him, "O *guru*, O *guru*," by prostrating oneself before the *guru*, by taking down every word uttered by the *guru*, going through those notes again and again and even telling others the same, by casting out demons as the *guru* did, or by doing something great, one does not become either a true disciple or truly enlightened. On the other hand, one who perceives *Brahman* (the Father in heaven) as the real Substance in one's own being as well as in the being of everything in all the worlds, one who knows that all the actions oneself performs in life, as well as all the activities going on everywhere in all the worlds, happen as willed by that one Reality, one who lives in this world as a manifest form of that Reality or as the embodiment of this wisdom, alone is a true *jñānin*. Those who are in search of this wisdom are the true seekers. Such persons normally will have no complaint to tell the *guru*. Those who are not true disciples might make complaints because they have not obtained wisdom, perhaps even after being with the *guru* for a long time. To them the *guru* may reply: "Though you were always living with me, what you perceive is not the Reality that I see within me. You see everything as externally existing objects. You consider even the self (*ātmā*) likewise. Such persons are not my true disciples. Therefore I say, I do not know you, depart from me."

The main point that Jesus underscores in his Sermon on the Mount is that there exists an imperishable supreme Reality (the Father in heaven) which is ever new and yet is subject to no change. The details of the wisdom of this Reality could be seen scattered in the rest of the chapters of the Gospel. This Reality, as the unchanging one, in Vedānta, is called *kūṭastha* (well fixed as the topmost). The indication is also that this wisdom is the firm foundation for the existence of the individual's life, as well as for that of the phenomenon of life in the universe in general. A house built on a firm rock never collapses even in heavy wind and storm. Likewise, the life built on the firm basis of this wisdom always remains firm and happy. Jesus makes all this clear in verses 24 to 27 of chapter 7. This section begins:

> Therefore whoever hears these sayings of Mine, and does them, I will liken him to a wise man who built his house on the rock. — 7.24

The Sermon on the Mount ends with verse 27 which answers the question concerning what life is like. For the one who does not have this firm foundation to support that life, it is like a house built on loose sand. Jesus says:

> and the rain descended, the floods came, and the winds blew and beat on that house, and it fell. And great was its fall. — 7.27

As Jesus concluded his Sermon on the Mount one thing became clear to those who were around, that

> He taught them as one having authority, not as the scribes. — 7.29

Teaching spiritual lessons could be done in two ways. One is, learning the text of the scriptures, and teaching others what was understood from these. The other is, realizing the Reality directly and imparting that realization through words or some other means. The scriptures taught in the former way only derive their authority from those who became enlightened in the latter way. The texts of such scriptures, in fact, are the collections of words of those realized souls of the past. Therefore, the enlightened ones (*jñānin*s) do not have to rely on scriptures. On the contrary, the scriptures derive their existence and authority from the realized souls. It is not as those who teach the texts of the ancient scriptures that Jesus appears here; on the contrary, his words will become scriptures. But scribes simply teach people the scriptural texts.

1.11

The Hard Life: Death and Immortality

Chapter 8 of the Gospel deals mainly with the miracles performed by Jesus. We have already seen how such phenomena in the life of the enlightened spiritual masters are to be understood. Though the disease of a leper who had full faith in Jesus was cured just by his touch, Jesus tells him as a precaution:

> See that you tell no one; but go your way, show yourself to the priest, and offer the gift that Moses commanded, as a testimony to them.
> — 8.4

The next miracle is the curing of the paralysis of a centurion's servant. Centurions were officials of Roman emperor who dominated the Palestinian region then; naturally they were despised by the Jews. It could be for this reason that this particular centurion tells Jesus:

> Lord, I am not worthy that you should come under my roof. But only speak a word, and my servant will be healed. — 8.8

These words indicate the centurion's full faith in Jesus, though he was not a disciple of Jesus, nor a Jew, and was likely even despised by the Jews, the community Jesus belonged to. In spite of these negative factors, his faith was fruitful. It so happens with many great Masters that those who are very close to them do not have full faith in them and do not fully understand them, whereas those who keep themselves at a distance understand them and have full faith in them. In the case of Jesus also, the faithlessness of his disciples is seen in the next miracle narrated in verses 23 to 27. They face a dangerous situation simply because they lacked faith, and so Jesus rescued them, thereby infusing a fuller faith in them.

Though unworldly events like the curing of diseases and the driving away of demons happen in Jesus's life, all such are a result of the full faith of those who are benefitted thereby. Jesus is a *jñānin* who constantly experiences full identity with everything and the one causal Reality that underlies everything. For such *jñānin*s to actually live in this world is, so to speak, a miracle. This miracle and the faith one has in such a miraculous person, these two fuse together to become one actual life-experience, and that fusion appears as a miraculous event of the sort mentioned above.

Now when Jesus saw great multitudes about him, he gave a command to depart to the other side. Then a certain scribe came and said to him, "Teacher, I will follow you wherever you go". And Jesus said to him:

> Foxes have holes and birds of the air have nests, but the Son of Man has nowhere to lay His head. — 8.20

Scribes are a group of people who lead a pleasant life by teaching people the Commandments of Moses true to the letter. Therefore, what Jesus would tell a scribe who intends to follow him would be somewhat like this, "You made a mistake if you think you can have a pleasant life by following me. Foxes have their holes in forests to live in, birds flying in the sky similarly have their own nests in which to rest at night. I do not have even that." Real *guru*s have nothing of their own, or rather they do not consider anything as theirs. It is equally true to say that they consider everything to be theirs. Those who follow such a *guru,* on being attracted by his or her wisdom or ideals, cannot expect to enjoy a comfortable life. On the contrary, many hardships will have to be endured by them. Such a life with a *guru,* in India, is qualified as *gurukula-kliṣṭa* (hard life with a *guru* in his abode).

Though enduring hardships that may prompt many to withdraw, only the few, who follow a *guru* with all firmness of mind and without looking backward, attain what one is to expect from a *guru.* Another incident reminiscent of this is given next. One disciple said to Jesus:

> Lord, let me first go and bury my father.

But Jesus said to him:

> Follow Me, let the dead bury their own dead. — 8.21-22

A *guru* is a person who leads his disciple to the realm that is birthless and deathless. Only to those who live in the world of ignorance (*ajñāna*) are both birth and death relevant. It is in that world of birth and death that it is considered a son duty bound to decently bury his father's dead body. But it is only by virtue of ignorance that one considers the many to be real, and that life begins with birth and ends with death. Those who live with such an understanding are virtually already dead. "Let such bury the dead body of the dead, but you, being intent on attaining eternal life, follow me." Such is the direction Jesus gives his disciple here.

These words of Jesus may be seen as a variant of the Upaniṣadic utterance:

yaḥ paśyatīha nāneva mr̥tyoḥ sa mr̥tyum gacchati ।
— *Kaṭha Upaniṣad* 4.11

(He who perceives the many as real goes from death to death.)

1.12

The Harvest and the Harvesters

IMPARTING wisdom is the natural function of a *guru*. Such imparting becomes meaningful only to the ignorant. Immersed as they are in ignorance, they may be found immersed in evils and wrong-doings likewise. Such persons, if willing to be corrected and to be led towards good, will be loved by a *guru*. The following incident clearly portrays this truth:

> Then as Jesus passed on from there, He saw a man named Matthew sitting at the tax office. And he said to him, "Follow Me." And he arose and followed him.
>
> And so it was, as Jesus sat at the table in the house, that behold, many tax collectors and sinners came and sat down with Him and His disciples.
>
> And when the Pharisees saw it, they said to His disciples, "Why does your Teacher eat with tax collectors and sinners?"
>
> But when Jesus heard that, He said to them, "Those who are well have no need of a physician, but those who are sick."
>
> But go and learn what this means: "I desire mercy and not sacrifice." For I did not come to call the righteous, but sinners, to repentence.
>
> Then the disciples of John came to Him, saying, "Why do we and the Pharisees fast often, but your disciples do not fast?"
>
> And Jesus said to them, "Can the friends of the bridegroom mourn as long as the bridegroom is with them?" But the days will come when the bridegroom will be taken away from them, and then they will fast.
>
> No one puts a piece of unshrunk cloth on an old garment, for the patch pulls away from the garment, and the tear is made worse.
>
> Nor do people put new wine into old wineskins, or else the wineskins break, the wine is spilled, and the wineskins are ruined. But they put new wine into new wineskins and both are preserved. — 9.9-17

Fasting is a religious observance. It indicates man's willingness to suffer for the cause of Truth. That the path of Truth and God gets cleared not through indulgence in worldly pleasures, but through relinquishment, is the message this observance gives. Observing such instructions normally originates from enlightened *gurus* and prophets. Even after they depart from this world, the religious practices they enjoined continue to be observed. Such practices, in course of time, assume a part of the religion concerned. When the *guru* or prophet who is enlightened enough to give such instructions does actually live among disciples, their observation of such practices does not strictly make much sense, for the presence of the *guru* itself enables and inspires them to decide then and there what to do and what not to as each situation demands. But after the departure of the *guru*, the disciples may not find themselves enlightened and discriminative enough to make such free decisions. They then will have to follow the instructions of the departed *guru* without any sense of freedom to make amendments. Their successors will also continue to live in strict adherence to these practices. The situation in which the *guru* lives among the followers is compared here to that of a bridegroom amongst his friends. A bridegroom, at a marriage gathering, is usually surrounded by his closest friends and so they crack many jokes with him. They will not make such jokes in the absence of the bridegroom. It is such a situation that is here likened to the future events in which Jesus's disciples will have to live without his guidance.

The wisdom teaching of a living *guru* is always a living one. It is itself a living experience. The life of the disciples who imbibe the teachings also becomes dynamic. But after the *guru*'s time, if the disciple who succeeds him happens to be not sufficiently enlightened, he would understand and interpret the teachings of the *guru* only true to their letters or from a parochial point of view. One who lives following such an interpretation attains a sort of inertness in life, as do the teachings as well. Then such a one may begin to feel that not strictly adhering to religious practices is something sacrilegious. In short, in the case of a *jñānin* adhering to the prevailing religious practices is of no relevance, whereas the ignorant may find themselves unable to live without strictly practising such observances.

We often make the mistake of mending the way of living in view of the enlightenment within, that does not care much for religious observances, with the practice of giving full credit to religious customs. This is compared by Jesus to the act of patching an old garment with a piece of unshrunken new cloth. In this comparison we have to see the old garment in the place of the existing way of religious life that adheres strictly to all customs and observances, and in the place of unshrunk cloth the ever-new and living wisdom of a living *guru* like Jesus. If the existing rigid religion is patchworked with the unshrunk cloth of the living wisdom of Jesus, it endangers the old garment or old religion alone — the patch becomes enlarged. That means, the old religious practices would be found to be of little relevance. At the same time, when evaluating the wisdom teaching on its own, the same teaching would be seen underlying the prevailing religious observances enjoined by the forgone *guru*s as well. In short, a new and living wisdom teaching should never be evaluated in the light of the existing religion and its practices. On the contrary, only the other way would show how meaningful such religious observances are. Indicating the same truth, Jesus says again: "Nor do people put new wine into old wineskins; or else the wineskins break, the wine is spilled, and the wineskins are ruined. But they put new wine into new wineskins and both are preserved."

The new all-inclusive and dynamic wisdom or the new gospel now revealed by Jesus is likened here to new wine. New wine is more powerful, and it ferments. It has to be kept in a bottle strong enough to withstand these pressures. (The Mediterranean region is famous for grape cultivation and wine. In the days of Jesus, wine used to be kept in bags made of animal skin.) Similarly, the wisdom Jesus intends to impart to his disciples is very strong in its content and effect. It is not to be evaluated by pouring it in the old wineskin of the existing religious customs. If done so, the brightness and freshness of the new teaching go unnoticed and the inertness and outdatedness of the existing customs become more evident. This is a double loss. Therefore, the new wisdom is to be seen as new and related to its own natural background. In short, the double loss is to be avoided and double gain attained.

Verses 18-34 of chapter 9 describe a few more miraculous acts of Jesus. The relevance of such acts has already been examined. The result of such miracles, as was noticed by Jesus, was that multitudes gathered around him. He was moved with compassion for them, because they were weary and scattered, lacking in spiritual guidance, like sheep having no shepherd. Then he said to his disciples:

> The harvest truly is plentiful, but the labourers are few.
>
> Therefore pray to the Lord of the harvest to send out labourers into His harvest. — 9.37-38

The multitudes gathered around Jesus were inquisitive about the new teaching for the sole intention of making their lives more secure and peaceful and are compared here to a crop ready for harvest.

Teaching them this wisdom requires enough disciples who have comprehended the essential content of it as taught by the *guru*, in this case Jesus. They should also be willing to go among the people and teach them. Such disciples are likened here to harvesters. Even a truly enlightened *guru* is helpless to create such disciples. They have to come to him on their own in search of wisdom, as if so desired by God. Therefore Jesus asks the few disciples around him to pray to God to send more harvesters. The *guru* of the Śikṣā Vallī, chapter I of *Taittirīya Upaniṣad* also makes such a prayer as follows:

āmāyantu brahmacāriṇaḥ svāhā ।
vimāyantu brahmacāriṇaḥ svāhā ।
pramāyantu brahmacāriṇaḥ svāhā ।
damāyantu brahmacāriṇaḥ svāhā ।
śamāyantu brahmacāriṇaḥ svāhā । — 1.4.2

(Hail! May seekers of Truth approach me! Hail! May seekers of Truth approach me variously! Hail! May seekers of Truth approach me properly! Hail! May seekers of Truth approach me undisturbed by external influences. Hail! May seekers of Truth approach me with mental self-control! Hail!)

1.13

Directives to the Disciples

THE entire content of chapter 10 consists of the directives given by Jesus to his twelve disciples who were to travel among people as good harvesters. The basic message they have to give the people, is,

> "The kingdom of God is at hand." (10.7)

The message, in other words, is this: "The domain of wisdom that makes you free is opened before you, be ready to own it; enter it and make your life absolutely meaningful." Besides the power to convey this message they are also given the power to perform miraculous deeds like healing all kinds of diseases and the casting out of evil spirits. That means, Jesus gives them permission and power to do everything that he does, beginning with things that are of value in this world and ending with those of transcendental value. We have already examined the meaning and relevance of all these.

The disciples are categorically asked to do all this as those who have renounced everything and are not expecting anything in return. Such renunciates in India are called *tyāgīs*. Jesus says:

> Heal the sick, cleanse the lepers, raise the dead, cast out demons.
> Freely you have received, freely give.
>
> Provide neither gold nor silver nor copper in your money belts.
>
> Nor bag for your journey, nor two tunics, nor sandals, nor staffs.
>
> — 10.8-10

If nothing is to be desired, how will one's daily needs like food be met? Jesus clears this doubt with the words,

> "a worker is worthy of his food" — 10.10.

The disciples are to travel all over the region with the sole mission of bringing to the people the good news that the kingdom of God is before them to be accepted. They will also have to teach them about the nature of that kingdom. People who are benefitted by the high value of that wisdom will support its providers without being asked. This is equivalent to saying that the kingdom of God itself will support them. The same assurance is given in *Bhagavad-Gītā* also with these words:

ananyāś cintayanto mām ye janāḥ paryupāsate ।
teṣām nityabhiyuktānām yogakṣemam vahāmyaham ॥ — *IX.22*

(People who meditatively adore Me with the awareness that I am not different from themselves, are there. The yogic easement of life of those eternally united ones, I do take care of.)

In the beginning people may ask many critical questions to those who approach them with a new wisdom of the ultimate Reality, which is quite unfamiliar to them, especially to those who dislike any change from the prevailing traditional attitudes towards life. Jesus assures his disciples that they do not have to think in advance how such situations will be dealt with. The wisdom secret itself will yield to them proper ideas and words as and when needed. Jesus says:

But when they deliver you up, do not worry about how or what you should speak. For it will be given to you in that hour what you should speak.

For it is not who speak, but the Spirit of your Father who speaks in you. — 10.19-20

Those who are well aware of the secret of the Father in heaven, that means, those who are enlightened, perceive everything in life in the light of that secret or Reality, and find solutions to all problems with that Reality as their firm basis. The secret they have realized unfolds itself in them in the form of the proper words and ideas that will enable them to encounter any situation related to it. *Chāndogya Upaniṣad* says:

Words yield the milk of their meaning, to the one who knows thus.
— 1.13.4, 2.8.3

Those who dedicate themselves to the cause of the kingdom of God or the ultimate Reality will have to face much pressure, mostly from their close relatives, causing much agony to them. For those who are not firm enough in their minds in respect of their dedication, spiritual life will always remain an unrealized dream. A son might have to disregard the wishes of his father. Critical or even dangerous situations may arise. Only those who can withstand all such difficulties with a firm mind will attain wisdom, and so become well qualified to travel among the people to teach them the new gospel or wisdom. Jesus says these things to his disciples as a sort of forewarning thus:

Now brother will deliver up brother to death, and a father his child; and the children will rise up against parents, and cause them to be put to death.

> And you will be hated by all for My name's sake. But he who endures to the end will be saved. — 10.21-22

As such carriers of the new Gospel reach any new place, the local people need not necessarily receive them readily; they may even create obstructions for them, or they could even persecute them. The best way to face such situations is by leaving that place with a sense of endurance (*titikṣā*) within. These newcomers may also be received gladly at certain places. Then they will also have to leave that place for the next village or town, after giving the people the news of wisdom. Whether accepted or rejected, they are thus meant to travel to every village and town of the country. Thus, this becomes their way of life. Ordinary people may not be able to even think that anyone can live like that.

How do these new messengers of the Gospel find it easy to take up such a way of life? What is the strong motivating force behind it? The birthless and deathless Reality assumed the form of a living mortal man, a *guru*, in this world, and he revealed that Reality to them; and the strength they derived from this new revelation enabled them to follow such a way of life. That revelation itself is their sole wealth. Unless thus enlightened, they would never be able even to think of such a life. The instructions Jesus gave his disciples in this regard apparently resemble the life pattern of the mendicant monks (*parivrājaka*s) of India. Jesus says:

> But when they persecute you in this city, flee to another. For assuredly, I say to you, you will not have gone through the cities of Israel before the son of Man comes. — 10.23

Jesus here is a *guru*. Extending the wisdom teaching of the *guru* to everyone who was keenly interested in it anywhere in this world was the duty assigned to the twelve disciples. Jesus reminded them as to the attitude with which they should take this message to the world, thus:

> A disciple is not above his teacher, nor a servant above his master.
>
> It is enough for a disciple that he be like his teacher, and a servant like his master. If they have called the master of the house Beelzebub, how much more shall those call those of his household? — 10.24-25

Jesus's words, "A disciple is not above his teacher" do not denote that a disciple who comes in a particular *guru*-disciple succession should never be a more knowledgeable person than his predecessor. Rather it is to be understood in the philosophical sense.

A *guru* is an embodiment of wisdom, an embodiment of the ultimate Reality, in the form of a mortal man in flesh and blood. What an embodiment of Reality teaches is always the nature and content of that Reality. There is no knowledge above this knowledge. For this reason, this knowledge is referred to as the finalized knowledge or wisdom, called Vedānta in Sanskrit. *Veda* means knowledge, and *anta* means the end or finalized position. No knowledge that transcends this is attainable to anyone. Even if a disciple is a more erudite person than his *guru* (predecessor), he still can never cross this limit of knowledge and go beyond it.

A *guru* is a person who has already reached this limit; what a disciple can aspire for in life is to somehow reach that limit himself or herself, and make it his or her own living experience. A disciple may have to face many difficulties and undergo many sufferings in order to attain this goal. One thing such a disciple always has to remember on all such occasions could be rephrased somewhat like this: a *guru*'s words, "I am the master of this house. Even I am rebuked by people. How much you, the members of my household, will have to suffer it then!" This thought transforms such trials and tribulations into a meaningful and valuable experience.

The instructions Jesus gives his disciples in verses 26-35 are mainly centred round the need to remain without any fear of the world. One of the strongest forces that stands in the way of spiritual life is one's worldly impulses. The need for deliberately getting rid of these impulses is stressed by Śaṅkara in his *Vivekacūḍāmaṇi* (Crest-jewel of Discrimination). He calls such impulses (*lokānuvartana*). As one frees oneself from these impulses, one finds oneself also free from fear of the world. Tempted by these impulses, disciples may distort the teaching of the *guru* or dilute it. One may even deny one's own *guru* as happened in the case of Jesus himself. Such instances are many in history.

What does a true disciple, who follows the *guru* strictly to the spirit of the *guru*'s teaching, gain in life? Such a person attains the unconditioned Happiness of having dominion over the kingdom of the Self or *Ātmā*, called *svarājya* in the Upaniṣads. Such an experience is indicated by Jesus by these words:

> Therefore whoever confesses Me before men, him I will also confess before My Father who is in heaven. — 10.32

He also speaks clearly about those who deny their own *guru* because of their fear for the world, thus:

> But whoever denies Me before men, him I will also deny before My Father who is in heaven. — 10.33

The following words of *Bhagavad-Gītā* contain the same message given in a different tone:

> *śraddhāvān labhate jñānam* — 4.39
>
> (Only one endowed with faithful attention (*śraddhā*) obtains wisdom.)

and

> *saṁśayātmā vinaśyati* — 4.40
>
> (The one who is an embodiment of doubt, perishes.)

Verses 34-39 once again emphasize the fact that those who consider worldly relations and blood relations to be of the highest value, will not find themselves on the path of Reality or the Absolute, also called *Brahman*. In other words, such persons do not become true *brahmacārin*s (those who walk on the path of the Absolute). They usually consider their own personality and personal interests to be most important in life. Those who can sacrifice such interests for the sake of knowing the one Reality, which is life's highest value, finally perceive the very same Reality as forming the essential content of their own being. They constantly experience the inseparable oneness between themselves and the Reality they are in search of. Such is the way the words of Jesus,

> "He who finds his life will lose it and he who loses his life for My sake will find it" — 10.39

will be understood by a Vedāntin.

A person who goes among the people as a messenger of a *guru* may be very simple and humble. Still he will be recognized and accepted by people who stand for higher values. Really it is the *guru* and his teaching that is thus honoured and accepted. The *guru* on his part became a *guru* as the ultimate Reality became incarnate. Thus the greatness and acceptance of this Reality are to be seen in the recognition and acceptance that the simple messenger gets.

What is the benefit people get by honouring and accepting the ultimate Reality through a simple messenger as medium? It is nothing other than the experience of an undisturbed peace in life; and it surely is attained. Such is the essence of Jesus's teaching in verses 40-42 of chapter 10. With this note comes to a close Jesus's instructions to his twelve disciples on the eve of their mission to go among the people as messengers.

1.14

The Hidden Nature of Wisdom

VERSES 1-8 of chapter 12 narrate an event that shows how enlightened persons (*guru*s) are the source of all religious customs, and for this reason they are not bound to obey such laws. Jesus and his disciples went through some grain fields on the Sabbath. The disciples, being hungry, began to pluck the heads of grains and eat. The Pharisees, on seeing this, questioned them asking,

> Lord, your disciples are doing what is not lawful to do on the Sabbath.
> — 12.2

That no work should be done on the Sabbath is a Jewish law. All such religious customs originate from the enlightenment of the prophets. That means, prophets are not bound to live following religious laws. Therefore Jesus replies:

> The son of Man is Lord even of the Sabbath. — 12.8

Though Jewish law prohibits doing any work on the Sabbath, such laws do not apply to doing something that saves humans from their afflictions. This point is clarified in verses 9-13.

Renunciates (*tyāgī*s) and *saṁnyāsins* are persons who live dedicating themselves to the Absolute (*Brahman*). Worldly relations like father, mother, brothers, have no place in their life. Rather, such persons consider their close relatives to be those who dedicate themselves for, or honour the cause for which they live. An episode in the life of Jesus that clarifies this principle is narrated in the Gospel as follows:

> While He was still talking to the multitudes, behold, His mother and brothers stood outside, seeking to speak with Him.
>
> Then one said to Him, "Look, Your mother and Your brothers are standing outside, seeking to speak with You".
>
> But He answered and said to the one who told Him, "Who is My mother and who are My brothers?"
>
> And He stretched out His hand towards His disciples and said, "Here are My mother and My brothers!"

> For whoever does the will of My Father in heaven is My brother and sister and mother. — 12.46-50

A *guru,* being enlightened about the ultimate Realtiy, may try his best to clarify that wisdom with a scientific-like precision to those who are around him, yet not all of them will necessarily comprehend or visualize it. For a listener to become capable of doing so depends mainly on his or her competence, called *adhikāra*. Therefore, when great multitudes gathered around him, the first thing Jesus did was to get into a boat that lay a bit away from this crowd (13.2). One of the peculiarities always seen in *guru*s is that, while they are intent on teaching wisdom to the people, they also like to distance themselves from the crowd. This quality is designated in *Bhagavad-Gītā* as *aratir jana-samsadi* (a distaste for being in the crowd) (12.10).

Jesus was well aware that those who gathered there were not all fit to comprehend what he intended to teach. This fact is clarified by himself through a parable thus:

> Then He spoke many things to them in parables, saying: "Behold, a sower went out to sow.
>
> And as he sowed, some seed fell by the wayside; and birds came and devoured them.
>
> Some fell on stony places, where they did not have much earth; and they immediately sprang up because they had no depth of earth.
>
> But when the sun was up they were scorched, and because they had no root they withered away.
>
> And some fell among thorns, and the thorns sprang up and choked them.
>
> But others fell on good ground and yielded a crop: Some a hundred-fold, some sixty, some thirty.
>
> He who has ears to hear, let him hear." — 13.3-9

The words "He who has ears to hear, let him hear" indicate that Jesus is well aware of the fact that, though many are gathered to listen him, all are not equally capable of comprehending what he says. Jesus himself later explains to his disciples the meaning of the above parable.

The secret of the kingdom of God (the secret of wisdom) taught by a *guru* might be heard by some again and again as if with much interest, but without seriously comprehending anything. The *guru*'s words, in their case, become seeds that fall on the wayside with no chance to sprout. Such people are very often misled by the evil-minded and those of vested interests who are like birds that devour the seeds that fell on the wayside.

Some others listen to the words and grasp them; yet what they understood does not strike roots in their life. In their actual life they simply forget those lessons. Even if remembered, they would not be willing to suffer for its sake. In their case, the words of the *guru* are like seeds that fell at a stony place. They sprout, but wither away when the sun is up.

There are some others who listen to the words with much interest and understand the teaching, but when pressed by worldly interests, greed for wealth and the like, they then ignore the *guru*'s teachings. The words of wisdom, in their case, are like seeds that fell among thorns.

There are few others who listen to the words of wisdom attentively, cogitate upon them, and finally the wisdom teaching becomes fruitful with them. With them the teachings are like seeds that fell upon good ground to yield eventually a hundredfold, sixtyfold or thirtyfold crop. That even among such there is a gradation is indicated by the mention about a hundredfold, sixtyfold or thirtyfold crop. Such are called *uttama-adhikārī*s (the best among the competents) in Vedānta. The previously mentioned types could then be considered *anadhikārī*s (non-competent), *manda-adhikārīṣ* (the weakest among the competent), and *madhyama-adhikārī*s (competent of the medium order). This explanation is given by Jesus himself in verses 18-23 of chapter 13.

> And the disciples came and said to Him, "Why do you speak to them in parables?"
>
> He answered and said to them, "Because it has been given to you to know the mysteries of the kingdom of heaven, but to them it has not been given.
>
> For whoever has, to him more will be given, and he will have abundance; but whoever does not have, even what he has will be taken away from him.
>
> Therefore I speak to them in parables." — 13.10-13

Those who were around Jesus hence were of two categories: one, the close disciples, and the other, the newly-arrived multitudes. The words spoken by the *guru,* meant for both, would have differing effects upon them. These words, in the case of the disciples who had already been taught, became helpful for the teaching to become more well-founded, and to gain broader and deeper dimensions. It is in this sense Jesus says, "For whoever has, to him more will be given."

But the newly-arrived multitudes are ordinary, ignorant people; they possess nothing related to wisdom. For them, the words of the *guru* are something very new. These words eventually may drive away the ignorance, their sole possession, and their attention may turn to wisdom. Therefore Jesus says, "Whoever does not have, even what he has will be taken away from him."

Jesus indicates also how rare and of what a hidden nature is the wisdom he teaches. He says:

> Seeing they do not see, and hearing they do not hear, nor do they understand. — 10.13

The ultimate Reality is not apparently visible; rather it remains hidden from our view. For this reason, the wisdom about this Reality is termed *upaniṣad* in India, a term meaning also, "secret wisdom." *Bṛhadāraṇyaka Upaniṣad,* in its *mantra*s from 4.3.23 onward says:

> *yad vai tan na paśyati*
> *paśyan vai tan na paśyati . . .*
>
> *yad vai tan na jighrati*
> *jighran vai tan na jighrati . . .*
>
> *yad vai tan na rasayati*
> *rasayan vai tan na rasayati . . .*
>
> (He in that state does not see. . . . Even when seeing . . . he does not see it. . . . He in that state does not smell . . . . Even when smelt he does not smell it. . . . He in that state does not taste. . . . Even when tasted . . . he does not taste it. . . .)

But his own disciples are differentiated from the multitude by Jesus, thus:

> But blessed are your eyes for they see, and your ears for they hear.
>
> For assurely, I say to you that many prophets and righteous men desired to see what you see, and did not see it, and to hear what you hear, and did not hear it. — 13.16-17

The secret nature of this wisdom is specifically stated in *Bhagavad-Gītā* (15.20) when it says, *"iti guhyatamam śāstram"* (this most secret science). Similarly, *Muṇḍaka Upaniṣad* also says:

nāyam ātmā pravacanena labhyo
na medhayā na bahudhā śrutena ।

This self is not attainable by instruction;
Nor by intellectual power,
Nor even by much scriptural learning. — 3 .2.3

Why is this wisdom a secret? This wisdom is not concerning an object of knowledge. On the other hand, it is merely a realization one attains through interiorizing one's perception and seeing that what is real in oneself is the ultimate Reality or God. The knower here becomes himself the known; the subject becomes the object; the two merge in a non-dual experience. This realization is not attained simply through hearing the words of instruction from a *guru*. Hearing (*śravaṇa*) is to be followed by cogitation (*manana*), eventually ending in the realization of oneness (*nididhyāsana*). The spiritual discipline that includes all these stages together is known as *tapas*, literally "heating up," for it is a self-heating process. For those who lack *tapas*, this wisdom remains unattainable. It is in this sense that Jesus says: "Many prophets and righteous men desired to see what you see, and did not see it, and to hear what you hear, and did not hear it."

1.15

The Priceless Value of Wisdom

JESUS next narrates yet another parable:

> The kingdom of heaven is like a man who sowed good seed in his field,
>
> but while men slept, his enemy came and sowed tares among the wheat and went his way.
>
> But when the grain had sprouted and produced a crop, then the tares also appeared.
>
> So the servants of the owner came and said to him, "Sir, did you not sow good seed in your field? How then does it have tares?"
>
> He said to them, "An enemy has done this." The servants said to him, "Do you want us then to go and gather them up?"
>
> But he said, "No, lest while you gather up the tares you also uproot the wheat with them."
>
> Let both grow together until the harvest, and at the time of harvest. I will say to the reapers, "First gather together tares and bind them in bundles to burn them, but gather the wheat into my barn."
>
> — 13.24-30

Wisdom is to be handed down from a true *guru* (*sad-guru*) to a true disciple (*sacchiṣya*). The value of this wisdom transcends all worldly values and is eternal and unworldly. Yet both the *guru* and disciple are destined to live in this world where many unavoidable necessities and worldly impulses may arise, obstructing the spiritual path of imparting wisdom.

A spiritual life fully devoid of such obstructing factors is rather impossible. Necessities like having to eat and having an abode exist for those who lead a spiritual life also. Even the thought, "I am a person who leads a spiritual life" contains an element of egoism that obstructs the very same spiritual life.

Such unavoidable counteractive factors are caused by some inimical tendencies within ourselves. With this understanding, we can only helplessly allow such factors to remain with us, just like weeds that grow along with the planted crops. Such counteracting elements, in fact, grow within us without our knowledge, as is suggested by the parable that the seeds of the weeds were sowed in the wheat field by an enemy at night when all men were asleep. We may have the intention to weed out such elements completely from within ourselves. Most likely, though such attempts also uproot those factors in us that are conducive for wisdom to strike root, sometimes resulting in the loss of the firmness of mind necessary for wisdom to become well-founded. *Muṇḍaka Upaniṣad* (III.2.4) warns us again:

> *nāyam ātmā balahīnena labhyaḥ*
>
> (This *ātmā* is not obtainable to the one who is not firm in mind.)

Therefore, as discriminative seekers, we must bear with the elements in ourselves that may cause obstruction to the attainment of our spiritual goal, as an unavoidable necessary evil that forms part of our actual life. A good farmer, when the harvest time comes, separates the weeds from the wheat. The tares are burned, and wheat is collected in the barn. Likewise, when a competent seeker's time of fulfilment comes, wisdom alone is given value and is made use of to enrich one's life, whereas all the necessary evils one had to endure in actual life are simply ignored.

Both the friend and foe in this case are within us. The inimical aspect within us has to be differentiated and gotten rid of, and the friendly aspect to be nurtured and utilized for self-upliftment. *Bhagavad-Gītā* says:

> *uddhared ātmanātmānam nātmānam avasādayet* ।
> *ātmaiva hyātmano bandhurātmaiva ripur ātmanaḥ* ॥ — VI.5
>
> (Let one uplift oneself by the self. Let one not let oneself down. Oneself, verily, is the friend of oneself; oneself is one's own enemy as well.)

Jesus provided another parable also about the kindgom of God:

> The kingdom of heaven is like a mustard seed, which a man took and sowed in his field,
>
> which indeed is the least of all the seeds, but when it is grown it is greater than all the herbs and becomes a tree [*sic*], so that the birds of the air come and nest in its branches. — 13.31-33

Wisdom is very minute or subtle, while it is also all-inclusive. It is also beneficial to everyone. All this is indicated by the present parable. Attaining the kingdom of heaven, as we have already seen, means attaining the wisdom of the Self (*Ātmā*). *Ātmā* is an extremely minute reality. This minuteness could be understood from two perspectives.

As a substance, it is inconceivably small because it has no measurements, and is thus invisible. But when realized as the Substance in one's own being, it also becomes evident that it is the same Substance that underlies the being of everything in all the worlds. It is for this reason that *Kaṭha Upaniṣad* (I.2.20) portrays *Ātmā* as

> *anor anīyān mahato mahīyān*
> (Smaller than the smallest and larger than the largest.)

The smallness of the kingdom of heaven could be understood in yet another way. No knowledge about anything in the world is so easy, so direct, as knowing oneself. Self-knowedge, in that sense, is extremely minute. The Self is pure Consciousness in essence. The Consciousness that functions as "I" is what unfolds itself as all the worlds and as the knowledge about everything in all the worlds. There is no object anywhere in any of the numerous worlds, no science, no branch of knowledge, that is not within the ambit of the function of Consciousness. We can thus say, Consciousness, *Ātmā,* the kingdom of heaven, is a huge tree that allows all the worlds, all the sciences, all the branches of knowledge, to nest within itself.

The knowledge you have about anything external serves the purpose only of putting out the fire of your curiosity about it, or to sometimes derive some pleasure from it; but it never makes your life peaceful. Entirely different is the case of knowing *Ātmā* or knowing the kingdom of heaven. It not only makes your life well-founded and full of peace, but the Peace and Happiness you experience in life console everyone around you also. It is like a huge tree that provides room for numerous birds to nest and for many passersby to rest in its shade.

Jesus in yet another parable says:

> The kingdom of heaven is like leaven, which a woman took and hid in three measures of meal till it was all leavened. — 13.33

Fermenting dough for the sake of making bread is a common practice. It makes the bread soft and chewy. It is done by adding a little bit of yeast to the dough. The same also is the nature of Self-knowledge. Though very subtle and minute, it helps the dough of your entire life become fermented, leavened and happy. The Happiness you derive from Self-knowledge is not to merely have known the Self, it also makes your life happiness (*ānanda*) in essential content, whatever be the field of your activity.

Jesus also says:

> The kingdom of heaven is like treasure hidden in a field, which a man found and hid; and for joy over it he goes and sells all that he has and buys that field. — 13.44

A treasure hiding under the soil is not ordinarily visible to anyone. Likewise is the way the kingdom of heaven or *Ātmā* hides within oneself, and in the usual course, remains unseen by anyone. This kingdom of heaven, if searched for as though it exists somewhere else, is never found even after a life-long search for it. Sometimes it is by chance that a seeker, with the guidance of a *guru* or on his own, finds the Reality in himself as the Substance of his own being. On realizing "I am that Reality," he finds all other knowledge and all other wealth to be of little value or of no value at all. He therefore ignores all these and attains the highest Happiness of becoming identified with the plenitude of the kingdom of heaven or of the Self. This experiential plenitude of Happiness is termed *bhūmā* in *Chāndogya Upanisad* (7.23.1, 7.24.1). All this can be seen suggested in the analogy of the treasure hidden in the field, and of the man who finds it, selling all his other possessions and buying this field. The same message is repeated in yet another analogy as follows:

> Again, the kingdom of heaven is like a merchant seeking beautiful pearls,
>
> who, when he had found one pearl of great price, went and sold all that he had and bought it. — 13.45-46

The kingdom of heaven or pure wisdom transcends all notions such as good and evil, moral and immoral. That means, *jñānins* like Jesus live in a realm that is beyond the bounds of customary ethical codes. Yet the deeds they perform in life naturally happen to be righteous. This happens, not because of their sense of duty to obey the prevailing moral codes, but because they cannot perceive their own existence and life as separate from the overall system that supports the universal life, and thus from the existence of other beings. In India, this overall system is really to be termed *dharma* which literally means "that which supports." Such great souls prefer to ignore certain lesser values in life. Yet such values are considered high by most. It is this value-world in which such people live that is really to be counted as hell (*naraka*). They too aspire to make life happy, but what they actually achieve are the trials and tribulations of a hell of their own making. Indicative of all this is the next parable of Jesus:

> Again, the kingdom of heaven is like a dragnet that was cast into the sea and gathered some of every kind,
>
> which, when it was full, they drew to shore and they sat down and gathered the good into vessels, but threw the bad away.
>
> So it will be at the end of the age. The angels will come forth, separate the wicked from among the just, and cast them into the furnance of fire.
>
> There will be wailing and gnashing of teeth. — 13.47-50

The last analogy that Jesus utters in this context runs thus:

> Therefore every scribe instructed concerning the kingdom of heaven is like a householder who brings out of his treasure things new and old. — 13.52

Householders bring out everything inside their houses at least once a year to clean up the entire residence. Such a cleaned house is here compared to the state of mind of the scribes instructed on the kingdom of heaven. The scribes intended here are not the ordinary ones who are fanatic about their allegiance to the Jewish tradition and customs. They, on the other hand, are the ones who are so open-minded as to cleanse their mind of all that has settled there as sediments, either as part of their inborn inner propensities or acquired knowledge, habits and impulses. They, in other words, have undergone the mental process of de-educating themselves.

Scribes customarily are those who are well-learned in Jewish spirituality and its scriputres. Those who lived in the days of Jesus, while honouring the scriputres true to their letters, were unmindful of their real spirit, which is of wisdom significance. The scribes mentioned here, on the other hand, are of the type who are already well-instructed in wisdom. That means, familiarity with scriptures and experiential wisdom find unity in them. Tọ use the Upaniṣadic terminology, they are *satyadharma*s (*Īśa Upaniṣad* 15) (those in whom enlightenment of Reality and righteous behaviour pattern are in unison).

1.16

The Value of Faith

A GURU lives as wisdom embodied. He does not think how his daily needs such as food and clothing will be met. The Reality, of which he is a manifest form, looks after all such things; such is the only possible explanation on this matter. Just as a *guru* does not care for such matters, we also do not have to worry about them. We have only to remain aware that such needs of the *guru*s are somehow met, and our needs also will somehow be met.

Seekers naturally follow the footsteps of such Masters. They also do not think, "Will I get the food I need?", "Will I get a place to sleep?" and so on. They follow a *guru* unmindful of all such matters. Still all such needs are somehow provided at least in the bare minimum. We can only say that it happens as willed by the greatness of the wisdom they are in search of, or by the mysterious power of the ultimate Reality or God.

In India it is customary to give free food to all visitors at temples and *āśrama*s. In certain *āśrama*s there are annual functions in which all the seekers and devotees get together, make serious studies, live together, and return home with a mind spiritually refreshed. They feel satisfied in eating together along with learning together. No one would know who co-operated to run the free kitchen and all the other affairs, and who did not. When everything is over, it may be found that there is provision enough for a few more days for the regular inmates of the *āśrama*. The same phenomenon could be seen in the life of Jesus as well. Indicative of all this is the episode narrated from verses 13-21, chapter 14 of the Gospel. More than 5,000 people had the satisfaction of having eaten and learnt together, while the stock of food readily available was merely five loaves of bread and two fish. Still, there was enough left-over at the end of the mass feeding to fill twelve baskets.

Feeding more than 5,000 people when the food articles available readily at hand were simply five loaves of bread and two fish, became possible merely because of the absolute faith Jesus and his followers had in the one absolute Reality or God. The event narrated that ensues after the above-mentioned one further underscores the value of this faith.

> Immediately Jesus made His disciples get into the boat and go before Him to the other side, while He sent the multitudes away.
>
> And when He had sent the multitudes away. He went up on a mountain by Himself to pray. And when evening had come, He was alone there.
>
> But the boat was now in the middle of the sea, tossed by the waves, for the wind was contrary.
>
> Now in the fourth watch of the night Jesus went to them, walking on the sea.
>
> And when the disciples saw Him walking on the sea, they were troubled, saying, "It is a ghost." And they cried out for fear.
>
> But immediately Jesus spoke to them, saying, "Be of good cheer! It is I, do not be afraid."
>
> And Peter answered Him and said, "Lord, if it is You, command me to come to You on the water."
>
> So He said, "Come." And when Peter had come down out of the boat, he walked on the water to go to Jesus.
>
> But when he saw that the wind was boistrous, he was afraid, and beginning to sink. He cried out, saying, "Lord, save me!"
>
> And immediately Jesus stretched out His hand and caught him, and said to him, "O you of little faith, why did you doubt?"
>
> And when they got into the boat, the wind ceased.
>
> Then those who were in the boat came and worshipped Him, saying, "Truly You are the Son of God". — 14.22-33

The scene introduced here has two sides. One consists of the darkness that spreads out over the sea, where the disciples sit in the boat. Darkness indicates the ignorance the disciples are in, and the vast sea the transactional world called *vyāvahārika* in Vedānta. It is horizontal in significance. The other side is the top of the high mountain where Jesus climbs up and sits alone meditating and praying. This represents the realm of the ultimate Reality (*pāramārthika*) of vertical significance. The ultimate Reality is one, whereas the transactional world is of the many. In this latter world, events could take place favourably or unfavourably, suggested by the contrary wind that tosses the boat about. When this occurs, the disciples, already in ignorance, began to falter and fear. Fear is an emotion normal in the ignorant living in the transactional world. All the same time, Jesus sits alone, and although in external darkness, is filled inside with the brightness of wisdom, fully identified with the Absolute (*Brahman*), pure effulgence in essence. Therefore it was not in the least difficult for him to climb down the hill and reach the disciples to help them, though fully surrounded by an external darkness. Jesus had no worries about the way to reach the disciples in that darkness, for he was fully absorbed in the Absolute. An embodiment of the Absolute, he intended to bring his disciples closer to him. It so happened at that ecstatic moment that he did so by walking on the sea. Its possibility was no problem for Jesus, but for the disciples it was a mystery.

A *jñānin* always lives in complete identity with the all-underlying Reality; he always experiences all the worlds as the unfoldment of himself. This experience is portrayed as *ātmata evedam sarvam* (everything originates from myself) in *Chāndogya Upaniṣad* (7.26.1). What is possible and what is impossible for the one ultimate Reality (*Ātmā*) can never be determined by mere human mind. The role of a human being and his mind is like that of a leaf that appears and disappears upon some remote corner of an everlasting huge tree. A fleeting leaf can never comprehend the nature of the overall tree, though it forms an integral part of it. A human can only conceive the idea that all that is thinkable and unthinkable are possible with *Ātmā*. In short, nothing is unworldly and impossible in the overall system of the phenomenal world, nor with the one who experiences his full identity with that system. Expounding this experiential identity and the possibility of everything, Narayana Guru says:

> Everything is possible because
> You always, as pure Consciousness,
> Exist in the mind giving out
> Constantly what is proper
> To all the worlds. O Mother!
>
> — *Mannamtala Devī Stavam,* verse 4

The disciples are quite ignorant of this secret, and therefore upon their seeing Jesus walking on the sea, he remains hidden from their view, and instead they see a ghost. Perceiving the one Reality (*Ātmā*) as this ghost-like world is normal with the ignorant.

Why did the disciples not recognize their own *guru* with whom they were living everyday? The first answer that comes to mind would be that it was dark then. The suggestion is that the disciples remained in the darkness of ignorance. What the ignorant can do with regard to the enlightened and their grandeur is but look at them in amazement, yet never to understand them.

Naciketas, the disciple in *Kaṭha Upaniṣad,* had to wait at the gate of the Guru Yama, for three days eating nothing. To compensate for this torment, Yama granted him three boons. The first boon the boy Naciketas chose was that he should be recognized and gladly received by his father upon his return home from the abode of Yama after receiving instruction on the secret wisdom. Why couldn't a father recognize his own son? Naciketas would be returning home after becoming enlightened and attaining immortality, whereas his father would still remain ignorant in the world of Vedic ritualism. The difference between the enlightened and the ignorant exists in this case between the son and the father. Seldom does an ignorant person properly recognize an enlightened one. This is why Naciketas chose this first boon. This choice also implies the prayerful wish in the mind of Naciketas that his father would also rise up into the realm of higher wisdom.

Here as well, the enlightenend Jesus tells his ignorant disciples, "Be of good cheer! It is I, do not be afraid."

The words "It is I" of Jesus, as a Vedāntin perceives, mean, "It is the Self (*Ātmā*) that you see". That means, everything perceived is nothing but the Self (*Ātmā*) become manifest. The one who is well aware of this reality is never disturbed by fear, for one sees himself alone everywhere; hence the words of Jesus, "Do not be afraid."

But realizing this Truth requires full faith in the one Reality and the conviction "I am that Reality." This awareness was lacking in the disciples of Jesus, and thus they were of "little faith." Therefore, the words of Jesus "It is I" were not understood by each of the disciples, "It is myself," as they should be, but as "It is Jesus." Peter, as the representative of such disciples says, "If it is You, command me to come to You". These words "If it is You" of Peter show a sort of doubt in his mind as to the veracity of Jesus's words, and he attempts to remove that doubt. The firm word "Come" of Jesus shows his intense desire to bring his doubting disciples to his side of full faith.

"Everything is possible" is simply natural with those who have full faith in the one ultimate Reality, who dedicate themselves to and find identity with that Reality. But so long as even a little bit of doubt remains in one's mind, the wind of fate will certainly blow in an unfavourable direction, or at least it will feel so. This is indicated by the event in which the wind becomes boistrous when Peter begins to walk on the sea. So then he becomes afraid, and he begins to sink, he cries out, "Lord, save me!"

Anyone, when faced with such a situation, will cry out, "O God, save me!" As this happened, Jesus, as the embodiment of God, stretches out his helping hand of faith to catch him and says, "O, you of little faith, why did you doubt?" On stepping into the safe boat of faith, the adverse wind subsides and the disciples become fearless.

The faith mentioned is equal to the *śraddhā* of Vedānta. *Bhagavad-Gītā* (IV.39-40) emphatically says: *"śraddhāvān labhate jñānam"* (the one of full faith attains wisdom), and *"saṁśayātmā vinaśyati"* (the doubting one perishes). It is the realization of complete identity with the Absolute (*Brahman*) that raises Jesus to the status of being the Son of God. And this is indicated by the words of the disciples sitting in the boat, "Truly You are the Son of God".

1.17

Tradition, Purity

CHAPTER 15 of the Gospel begins thus:

> Then the scribes and Pharisees who were from Jerusalem came to Jesus, saying,
>
> "Why do Your disciples transgress the tradition of elders? For they do not wash their hands when they eat bread."
>
> But He answered and said to them, "Why do you also transgress the commandment of God because of your tradition?
>
> For God commanded, saying, "Honour your father and your mother," and "He who curses father or mother, let him be put to death."
>
> But you say, "Whoever says to his father or mother", "Whatever profit you might have received from me has been dedicated to the temple" —
>
> 'is released from honouring his father or mother.' Thus you have made the commandment of God of no effect by your tradition.
>
> Hypocrites! Well did Isaiah prophesy about you, saying:
>
> 'These people draw near to Me with their mouth, and honour Me with their lips, but their hearts are far from Me.
>
> And in vain they worship Me, teaching as doctrines the commandments of men.'"
>
> Then He called the multitude and said to them, "Hear and understand:
>
> "Not what goes into the mouth defiles a man; but what comes out of the mouth, this defiles a man." — 15.1-11

A popular Indian custom demands that people should wash their hands before eating. It is but a hygienic habit that hands should be clean when eating with one's fingers. The same custom existed amongst the Jews also. It is for not adhering to it that the scribes and Pharisees find fault with the disciples of Jesus.

This custom came into vogue not as commanded by God, but was only a creation of man-turned tradition. Its value pertains simply to bodily hygiene. Eating with your fingers without washing your hands only results in a little bit of dirt entering your mouth. Much higher than such down-to-earth values are those pertaining to noble social morality. And in that realm comes the responsibility of honouring and looking after one's parents. Jesus points out that there are also higher commandments of God that pertain to this matter. But such commandments become ignored by Jews in the face of certain traditional customs. According to one such, if you have made enough offerings to God, you are not bound to honour and look after your own parents. Promiscuously mixing up these two value worlds is the error that vitiated the Jewish tradition. It allows people to forgo their responsibility to their parents on the grounds that they show full devotion to God. Ignoring noble things, though of lower value, on the claim that other noble things of a higher value are being honoured, is not justifiable, and it is not the proper way of being religious. The love for God, on the other hand, should become reflected in actual life as the love and regard for one's parents as well as for everyone. *Taittirīya Upaniṣad* (1.11.2), in this sense, instructs, *"mātr̥ devo bhava"* (become one for whom mother is a god), *"pitr̥devo bhava"* (become one for whom father is a god), *"ācāryadevo bhava"* (become one for whom teacher is a god *"atithidevo bhava"* (become one for whom guest is a god). That the love and devotion one has for one's mother, father, teacher and guest are equal to the ones for God is the message given in this Upaniṣadic teaching. Social justice and responsibilities are there, and one's faith and devotion to God also prevails. The latter is of higher value than the former. Still, ignoring the former is not proper. Customs related to bodily hygiene are still lower in value than social morality. In short, it is the same people who transgress in the realm of social morality that finds fault with those who ignore customs related to bodily hygiene.

How does this happen? It happens simply because tradition as well as the commandments of God are honoured true only to the latter, while people remain completely ignorant of their true spirit. That is why Jesus quotes the cursing words of the prophet Isaiah thus: "These people draw near to Me with their mouth, and honour Me with their lips, but their hearts are far from Me. And in vain they worship Me, teaching as doctrines the commandments of men. Then He called the multitude and said to them, "Hear and understand:" Not what goes into the mouth defiles a man, but what comes out of the mouth, this defiles man."

Jesus explains this to his disciples himself thus:

Do you not yet understand that whatever enters the mouth goes into

> the stomach and is eliminated?
>
> But those things which proceed out of the mouth come from the heart, and they defile a man.
>
> For out of the heart proceed evil thoughts, murders, adulteries, fornications, thefts false witness, blasphemies.
>
> These are the things which defile a man, but to eat with unwashed hands does not defile a man. — 15.17-20

What goes into the mouth of man is simply food. The dirt in it is eliminated. But what comes out of the mouth are words. These reflect one's thought and understanding. Should these go wrong with you, everything goes wrong with you.

When the scribes and Pharisees were encountered by Jesus thus, his disciples asked him:

> Do you know that the Pharisees were offended when they heard this saying?
>
> But He answered and said, "Every plant which My heavenly Father had not planted will be uprooted.
>
> Let them alone. They are blind leaders of the blind. And if the blind leads the blind, both will fall into a ditch." — 15.12-14

The stand of Jesus here is that of an *jñānin* who is an absolutist. As a *jñānin* adopts a firm stand in life, he does not care for the public opinion about it, nor even for the infamy it causes. Those who are afraid of disrepute, and change their stand, are not well-founded in their vision of Reality. Such are to be considered ignorant. The scribes and Pharisees mentioned here, though leaders of the Jews, are simply ignorant, as are the people led by them. The blind leading the blind results simply in both falling into a pit. In order to avoid this danger, what the ignorant have to do is accept the leadership of the enlightened. But this happens only in the case of those ignorant ones who are well-aware of their ignorance.

A *jñānin* finds acceptable only what agrees with the one Reality, what agrees with the total system of life. That means only what has God's consent. Everything else is ignored by him. This is the sense in which Jesus says: "Every plant which My heavenly Father had not planted will be uprooted."

The analogy of the blind leading the blind appears in *Muṇḍaka Upaniṣad* (1.2.8) as well as in *Kaṭha Upaniṣad* (2.5). The comparable instance seen in the Upaniṣads is that of the ignorant who are interested in Vedic rituals being led and exploited by the equally ignorant priests. That means that the Vedic ritualism known as *karma-kāṇḍa* appears in the Upaniṣads as the anterior position (*pūrva-pakṣa*) that is meant to be corrected (*siddhānta-pakṣa*) by the wisdom of the Upaniṣad known as *jñāna-kāṇḍa*. The Pharisees of the Jewish context in Jesus's day were almost equal to the ritualists of Vedism.

1.18

A Peep into the Core of Wisdom

> The Pharisees and Sadducees came, and testing Him asked that He would show them a sign from heaven. — 16.1

He answered:

> A wicked and adulterous generation seeks after a sign, and no sign shall be given to it except the sign of the prophet Jonah. — 16.4

The Pharisees and Sadducees who approached Jesus demanded of him a sign from heaven. In their perception, heaven was a world that existed somewhere above this world. But it is within himself that a *jñānin* like Jesus perceives heaven, as stated clearly by Jesus himself in yet another context. Such a heaven is nothing other than the kingdom of the Self (*svārājya*) conceived by the Upaniṣads. A *jñānin* has no sign to show others what he experiences within himself. Jesus, for this reason, said, "A wicked and adulterous generation seeks after a sign."

The enlightened state one experiences within himself may only be either believed or disbelieved by another.

The Book of Jonah in the Old Testament makes it clear that there is no other alternative than to obey the commands of God, whether for a prophet or for those to whom the prophet was sent. Jesus replies likewise to the ignorant Pharisees and Sadducees who demanded a sign from him. To them Jesus said, "An evil and adulterous generation seeks after a sign, and no sign will be given to it except the sign of the prophet Jonah." In other words, Jesus compared their faithless demands to the faithless demands of Jonah. Jonah was called upon by God to prophesy to the city of Nineveh. He then tried to avoid the command of God, without success. Though living unmindful of God's will, and so living unrighteous, the city changed its ways upon hearing the word of God from Jonah's lips. Such a willingness to accept God's will saved them from destruction. None the less, Jonah himself remained reluctant to accept God's will at the end of the story.

Jesus was not so. He had no alternative but to teach the Jews among whom he was sent, and he knew this well. He was fully willing to abide by the command of God. Like all prophets, his mission was to inspire people to live according to the same understanding and faith. The only viable option before the Jews then was to accept God's message sent through Jesus, the un-reluctant prophet. This message was, as we know, that the kingdom had come. If the people of Nineveh were willing to accept a reluctant prophet, how much more should the Jews accept an un-reluctant prophet? Yet certain Pharisees and Sadducees were not willing to accept the will of God as sent through His messenger Jesus. Instead, they sought a sign from him. But wisdom being pure and absolute, it needed no external sign. To put the same verity in theological terms, there is no relevance for a third factor when establishing the right relation between man and God. Those ignorant of this verity seek a sign. Just as God did not bend his will to the demands of the faithless Jonah, so the Pharisees and Sadducees here will not have the kind of sign they demanded. As such, they only received the sign of Jonah.

It could be asked, "Had not Jesus shown signs of heaven when he fed 4,000 people with merely seven loaves of bread, when he healed many of their diseases, and on many such occasions?" Such signs were shown not before the people who came to test him, but for the benefit of those who had full faith in him. Jesus, on all such occasions, repeatedly tells the beneficiaries, "Your faith saved you." A genuine *guru* never testifies as to his merits before those who approach merely to test him. At the same time, such a one reveals his wisdom, the kingdom of heaven, to those who approach with full faith. This fact is also implied in the present episode.

Verses 5-12 of chapter 16 underscore the importance of the faith that disciples should have for their *guru.* Lacking in this faith, they may worry about their food when travelling with the *guru*, and what's more, they may remain incapable of comprehending the deeper significance of the *guru*'s words. The necessity of faith in one's *guru* thus has two facets. One pertains to the horizontal world of our daily bread, and the other is related to understanding what the *guru* means when uttering certain words of wisdom. This latter facet has a vertical dimension.

Thereafter,

> When Jesus came into the region of Caesarea Philippi, He asked His disciples, saying, "Who do men say that I, the Son of Man, am?"

> So they said, "Some say John the Baptist, some Elijah, and others Jeremiah or one of the prophets."
>
> He said to them, "But who do you say that I am?"
>
> And Simon Peter answered, and said, "You are the Christ, the Son of the living God."
>
> Jesus anwered and said to him, "Blessed are you, Simon Bar-Jonah, for flesh and blood has not revealed this to you, but My Father who is in heaven.
>
> And I also say to you that you are Peter, and on this rock I will build My church, and the gates of Hades shall not prevail against it.
>
> And I will give you the keys of the kingdom of heaven and whatever you bind on earth will be bound in heaven, and whatever you loose on earth will be loosed in heaven." — 16.13-19

Jesus evidently was honoured by everyone here. Some saw him as a prophet equal to John the Baptist. For certain others, he was equal to the Prophet Elijah. Still others thought of him as the Prophet Jeremiah reborn. There were also those who saw him as equal to certain other prophets. Jesus came to know all this from his own disciples. But his interest was not in public opinion but on knowing what his own disciples thought of him. Asked directly by Jesus of this, Peter, with no hesitation, said, "You are the Christ, the Son of the living God."

The word "Christ" means, "the anointed one." Anointing means pouring oil, milk, water or some other liquid ceremoniously on someone, as a sign of consecration. But no Gospel story tells us that Jesus underwent any such anointing ceremony. Then who anointed Jesus, to make a Christ of him? The anointing ceremony in the case of Jesus, it is to be presumed, was merely virtual, not actual. And this virtual anointing must have been officiated by God himself. That means, Jesus was filled inside and outside with the being of God. This was the way he was virtually anointed by God with the spirit of God. Peter himself indicates in what sense Jesus became anointed, by the words, "the Son of the living God."

Had Jesus been the Son of God in the biological sense, Peter would not have qualified him as the "the Son of the living God." A non-living being, we know, cannot beget children. "The living God", therefore, is to be understood in the philosophical sense. Put in Vedāntic terms, God is the imperishable living Reality that unfolds itself as all the worlds. The entire cosmic system admittedly being a living entity, the Reality underlying it also has to be a living one which is the reason why Peter qualifies God as "the living". A human being is simply a tiny speck of the countless and boundless manifestations of that one undecaying Reality, called God here. A man, upon knowing himself to be so, becomes the Son of God. Such knowers of Reality in Vedānta are known as *jñānins*. Jesus here is not merely such a *jñānin,* but is a *guru* as well. A *guru* is a person who is enlightened about the one Reality, and readily willing and expert to impart to a seeker what he or she has realized. Such a Son of God is Jesus, as perceived by Peter. The implication is that the secret wisdom that transformed Jesus into a *guru* has become revealed to Peter. Yet so far in this Gospel we have not seen Jesus revealing this secret anywhere either to Peter or to any other disciple. Though it was stated by Jesus in verse 11 of chapter 13, "it has been given to you to know the mysteries of the kingdom of heaven," that mystery was not seen before as given to them to know. We can see the wisdom secret implied in this scene.

Gurus in the usual course teach with words as the medium. But as the subtlest core of wisdom is reached, words fail to give expression to it. About that stage, *Taittirīya Upaniṣad* (II.9) therefore says:

> That state from which words along with the mind, withdraw incapable of attaining.

Narayana Guru describes it as a "Silence that resounds and re-echoes in its neutral fullness of meaning" (*Devīstavam*, verse 1). The *ṛṣi* of *Īśa Upaniṣad,* after expounding the dialectical secret of wisdom to the ultimate limit possible by the use of words, virtually says: "What has been revealed so far was only the golden casket within which was kept the valuable gem most worthy of being sought out. The casket, being made of gold, could be mistaken for the valuable thing we are after. Upon recognizing that it is only a casket, one will try to open it, which requires the Grace of God also."

The actual words of the *ṛṣi* are:

> *The face of the Reality is veiled*
> *By a golden casket.*
> *O God, please open it so that*
> *This one who is an aspirant of Reality*
> *And stands for righteousness*
> *Could perceive it clearly.*
>
> — *Mantra* 15

Very similar is the meaning implied by the words of Peter also. Yet for this secret wisdom to be stated more explicitly we have to wait until the Gospel according to John is reached, where Jesus states, "I and My Father are one." The implications of this statement will be examined as we comment on that Gospel.

The secret that was not directly stated by Jesus was visualized by Peter with the words of Jesus themselves as a means. That is to say, Peter perceives in the words of Jesus, more than what they literally signify. And that is the way Peter happened to recognize Jesus as "the Son of the living God." It does not mean that Jesus biologically was the Son of God. Jesus, upon recognizing that Peter intuitively perceived the secret wisdom that fills his (Jesus's) being, gladly declares to Peter, "Blessed are you Simon Bar-Jonah, for flesh and blood has not revealed this to you, but My Father who is in heaven."

It has always been an indomitable urge with almost all the enlightened ones to somehow convey to posterity what they visualized. In order to accomplish it, they very often make some heirarchical arrangements as well. This peculiarity in one sense is a sort of extended form of the human instinct to share what one knows and experiences. This arrangement, in the case of Jesus, took the shape of the institutionalized Christian church. This church, though originally started with the intention of propagating the catholicity of the wisdom-teachings of Jesus, in course of time, became transformed sometimes as a rigid and closed religion, often fanatically arguing that only those who believe in Jesus Christ the person are saved. There is no reason to believe that such was the intention of Jesus. So open-minded and of such universal significance was the vision of Jesus, as well as his words which reflect that vision, that the very opposite can be presumed.

Anyhow, Jesus also had the intense desire that the secret wisdom he became enlightenend upon should be handed down through generations for the benefit of the people at large. Fulfilling such a desire requires at least one disciple who has gone deep into the core of the secret wisdom. Jesus finds such a disciple in Peter. He therefore says, "You are Peter, and on this rock I will build my church."

A true disciple (*sacchiṣya*) can fulfil such a mission only if he is endowed with a transparent vision of the one Reality and the firmness of mind to stick to it at all cost. Jesus is now fully convinced that these qualities exist in Peter. This is why he compares Peter with a firm rock. This is also a pun as Petros (Peter in Greek) means "stone."

Anything built on such a rock will definitely be stable. The value of a *guru*'s vision transcends the limitations of time. It is this Reality that Vedāntins perceive as the birthless and deathless *Ātmā* (the Self) or *Brahman* (the Absolute). Whether a *guru* or a disciple, the one who lives constantly with the awareness "I am that Reality" has already attained immortality. A life well-founded on such an enlightened conviction also crosses the bounds of birth and death. The one who lives thus is never touched by the fear of death. That is why Jesus said, "The gates of Hades shall not prevail against it."

The kingdom of heaven, as has already become clear by now, is the inner secret of wisdom. Big palaces usually have secret chambers in them, to be opened only with special keys by the specially trained personnel. The inner chambers of wisdom also require certain special keys to open them. Jesus here tells Peter, "I will give you the key of the kingdom of heaven."

This secret key to wisdom, in India, is known as *yoga-buddhi*, and in the West "dialectics." *Yoga-buddhi* is profusely made use of in *Bhagavad- Gītā* which claims itself to be a *yoga-śāstra* or the science of dialectics). No scene has so far been described in this Gospel in which Jesus disclosed the key to the secret wisdom to his disciples. But now, upon seeing in Peter a rock-like firm-minded disciple, Jesus tells him, "I shall give you the key to the secret wisdom."

What is the nature of this dialectical method of revealing the non-dual Reality? Reality has two aspects in it. One is the ultimate, abstract and invisible Reality which can merely be understood philosophically. This Reality, when, owing to its own indomitable creative urge and will, becomes self-manifest, it appears as all the worlds. This visible concrete world is the other aspect. Whatever has appeared as gross or subtle in these worlds, whatever appears now, whatever will appear in future, the potential for all such remains latent in the abstract Reality. Whatever is not latent in that Reality may not become manifest in the world, and whatever does not find expression in the visible, concrete world remains latent in the abstract Reality. A sort of one-to-one correspondence exists between the one abstract and absolute Reality and the countlessly multitudinous apparent, concrete worlds. This bipolarity exists between these two, in spite of the two being opposite in nature. Perceiving that the one does not exist without the other, constitutes the core of non-duality. How this non-duality of the two is to be intuitively perceived by adopting such a method is indicated by Jesus in these words, "Whatever you bind on the earth will be bound in heaven, and whatever you loose on earth will be loosed in heaven."

The nature of the non-dual Reality and the way of realizing it are revealed by a *guru* only to his closest disciple or disciples who have established a fully dedicated bipolarity with him. A *guru* never prefers to teach it to the general public. Even if taught they do not understand it, because they are not yet competent for such lessons. A *guru*, therefore, when facing the general public, says something only that touches the peripheral aspects of the wisdom and its value. It is by considering the secret nature of the core of wisdom that Jesus commanded his disciples to tell no one that he was Jesus the Christ. It may at first sight be presumed that Jesus knew in advance that the elders, scribes and Pharisees together would cause his crucifixion, and it was for this reason that he made this command to his disciples. But it becomes quite evident in verse 23 that follows that Jesus was not at all afraid of such an eventuality; he did not even desire to avoid it.

1.19

The Insuperable Will of the Absolute

A SELF-REALIZED *guru* perceives his own existence and life simply as part of the mysterious unfoldment of the Self, which we call "Nature" (*prakṛti*). The events that take place in nature can be understood only as being guided by the will of the Absolute, called here God or the Father in heaven. All the events in nature, in short, happen as willed by God. A *jñānin* lives fully in unison with such a will of God, and never desires to have a course of life that deviates from the course of events of nature. Even if he has to face an untimely death as part of it, a *jñānin* never desires to somehow stop it.

For close disciples to desire avoiding the possibility of death of their dear *guru* is but natural and noble conduct on their part, looked at from a worldly perspective. Simply for having such a noble desire, a disciple or his desire might be deridingly named "Satan" without hesitation by a real *guru*. Verses 21-23 of chapter 16 of the Gospel show this aspect very clearly. Such disciples, who desire to save their *guru* from what happens inevitably as nature's unfoldment, care only for the will of men, not for the will of God; they treat human values higher than divine ones. It is evident from the following sentences that Jesus was not at all afraid of what was going to happen during his life.

> From that time Jesus began to show to His disciples that He must go to Jerusalem, and suffer many things from the elders and chief priests and scribes, and be killed, and be raised again the third day.
>
> Then Peter took Him aside and began to rebuke Him saying, "Far be it from You, Lord, this shall not happen to You!"
>
> But He turned and said to Peter, "Get behind Me, Satan! You are an offence to Me, for you are not mindful of the things of God, but the things of men." — 16.21-23

Jesus has already disclosed to his disciples that he would soon be crucified. We will shortly see the scene of Jesus himself carrying the cross in which he was to be crucified. Spiritual life is not an easy one. It sometime ends up in tragic situations. A *jñānin*, unmindful of all such dangers, desires only to tread the path of God or (*Brahman*). The disciples that follow such a *guru* also should be prepared to undergo such tribulations and persecutions. Perhaps one may have to sacrifice one's own life for this cause. The instinct for self-preservation is meant to save one's own life. But those who are willing to sacrifice their own lives become blessed with realizing the Self or perceiving the kingdom of God. In fact, such an attainment implies obliteration of the individual self. Jesus therefore tells his disciples:

> If anyone desires to come after Me, let him deny himself, and take up his cross and follow Me.
>
> For whoever desires to save his life will lose it. — 16.24-25

Different is the case of those who incessantly experience their oneness with the ultimate Reality. They see their being in the being of the Supreme Self. Therefore, it is that Reality that makes their lives meaningful. This experience of life being filled with meaning, runs throughout their lives. By relinquishing their own individuated mode of existence into the all-inclusive Reality, they do not really lose their lives, but that Reality becomes theirs. Therefore Jesus says,

> Whoever loses his life for My sake will find it. — 16.25

The words "for My sake" of Jesus are understood by a Vedāntin in the sense that Śrī Kṛṣṇa says *mayi* (in Me) in *Bhagavad-Gītā*. In short, the experiential aspect in the life of a *jñānin* is that of offering himself as an oblation into the sacrificial fire of the Absolute, and then living as the Absolute.

Attaining immortality (*amṛtatva*) is the ultimate goal of the Vedāntic search for Reality. This goal is attained by realizing oneself to be nothing other than the birthless and deathless *Ātmā* or *Brahman*. This realization is attained by a disciple when the *guru* reveals to him the secret wisdom. This secret becoming revealed means that the Self-experience of the *guru* becomes the Self-experience of the disciple. This event means that the Son of Man enters the kingdom of the Self for the disciple as with the Master. Jesus indicates that certain other disciples who are competent to attain this immortality are also there. This statement could be considered a sort of encouragement given by Jesus to his disciples besides Peter. Jesus says:

> Assurely I say to you, there are some standing here who shall not taste death till they see the Son of Man coming in His kingdom.
>
> — 16.28

The words "coming in His kingdom" could be interpreted as Jesus going back and becoming absorbed to his real kingdom of God (*Brahman*). The meaning as such is, there are certain disciples who attain immortality upon Jesus becoming absorbed in *Brahman*. When the disciple realizes Reality, his Kingdom of the Self and the *guru*'s Kingdom of the Self are not two. Therefore "His kingdom" could also be treated as related to the disciple.

1.20

Transfiguration, Faith

VERSES 1-13 of chapter 17 describe the scene of Jesus becoming transfigured on a high mountain in the presence of Peter, James and John. His face shone like the sun; his clothes became as white as the light. The prophets Moses and Elijah also appeared to them as talking with Jesus. The three disciples decided to make three tabernacles on that spot in memory of the divine vision they had of the three prophets together.

This event shows the devotion and worshipful attitude the disciples had developed towards Jesus, and that Jesus had acknowledged it and valued it. That means, full bipolarity between the *guru* and the three disciples had become firmly established. The unworldly vision the disciples had was a reflection of that mutual rapport. According to the text of the Gospel, it is difficult to say definitely whether this vision was merely seen by the disciples in Jesus, or shown deliberately by Jesus. Such visions are seen to be found in the lives of some who follow the spiritual path. To disclose to another that you had such a vision, would most likely be taken as a sign of insanity. Just because someone else rejects such a vision as absurd, the vision as such does not become false. Only a mind that is fully prepared can have an enlightened vision. That preparedness need not be there in the minds of others, and therefore others need not perceive it.

Such a vision normally relates to something that your mind is fully devoted to with the greatest interest. In the present case, the minds of the three disciples feel amazed by the purity of insight contained in the wise words of Jesus. That purity of insight is reflected in seeing the clothes of Jesus as white as the light. They perceive this divine nature of Jesus as a continuation of the traditions of Moses and Elijah. They see him as the one who revalued the teachings of these previous prophets and restated them in a new way that is more open-minded and universal. That the experience of this vision was for these disciples alone, and not something that others also should or may have, is indicated by these words of Jesus:

> Tell the vision to no one until the Son of Man is risen from the dead.
> — 17.9

It was because of it, they became incapable of curing the epileptic boy whom Jesus could cure. Still they were his disciples and Jesus did not hesitate to address them deridingly as "O faithless and perverse generation". On the other hand, "everything is possible", would be the byword for the person of full faith.

Verses 24-27 of chapter 17, show how even the worldly obligations of the enlightened are also taken care of by God, and read thus:

> And when they had come to Capernaum, those who received the temple tax came to Peter and said, "Does your Teacher not pay the temple tax?"
>
> He said, "Yes." And when he had come into the house, Jesus anticipated him saying, "What do you think, Simon? From whom do the kings of the earth take customs or taxes, from their own sons or from strangers?"
>
> Peter said, to Him, "From strangers." Jesus said to him, "Then the sons are free.
>
> Nevertheless, lest we offend them, go to the sea, cast in a hook, and take the fish that comes up first. And when you have opened its mouth, you will find a piece of money, take that and give it to them for Me and you."

Kings do not collect taxes or customs duties from their own children. Likewise, no temple tax is to be collected from the Son of God, for a temple is the abode of God. *Gurus* and prophets are those who live for God or the Absolute, as the embodiment of God. Therefore, a *guru* is not bound to pay temple taxes. Explaining this principle to the tax collecting officials would simply confuse them. Jesus, for this reason, decides to pay the temple tax, but not with any money that he earned, but with the money he received purely because of the glory of God. Not only the money for paying taxes, but everything required for day-to-day sustenance also naturally reach a *guru,* simply because of the glory of God. This glory of God is apparent in the event where Jesus gets the money for paying the temple tax from the mouth of a fish. Śrī Kr̥ṣṇa, the *guru* of *Bhagavad-Gītā* also tells Arjuna:

> Do not create confusion in the minds of the ignorant attached to actions. The wise should encourage such people by being engaged in actions as one in full identity with the Absolute. — III.23

The event narrated in verses 14-20 shows, that, in spite of their full faith in the supreme wisdom of Jesus, the disciples were not yet fully convinced of their having made it their own so that it is seen reflected in their own actual lives.

1.21

Humility, Compassion

THE disciples now feel, they have not yet entered the kingdom of heaven. therefore, Verses. 1-4 of chapter 18 read as follows:

> At that time the disciples came to Jesus, saying, "Who then is greatest in the kingdom of heaven?"
>
> And Jesus called a little child to Him, set him in the midst of them,
>
> and said: "Assuredly I say to you, unless you are converted and become as little children, you will by no means enter the kingdom of heaven."
>
> Therefore whoever humbles himself as this little child is the greatest in the kingdom of heaven.

By "the greatest in the kingdom of heaven" we mean, the one who has reached the purity and clarity of wisdom. The question, in other words, is, "Who is fully competent (*uttama-adhikārī*) to attain wisdom?" Jesus answers straightaway, those who become converted in their minds and become like little children are fully competent.

Ordinarily, people live with a heap of acquired ideas and the memories of previously lived experiences. The colourings of all such ideas and experiences are already imprinted in their minds, shaping their way of thinking and the concepts they formulate. As such, people's concept of life and of Reality is vitiated by such coloured perceptions. In short, the true nature of Reality is not seen by anyone. Put in Vedāntic terms, each has knowledge conditioned by *avidyā* (ignorance). Avoiding this danger and perceiving Reality as it is requires one to mentally become deconditioned through de-education and become as pure and innocent as a child. A child's mind is untainted by any kind of conditioned conceptualization and formulation of parochial ideas. One's mind, in other words, has to become like a clean slate. In such a mind alone does the true visualization of Realtiy become well-founded.

The ideas and ideals that give shape to such conditioned ways, often make many into egoistic self-admirers. But true knowledge makes man humble; as is underscored by the words of *Bhagvad-Gītā* (5.18): *vidyā-vinaya-sampanne* (in the case of the one who has become rich with humility through acquiring knowledge). Such humility, in the case of elders, is to be cultivated through practice, whereas with children this humility and unconditioned state of mind are simply natural. This is the reason why Jesus says, "Whoever humbles himself as this little child is the greatest in the kingdom of heaven." It is as true to say those who are humble enter the kingdom of heaven, as it is to say, those who enter the kingdom of heaven naturally become humble.

Verses 5-6 of chapter 18 are as follows:

> And whoever receives one little child like this in My name receives Me.
>
> But whoever causes one of these little ones who believe in Me to sin, it would be better for him if a millstone were hung around his neck, and he were drowned in the depth of the sea.

What is meant by "child" here, as we have already seen, is the one whose mind has become pure and innocent like that of a child. It was also seen that only those of such a mind are admitted to the kingdom of heaven. Such entry invariably requires the guidance of a *guru* like Jesus. Jesus's words, "receives one little child like this in My name" signify the mind of the seeker that becomes pure and innocent on the one hand, and on the other, keeps it attuned to the *guru* with a full bipolarity. In short, the difference, in principle, between a fully competent seeker who has also found his *guru* and established an intimate rapport with him on the one side, and the *guru* on the other side, is quite insignificant. This principle is implied in these words of Jesus: "Whoever receives one little child like this in My name receives Me."

A notion prevails in India amongst the pious people of the Vaiṣṇavite and Śaivite sects that worshipping Viṣṇu or Śiva (God) and worshipping their devotees are of equal value. Almost a similar attitude is seemingly acknowledged by Jesus here. But those who cause troubles to such innocent seekers are the types that do not value wisdom. Though living biologically, they are as if already dead. Such are the implications of verse 6.

Verses 7-9 read thus:

> Woe to the world because of offences! For offences must come, but woe to that man by whom that offence comes!
>
> And if your hand or foot causes you to sin, cut it off and cast it from

> you. It is better for you to enter into life lame or maimed, rather than having two hands or two feet, to be cast into the everlasting fire.
>
> And if your eye causes you to sin, pluck it out and cast it from you. It is better for you to enter into life with one eye, rather than having two eyes, to be cast into hell fire.

The "offences" as understood here and in the last verse are the factors that stand against one's attainment of the final goal. The main cause of woes in life for humans is their ignorance. Therefore, gaining wisdom is what one ultimately needs to make life without woes. And whatever stands against this attainment is the worst of all evils. Even though no one likes evils, avoiding evils altogether in life is practically impossible. Hence the words of Jesus, "For offences must come."

Naturally occurring evils are different from man-made evils. The worst of all such man-made evils is obstructing the wisdom path of humble and innocent seekers. Jesus asks those who cause such obstructions to cut and throw away the organ that was instrumental in doing this, so that they might enter real life even as maimed persons. The moral lesson Jesus gives here is very forceful indeed. The strong suggestion in these words is that mental vices and the evils caused by them, are much worse than if we remain physically impaired.

Verses 10-14 are as follows:

> Take need that you do not despise one of these little ones for I say to you that in heaven their angels always see the face of My Father who is in heaven.
>
> For the Son of Man has come to save that which is lost.
>
> What do you think? If a man has a hundred sheep, and one of them goes astray, does he not leave the ninety-nine and go to the mountains to seek the one that is straying?
>
> And if he should find it, assuredly, I say to you, he rejoices more over that sheep than over the ninety-nine that did not go astray.
>
> Even so it is not the will of your Father who is in heaven that one of these little ones should perish.

It is a very common habit in society to treat children as being of little significance. So is deriding those who live as seekers with innocent minds. Such are even dubbed "crazy" sometimes by those who consider themselves to be respectable gentle folk. But it is these insignificant and ignored ones who become blessed with the possibility of entering the abode of the Father in heaven (the realm of higher wisdom). This secret is stated by Jesus in terminology familiar to the Semitic religions thus: "In heaven their angels always see the face of My Father who is in heaven." Jesus then warns us, "Take heed that you do not despise one of these little ones."

He then declares the nature of his life-mission thus: "The Son of Man has come to save that which is lost." He then narrates the parable of the lost sheep. Who really is the lost sheep as understood by Jesus here? It should be "one of these little ones" as already stated. How did such a one become lost? There was reference earlier to those who cause offences. Those who consider themselves important people in the society often become readily willing to frighten, insult or even to tempt those who lead simple lives as seekers. Such simple people who thus happen to go astray are here compared to lost sheep. The relevance of this parable is to be related to the way of life of many Jews of that time who worked as shepherds. Jesus thus makes clear that bringing the one that happens to be lost, back to the path of wisdom, is more important for him, and is what makes him happier, than teaching the ninety-nine disciples already with him. Such an interest of a living *guru* is not merely a personal whim. It is rather the fulfilment of the will of God, as indicated in verse 14.

Verses 15-20 of chapter 18 run as follows:

> Moreover if your brother sins against you, go and tell him his fault between you and him alone. If he hears you, you have gained your brother.
>
> But if he will not hear you, take with you one or two more, that by the mouth of two or three witnesses every word may be established.
>
> And if he refuses to hear them, tell it to the church. But if he refuses even to hear the church, let him be to you like a heathen and a tax collector.
>
> Assurely, I say to you, whatever you bind on earth will be bound in heaven, and whatever you loose on earth will be loosed in heaven.
>
> Again I say to you that if two of you agree on earth concerning anything that they ask, it will be done for them by My Father in heaven.
>
> For where two or three are gathered together in My name, I am there in the midst of them.

Verses 15 and 16 give instructions on the best way to handle, with a worldly point of view, the wrong that one person does to another. This way takes into account only the values of this world.

Yet there is another way that respects both the here and the hereafter. According to it, whatever happens in this world is considered as existing in the other world also — in the ultimate Reality also — as latent possibility. Nothing that is not latent in that Reality can happen here in this world. We have seen the same principle stated in verse 19 of chapter 16. Here the shift is only to the moral application of understanding Reality rather than on the Reality itself. Accordingly, whatever we do in this world should have the assent of the ultimate Reality, and whatever ethical values are ignored in this world would be felt to be lost in the world of Reality or Supreme Happiness also. If two persons with this perception get together and think of something agreeable to this world as well as to the other, it would be fulfilled by the very same Reality they had relied on. For, nothing that does not agree with the ultimate Reality would be thought of as desirable by them, or whatever they desire would naturally be something agreeable to the ultimate Reality or God. For the gathering together of two or three in the name of the one Reality to happen, needs the proper guidance of a *guru* who points out to them that what is Real in all the worlds is what is Real in oneself also. That *guru*, here, is Jesus. Therefore, two or three gathering together in the name of the one Reality or God, and in the name of the *guru*, in principle and in effect, mean the same.

> Then Peter came to Him and said, "Lord, how often shall my brother sin against me, and I forgive him? Up to seven times?"
>
> Jesus said to him, "I do not say to you, up to seven times, but up to seventy times seven". — 18.21-22

Peter asks, how many times can one do wrong against another, according to the law acceptable to Jesus, that he should be forgiven. For Jesus to give a difinite answer as to how many times, would in effect mean creating a new law. But the intention of Jesus was not to bring into vogue a new set of worldly laws to replace ones of the same nature, already in existence. On the other hand, he preferred to look at the pettiness of the problems in human life, in the light of wisdom, or in the light of the one ultimate Reality. Such an intention is there with all *jñānin*s anywhere in the world. Viewed thus, forgiving seventy times seven would be but natural. A Self-realized person sets no limit to his pardoning the wrongs done unto him. Though Peter's question arose from the worldly point of view, Jesus answered it by taking his firm stand on the ultimate Reality.

The message contained in the parable narrated in verses 23-35 is given in verse 35 as follows:

> So My heavenly Father will also do to you if each of you, from his heart, does not forgive his brother his tresspasses.

A king from whom a servant had borrowed a large amount forgave his debt on realizing the miserable condition of the servant. This servant in turn is bound to forgive a small loan he had given to another fellow servant. Likewise, the one who enjoys the concession granted by God or the ultimate Reality is bound to allow the same concession towards his fellow beings. Put otherwise, those who are aware that they live in dependence upon the mercy of God are bound to show the same mercy to their fellow beings as well.

That means, the love and compassion one gets from God should become reflected in actual life in the form of the love and compassion that is shown to other living beings. The mercy of God has a vertical dimension, whereas the mercy one shows to others is of a horizontal or transactional significance. So then, when one experiences life in both principle and practice, we may say that both the vertical and horizontal dimensions of life meet upon a neutral, non-dual ground. As such, a theory or principle then becomes transformed into a life value.

1.22

Marital Relationships, Giving Up Attachments

THE problem dealt with in verses 1-9 of chapter 19 regards when a husband can legally and morally divorce his wife. A man and woman, as perceived by Jesus, become husband and wife inevitably as part of the function of nature in order to ensure the continuity of human life. In that sense, their union is arranged by the will of God or the Absolute. The transactional minds of men have no right to separate such a union. The marital relationships, apparently is not seen by Jesus merely as a social institution, but an inevitable part of the absolute will of God. Jesus therefore says,

> What God has joined together, let not man separate. — 19.6

The suggestion is that, in the context of marital relationships as elsewhere, man should raise himself up to the absolute level of realizing identity with God. Jesus again says,

> Moses command to give a certificate of divorce and to put her (your wife) away. — 19.7
>
> Because of the hardness of your hearts. — 19.8

Verses 10-12 are as follows:

> His disciples said to him, "If such is the case of the man with his wife, it is better not to marry."
>
> But He said to them, "All cannot accept this saying, but only those to whom it has been given.
>
> For there are eunuchs who were born thus from their mother's womb, and there are eunuchs who were made eunuchs by men, and there are eunuchs who have made themselves eunuchs for the kingdom of heaven's sake. He who is able to accept it, let him accept it."

The conjugal relationship is a must for generations to progress without break. Though such unions happen as if willed by God, for reasons caused by human volition, or because a particular union was mispaired, certain marital relationships end up as tragedies, sometimes even resulting in divorce. On such occasions, at least a few may feel it would have been better to live unmarried. This feeling becomes all the more forceful as they see that most of those who lead a spiritual life remain unmarried. It may become difficult to decide which way of life is recommendable and which is not. Jesus therefore says, "All cannot accept this saying, but only those to whom it has been given."

No clear-cut universal rule is available to decide whether living married or unmarried is better. It varies according to the psychological make-up, will-power, self-restraint, value notions and circumstances of the life of each person concerned. Jesus indicates that only those who are capable of evaluating all such factors themselves will understand this. In general it can only be said that there are born-eunuchs; there are people who are made eunuchs by others; and there are those who make themselves eunuchs for the sake of wisdom and the Supreme Happiness that goes with it.

Only those of the first type are eunuchs in the literal sense, the others are really not eunuchs, but are allegorically called so, because they live without making use of their reproductive capacity. Of these, the second type happen to live unmarried either as compelled by circumstances, or for the sake of certain ideals forced upon them by others. Such may feel disappointed in life at a certain stage. The third kind of people deliberately ignore the necessity of having a married life, because they intend to dedicate themselves for the cause of higher wisdom. When this wisdom is attained, they experience the Supreme Felicity, which is of much higher value than that of family life. Therefore they feel no disappointment at all in remaining unmarried. Had they married, it would have perhaps denied them the Supreme Happiness of attaining wisdom. Such are the people who have made themselves eunuchs. Without taking all these into account, it would not be possible to say in a clear-cut manner whether unmarried life or married life is better.

Almost all religions conceive the idea that the good deeds performed in this life enable one to reach heaven in the hereafter. Such good deeds could be seen enumerated in all the moral codes (Dharma-śāstras) and the commandments of God. Will a person who follows all such instructions strictly attain heaven? No one knows. Jesus revises and sublimates the very notion of attaining heaven as "attaining eternal life." Attaining eternal life philosophically means, one reaches the fullness of wisdom, realizing that oneself is the eternal Self (*Ātmā*) in essence, and so lives as the Self embodied. Simply obeying the commandments of scriptures in their literal sense is not enough to attain this eternal life. All the commandments are worth obeying because of the wisdom behind them. Aiming at this wisdom is much superior to merely obeying the commandments. The intense yearning for this wisdom naturally makes a seeker uninterested in worldly pleasures, because all such have only a fleeting value. There is another side of this sense of detachment towards worldly pleasures: One's mind always remains attuned to God or the Absolute, which is of the highest and eternal value. This Reality of the ultimate value is referred to as "That" (*tat*) in Vedānta, and the state of mind being attuned to *tat* is called *tat-paratā*; whereas the sense of detachment towards all that is fleeting is known as *vairāgya*. These two, *tat-paratā* and *vairāgya*, are mutually complementary and compensatory. It means that cultivating a sense of detachment towards things of lesser and fleeting value requires that the mind becomes attuned to *tat* of the highest and eternal value. And the mind that become fully attuned to *tat* needs to become deliberately withdrawn from things of lesser and transient value. Eternal life or immortality is attained only by those in whom *vairāgya* and *tat-paratā* are in unison. This very important principle that guides spiritual life is revealed in verses 16-22 as follows:

> Now behold, one came and said to Him, "Good Teacher, what good thing shall I do that I may have eternal life?"
>
> So He said to him, "Why do you call Me good? No one is good but One, that is, God. But if you want to enter into life, keep the commandments."
>
> He said to Him, "Which ones?" Jesus said, "You shall not murder," "You shall not commit adultery," "You shall not steal," "You shall not bear false witness."
>
> "Honour your father and your mother", and "You shall love your neighbour as yourself."
>
> The young man said to Him, "All these things I have kept from my youth. What do I still lack?"
>
> Jesus said to him, "If you want to be perfect, go, sell what you have and give to the poor, and you will have treasure in heaven; and come, follow Me."
>
> But when the young man heard that saying he went away sorrowful, for he had great possessions.

In the case of those who ignore worldly possessions and live possessed by wisdom or God, their worldly needs are taken care of by the very same wisdom or God. This truth is emphasized by Jesus when he says, "You will have treasure in heaven." Many usually have more trust in their own capabilities and in the wealth that can be amassed by them, than on God or the Reality. For them, the attainment of wisdom or to enter the eternal life can hardly happen.

The famous words of Jesus which stress the important role played by *vairāgya* or *nissaṅgatva* (having no attachment with anything) in the attainment of wisdom are as follows:

> And again I say to you, it is easier for a camel to go through the eye of a needle than for a rich man to enter the kingdom of God.
>
> When His disciples heard it, they were exceedingly amazed, saying, "Who then can be saved?"
>
> But Jesus looked at them and said to them, "With men this is impossible, but with God all things are possible." — 19.24-26

Vairāgya (sense of detachment towards worldly possessions) is a habit that can be cultivated in life by those who are interested in wisdom. But wisdom is not attained by cultivating this habit alone. As was indicated by Jesus earlier, one has also to follow an enlightened *guru*. One may become interested in wisdom or may remain uninterested in it. Either way, it does not happen through one's own control. It simply happens as part of the rolling wheel of nature (*prakṛti*) which is really in no one's control. Even if by chance or as if decided by God, one becomes a true seeker, the attainment of one's goal does not materialize unless one finds a real *guru* to be guided by. This latter case also does not take place by one's own control. Taking all this together, it is evident that to obtain wisdom, or to be saved, is something that happens completely beyond the bounds of any human effort. At the same time, all this will happen easily if God wills it so. That means, nothing is impossible if the vagaries of nature turn out by chance to be favourable. Jesus therefore says "With men this is impossible, but with God all things are possible."

> Then Peter answered and said to Him, "See, we have left all and followed You. Therefore what shall we have?"
>
> So Jesus said to them, "Assuredly I say to you, that in the regeneration, when the Son of Man sits on the throne of His glory, you who have followed Me will also sit on twelve thrones, judging the twelve tribes of Israel". — 19.27-28

Peter here speaks as the representative of all twelve disciples. Having become unattached to all worldly matters, they have taken refuge fully in the Guru Jesus alone. The question Peter asks is, what do they gain by such a renunciation and by following Jesus. It has already been made clear that it is the kingdom of heaven that they gain. The intention of the question should be therefore to know the details of that kingdom. Jesus begins to answer with reference to a "regeneration." A regeneration happens in the life of a person who has left behind all worldly interests, and with full dedication follows the wisdom path of a *guru*. The concept of *dvija* (twice-born) exists in Indian spirituality. There we see that one birth is of the womb of a mother, and the other consists of coming out of the worldly interests and entering the empire of wisdom or *Brahman*. The regeneration mentioned here could be understood as pertaining to this context. Whose regeneration is intended by Jesus's words "in the regeneration, when the Son of Man sits on the throne of His glory?" Is it that of Jesus or his disciples? Jesus is already in the empire of wisdom; so it is to the disciples that the regeneration should happen. Only upon attaining this regeneration or second birth, and so becoming enlightened themselves, do they realize the real glory of the throne upon which Jesus is seated, and that they too have already become raised to that glory.

Jesus here admittedly is the first *guru* in the line. The guruhood of Jesus in the biblical context is to be seen as related to the entire nation of Israel. The people of Israel once consisted of twelve separate tribes. The number of disciples Jesus chose was also twelve. Number twelve, in the Jewish culture, is a symbol of fullness. This fullness, in the case of the people of Israel, was divided into twelve separate tribes, and the twelve disciples, as intended by Jesus, were to lead each of these tribes. Philosophically seen, Jesus intends to transform his own fullness into another fullness formed of twelve segments.

Verse 29 reads as follows:

> And everyone who has left houses or brothers or sisters or father or mother or wife or children or lands, for My name's sake, shall receive a hundredfold, and inherit everlasting life.

As we have already seen, only those who willingly ignore blood relations and worldly possessions, and follow a *guru*, gain the wisdom secret. If it is one's own house that has been given up for the sake of following the footsteps of a *guru*, then upon enlightenment one experiences the satisfaction that all houses have become one's own. One who gives up one's own brothers and sisters, similarly gains the contentment that all are one's own brothers and sisters. It is similar with everything that one gives up for the sake of wisdom. Above all this, one attains the final liberation called *mukti* or *mokṣa* in India, and "eternal life" by Jesus. This final attainment is known also as *parama-puruṣārtha* (the highest of all human values).

Verse 30 reads as follows:

But many who are first will be last, and the last first.

Those who give up everything worldly and follow the wisdom-path of a *guru* alone have the right to attain *mukti* (eternal life). The intensity of this urge for giving up and following a *guru,* among seekers, is normally of different grades. Some in this respect may be seen in the front line and some remaining in the back row. It may so happen that some in the back row suddenly find themselves in the front row in respect of the depth and subtlety of their perception, speculation and dialectical thinking. Finally when such seekers give up everything and attain the final goal, those who were earlier in the front line may be seen dragging behind. The "first" and the "last" understood here could be taken as time related also. Those who give up everything and follow a *guru* at an early stage in life may be lagging behind, while some others who do so only very late in life may attain wisdom with not much delay. All these take place in accordance with no set rules, but depend mainly on the nature of the person concerned, the circumstances in which one happens to live, certain chance elements and many other factors.

There are scholars who are experts in philosophical thinking. They easily understand the nuances of the world of philosophy, whether theological or Vedāntic. They are good in teaching philosophy as well. In these respects they are in the front line. But there are those who, with no help of any philosophical speculation, simply by making use of their common sense and austere self-discipline (*tapas*), realize, "I am not separate from the whole; what is Real in the total is what is Real in me as well." Though in the back row in respect of scholarliness, they are in the front row with regard to Self-realization.

1.23

Exegesis

THE seekers of the first order who become the last, and those who are last and become the first, are there not as decided by human will, but as dictated by God's will. It is as if by God's generosity that the last becomes the first. The parable described in verses 1-16 of chapter 20 highlights this subtle truth.

What we understand from the event narrated in verses 20-28 is this: Of Jesus's twelve disciples two were brothers. Their mother comes to Jesus and asks, "Grant that these two sons of mine may sit, one on Your right side and the other on the left, in Your kingdom." (20.21)

Jesus has a kingdom of his own, but it is not the geographical region known as Israel, though he was acclaimed as the king of Israel. The entire people of Israel were seen by Jesus as representing of the whole of the human race, and the kingdom of wisdom he reveals is meant for all humans. Jesus is the overlord of that kingdom. It is in this sense that Jesus becomes the king of Israel. But the punishment meted out to him was on the allegation that he claimed to be the king of the political territory known as Israel. In the kingdom in which Jesus is the king, those who are fit to sit at his side as his confidants should be his closest disciples. The favour asked by the mother of Zebedee's sons is that these two be seated as the closest disciples or successors of Jesus.

The mistake of the mother here is that she indiscriminately mixes up two worlds of value. One value world is that of blood relations or of relativism, and the other that of spiritual wisdom or Absolutism. In the first one, it is but natural for a mother to wish that her children attain the highest possible positions, even if it be in the spiritual context. In the second, the competence of one to sit nearby a *guru* depends on the fullness and clarity of the philosophical vision one has imbibed from the *guru*. This never happens as wished by the parents or other blood relations. At the end of chapter 19 itself, it was seen that many who are the first will be last and last the first. Some of those who were pushed behind the front line of the society may come to occupy the front row in the context of wisdom. This does not happen as the result of human effort alone. The most important deciding factor, as was already stated, is the will of God or the favourable coming together of many accidental events. For a mother to ask a *guru* for the favour of her sons to become his immediate successors is not at all proper. Jesus therefore says to the mother, "You do not know what you ask" (20.22).

Jesus also asks a question to them: "Are you able to drink the cup that I am about to drink?" The question evidently was aimed at both the mother and the sons. By "the cup that I am about to drink," Jesus meant the tortures he was about to suffer as was indicated in verses 17-19. But they took it to mean the ordinary cup from which Jesus used to drink wine or water. That must be the reason why they readily said, "We are able." Jesus then says:

> You will indeed drink My cup, and be baptized with the baptism that I am baptized with; but to sit on My right hand and on My left is not Mine to give, but it is for those for whom it is prepared by My Father. — 20.23

Despite all this, the other ten disciples felt a grudge towards the two sons of Zebedee. This indicated a sort of greed for position, and the possibility also of envy and hatred to develop amongst them. Of course, Jesus noticed it and He therefore tells them:

> Whoever dlgesires to become great among you, let him be your servant.
>
> And whoever desires to be first among you, let him be your slave —
>
> just as the Son of Man did not come to be served, but to serve, and to give His life as ransom for many. — 20.26-28

This incident is narrated as yet another way of elucidating the idea contained in the statement at the end of chapter 19, "so the last will be first, and the first last." Any high-position one attains in the realm of spirituality should never be something aspired for. On the other hand, such positions should come to them as a natural course. That is, on the strength of one's knowledge about spiritual matters, their willingness to give up everything, their willingness to serve and their dedication to the cause of wisdom. Jesus shows himself as a role model in this respect. There is no other better service to mankind than leading them to the world of wisdom, showing them who they really are and rendering their life fully meaningful. All this is indicated by the words, "to give His life as ransom for many."

Verses 29-34 narrate the story of Jesus as he and his disciples departed from Jericho, and Jesus gave eyesight to two blind men.

Now as they departed from Jericho, a great multitude followed Him.

> And behold, two blind men sitting by the road, when they heard that Jesus was passing by, cried out, saying, "Have mercy on us, O Lord, Son of David."
>
> Then the multitude warned them that they should be quiet; but they cried out all the more, saying, "Have mercy on us, O Lord, Son of David."
>
> Jesus stood still and called them, and said, "What do you want Me to do for you?"
>
> They said to Him, "Lord, that our eyes may be opened."
>
> So Jesus had compassion and touched their eyes. And immediately their eyes received sight, and they followed Him. — 20.29-34

Instead of going back happy, the blind men who had received their sight back decided to follow Jesus. Following a *guru* happens only with those who dedicate themselves to the cause of wisdom. That means, the sight they received did not only pertain merely to their ordinary external eyes, but also to the spiritual eye of wisdom. Seen thus, these two men are the last to attain wisdom from Jesus. This could be counted also to explain how "Many who are first become last, and the last first."

There is a section in the Indian Vedic scriptures known as *arthavāda*. In it, important righteous behaviour patterns are enjoined. After such a life pattern is explicated, *arthavāda* states the good arising from its proper observance, and also the evils that arise from its omission. In doing so, certain historical instances will be adduced as support. The Western equivalent to *arthavāda* is called "exegesis." Here also the chapter 20 in its entirety could be considered as forming a sort of *arthavāda* in support of what was stated at the end of chapter 19, "Many who are first become last and the last first."

1.24

A Humble King's Sovereignty

While not denying that Jesus is the king of Israel, verses 1-11 of chapter 21 elucidate how humble his sovereignty is. The general public receive him with great honour, as though he were a king. But it is on a donkey that this king of Israel rides royally. We have already seen in what sense the kingship of Jesus is to be understood. The people of Israel for Jesus represent the entire human race, and all his teachings are meant for them. Jesus thus is the king of the wisdom-kingdom of Israel or all human kind. The honour given by people to a *guru* is really much higher than that due to any king or political authority; yet a *guru* always remains humble. In one sense, humility and kingship find unity in a *guru*. It is in this sense that the scene in which Jesus rides royally on a donkey and where people receive him with all pomp and honour is to be evaluated.

Verses 12 and 13 portray the scene of Jesus entering the temple of God and driving out all those who were buying and selling in the temple, where he overturns the tables of money-changers and the seats of those who sold doves. A temple is the abode of God; it is not meant to be a marketplace. The value of a temple is of an absolutist order, and only things of that order should take place there. Ensuring this is the bounden duty of a prophet, who is the representative of God. He is one who knows the secret of God, and who is the king of that absolutist kingdom. When such prophets (*guru*s) witness things that are against such values, going on in the abode of God, a sort of moral indignation, called *dharma-roṣa* in India, wells up in their minds. This indignation filled the being of Jesus when he saw the abode of God being converted into a marketplace by greedy merchants and money-changers. Ensuring justice among the people of a country is the duty of that country's king. Ensuring justice in the kingdom of God, symbolized by the temple, is the duty of that kingdom's king. Jesus fulfils the role readily.

The incident narrated in verses 14-17 shows that, even as Jesus was vehemently driving out the greedy merchants from the temple of God, he remained fully tranquil in mind. He heals the blind and the lame with a composed mind. He indicates also that the perfectly blameless praise of higher values comes out of the mouths of innocent babes and nursing infants.

Verses 18-22 of chapter 21 describe the event of a hungry Jesus who sees a fig tree by the road, and then when going to it, only finds on it but leaves. He then says to it, "Let no fruit grow on you ever again." The fig tree immediately withered away.

The function of a fig tree, as forming part of the total system of life, is to yield fruits that satisfy the hunger of some other beings. Each human being, indeed each living being, similarly has its own role to play to ensure the sustenance of the overall system of life. Suppose a man or any other living being fails to fulfil this role. This would be equivalent to being non-existent. Jesus here represents the ultimate Reality that unfolds itself as the total system of life. It could well be said that he represents God. Jesus's curse to the tree results in the tree withering away immediately; this indicates that no individual entity in the world can exist without regard for the total existence. Every individual being, as part of the total system of life, has to yield some fruit, and this fruit should ensure the satisfaction of the hunger of at least some other being as part of the very same system of life. Such is the way the total life system is devised by God.

> Now when the disciples saw it, they marvelled, saying, "How did the fig tree wither away so soon?" — 2.20

So Jesus answered and said to them,

> Assuredly, I say to you, if you have faith and do not doubt, you will not only do what was done to the fig tree, but also if you say to this mountain, "Be removed and be cast into the sea," it will be done.
>
> And all things, whatever you ask in prayer, believing, you will receive. — 2.21-22

Jesus does not consider this event to have taken place by any spiritual attainment of his own, but to have happened as willed by God. Jesus is a *jñānin* who always experiences his existence as inseparably one with God. And therefore God's will and his will are not two. This state of identity is to be counted, in principle, as marking the zenith of one's faith. For those who have attained this state of faith, nothing is impossible for the simple reason that nothing is impossible for God. In one sense it could be said, this incident indicates how mysterious events appear to be in the life of those who experience their true identity.

Verses 23-27 read as follows:

23 Now when He came into the temple, the chief priests and the elders of the people confronted Him as He was teaching, and said, "By what authority are you doing these things? And who gave you this authority?"

24 But Jesus answered and said to them, "I also will ask you one thing, which if you tell Me, I likewise will tell you by what authority I do these things:

25 "The Baptism of John, where was it from? From heaven or from men?" And they reasoned among themselves, saying, "If we say, 'From heaven,' He will say to us, 'Why then did you not believe him?'"

26 But if we say, 'From men' we fear the multitude, for all count John as a prophet.

27 So they answered Jesus and said, "We do not know." And He said to them, "Neither will I tell you by what authority I do these things."

The question asked by the chief priests and the elders of the public is, who gave Jesus the authority to teach wisdom. Only two sources are thinkable for such a source of authority — either men or God. A person who got the authority from men has no right to teach anything about God. If the source is God, the nature of authority conceived may vary according to the nature of the concept of God that each has. The God thought of by Jews is a personalized form of Yahweh. Jesus's concept, on the other hand, as we have already noticed, is a philosophical and experiential one. For this reason, if Jesus claims that he got the authority from God, it could be condemned as heresy by the Jews upon the basis of the concept of God they have. Therefore, Jesus cleverly evades the question of the priests and elders, and so silences them. The question concerns the authority John the Baptist had. At the same time Jesus himself is about to make clear through certain parables what is the nature of the authority he has.

1.25

The Authority of Jesus

VERSES 28-32 of chapter 21 are as follows:

> But what do you think? A man had two sons, and he came to the first and said, "Son, go, work today in my vineyard."
>
> He answered and said, "I will not," but afterward he regretted and went.
>
> Then he came to the second son and said likewise. And he answered and said, "I go, sir," but he did not go.
>
> Which of the two did the will of his father? They said to Him, "The first." Jesus said to them, "Assuredly, I say to you that tax collectors and harlots enter the kingdom of God before you."
>
> For John came to you in the way of righteousness, and you did not believe him; but tax collectors and harlots believed him; and when you saw it, you did not afterward relent and believe him."

Jesus, through this analogy and the next one, tries to convince the chief priests and elders that something lacks in them tempting to ask about his authority to teach. He sees two sets of people around him. The first are not respectable in the perception of the orthodox Jews. Still they are earnestly intent on imbibing the wisdom teachings of Jesus. They are like the first son in the parable. The others are people like the chief priests and elders, they not only do not believe the words of Jesus, but also question his authority to come to the temple and teach. Still, they think, they are the true followers of the Jewish tradition and religion. What they do is simply learn the injunctions of the scriptures and teach people to follow these true to the letter; but they lack the gift of insight to perceive the philosophical principles behind such injunctions. They are like the second son who said to his father, "I go, sir", but did not go.

John the Baptist forewarned the people of two things. First, he encouraged them to repent and to come out of the closed religiousness they were practising. Second, he declared the greatness of the one who was to follow him. Those who claimed themselves to be fully religious could not heed either of these warnings, but those who were not at all respectable, like tax collectors, harlots and fishermen could.

These latter repented and followed the wisdom-path of Jesus. They did not even think of asking Jesus who had given him the authority to teach because his teaching was so transparent. But those who claimed themselves to be true religionists, scholars, priests and elders of the society dared to question the authority of Jesus, simply because they were not willing to come out of their closed religiousness. Even those who ordinarily are hated for belonging to the lowest rung of society, but endowed with an open mind, do experience the blissful tranquillity in life just by listening to the words of wisdom of Jesus. Even upon witnessing this, it becomes impossible for those who are thought of as respectable to repent and become seekers. For the poor and the lowly to become open minded, and the rich and the scholarly to merely stick to orthodoxy, is but common in the world.

Jesus tells them one more parable:

> There was a certain landowner who planted a vineyard and set a hedge around it, dug a winepress in it and built a tower. And he leased it to vinedressers and went into a far country.
>
> Now when vintage-time drew near, he sent his servants to the vinedressers, that they might receive its fruit.
>
> And the vinedressers took his servants, beat one, killed one, and stoned another.
>
> Again he sent other servants, more than the first, and they did likewise to them.
>
> Then last of all he sent his son to them, saying, "They will respect my son."
>
> But when the vinedressers saw the son, they said among themselves, "This is the heir. Come, let us kill him and seize his inheritance."
>
> And they caught him, and cast him out of the vineyard, and killed him.
>
> Therefore, when the owner of the vineyard comes, what will he do to the vinedressers?
>
> They said to Him, "He will destroy those wicked men miserably, and lease his vineyard to other vinedressers who will render to him the fruits of their seasons."
>
> Jesus said to them, "Did you never read in the scriptures": 'The stone which the builders rejected has become the chief cornerstone. This was the Lord's doing, and it is marvellous in our eyes."
>
> Therefore I say to you, the kingdom of God will be taken from you and given to a nation bearing the fruits of it." — 21.33-43

The landowner of this parable represents God, and he could also be the original *guru,* for a *guru* can never be differentiated from the ultimate Reality or God. The vineyard planted by the landowner stands for the wisdom that is beginningless, and setting a hedge around it shows the same wisdom being protected by giving it the form of a scientifically conceived system of thought. The determination that this wisdom should become beneficial to future generations is signified by the winepress dug there. A line of successors entrusted with the duty of upkeeping the purity of this wisdom was also arranged for, represented in the parable by the vinedressers. But it so happened that such upkeepers of wisdom were people like the chief priests and elders now standing before Jesus. Instead of handing down the pure wisdom to posterity, they transformed it into a rigid religion meant for the Jews alone, and to safeguard their own self-interests.

God sent many prophets represented in the parable by the servants, in order to restore the purity of wisdom and make it again beneficial to the world at large; but all of them were either ridiculed and sent away or were even killed. At last God sent His own son (Jesus Christ). Then the custodians said among themselves, "This is the heir, let us kill him and seize his inheritance." These words of theirs show that Jesus received the right to teach from God Himself. But this Son was also cast out of the vineyard and was killed. This indicates the crucifixion about to happen to Jesus, simply because of the vileness of the chief priests, scribes and elders. Jesus therefore says: "I say to you, the kingdom of God will be taken from you and given to a nation bearing the fruits of it." Such an eventuality has also been prophesied in earlier scriptures which Jesus quotes thus, "The stone which the builders rejected has become the chief cornerstone."

The builders entrusted with the work, as seen here, are people like the priests and elders. They lack discriminative understanding, they lack the ability to differentiate the valuable from the valueless. The most important place in the construction of a building is that of the cornerstone. The present construction work signifies the line of prophets or *guru*s that ends with Jesus.

But they were rejected by the very people who were put in-charge of safeguarding them. Just because rejected so, *guru*s and the wisdom they represent do not become valueless. What happens when Jesus emerges as a perfect *guru* is that the chief cornerstone is rejected by the builders. This also takes place not because of the greatness of Jesus, but by the "Lord's doing."

Many may wonder, how do all these things happen, for all these happenings may appear mysterious. But for God nothing is mysterious. On seeing the many worldly things that happen each day about us, some may ask, "How does all this happen?" There is no one, in fact, who knows all of nature's secrets. Nor can anyone say definitely what is possible in this world and what is not. We usually count as mysterious everything that we cannot explain by making use of our mind's logic. That this very mind that thinks is a part of this mysterious world is often forgotten by us.

How can such a mind, a minute element of the total system, measure and know the Reality that underlies that very system? On realizing this, one realizes also that nothing is impossible in this world, for everything is possible to God. What each of us can do then is to see ourselves as simply forming a minute part of that great mystery and to see that this mystery underlies our very being and is the meaning content of our entire life. This perception is what makes our life really meaningful. This realization could be considered a kind of knowledge as well as a kind of non-knowledge. It is more an event of revelation than an event of knowing something else. And this revelation brings a state of unconditioned peace in life. This peace is the best fruit one should receive from the tree of wisdom. If the caretakers of this wisdom tree, represented here by the vinedressers of the parable, behave in such a way that this fruit is denied to the world, then God's mysterious way of acting will itself take away this responsibility from them in the same way, and hand it over to those who are worthy of it, and are sure to be fruitful. The fig tree mentioned earlier could be seen as representing any religious group that has become fruitless in the context of this wisdom teaching.

1.26

Who Becomes Enlightened?

JESUS adds yet another parable in verses 2-14 of chapter 22. Presumably this also happens in the very same scene seen at the beginning of the last chapter where Jesus was questioned by the chief priests and elders about the authority of Jesus to teach. The parable is as follows:

> The kingdom of heaven is like a certain king who arranged a marriage for his son,
>
> and sent out his servants to call those who were invited to the wedding, and they were not willing to come.
>
> Again, he sent out other servants, saying, "Tell them who are invited, 'See, I have prepared my dinner, my oxen and fatted cattle are killed, and all things are ready. Come to the wedding'."
>
> But they made light of it and went their ways, one to his own farms, another to his business.
>
> And the rest seized his servants, treated them spitefully, and killed them.
>
> But when the king heard about it, he was furious. And he sent out his armies, destroyed those murderers, and burned up their city.
>
> Then he said to his servants, "The wedding is ready, but those who were invited were not worthy."
>
> Therefore go into the higways, and as many as you find, invite to the wedding.
>
> So those servants went out into the highways and gathered together all whom they found, both bad and good. And the wedding hall was filled with guests.
>
> But when the king came in to see the guests, he saw a man there who did not have on a wedding garment.
>
> So he said to him, "Friend, how did you come in here without a wedding garment?" And he was speechless.
>
> Then the king said to the servants, "Bind his hand and foot, take him away, and cast him into outer darkness; there will be weeping and gnashing of teeth."
>
> For many are called, but few are chosen.

The kingdom of heaven, as made clear earlier, signifies the pure essence of wisdom. The dinner set ready stands for this wisdom rendered satisfying and attractive. The king who sets the dinner ready is none other than God or the origingal *guru* (*ādi-guru*). The servants that are sent out to bring in the guests to enjoy the dinner are the *guru*s and prophets sent to this world by God as His representatives. It is gentlemen of the society who are normally invited for wedding dinners. But those who considered themselves gentlemen, when invited to enjoy the dinner of wisdom, just made light of it, as very often happens, and preferred to keep themselves away from it. On such occasions the *guru*s or prophets may speak about the importance of having this wisdom in life, which is indicated by the king's words as to how grand was the dinner prepared and laid out for them. Such words may also be ignored by the gentlemen of the society. What they consider of value in life are their business, their farms and the comforts of life. They therefore pursue such worldly affairs. There may also be people who turn against the *guru*s and prophets, and insult or even kill them, perhaps upon charges of misleading the people. But what happens to those who turn away from the instructions of *guru*s and prophets, and what happens to those who torture or kill them, actually is that they make a ravaging hell of their own life, which is indicated by the king's sending his army out to destroy the murderers.

But when those who are found in the highways, without discrimination between the good and the bad, are invited, the dinner hall becomes filled with guests. This does not mean that everyone at that gathering has the right to own wisdom. Therefore some might have to be expelled from the dinner hall for a lack of competence to receive this wisdom. Some others may naturally find themselves outside that hall. All such, who are either expelled, or who are already outside, are trapped in the world of ignorance. The sufferings they have to undergo there are indicated by the "weepings and gnashing of teeth."

Though the right to wisdom is not denied to anyone, all do not attain it; only those who seek it earnestly gain wisdom. Even those who seek it earnestly may not necessarily get at the core of it; only those who are the most competent (*uttama adhikārin*) will own it. *Bhagavad-Gītā* (VII.3) also says:

> Among thousands of men, one perchance strives for the perfection of attainment. Even among those who strive thus and attain the goal, one perchance knows Me right to the core.

This is the reason why it is insisted upon in India that the wisdom feast should not be served in public, but should be taught only to the eldest son or the closest disciple.

The persecution which the servants of the king had to undergo indicates the harassments the prophets who came prior to Jesus had to suffer. It is also implied that the wisdom secret is not meant to be disclosed to an invited gathering that consists of people of every kind; yet at the same time that everyone, good or bad, has the right to seek it. A *guru* is not supposed to go in search of a disciple; on the contrary, a disciple has to seek out and find his proper *guru;* this is another indication in this parable.

Among such seekers there could be good and bad; there could also be gentlemen and lowly persons. All such matters are taken into account by a *guru* when imparting wisdom. What is most important in the context of this imparting is that the seekers should be fully interested in and dedicated to wisdom. This aspect is evinced by the incident of the guest who does not wear a wedding garment, who then is ousted from the wedding hall.

Yet another point is also suggested here. The twelve disciples of Jesus were not chosen from among the gentlemen of the society. Even among them was one who was not or gave up being a true seeker — Judas, the one who finally betrayed Jesus. He, at last, was thrown out of the context of real life and had to suffer.

1.27

Two Value Worlds

> Then the Pharisees went and plotted how they might entangle Him in His talk.
>
> And they sent to Him their disciples with the Herodians, saying, "Teacher, we know that You are true, and teach the way of God in truth; nor do You care about anyone, for You do not regard the person of men.
>
> Tell us, therefore, what do You think? Is it lawful to pay taxes to Caesar, or not?"
>
> But Jesus perceived their wickedness, and said, "Why do you test Me, you hypocrites?
>
> Show Me the tax money." So they brought Him a denarius.
>
> And He said to them, "Whose image and inscription is this?"
>
> They said to Him, "Caesar's." And He said to them, "Render therefore to Caesar the things that are Caesar's, and to God the things that are God's."
>
> When they had heard these words, they marvelled, and left Him and went their way. — 22.15-22

The Pharisees perceived the clarity and straightforwardness of the wisdom teachings of Jesus, and thus realized that trapping him in their own logical arguments would not be possible. They then decided to trap him in his own words. They sent their disciples to him along with the Herodians. These disciples are well-versed in the Judaic scriptures, customs and basic beliefs. And the Herodians were the servants of Herodotus who ruled Judea as the representative of the Roman emperor, Caesar. It is they who ask, "Is it lawful to give taxes to Caesar?" If he says, "It is lawful," it spells an approval of the Roman invasion of Israel, who were always disliked by the Pharisees and their disciples. Admitting Jesus to be the king of Israel and saying that giving taxes to Caesar is unlawful would in effect be treason in the eyes of Herodians.

Jesus perceives this trap, and the answer he gives to evade it, helps to differentiate the two value worlds as well. The coins then current in Judea were those issued by Ceasar, and had his seal inscribed on them. That means, those coins are viturally owned by the emperor. It is these coins that are given back to him as tax. Giving tax to Caesar, thus, only means, what is really owned by him is given back to him.

But Jesus is not a king of any kingdom in which such political and economic values are of any concern; he on the other hand is the king of the God's kingdom. The tax to be given in that kingdom is not in the form of any kind of money, but is one's own self itself. The value world in which money is considered most prized is of a horizontal nature, whereas the kingdom of God is vertical in nature. Those who planned to entangle Jesus in his own words were people unable to discriminate between these two value worlds. Not only did they fail to trap Jesus but this became an occasion for presenting a new lesson on discriminating between two value worlds and on the danger of mixing them up indiscriminately.

1.28

Resurrection

VERSES 23-33 of chapter 22 read as follows:

> The same day the Sadducees, who say there is no resurrection, came to Him and asked Him,
>
> saying, "Teacher, Moses said that if a man dies, having no children, his brother shall marry his wife and raise up offspring for his brother.
>
> Now there were with us seven brothers. The first died after he married, and having no offspring, left his wife to his brother.
>
> Likewise the second also, and the third, even to the seventh.
>
> And last of all the woman died also.
>
> Therefore, in the resurrection, whose wife of the seven will she be? For they all had her."
>
> Jesus answered and said to them, "You are mistaken, not knowing the scriptures nor the power of God.
>
> For in the resurrection they neither marry nor are given in marriage, but are like angels of God in heaven.
>
> But concerning the resurrection of the dead, have you not read what was spoken to you, by God, saying:
>
> I am the God of Abraham, the God of Isaac, and the God of Jacob? God is not the God of the dead, but of the living."
>
> And when the multitudes heard this, they were astonished at His teaching.

The Sadducees wrongly understood the scriptural utterances about the resurrection, which was the reason why they did not believe in it. The question they ask arises from their wrong understanding. According to their understanding, the dead will be reborn in this world or another, and will continue to have their own individuality, including male–female difference and personal relationships. It is from such ignorance that many basic questions, concerning life and afterlife arise. What is needed, then, is not a direct answer to the question, but the removal of the ignorance from which the question arose. Jesus also offers this.

The resurrection could be understood by relating it to the context of *dvijatva* (twice-born) already mentioned, as well as to the phenomenon of death. Jesus here reacts to the question from both the points of view.

The first kind of resurrection happens as one becomes enlightened. A *jñānin* perceives himself not as an individual, but as fully lost in the ultimate Reality (*Brahman*) that he has realized. That Reality was never born and never dies. The existence of individuals is not relevant there, nor is any personal relationship, nor any marriage. This experiential identity with the Absolute is the resurrected state. It is put in the language familiar to Semitic religious terms, "but are like angels of God in heaven."

Now let us look at the resurrection as related to the phenomenon of death. For this we should know what death is and what birth is. Individuated forms emerge from and merge back in the one absolute Reality or God just as individual waves arise, roll on for a while and disappear into the ever existent ocean. The emergence of wave-like individuals is what we call birth; for them to roll on for a while is called life; their disappearance back into what ultimately exists is called death. A wave's mergence back only means that it becomes the ocean. It, as it is, does not re-emerge as a new wave, at the same time new waves constantly emerge on the surface of the ocean. One such wave cannot be counted as the resurrection or the rebirth of a particular wave that appeared and disappeared previously. As the birth of waves occurs again and again; we can safely say, waves are reborn, but not in the sense that new waves are the reincarnations of past waves. The same is the case with the birth of individual beings in the ocean of the Absolute. All such emerge from and in the one Reality. Even when a wave exists as a wave, it is not different from the ocean. Similarly, individual beings, even when appearing as individuals, are one with the Reality or God. In that sense it is said, "God is not the God of the dead, but of the living."

The Absolute is a living Reality. The sign of this is that new manifest forms incessantly appear in it and the old ones incessantly disappear in it. An individual is one such manifest form that exists without being different from the Absolute. Each such individual entity also is a living one. That means, God is the living Reality that exists as the essential content in all the individual beings that also are living. In this sense also it could be said, "God is not the God of the dead, but of the living." When an individuated form disappears, and what is real in it merges with the Total Being, it may be considered the resurrection of the individual. The nature of life as a whole, as visualized here by Jesus, is summarily portayed by Narayana Guru thus:

> Individuated forms, like waves in the ocean,
> Emerge in sequence, and so do they merge.
> When will this process come to an end?
> Oh, this is nothing but the action
> In the process of creation ever unfolding within
> The ocean of primeval source-Consciousness!
>
> — *Ātmopadeśa Śatakam,* verse 56

1.29

Two Commandments

VERSES 34-40 of chapter 22 run as follows:

> But when the Pharisees heard that He had silenced the Sadducees, they gathered together.
>
> Then one of them, a lawyer, asked Him a question, testing Him, and saying,
>
> "Teacher, which is the great commandment in the law?"
>
> Jesus said to them, "You shall love the Lord your God with all your heart, with all your soul, and with all your mind."
>
> This is the first and great commandment.
>
> And the second is like it: "You shall love your neighbour as yourself."
>
> On these two commandments hang all the Law and the Prophets.

Of all the teachings of Jesus, these two are counted as the most important. These two are really the essential content of the ten commandments of Moses. How profound these two are becomes evident only as we see their mutual complementarity and the compensatory nature.

These two messages given in the language familiar to the Semitic religions, when translated to Vedāntic forms, would read as follows:

> Perceive constantly your oneness with the Absolute (*Brahman*). Then the love you have for yourself becomes the love you have for *Brahman* as well. You then perceive the entire worldly phenomena, including yourself, as the changeful fleeting manifest forms that appear and disappear in that changeless and unmanifest Reality. Then the love you have for yourself becomes extended as the love you have for every being.

The first of these two commandments insists on realizing one's identity with God (*Brahman*). This sense of identity becomes actualized in life only when it finds expression in the form of the second message as an accepted law. That means, it is when the love one has for oneself becomes transformed as the love for every being, that this identity becomes experiential and valuable in life. Likewise, the second commandment gains a dimension and value beyond any commendable codes of law for the society, but only when it is well-founded on the philosophical vision of the love of God contained in the first commandment. Jesus reminds us of the mutuality and importance of these two commandments thus, "On these two commandments hang all the Law and the Prophets."

Human life is value-based, and this is what differentiates it from mere animal life. When life is value-based, you are bound to decide what to do and not to do in different situations. When you feel you are incapable of taking this decision on your own, you may seek the advice of other knowledgeable persons concerning the particular matter. Such directives are what we call laws or codes of conduct in life.

Such directives generally have two sources available for humans. One consists of the laws of commandments given by the enlightened *guru*s or prophets, these forming part of the religious scriptures. Such codes and laws that are codified separately from the philosophical teachings are called Smṛtis in India, literally meaning "remembrances." It indicates that such codes of conduct are given shape by keeping in mind the ultimate Reality that governs life. On becoming enlightened of this Reality, the *guru*s codify these laws with this vision for their sound basis. These laws are considered to have the approval of God. The enlightened ones who reveal such God-given laws are called prophets, and their enlightenment is known as "revelation."

The other kind of laws are what originate from human minds. Neither revelation nor enlightenment of the prophets (*guru*s) is there to support these. These, on the other hand, are the result of human manipulation created in order to deal with social problems of a local and impermanent order. Such laws need not necessarily be infallible. There is only one way to decide, how impeccable such man-made laws are: to find the extent to which such laws agree with the God-given laws or the ultimate laws that govern nature and the phenomenon of life in it. Jesus's words, "On these two commandments hang all the Law" could be interpreted this way also.

Many prophets had emerged in the Semitic background, just as in the Eastern religions there were many *guru*s. Whether prophets or *guru*s, what became revealed to them, and what they had to expound, was the one secret that underlies all life. The phenomenon called life, and the world of which this phenomenon forms a part, together form one single Reality. The creative urge for self-expression in this Reality, and the phenomenon of the world that emerges as its expressed form, are all governed by one Law that is changeless. Be they prophets or *gurus*, those to whom this law became revealed had only one wisdom to teach. The essence of the present two commandments of Jesus shows how this one wisdom secret looks when translated into the day-to-day human life. Jesus therefore says, "On these two commandments hang all the Prophets."

These words are very peculiar in that, though they contain the essential content of his entire teaching, they were revealed by him as a means to silence his opponents, and not as a teaching given directly to his disciples. It could perhaps be because these words really were not his own. In order to defeat his opponents who followed the injunctions of the Old Testament to the letter, Jesus reintroduces the essential content of those very injunctions in the form of two new commandments. This incident implies also that Jesus was fully aware of himself as belonging to a long line of prophets in the Jewish tradition, as its latest revaluator.

The Pharisees asked the question to Jesus simply to trap him in his own words. They expected Jesus to give some new commandments that were different from those of Moses. For, Jesus to do so would have given them an opportunity to charge him with sacrilege. But what Jesus did was simply restate two of the ten commandments of Moses in a revised and revalued manner. This not only served as a means to silence the Pharisees, but also to introduce his own two commandments.

1.30

Christhood

THOSE who could not admit that Jesus was a prophet tried many tactics to trap him. But none of these worked. Now Jesus returns a question to them. Yet they find themselves unable to answer it. The concerned part of the Gospel is as follows:

> While the Pharisees were gathered together, Jesus asked them,
>
> saying, "What do you think about the Christ? Whose Son is He?" They said to Him, "The Son of David."
>
> He said to them, "How then does David in the Spirit call Him, "Lord," saying:
>
> "The Lord said to my Lord, "Sit at My right hand, till I make Your enemies Your footstool."
>
> If David then calls Him "Lord," how is He his Son?
>
> And no one was able to answer Him a word, nor from that day on did anyone dare question Him anymore. — 22.41-46

The word "Christ" means "the anointed one." A firm belief among the Jews is that a Christ as their saviour, anointed by God, will be born, as the son of David, i.e., as a descendant of David. According to Christianity, that Christ is Jesus himself, which the Jews do not officially admit. That is how Christianity became a religion separate from Judaism, or as an offshoot of it. The Jews believe, thus, the Christ is yet to come. The question asked here by Jesus is to be understood with this historical fact as the background.

Psalm 110 of the Old Testament refers to a context in which David, in a state of ecstacy, perceives Christ and calls him "Lord." Jesus here quotes the first two lines of this psalm. Well known is the fact that the Old Testament of the Bible of which Psalms forms a part, is acceptable both to Jews and Christians. Jesus's question is this: How is it possible that a person addressed by David as "Lord" be his own son?

The Christhood of Jesus is not as the biological son of David, but as the Son of God — as the one anointed by God. As we have already seen, a Son of God is the one who realized *Brahman* (God) and lives in full identity with that Reality. Such a Son of God is always considered

God-like by everyone, including those in whose genealogical line he is biologically born. This is the reason why David, when in a state of trance or self-realization, addresses the Christ as "Lord." But the Pharisees were incapable of differentiating the Lordship of Jesus as an enlightened *guru* from the state of being the son of David. The present context is also one in which Jesus acknowledges his Christhood, though indirectly. No enlightened person directly acknowledges to be so.

1.31

The Moral Indignation of Jesus

THE message contained in verses 1-12 of chapter 23 could be summarized as follows:

The scribes and the Pharisees boastfully think that they occupy the seat of Moses and that they teach the words of God as revealed through Moses. But Jesus knows how mechanical and soulless their way of teaching is. He, therefore, warns the multitudes and disciples that follow him thus:

> Whatever they tell you to observe, that observe and do, but do not do according to their works; for they say and do not do. — 23.3

What they teach are scriptural injunctions, but what they do themselves does not respect the very injunctions they teach. The basic interest of such teachers evidently is not in the scriptural teachings which guide the life of the ordinary people and thus bring peace to their lives; but their own interest in being honoured as teachers.

> They love the best places in feasts, the best seats in the synagogues, the greetings in marketplaces, and to be called by men, "Rabi, Rabi." — 23.6-7

Jesus, on the other hand, directs his disciples:

> But you, do not be called "Rabi," for One is your Teacher, the Christ, and you are all brethren. — 23.8

There is a reference made here by Jesus himself to "the Christ," but there is no sign here that he claims himself to be "the Christ." A Christ-concept already existed within the Jewish tradition. This conceptual Christ, which is acceptable to everyone and signifies the eternal saviour, could be what Jesus refers to here. All the living prophets are to be treated as various forms in which this one Christ or Teacher has become incarnate.

Indian traditions also admit one eternally existing *guru,* and the actual *guru*s that appear frequently in history are to be treated as the temporal manifest forms of that one eternal *guru.* Similar is the perception of Jesus here. The teachings of each such *guru* may vary in respect to the actual problems of the local and passing import they deal with, and the cultural background that forms their way of expression, and of the people to whom they are immediately addressed. Such inevitable and necessary aspects are to be set aside, and the wisdom secret packaged within such factors is to be sought out. The discovery of wisdom never makes us self-important, but instead allows us to realize just how insignificant each of us is. This realization makes us humble. *Bhagavad-Gītā* (V.18) also underscores the value of wisdom in making our life rich with humility. The same is seen in these words of Jesus:

> But he who is greatest among you shall be your servant.
>
> And whoever exalts himself will be abased, and he who humbles himself will be exalted. — 23.11-12

The rest of chapter 23, from verse 13 onwards, clearly portrays the moral indignation Jesus felt towards the scribes and the Pharisees; and it finds expression in a forceful language. Both the scribes and Pharisees are the proponents of the Jewish spiritual tradition, but the spirituality they are familiar with has already become lifeless during its passage through many generations. They are neither willing to understand what they lack nor to correct themselves. They think, whatever spiritual teaching is there outside what they know is heresy, and thus is sacrilegeous.

Jesus is a *guru* or the Son of God, who emerged to restore the purity and liveliness of wisdom, by cleansing the Jewish spirituality of the degeneration it had already undergone. This degeneration happens whenever pure wisdom is transformed into a religion. (The same degeneration happened to the wisdom teachings of Jesus also as it took the shape of a rigid religion.) Jesus counts one by one all the vicious aspects that have found place in the customs, lifestyles and way of thinking of the Jews as a result of this degeneration. And he derides in a very forceful but mannerly fashion the scribes and the Pharisees who have caused it.

A peculiarity is to be noticed here. This is the first time Jesus boldly confronts the scribes and Pharisees who were constantly troubling, questioning and despising him. In the beginning Jesus simply evaded them. Next, their arguments were cleverly answered. In silencing them, Jesus made use of such occasions to teach his wisdom. But now Jesus confronts them by boldly bringing to light all their weaknesses and faults as perceived by a perfect Master. As a result, he was immediately going to be caught and crucified by them.

Jesus's words of censure cool down and end as he concludes:

> I say to you, you shall see Me no more till you say, "Blessed is He who comes in the name of the Lord." — 23.39

It is an enlightened *guru* who realizes the ultimate Reality or Lord as the one Substance in the being of everyone of us, who also reveals this wisdom to the world, that is to be considered as coming in the name of the Lord. The scribes and the Pharisees represent the kind of people who think that what they understand as the meaning of the scriptural utterances alone is right, yet who remain ignorant that those words have meanings beyond what they comprehend. The vision of a *guru* like Jesus crosses the bounds of the literal sense with which they are familiar and reveals the eternal living wisdom hiding within the words of scriptures. The Blessed One who comes in the name of the Lord, referred to by Jesus, could be understood as indicating himself, or as all the prophets and *guru*s like him who have previously emerged, as well as those yet to come. One thing is definite: those who are aware that the words of scriptures contain meanings that are beyond what they comprehend of them on their own, those who are determined to find them out, and those who are well aware that it becomes possible only with the guidance of an enlightened Master, can alone understand the greatness of a *guru* and honour a *guru.* As implied in the concluding words of Jesus, unless and until this is felt by them, the scribes and the Pharisees will never know Jesus and can never admit him as their Master. The strong words, "Woe to you" which we see in the beginning, though not repeated at the end, are also to be seen as hinting at this.

1.32

A Seeker's Path

Verses 1-2 of chapter 24 are as follows:

> Then Jesus went out and departed from the temple and His disciples came to Him to show Him the buildings of the temple.
>
> And Jesus said to them, "Do you not see all these things? Assuredly, I say to you, not one stone shall be left here upon another, that shall not be thrown down."

The whole of chapter 24 compares the things we ordinarily value in life, with the value of wisdom. In doing so, it becomes clear just how valueless and unimportant are the things we usually find valuable and important when they are placed side by side with the value of wisdom. The present scene is introduced as if to mark the beginning of this lesson. The disciples of Jesus themselves show him the architectural beauty of the temple from which he exited. A temple really is meant to make known and to glorify God or the ultimate Reality. As the greatness of this wisdom becomes experientially transparent, one realizes of what little value are the supposedly beautiful buildings of the temple built of ordinary stone. One feels upon attaining this wisdom as if the building that was until then considered as beautiful and durable is but a crumbling thing.

Verses 3-8 read as follows:

> Now as He sat on the Mount of Olives, the disciples came to Him privately, saying, "Tell us, when will these things be? And what will be the sign of Your coming, and of the end of the age?"
>
> And Jesus answered and said to them: "Take heed that no one deceives you.
>
> For many will come in My name, saying, "I am the Christ," and will deceive many.
>
> And you will hear of wars and rumours of wars. See that you are not troubled; for all these things must come to pass, but the end is not yet.
>
> For nation will rise against nation, and kingdom against kingdom. And there will be famines, pestilences, and earthquakes in various places.

All these are the beginning of sorrows.

Jesus had already mentioned the event by which the temple will come crumbling down without a stone remaining one over another. Is this event going to happen to the actual temple that the disciples referred to, or does it amount to some radical change that has to take place in their perception of the temple of life? It is to be presumed from the questions the disciples ask, that they were not sure about this themselves.

The previous chapter brought forward the concept of the Christ; and Jesus admitted in an indirect way that he himself was the Christ. It must be the coming of Jesus as Christ that the disciples meant when they referred to "Your coming" in their question. Were it his coming as Jesus himself that they meant, it has already happened. Moreover, they fully believed that the coming of Christ would mark the end of an age, as is generally admitted by the Jewish tradition. They therefore are eager to know what are the signs of the end of the age. These passages at first might seem to refer to the end of the world as an historical event. But really these indicate the internal feelings of those who have strayed from the path of true spirituality and the self-discipline it enjoins. Jesus therefore warns at the very beginning, "Take need that no one deceives you."

It is an event sort of like birth pains that verse 8 signifies when it says, "Nation will rise against nation, and kingdom against kingdom." It also says, "And there will be famines, pestilences and earthquakes in various places." A seeker's spiritual search for Reality implies a sort of labour pain in which a war is involved between two value worlds. One world is that of the enjoyable objects spread out before us, and of the living comforts that can be amassed. On the other side is the world of wisdom and the Supreme Peace that is experienced in life when it is attained. There is room for greed, competition, rivalry and mistrust in the former world. Yet those who are fully immersed in that world also may feel at rare moments that something of great value is missing in their lives, so that they experience the famine of something. This famine is not merely of the shortage of ordinary food, but of the food of peace, a feeling that life lacks real meaning. Those who feel this kind of famine may then turn their attention to the other world which ensures peace in life, which makes life fully meaningful. Such people will have to pass through an internal struggle that results from these two value worlds, pulling them in two opposite directions. Should the world of wisdom gain in this struggle, it causes a sort of earthquake-like transformation to occur in their life.

In rare cases, even in their youth they discriminate between these two value worlds and firmly fix their interest in the world of wisdom, dedicating themselves to this cause. They too are always tempted by the force of the other value world. Even when all such forces are conquered, the strong force of sex still remains to drag them behind it. The coming of Christ or enlightenment, that marks the end of the world, becomes an actual experience in life only to those who subdue or sublimate these forces and fully attune themselves to the ultimate goal of attaining wisdom. Those who take this kind of drastic decision in life also experience an agony that is like an inner earthquake.

The struggle between these two forces in the life of Jesus himself has already happened, as was seen in chapter 4 of the Gospel. Satan came to tempt Jesus when he (Jesus) was totally emaciated as a result of forty days' fasting. We have already noticed how Jesus conquered satan in this battle. Spiritual life, in fact, is not possible unless one passes through such an internal struggle, and the interest in wisdom reigns victorious. Such are the warring nations or kingdoms mentioned here, which *Bhagavad-Gītā* conceived as *āsurī-sampat* (demonic values) and *daivī-sampat* (divine values), in the whole of its chapter XVI. One should first find for oneself, of what nature are the *āsurī-sampat* and *daivī-sampat* in oneself, and then the *āsurī-sampat* should be defeated by diligently making use of the *daivī-sampat*. If the *āsurī-sampat* in oneself is very strong, then the conquering of it is felt as a sort of earthquake and as if a severe famine is felt in the worldly aspect of life. Such struggles sometimes have to be faced by seekers literally gnashing their teeth and clinching their fists. We are going to see more of this now.

Those who unerringly tread the path of wisdom finally reach the stage of enlightenment. Two things then happen to them. For one, instead of perceiving one's *guru* (here Jesus) as an individual human being, one sees him as the eternal *guru*. This awakening, as far as the disciples of Jesus are concerned, is the coming of Christ. And two, this marks the end of the age, or the end of the world. That means, the apparent world then ceases to exist as real, because the constantly changing phenomenal world is realized to be nothing other than the manifest forms that appear and disappear in the one changeless Reality, called *Brahman* in Vedānta and God in theology. This appearance happens simply because of the *māyā* inherent in that Reality. In short, the realness of the world comes to an end then, and what then alone remains as existing is the realness of God (*Brahman*).

A spiritual life aimed at this attainment is not at all easy. Those who dare to choose such a path may be derided by many of society. They may even be dubbed as "parasites" and thus the enemies of society. Many who were very close once distance themselves. They may also be approached by false *guru*s on the pretext of showing them some other spiritual path claimed to be better than the one they have chosen. Only in the life of those who go forward along the true spiritual path as guided by the true *guru,* evading all these obstructions and temptations, does the true coming of Christ happen. Only on one's becoming well-founded in this experience of the coming of Christ, does one realize that the end of the perceptible world has come. Such an enlightened one feels the urge to declare to the world the gospel of this Reality — the coming of the kingdom of God. All this is indicated in verses 9-14 which are as follows:

> Then they will deliver you up to tribulation and kill you, and you will be hated at by all nations for My name's sake.
>
> And then many will be offended, will betray one another and will hate one another.
>
> Then many false prophets will rise up and deceive many.
>
> And because lawlessness will abound, the love of many will grow cold.
>
> But he who endures to the end shall be saved.
>
> And this gospel of the kingdom will be preached in all the world as a witness to all the nations and then the end will come.

The reference of Jesus to his disciples in verse 9 is in the plural as "you." But as far as the context of reaching the final goal by enduring all obstructions, conflicts, persecutions and tribulations to come, the reference is in the singular as "he who endures to the end." The suggestion is that a *guru* may have many disciples to follow him, but following the true path of wisdom according to his guidance becomes possible for one or two of them.

And the statement "the end will come" is to be understood in two senses. One, this experience marks the end of the seeker's quest. Two, considering this visible world as real in itself ends with this attainment of the coming of Christ. In fact, these two are experienced simultaneously like two sides of the same coin.

1.33

Hard Life and Attainment

VERSES 15-28 of chapter 24 in this Gospel portray the difficulties and trials that spiritual seekers may have to endure in life. But apparently this section looks like a description of the end of the world, which is a normal subject for the Semitic religions. But it is clearly said at the end.

> As the lightning comes from the east and flashes to the west, so also will the coming of the son of Man be. — 24.27

Very similar is the description of the same experience given by Narayana Guru thus:

> Like ten thousand suns rising all at once
> Dawns the discriminative enlightenment,
> That really is the original sun that cuts through
> The ephemeral māyā-darkness which puts a veil
> Over the pure and unconditioned Consciousness.
> — *Ātmopadeśa Śatakam*, verse 35

These verses of the Gospel could in general be considered to simply give the details of the inner process "that cuts through the *māyā*-darkness."

"The abomination of desolation spoken of by Daniel the prophet, standing in the holy places," referred to in 24.15, reminds us of an earlier scene in which Christ drove away all the merchants and money changers from the temple of God. Likewise, choosing a spiritual path in life becomes meaningless if one is incapable of driving away all the elements of abomination from the temple of life. There will remain a few clear and pure elements in us when all such impure elements are driven away. Some such elements may look neither good nor evil, and certain others will be found to lean towards goodness. Both these elements, when specified, have to be given a direction aimed at the ultimate goal of attaining wisdom and Happiness. This is indicated by the statement, "then let those who are in Judea flee to the mountains" (24.16). Spiritual disciplines become fruitful only for those who detach themselves from all that is abominable and attach themselves to all that is of the highest value in life.

Those who have chosen with determination such a harsh spiritual path, should not look backwards. That means, they should not think of or become worried about the unfulfilled obligations in ordinary life, because entering the spiritual path after fulfilling all such obligations would not be possible. The attachment towards friends and relatives also should not attract them. Indicative of this decision are the words:

> Let him who is on the housetop not come down to take anything out of his house.
>
> And let him who is in the field not go back to get his clothes.
>
> — 24.17-18

We have seen earlier also the words of Jesus to his disciples, "Let the dead bury the dead" which convey the same message. Such firm decisions taken by spiritual aspirants may at times cause trouble for some people who were dependent on them and who are caught in certain unavoidable situations in life, for example, "those who are pregnant and those with nursing babies" (24.19).

Miserable will be the plight of those who take to a spiritual path in life, if they do not find a proper *guru,* in spite of enduring all the above-mentioned trials and tribulations. Many agents may come to them in order to lure them into certain popular spiritual cults or movements, saying, "Such and such a *siddha* is there," "Such and such a *yogī* is there," "Such and such a meditation centre is there where you can learn meditation techniques and the like". One must turn a deaf ear to all such tempting offerings, and stick with full faith to the guidance of the true *guru* whom one could find simply by the grace of God. Such a seeker reaches the true final goal referred to here as the "coming of the son of Man." Eagles gather around wherever there is a carcass. Likewise, as long as the spiritual quest is a part of human life and interest, so-called spiritual movements and cults intent on luring such seekers to their camps will continue to prevail. The nature of such movements or their agents is compared here to eagles or vultures that gather around carcasses.

Verses 29-30 portray the inner agonies and transformations that find place in the seeker or disciple, upon his treading the path of spiritual discipline as properly guided by a *guru.* The sun, as modern science teaches us, is the great source of energy for all the living beings on this planet. But it becomes clear upon realizing the ultimate Reality, that there is a supreme source-Consciousness that systematizes the sun itself and the energy it gives to the world, as well as our life and the life of all beings and all the worlds. Inhering within that Reality is the limitless potential to emanate all the worlds from itself. All the worlds, the sun, the moon and stars, the phenomenon of life and everything else are nothing more than mere spark-like emanations that come from the one causal Consciousness, called *cit* in Vedānta. The sun has no power to shine without respecting the systematization arranged by that Reality. So too with the moon and stars. We also have no power to live independently of it, as we have no existence apart from it. *Taittirīya Upaniṣad* (II.viii.1) therefore says:

> Being afraid of Him the wind blows.
> Being afraid (of Him) the sun shines.
> Being afraid of Him the fire and Indra function. And Death too runs as the fifth.

All the concepts we have formulated so far about what controls life, thus, are turned upside down. It is then felt that, until that moment, all things that were considered as valuable like wealth, good family, social relations and all such, no longer make life meaningful. What then remains to exist, and to be of the highest value, is the one ultimate Reality, pure effulgence in essence, referred to here as "the Son of Man." All this is indicated in verses 29-30 which read as follows:

> Immediately after the tribulation of those days the sun will be darkened, and the moon will not give its light; the stars will fall from heaven, and the powers of the heavens will be shaken.
>
> Then the sign of the Son of Man will appear in heaven, and then all the tribes of the earth will mourn, and they will see the Son of Man coming on the clouds of heaven with power and great glory.

"The tribulation of these days" point to the hardships that the seekers are compelled to go through. The heaven in which the Son of Man will appear is the *cidākāśa* (the space of Consciousness) understood in Vedānta. "The tribes of the earth who will mourn" are those who live in the world of relativism indicated by the word "tribes." Those who are in that world count family ties, tribal unity and social obligations to make life meaningful. Those who live by identifying themselves with tribes and clans and other traditional values, in the event of realizing the Reality, the real meaning-content of life, lament the meaninglessness of the values they were until then holding high. If they remain unrealized, their lamentation will be on their incapability of attaining higher wisdom. This phenomenon could well be seen in situations such as when those who are considered rich and important people in society will sometimes come before enlightened persons and lament before them, exposing all the problems they face in life.

A *guru* who lives as the torch bearer of wisdom, always longs to hand it down to a fully competent successor-disciple. A *guru* truly becomes a *guru* only when a true disciple has approached him in search of wisdom. Otherwise he remains just a *jñānin*. A *jñānin* when fully intent on handing down his wisdom, remains with a prayer for the coming of such disciples. Therefore, the *guru* in chapter I of *Taittirīya Upaniṣad* openly prays thus:

> May seekers of Truth approach me variously; Hail! May seekers of Truth approach me properly; Hail! May seekers of Truth approach me undisturbed by external influences; Hail! May seekers of Truth approach me with mental self-control; Hail! — I.iv.2

The following words of Narayana Guru, though addressed to the god Subrahmaṇya, could well be interpreted to be related to the present context also:

No one do I see
To share this with, wherein
Even the humming sound
Of the bee that sucks honey
Day and night, is not heard.
O come and enjoy this sweetness!
— *Subrahmaṇya Kīrtanam,* verse 7

We have already seen the trials and tribulations a seeker has to go through in his effort to attain the final goal of realizing the eternal Reality. Such hardships do not last long, and moreover, such are indicative of having reached the threshold of their goal. And this attainment is not usually accomplished without passing through such trials. As heaven and earth do not exist eternally, so too the hardships felt by a seeker also are not eternal. An eternal Reality underlies the appearance of all that is transient, and it is that Reality that effects these fleeting appearances. Likewise, attaining the secret of the Eternal involves some fleeting hardships. The words of wisdom of every *guru* are verbal expressions of this one eternal Reality, and such words are also of an eternal nature. Indicative of all this are verses 32-35, which read as follows:

> Now learn this parable from the fig tree: When its branch has already become tender and puts forth leaves, you know that summer is near.
>
> So you also, when you see all these things, know that it is near, at the very doors.
>
> Assuredly, I say to you, this generation will by no means pass away till all these things are fulfilled.
>
> Heaven and earth will pass away, but My words will by no means pass away.

The necessity for a seeker to remain fully alert and attentive is underscored in verses 36-44 which run as follows:

> But of that day and hour no one knows, no, not even the angels of heaven, but My Father only.
>
> But as the days of Noah were, so also will the coming of the Son of Man be.
>
> For as in the days before the flood, they were eating and drinking, marrying and giving in marriage, until the day that Noah entered the ark,
>
> and did not know until the flood came and took them all away, so also will the coming of the Son of Man be.
>
> Then two men will be in the field: one will be taken and the other left.
>
> Two women will be grinding the mill: one will be taken and the other left.
>
> Watch therefore, for you do not know what hour your Lord is coming.
>
> But know this, that if the master of the house had known what hour the thief would come, he would have watched and not allowed his house to be broken into.
>
> Therefore you also be ready, for the Son of Man is coming at an hour when you do not expect Him.

As was made clear earlier, even as the seekers go through all hardships, they must keep in mind the definite goal to be attained. Having full faith in that goal and its attainment, a firmness and determination to not back out until it is attained, and a one-pointedness of attention to the goal, are to be maintained by the seekers. These qualities together are called *samādhāna* by Śaṅkara in his *Vivekacūḍāmaṇi* (The Crest-Jewel of Discrimination). *Samādhāna* is one of the six self-imposed disciplines, called *śamādi-ṣaḍka-sampatti* that the seeker has to develop in himself as conceived by Vedānta. Śaṅkara defines *samādhāna* as follows:

> Keeping the thinking mind (*buddhi*) properly fixed in pure *Brahman* constantly is spoken of as *samādhāna*. — verse 27

It would be at an unexpected moment that the nature of Reality becomes revealed to the seeker who subjects himself thus to an austere self-discipline generally known as *tapas* (self-heating up). When such an attainment is noticed by the public, they become divided into two camps: one, those who deny it and despise the attainer, and the other, those who faithfully admit it. All this can be seen indicated in the above passages.

Verses 45-47 are as follows:

> Who then is a faithful and wise servant, whom his master made ruler over his household, to give them food in due season?
>
> Blessed is that servant whom his master, when he comes, will find so doing.
>
> Assuredly, I say to you that he will make him ruler over all his goods.

An enlightened *guru* or prophet should have at least one disciple who is capable of imbibing the true spirit of his wisdom and of handing it down to posterity without losing its essential content and clarity. It will be the disciple who is chosen by the *guru* to be his successor, and this one will be entrusted with the entire responsibility related to it. This could be seen to have happened in the life of all the *guru*s and prophets. The present parable compares the *guru* with the master, and the true disciple with the faithful servant. All the disciples that gather around a *guru* need not necessarily be fully competent or be true seekers; others could also be among them. The character of this latter type of disciples lacks in the above-mentioned quality of *samādhāna*. Such persons naturally find themselves left out from the actual context of wisdom attainment. They are likely to lament later like this, "I lived for this *guru* so many years; but what I got is nothing." All this is indicated in verses 48-51 which read as follows:

> But if that evil servant says in his heart, "My master is delaying his coming,"
>
> and begins to beat his fellow servants, and to eat and drink with the drunkards,

the master of that servant will come on a day when he is not looking for him and at an hour that he is not aware of,

and will cut him in two and appoint him his portion with the hypocrites. There shall be weeping and gnashing of teeth.

1.34

Incomparable Grades of Happiness

JESUS presents three parables in chapter 25. The first one comes in verses 1-13 which are as follows:

> Then the kingdom of heaven shall be likened to ten virgins who took their lamps and went out to meet the bridegroom.
>
> Now five of them were wise, and five were foolish.
>
> Those who were foolish took their lamps and took no oil with them,
>
> but the wise took oil in their vessels with their lamps.
>
> But while the bridegroom was delayed, they all slumbered and slept.
>
> And at midnight a cry was heard, "Behold, the bridegroom is coming, go out to meet him!"
>
> Then all those virgins arose and trimmed their lamps.
>
> And the foolish said to the wise, "Give us some of your oil for our lamps are going out."
>
> But the wise answered, saying, "No, lest there should not be enough for us and you; but go rather to those who sell, and buy for yourselves."
>
> And while they went to buy, the bridegroom came, and those who were ready went in with him to the wedding; and the door was shut.
>
> Afterward the other virgins came also, saying, "Lord, Lord, open to us!"
>
> But he answered and said, "Assuredly I say to you, I do not know you."
>
> Watch therefore, for you know neither the day nor the hour in which the Son of Man is coming.

The kingdom of heaven or the context of gaining wisdom from a *guru* is compared here to ten virgins who wait to receive a bridegroom. There are not many who are desirous of and willing to live in the heaven of wisdom. Therefore the number of such virgins is here limited to ten. These virgins are to be seen as ten disciples who have approached a *guru*. All those who come to a *guru* need not necessarily be genuine seekers capable of imbibing the spirit of true wisdom. The analogy of the five wise virgins and the five foolish ones indicates that a few of the disciples may be competent for wisdom and others incompetent. The aim of both, still, remains entering the wedding hall of wisdom by receiving the bridegroom of enlightenment, and enjoying the wedding feast of Supreme Happiness. The lamps carried by the virgins signify the method one adopts for gaining wisdom, and the oil stands for the mental propensities that enable one to make use of such methods beneficially and properly. They should wait fully awake with this lamp lit.

To remain awake unceasingly; in the literal sense, is not possible for anyone. The waking state is always followed by the sleeping state. But one should be fully prepared internally so that such alternating states of consciousness do not in any way affect the lively internal yearning for wisdom. This is indicated by the five wise virgins carrying enough oil with them. One seeker's internal preparedness can never be shared with another as indicated by the words of the wise virgins, "No, lest there should not be enough for us and you."

Enlightenment is an inner event that happens unexpectedly in the true seeker as he passes through the intense self-heating (*tapas*) of spiritual discipline; no one can predict when it will happen. Those, who remain ever watchful and on the look out, will directly enter the wedding hall of wisdom. But even on being the disciples of a *guru*, those who do not remain fully alert and in readiness because of the inert and dark elements (*tamas*) in their character, become ousted when the real hour of attaining the goal comes. Their lamentation from the outside would be responded to by wisdom itself as, "Assuredly, I say to you, I do not know you." That means, lazy and drowsy seekers find real wisdom to be alien to them.

The second parable reads thus (verses 14-30, chapter 25):

> For the kingdom of heaven is like a man travelling to a far country, who called his own servants and delivered his goods to them.
>
> And to one he gave five talents, to another two, and to another one, to each according to his own ability; and immediately he went on a journey.
>
> Then he who had received the five talents went and traded with them, and made another five talents.
>
> And likewise he who had received two gained two more also.
>
> But he who had received one went and dug in the ground, and hid his lord's money.
>
> After a long time the lord of these servants came and settled accounts with them.

> So he who had received five talents came and brought five other talents saying, "Lord, you delivered to me five talents; look, I have gained five more talents besides them."
>
> His lord said to him, "Well done, good and faithful servant, you were faithful over a few things, I will make you ruler over many things. Enter into the joy of your lord."
>
> He also who had received two talents came and said, "Lord, you delivered to me two talents; look, I have gained two more talents besides them."
>
> His lord said to him, "Well done, good and faithful servant, you were faithful over a few things. I will make you ruler over many things. Enter into the joy of your lord."
>
> Then he who had received the one talent came and said, "Lord, I know you to be a hard man, reaping where you have not sown, and gathering where you have not scattered seed.
>
> And I was afraid, and went and hid your talent in the ground. Look, there you have what is yours."
>
> But his lord answered and said to him, "You wicked and lazy servant, you knew that I reap where I have not sown, and gather where I have not scattered seed.
>
> Therefore you ought to have deposited my money with the bankers, and at my coming I would have received back my own with interest.
>
> Therefore take the talent from him, and give it to him who has ten talents.
>
> "For to everyone who has, more will be given, and he will have abundance; from him who does not have, even what he has will be taken away.
>
> And cast the unprofitable servant into the outer darkness. There will be weeping and gnashing of teeth."

The master of this parable stands for the *guru* who is about to depart from this world, and the servants represent the disciples. A *guru* before dying, always tries somehow to hand down his wisdom secret to at least some disciples, as is signified in the parable of the master sharing out his wealth among his servants. A *guru* admittedly has no wealth greater than wisdom. Though it is one wisdom alone that is taught to all the disciples each imbibes the spirit of it according to their own capacity and competence. The servant who got five talents represents the disciple who has taken in the entire spirit of the wisdom. He absorbs it into his own life and imparts it to the seekers who approach him. It thus becomes beneficial both to him and to the world.

It in effect becomes a double gain. This is suggested where the servant trades with the five talents, letting it grow twofold.

Some of the other disciples grasp the content of the wisdom which they were taught only in its general outline. They too perceive their own life accordingly and teach others to perceive life so. What they gained, though of a lesser order, also thus grows twofold. But the disciples of the last type remain afraid of the subtlety of the wisdom they were taught. They therefore remain without grasping the real content of the wisdom, and for the same reason become compelled to hide it from others, for they find themselves unable to imbibe and teach it. Such disciples, sometimes by keeping in mind only the literal sense of what the *guru* taught, may even make attempts to establish religious cults or churches in the *guru*'s name. Such movements, in effect, will only be something like the blind leading the blind, as Jesus pointed out earlier himself. Such organizers may remain in the top positions of these cults or movements, which only ends up boosting up their own egos. All this ends up in a situation where the leader and the led reach a blind alley. Weeping and gnashing of teeth instead of joy are normal there.

The part of the parable where the master comes back and settles the accounts stands for when the disciples themselves look back at themselves and evaluate how far the wisdom they were taught became beneficial in making their own lives and the lives of others meaningful and peaceful. This allows them to decide whether they are fully content with it or not.

Nowadays, equality is one of those modern ideals given a very high value, particularly in politics. But this ideal has no respectable place in the world of spirituality, especially when related to the stage of attainment. The Happiness and Peace experienced by each as a result of their own spiritual quest are of differing orders. Life is experienced to be Happiness in essence by those who perceive their personal happiness and the happiness of the world as one Happiness. This is indicated by the words, "To everyone who has, more will be given." But there are those who live ignoring the wisdom-teaching or do not grasp the real content of wisdom. They make use of spirituality to boost up their own egos. They lead people to untruth in the guise of leading them to truth. Such people, though apparently happy, within themselves, remain full of fear and unhappiness. The experience in store for such people is indicated by the statement, "from him who does not have, even what he has will be taken away." They inwardly weep and gnash their teeth.

1.35

A Criterion for Good and Evil

In verses 31-46 of chapter 25, Jesus presents a vision of a highly ethical significance. It runs as follows:

> When the Son of Man comes in His glory, and all the holy angels with Him, then He will sit on the throne of His glory.
>
> All the nations will be gathered before Him, and He will separate them one from another, as a shepherd divides his sheep from the goats.
>
> And He will set the sheep on His right hand, but the goats on the left.
>
> Then the King will say to those on His right hand, "Come, you blessed of My Father, inherit the kingdom prepared for you from the foundation of the world,
>
> for I was hungry and you gave Me food; I was thirsty and you gave Me drink; I was a stranger and you took Me in;
>
> I was naked and you clothed Me; I was sick and you visited Me; I was in prison and you came to Me."
>
> Then the righteous will answer Him, saying, "When did we see You hungry and feed You, or thirsty and give You drink?
>
> When did we see You a stranger and take You in, or naked and clothe You?
>
> Or when did we see You sick, or in prison, and come to You?
>
> And the King will answer and say to them, "Assuredly, I say to you, inasmuch as you did it to one of the least of these my brethren, you did it to Me."
>
> Then He will also say to those on the left hand, "Depart from Me," you cursed, into the everlasting fire prepared for the devil and his angels;
>
> for I was hungry and you gave Me no food; I was thristy and you gave Me no drink.
>
> I was a stranger and you did not take Me in, naked and you did not clothe Me, sick and in prison and you did not visit Me."
>
> Then they also will answer Him, saying, "Lord, when did we see You hungry or thirsty or a stranger or naked or sick or in prison, and did not minister to You?"

Then He will answer them, saying, "Assuredly I say to you, inasmuch as you did not do it to one of the least of these, you did not do it to Me."

And these will go away into everlasting punishment, but the righteous into eternal life.

Jesus here seats himself on the throne of the kingdom of wisdom. The suggestion in the present context is that wisdom itself is to be seated in the honoured seat of justice, which is the criterion to differentiate good and evil, the just and the unjust. Seen from wisdom's point of view, those who live fully in accord with the essence of wisdom are to be called the good and the just, and those who do not do so are bad and unjust. The essence of wisdom is this much: Reality is one alone; and that Reality is what manifests as everything apparent. A *jñānin* (an enlightened one) is one who sees one Reality alone in himself and everything else, or in everything. Every action of the one who lives with this perception, while being aimed at his own happiness, ensures the happiness of others as well, for the simple reason that what is counted as others are not really different from himself. The Self, for the happiness of which a *jñānin* performs actions, thus, covers himself and others. A *jñānin* perceives the sufferings of others as his own. But in the case of those who live unaware of this wisdom secret, their actions are aimed at their personal happiness alone and are unmindful of the happiness or sufferings of others. The result of this outlook on life is that eventually they suffer. The life of a *jñānin* is always filled with Happiness (*ānanda*), while the life of others are filled with hellish torments. What this section of the Gospel portrays is merely a variant of the following verse of *Īśa Upaniṣad*:

When, to one who knows, all beings have verily become one with his own self, then what delusion and what sorrow can be in him who has seen the oneness? — verse 7

Narayana Guru also, following the same line of thought, says in his *Ātmopadeśa Śatakam*:

The happiness of another is the happiness of mine,
And my happiness is the happiness of others too
With this guiding principle.
Actions performed to ensure the happiness of oneself
Should secure the happiness of others as well. — verse 22

Any action that ensures one's happiness
And causes another's suffering, remember well,
Goes against the principle of the oneness of ātmā,
Those who cause misery to others surely fall
Into the fiery ocean of hell and suffer. — verse 25

1.36

The Final Homage

VERSES 6-13 of chapter 26 are as follows:

> And when Jesus was in Bethany at the house of Simon the leper,
>
> a woman came to Him having an alabaster flask of very costly fragrant oil, and she poured it on His head as He sat at the table.
>
> But when His disciples saw it, they were indignant, saying, "To what purpose is this waste?
>
> For this fragrant oil might have been sold for much and given to the poor."
>
> But when Jesus was aware of it, He said to them, "Why do you trouble the woman? For she has done a good work for Me."
>
> For you have the poor with you always, but Me you do not have always.
>
> For in pouring this fragrant oil on My body, she did it for My burial.
>
> Assuredly, I say to you, wherever this gospel is preached in the whole world, what this woman has done will also be told as a memorial to her."

The values of both philanthropy and the love of wisdom are admirable. But when seen in the light of the wisdom, as stated at the end of the last chapter, these two values are of two orders. Though both are to be honoured, one's place in life should not be given to the other. Philanthropy pertains to the level of benevolence. It consists of doing good things beneficial to other members of society, particularly to the poor and meagre section. But the love of wisdom, indicated by honouring a *guru* who lives as the embodiment of the wisdom effulgent, and who radiates that effulgence to the world, is of a different order. The former is a worldly value; thus it is of a horizontal dimension. But paying homage to a *guru* signifies honouring the glory of the wisdom he represents. Moreover, it is your intense interest in wisdom that inspires you to honour a *guru*. Doing so makes you happy, but that happiness has a different dimension, in no way attached to worldly affairs. This Happiness, to be written with a capital H, could be said to be of a vertical order. Mixing up these two value-worlds is hazardous.

Guruhood, as a principle, can be deified by us by always keeping it within ourselves as the highest value. But honouring an actual living *guru* is only possible when he is alive. And in the case of Jesus, his days are already numbered; two days only remain for him to live in this world. Thus, this is the last homage Jesus receives as a living *guru*. The virtuous work of doing good to others could be done as and when we like, for there is no time or country in which there is no one living in poverty. Seen a bit differently, you may not always get a chance to honour wisdom and to acquire wisdom. But to be philanthropic is always possible.

The names of philanthropists are not always remembered with honour by posterity. Though this is true, there are many who desire to be known in the future as benevolent persons; so their names are inscribed on some plaques after performing a good work of a philanthropic nature or for the public's benefit. Now inscribing the philanthropist's name on a memorial or a tomb is the highest honour that may be given him. But the *guru*'s glory is not like that. He is always remembered for his wisdom teachings. The one who gets a chance to pay homage to such a living *guru*, by really treating him as a *guru*, with all the people around to witness, will also be remembered for ever by doing so. Jesus is the Christ. The word "Christ" means "the anointed one." By anointing him with a costly fragrant oil, the woman was here literally making him a Christ.

1.37

The Last Supper and Dialectics

VERSES 14-29 of chapter 26 describe the Last Supper. It is on this occasion that Jesus tells his twelve disciples that one of them will betray him. Verses 26-29 read thus:

> And as they were eating, Jesus took bread, blessed it and broke it, and gave it to the disciples and said, "Take, eat; this is My body."
>
> Then He took the cup, and gave thanks, and gave it to them, saying, "Drink from it, all of you."
>
> For this is My blood of the new covenant, which is shed for many for the remission of sins.
>
> But I say to you, I will not drink of this fruit of the vine from now on until that day when I drink it new with you in My Father's kingdom.

This, in fact, is the last time Jesus sits alongside his disciples. It is here that he gives his own body and blood to his disciples in the form of bread and wine. In a sense, what Jesus does here is to entrust himself to the disciples. Jesus, as stated earlier, is the embodiment of eternal guruhood. To entrust the *guru* to his disciples does not simply mean that the individual is put into their charge; it is the wisdom itself or the principle of eternal guruhood, in its new form, that is put into their charge.

Jesus by now has already taught his disciples whatever wisdom he intended to teach. And this teaching has an orderly form of its own. So it too has a meaning-content that flows, that is transmitted through generations. The flow of this meaning-content, as held by the Jewish tradition, began with Abraham. Such traditions do exist in many cultural milieus. India is no exception. In India too, a wisdom tradition passes through generations, while its external form undergoes certain modifications. Likewise, Jesus also has just given a newly-modified and revised form to the already existing body of Jewish wisdom and religion. What Jesus does here really is to entrust his disciples with the wisdom secret that cannot be confined to any particular form, by giving it the bodily shape of a teaching. It is this body and its ever-flowing meaning-content that Jesus hands over to his disciples in the form of bread and blood.

It is after giving himself to the disciples that Judas, one of the disciples, betrays him. He tells his disciples after entrusting himself to them, "I will not drink of this fruit of the vine from now on until that day when I drink it new with you in My Father's kingdom." A suggestion is also here in these words that this is the last time he will be eating in his life.

In the kingdom of his Father, i.e. in the kingdom of wisdom, *guru* and disciple are equals; for there can be no *guru* without any disciple, and no disciple without a *guru.* Wisdom is what links them together in that kingdom. When both find themselves in that kingdom, the wisdom of the *guru* becomes the disciple's. The two thus become equal in status, and both realize their oneness in the kingdom of wisdom. In such a kingdom, the ordinary bread and blood are of no significance. All these ideas can be seen suggested in the above words of Jesus.

The section of the Gospel covered in verses 36-46 contains two basic principles that should be noticed. Jesus sits at a lonely place, and prays to God with an exceedingly sorrowful soul, and then instructs the disciples. The prayer is thus:

> O My Father, if it is possible let this cup pass from Me, nevertheless, not as I will, but as You will. — 26.39

He repeated this prayer three times, but during this entire time the disciples who accompanied him were asleep. Jesus went to them, woke them up, and said:

> Watch and pray lest you enter into temptations. The spirit indeed is willing, but the flesh is weak. — 26.41

We have noticed all through this Gospel that Jesus Christ has two faces: one as the son of Man and the other as the Son of God. As the son of Man, he is like everyone of us. Wishing to avoid death is a natural instinct in all beings including humans. It is as the son of Man that Jesus prays, "O Father if it is possible, let this cup pass from Me." Put in Vedāntic terms, Jesus utters these words by remaining under the spell of *māyā*. It is under *māyā*'s influence that this beginningless and endless world, and the phenomenon of life in it, seem to be real. Birth and death are also felt to be real then, and trying to avoid death is but natural. This instinct shows our love for life. That everything is real, is the way we understand the world in this state.

If everything is real, the question arises, "What is real in everything?" The answer is, "It is the one ultimate Reality or Father."

What appears as all this is but one Father or God alone, called *Brahman* or *Ātman* in Vedānta. The whole of the worldly phenomena is nothing but the will of God having found expression. The world and ourselves, thus, have existence only as fleeting manifest forms of that Reality or God. In that sense, we are all the sons of God. But we live completely ignorant of this truth. What differentiates Jesus from us is that he is fully aware of this truth. And for this reason he alone is glorified as the Son of God — the Son of God is he who knows the secret of God. In this capacity he says, "nevertheless, not as I will, but as You will." This is the first principle to be noticed in this section.

The second principle is this: Two aspects of the Guru Jesus are to be differentiated here. One is the individual human being who is subject to *māyā*, who is changeful and impermanent, and who also is one among the ephemeral worldly phenomena. The other is the one eternal Reality, the eternal *guru*, that transcends *māyā*, that is changeless. Now there is a realm of experiential awareness that exists where these two meet at a neutral ground and become inseparably one. Jesus as the Christ pertains to that realm, as the eternally living *guru*, who is to be intuitively perceived. It is in order to attain that realm of perception that the disciples, as intended by Jesus himself, were to remain fully awake; yet right at that moment they fell asleep. Perhaps it is for this reason that, later, when these disciples builtup the Christian church, it lost much of its dialectical and non-dual flavour, and became a more mechanistically functioning religious institution.

Seen thus, the prayer, "O My Father, if it is possible, let this cup pass from Me" indicates the former aspect of Jesus the *guru*. Immediately he neutralizes it himself with the latter aspect when he says, "nevertheless, not as I will, but as You will." The dialectical oneness of these aspects in the living *guru* Jesus is to be meditatively perceived.

When praying to God, we usually forget to say "O God, thy will be done." Moreover, we pray for the fulfilment of our personal desires and gains, and very often we also make offerings to God in order to attain our goals. Mostly it is money that is offered, and it is money that is prayed for also. In fact, it is to be doubted whether God knows what money is, for it is simply a man-made device. All the natural products such as rice, wheat, fruits and vegetables are well known to God as His own creations. If such are the objects we pray for, then God may understand our prayer. But when asked for money, God may smilingly reply, "Money? I don't know what it is."

Unless the above-mentioned two sides are discriminated between and their dialectical oneness perceived, every possibility is there to be tempted by the side of the ephemeral bodily aspect. Jesus therefore warns his disciples "Watch and pray, lest you enter into temptation. The spirit indeed is willing, but the flesh is weak." In short, Jesus as a *guru,* prays to God with a clear understanding of this dialectical secret and in doing so makes dialectical counterparts stand out clearly. Again, as a *guru,* he virtually reminds his disciples not to forget this dialectical secret.

1.38

A Guru Does not Desire to Avoid Death

THE agents of the chief priests and elders laid hands on Jesus and took him, as he had been betrayed by Judas. Suddenly one of those who were with Jesus stretched out his hand and drew his sword, struck the servant of the high priest and cut off his ear. Then Jesus said to him:

> Put your sword in its place, for all who take the sword will perish by the sword.
>
> Or do you think I cannot now pray to My Father, and He will provide Me with more than twelve legions of angels?
>
> How then could the scriptures be fulfilled, that it must happen so?
> — 26.52-54

The Son of God could very well have prayed to his own Father to save him from death, as Jesus himself makes clear. Or else, Jesus, who had brought many dead back to life, who had walked on the sea, could have used the same miraculous power to save himself. But he does not do so. He intended rather that the predictions in scriptures, that this had to happen in his life, should be fulfilled.

The ideas expressed here in terms familiar to Semitic religions could well be understood in Vedāntic terms thus: *Jñānin*s are those who constantly perceive the beginningless and endless flow of the world, as the incessant stream of manifest forms that emerge in the one ultimate Reality, as the unfoldment of the mysterious creative urge inherent in itself. No *jñānin* desires to stop any event that has to happen as part of this flow, even to save his own life. That is why Jesus, even when death confronts him, does not try to avoid it though doing so was possible. The enlightened always wish their life to flow along with the overall flow of nature. Morover, Jesus makes use of his own impending death to teach a new lesson about what happens to those who react violently.

An event of a similar nature happened in the life of Narayana Guru. He had healed the illnesses of many as if miraculously. But when he himself lay sick in his last days, one of his devotees asked him, "You have healed the diseases of many; why don't you heal your own disease?" The Guru's response was. "Is it for the sake of this body?" The Guru healed the diseases of those who thought of themselves, "I am this body." It was not the recovery *of the body* that they felt then; they felt *their own* recovery. Even if the body's sickness is healed for the time being, it will perish in due course. The Guru on the other hand, had freed himself from the sense of identity with the body, and therefore he would not do anything to save the body, which really is meant to perish, from perishing.

Jesus knew as Judas approached him, that he was going to betray him. Still, he addressed him as "Friend." It shows that Jesus did not see Judas simply as a betrayer, but as an incidental instrument for what unavoidably had to happen in life. Judas, as part of nature, is deputed by the very same nature to implement one of its decisions. Jesus, on whom this decision is implemented, is also part of the same nature. Then what else can Jesus do other than call him a "Friend?"

Verses 3-10 of chapter 27 mainly describe how Judas, who betrayed Jesus, becomes remorseful on seeing that Jesus was condemned, saying, "I have sinned by betraying innocent blood," and finally he hangs himself. Judas, though one of the twelve disciples of Jesus, evidently could not strictly stick to his discipleship of remaining true to its spirit by honouring the high values which his *guru* uncompromisingly stood for. Nor could he stick to the value-world that tempted him to betray Jesus. The words "Then Judas, His betrayer, seeing that He had been condemned, was remorseful" (27.3) suggest that he did not expect Jesus to be condemned, perhaps because he expected Jesus to save himself by making use of his unworldly powers. In that case, Judas had a wrong understanding of the teachings of his *guru*. Anyway, he was rejected from the value-world that Jesus represented and also from the one represented by the thirty pieces of silver which he finally brought back to the chief priests and elders. Thus, he, in effect, became thrown out from both the worlds, eventually leading him to hang himself. Such persons are called *ubhaya-bhraṣṭa*s (thrown out from both). *Bhagavad-Gītā* also emphatically says, *saṁśayātmā vinaśyati* (the one of doubtful mind perishes).

Verses 11-23 summarize the scene in which Jesus was examined by the Governor Pontius Pilate. Earlier when the chief priests and elders accused him of the blasphemy for saying, "I am able to destroy the temple of God and rebuild it in three days," he did not answer anything. Here also, the governor, while sitting on his seat of justice, asks Jesus, "Do you not hear how many things they testify against you? But Jesus answered not a single word, and the governor marvelled greatly at it." — 27.13-14

Why is it so? In one sense, Jesus knew what was going to happen to him, and that he was himself unable to stop it. Looked at another way, Jesus did not live in the world where man-made laws and human sense of justice were valid. Such laws and such a sense of justice have no place in the kingdom of heaven where he lived and where he was the king. Therefore, he did not answer any of the questions that came from the world of man-made laws and of the human sense of justice. Those who are familiar with that world alone may marvel at such a reaction, or rather a lack of reaction from an accused in a court of law.

1.39

Crucifixion, Resurrection

VERSES 32-44 describe the scene of crucifixion. This, in a way, is one of the glaring examples that portray what happens when wisdom (*jñāna*) totally disappears from human life and ignorance (*ajñāna*) rules. Those who become aware that this is the way things are, simply remain helpless witnesses, saying, "I am innocent of the blood of this just person." This phenomenon can be seen prominently in modern life.

Just when Jesus was about to die on the cross, he cries out, "My God, My God, why have you forsaken Me?" This lamentation, as was stated earlier, could be considered to come from Jesus as the son of Man, not as the Son of God. These words, in fact, are not his own, but he was simply repeating the words at the beginning of chapter 22 of the Psalms of the Old Testament. Thus, even at the time of his death, Jesus maintained the status as a continuator of an already existing spiritual tradition. Similarly, the words of some of the people who were present there were, "Let us see if Elijah will come to save Him" (27.49). These words also are a variant of verse 8 of the same psalm, which reads as follows: "He trusted in the Lord. Let Him rescue Him; Let Him deliver Him, since He delights in Him." In short, Jesus ends his life by doing nothing that infringes upon his status as a true continuator and revaluator of an ancient cultural stream.

Now what remains is the Resurrection described in chapter 28. No *guru* lives in his body forever. A pot, for example, is filled with space, and the same space becomes one with the all-filling space when the pot is broken. Similarly, when the *guru*'s external form as an individual ceases to exist, the Reality that was in him becomes one with the all-filling Reality or *Brahman*. When Cattampi Swami, a saint contemporary to Narayana Guru who lived in Kerala, attained *mahā-samādhi*, the latter wrote three verses as an obituary, in which he said in part,

niḥ svam vapum samutsr̥jya ।
svam brahma-vapur āsthitaḥ ॥

He, by giving away the body that was not really his own, attained the *Brahman*-body that is his own.

Such is the resurrection a *guru* attains upon leaving the physical body. The same is the case with Jesus also. The presence of Jesus thus resurrected then is felt by us even now.

Part II

The Gospel According to Mark

2.1

The Secret Nature of Wisdom

THE Gospel according to Matthew begins with the story of Jesus's birth as the Son of God, whereas the present one begins by introducing John the Baptist as Jesus's predecessor, and also by describing the scene in which Jesus becomes baptized by John. That means, this Gospel confines itself to only the story of Jesus as the prophet blessed by God or as an enlightened *guru.*

Jesus started his teaching mission at Galilee, and it happens after John the Baptist was put in prison. That means, he did not begin to teach so long as his predecessor lived as a free person. Thus he strictly honoured the *guru*–disciple succession. The first words of his teaching, therefore, are:

> The time is fulfilled, and the kingdom of God is at hand. Repent, and believe in the gospel. — 1.15

Wisdom-seekers usually feel, the kingdom of God is at hand when their time of attaining the maturity of wisdom arrives. The completion of this experience involves two aspects. One is identifying the evil factors and shortcomings in oneself, and driving them away. This aspect is here indicated by the exhortation "Repent." If this is the negative side of the situation, its positive counterpart is, "Believe in the gospel." That means,"Have full faith in the wisdom-path of a true *guru.*"

The scene where Jesus enters the synagogue at Capernaum and teaches there portrays this double-faceted nature of the coming of the kingdom of God in the guise of an actual event in life. People were astonished at his teaching, for they noticed that he taught them as one having authority, and not as the scribes did. Spiritual truth, as indicated here, could be taught in two ways. One method is quoting the scriptures and elucidating them. The other is where a realized *guru* reveals to true seekers what he realized as a living wisdom. It is the second sort of teaching that arouses the feeling in the listeners, "He teaches as one having authority." This is the positive side of imparting wisdom. Its negative side is, as was noticed earlier, what the exhortation "Repent" represents, i.e., driving away the evil elements in oneself. This latter aspect is represented by the driving away of the unclean spirit from the man who was in the synagogue (1.23-25). People were then amazed and they said among themselves:

> What is this? What new doctrine is this? For with authority He commands even the unclean spirits and they obey Him. — 1.27

The method of Jesus's teaching thus is perfect in its dialectical nature. It is for this reason that his fame immediately spread throughout all the region around Galilee (1.28).

Verses 35-38 run thus:

> Now in the morning, having risen a long while before daylight, He went out and departed to a solitary place, and there He prayed.
>
> And Simon and those who were with Him searched for Him.
>
> When they found Him, they said to Him, "Everyone is looking for You."
>
> But He said to them, "Let us go into the next towns, that I may preach there also, because for this purpose I have come forth."

When his followers searched for him, why did Jesus just reply, "Let us go into the next towns?" It may be because the followers went in search of him with the feeling that they did not attain the knowledge they had expected from him. Had not Jesus already taught what he intended to teach? Though it is not stated here what he taught in the synagogue, it created a feeling in the people that he was teaching as one with authority. This force of authority of his words is derived from nowhere else than the secret wisdom they contain. That means, though Jesus spoke there to reveal what real wisdom was, the listeners could not comprehend the inner meaning-content of those words. Therefore they felt, there was something more to obtain from their *guru*. He, on the other hand, was well aware that he did not have anything to teach other than the secret of the kingdom of God, which he had already taught. The inner secrets of the words of wisdom a *guru* speaks need not necessarily become clear immediately to the disciples nor to the ordinary people who happen to be there. As long as this secret remains unrevealed, the disciples may feel, something more remains to be taught by the *guru*.

Kena Upaniṣad also pictures an incident very similar to this. The disciple had asked a definite question that was very basic, and in answer to it, the *guru* had already taught him the inner core of *brahma-vidyā* (the science of the Absolute). After all this, the disciple asks the *guru* again, "Please teach me *brahma-vidyā.*" The *guru,* then tells him, "It is *brahma-vidyā* that I have just taught you." The present incident in the life of Jesus is a similar one.

People may run after a *guru* with the request, "Please teach us more," even after he has already taught them what he wanted to. Then all he can do afterwards is simply leave them and go to some other place.

Verses 7-12 of chapter 3 describe how a great multitude followed Jesus, and how he healed many a sick person. But when the time of his going up on the mountain comes (verse 13), only twelve disciples were there to accompany him. The mountain top stands for the high value and sublimity of wisdom. No ordinary person, interested in worldly gains such as the healing of their illnesses, would be ready to follow a *guru* when he ascends to the top of the mountain of wisdom. Only the select disciples would be there. It is normal for real *guru*s to teach those disciples the secret of wisdom or of the kingdom of God, and send them out into the world at large to be the messengers of this teaching. This is what verses 13-19 of chapter 3 indicate.

Jesus tells his disciples in verses 21-23 of chapter 4, the following:

> Is a lamp brought to be put under a basket or under a bed? Is it not to be set on a lamp stand?
>
> For there is nothing hidden which will not be revealed, nor has anything been kept secret but that it should come to light.
>
> If anyone has ears to hear, let him hear.

The words "If anyone has ears to hear, let him hear" show the secret nature of wisdom. A lamp, when lit, is never meant to be hidden somewhere; it is always kept in a place where its light becomes available unto a maximum area. Similar is the case with wisdom. A lamp set on a lamp stand shines on its own, shedding its light all round, but those who are properly sighted alone see it. Self-knowledge, the awakening of the knowledge one has of oneself, shines on its own, shedding its brightness to the people all around. The Self (*Ātmā*) is self-effulgent. Moreover, it is the Self-Reality that shines by assuming the form of all the worlds. Nothing is there in the Self that remains unmanifest and hidden. No one can keep the Self-Reality as a secret either, but seeing it requires a special eye.

The Upaniṣads to also claim that they contain a secret knowledge, one of the meanings of the word *upaniṣad* itself being "secret knowledge." In what sense is it a secret knowledge? If someone attempts to explicate it to someone else in a logically convincing way, or if someone tries to make it conveyable through the medium of words, then it remains a hidden knowledge. But when one becomes enlightened to the fact that it is the very same Reality searched for, that assumes the form of oneself who seeks, that oneself is that Reality, and that it is that Reality that functions as one's search for Reality itself, then one feels that nothing remains unrevealed. In this sense Jesus says, "Nor has anything been kept secret but that it should come to light."

Reality can never be kept a secret by anyone. Suppose one hesitates to divulge the secret aspect of wisdom on the plea that it is a secret knowledge. Even then, if the seeker is fully competent and endowed with the intense heat of the search, called *tapas* in Vedānta, the Reality becomes revealed with no secret hidden.

The above said passage could well be understood with the help of the *māyā*-concept of Vedānta also. Reality remains secret as long as the veiling effect of *māyā* prevails. It is *māyā,* then, that keeps the Reality as a secret or hidden. Becoming free from *māyā* is possible only by realizing that *māyā* itself is non-existent. On attaining this freedom, one realizes that nothing hidden remains to be known.

The above passage has two parts in it: the first part is, "There is nothing hidden which will not be revealed," and the second part is "nor has anything been kept secret but that it should come to light." This division becomes clear as we put together and read the various translations of the Bible and try to understand the implied meanings of the verse. The first part could be construed as referring to the Reality that remains hidden by itself, and the other part to the Reality that is veiled by something.

Removing these two veils together and realizing the non-dual reality has a secretness of its own. This secretness could be seen implied in the words of Jesus, "If anyone has ears to hear, let him hear." In short, the non-dual Reality never remains hidden because It is the one Substance in everything in all the worlds. And no one can keep the non-dual Reality veiled from anyone because we the perceivers are that Reality in essence. Verse 24 runs as follows:

> And He said to them, "Take heed what you hear. With the same measure you use, it will be measured to you; and to you who hear, more will be given."

We saw in the verse just prior that Reality or wisdom never remains hidden, and that no one can hide it. Such being the "secret" of wisdom, a disciple or seeker becomes awake to it only when he hears the words of a *guru* who is already awakened. Such a listener is to be counted as the one "who has ears to hear." Giving emphasis to this aspect, Jesus repeats, "Take heed what you hear." According to *Bṛhadāraṇyaka Upaniṣad*, such a hearing, called *śravaṇa,* is always to be followed by proper cogitation on what is thus heard (*manana*), and meditation followed by realization (*nididhyāsana*). Therefore, the words of Jesus "Take heed what you hear" could be taken to also imply the *manana* and *nididhyāsana* that should follow it.

The words "with the same measure you use, it will be measured to you" apparently look like a forceful moral lesson. But the verse that preceded and the one that succeeds are purely of wisdom import. A moral lesson coming in between these two statements, cannot be expected of a *guru* who is very careful about every word he utters when he teaches. Therefore, these words must have a significance within the context of teaching wisdom.

The present context is that of a true disciple listening to the words of a true *guru.* The actual revelation of the wisdom content in those words that occurs to a disciple depends mainly on the intensity of his faith in those words, called *śraddhā,* as well as the maturity of thinking and *tapas* he has attained. This should be what the words "with the same measure you use, it will be measured to you" signify.

There is another reason to assume that this is the implication of these words. The rest of the verse reads as follows: "To you who hear, more will be given." Jesus could be considered to be saying to his disciples this: The clarity with which Reality becomes revealed to each of you depends on your intensity of faith (*śraddhā*) in that Reality and in my words, and on the maturity of your reflections and *tapas.* In your case, you are all very attentive and faithful listeners. Therefore, the nature of Reality will become revealed to you fully. This revelation means that you will become capable of perceiving all the worlds to be but an eternal flow of fleeting manifest forms appearing in that one Reality, which you will realize to be yourselves. It, in effect, is an experience in which you feel that all the worlds are yours. That means, you gain the kingdom of God and gain this world as well. Thus "to you who hear, more will be given."

Verses 26-29 of chapter 4 read as follows:

> And He said, "The kingdom of God is as if a man should scatter seed on the ground,

> and should sleep by night and rise by day, and the seed should sprout and grow, he himself does not know how.
>
> For the earth yields crops by itself: first the blade, then the head, after that the full grain in the head.
>
> But when the grain ripens, immediately he puts in the sickle, because the harvest has come."

That we mean the wisdom secret when referring to the kingdom of God has already been seen. The man who scatters seed on the ground represents a *guru* putting the seeds of wisdom in the mind of a true disciple in the form of his words. The *guru* always observes how the disciple imbibes the teaching, how he makes it part of his searchful self-discipline, and how it transforms his life. The wisdom-seed that was planted into the mind of the disciple through hearing (*śravaṇa*) sprouts and grows within him through his cogitation (*manana*) and meditation (*nididhyāsana*). Neither the disciple nor the *guru* knows how it happens, but its growth is watched by both. The farmer in the parable also does not know how the seeds scattered in the field sprout, grow and become ready for harvest. The grains becoming ripe indicates the disciple's search for Reality has attained its term of fulfilment, and thus realizes the Reality to be what is Real in himself, as himself. It is then that the seeker experiences the contentment of having reached his goal. This contentment (*ānanda*), in effect, becomes his final emancipation (*mukti* or *mokṣa*) as well. This wisdom and the contentment he experiences become an inspiration for the world, and also a guidance for the world. This is indicated by the coming of the harvest in the parable.

2.2

Ignorance Vanishes in the Presence of Wisdom

VERSES 35-41 of chapter 4 read thus:

> On the same day, when evening had come, He said to them, "Let us cross over to the other side."
>
> Now when they had left the multitude, they took Him along in the boat as He was. And other little boats were also with Him.
>
> And a great windstorm arose, and the waves beat into the boat, so that it was already filling.
>
> But He was in the stern, asleep on a pillow. And they awoke Him and said to Him, "Teacher, do You not care that we are perishing?"
>
> Then He awoke and rebuked the wind, and said to the sea, "Peace, be still!" And the wind ceased and there was a great calm.
>
> But He said to them, "Why are you so fearful? How is it that you have no faith?"
>
> And they feared exceedingly, and said to one another, "Who can this be, that even the wind and the sea obey Him?"

Comparing worldly life to an ocean is very common in India. It is called *saṁsāra-sāgara* (the ocean of constant movement). This ocean is considered also to be the ocean of sufferings, and hence the ultimate goal of human life is to reach the other shore of this ocean. Indicative of this perception are Jesus's words, "Let us cross over to the other side."

The yearning to reach such a goal in life arises only in a very few in this world, as suggested by the words, "When they had left the multitude." To cross this *saṁsāra* and reach its other shore, again is well recognized in Vedānta, and is to be accomplished in the boat of wisdom (*jñāna*). Here also, the *guru* Jesus tries to take his disciples with him to the other shore of *saṁsāra* in the sturdy boat of the wisdom he has attained. An enlightened *guru* does not have any doubt of either his wisdom or in Reality. Therefore, he sleeps in the stern of the boat of wisdom peacefully. A boat is always controlled by the one seated at the stern. The disciples who accompany the *guru* with the intention of crossing the ocean are yet to attain that doubtfree attitude about Reality and the wisdom of their *guru*. Such are the ones who feel that the ocean of life is an ocean of sufferings and is turbulent with windstorms. Caught in the middle of such a danger, the disciples awaken the *guru,* their sole refuge in the middle of the sea of *saṁsāra* and say: "Do you not care that we are perishing?"

Life and the events in it are felt to be *saṁsāra-sāgara* by those who are ignorant. The enlightened, on the other hand, perceive the same as the wave-like agitative movements that arise in the ocean of Consciousness (*saṁvit-sāgara*). They feel constant Peace in life.

Jesus's words of exhortation to the sea and windstorms "Peace, be still!" are really addressed to the troubled minds of the disciples. To attain peace, the mind requires a proper awareness of Reality. This awareness is sometimes aroused by the spoken words of the *guru*, sometimes by his meaningful silence, and sometimes when he shows the wisdom gesture (*jñāna-mudrā*). Whatever be the means, the mind of the disciple that was turbulent, like a stormy sea, becomes calm. Such an event is a marvel indeed. This mysteriousness really belongs to the Reality thus realized or to the wisdom that was thus imparted. This mysterious wisdom lacking, one feels life to be fearsome. To gain this wisdom one needs full belief in the ultimate Reality as well as in the *guru*'s words about that Reality. This quality in a disciple is known in Vedānta as *śraddhā.* The need of this quality is indicated by Jesus's words "Why are you so fearful? How is it that you have no faith?" The sea obeying his words and immediately becoming calm are only the external signs of the calming down of the commotions going on in the minds of the disciples.

Verses 1-13 of chapter 5 are as follows:

> Then they came to the other side of the sea, to the country of the Gadarenes.
>
> And when he had come out of the boat, immediately there met Him out of the tombs a man with an unclean spirit,
>
> who had his dwelling among the tombs; and no one could bind him, not even with chains,
>
> because he had often been bound with shackles and chains. And the chains had been pulled apart by him, and shackles broken in pieces; neither could anyone tame him.
>
> And always, night and day, he was in the mountains and in the tombs, crying out and cutting himself with stones.
>
> But when he saw Jesus from afar, he ran and worshipped Him.

> And he cried out with loud voice and said, "What have I to do with You, Jesus, Son of the Most High God? I implore You by God that You do not torment me."
>
> For He said to him, "Come out of the man, unclean spirit!"
>
> Then He asked him, "What is you name?" And he answered saying, "My name is Legion; for we are many."
>
> And he begged Him earnestly that He would not send them out of the country.
>
> Now a large herd of swine was feeding there near the mountains.
>
> And all the demons begged Him, saying, "Send us to the swine, that we may enter them."
>
> And at once Jesus gave them permission. Then the unclean spirits went out and entered the swine (there were about two thousand); and the herd ran violently down the steep place into the sea, and drowned in the sea.

This incident, at first, may look like one of the miraculous acts of Jesus. But this story is more of a symbol. And it teaches the truth that, on the awakening of pure wisdom, all that seemed to exist because of ignorance (*avidyā*) just vanishes. Narayana Guru says:

> As knowledge of the Self shrinks
> So, nescience (avidyā) becomes prevalent.
> It, assuming names and forms
> In a most terrible fashion,
> Looms here as ghost-like. — *Darśanamālā* I.7

The world appears to be real as long as (*avidyā*) prevails. As this (*avidyā*) vanishes on the awakening of *vidyā* (wisdom), the world no longer exists as real; ghosts and devils no longer exist as real.

The life-interest of many who are trapped in the snare of *avidyā*, is in their wives, children, wealth, social status and the like. They find the meaning of their life in the welfare and secure existence of all such. As the brightness of wisdom shines, all such values are realized to be only of fleeting value. Yet there are those who are not willing to free themselves of these; and they fear the coming of wisdom. They too pray "Do not torment me," as the evil spirit did. Their prayer is also addressed to God or is in the name of God, as the evil spirit prayed to "the Son of the Most High God."

To the question of Jesus, "What is your name?" the evil spirit replies, "My name is Legion, because we are many." The word "legion" means "a very large number." The evil effects of *avidyā* are many; and what appears as real and is valued because of *avidyā* are also many. The evil spirit also says here, "We are many." These numerous evil spirits see the coming of the brightness of wisdom in the form of Jesus, and decide that the only thing they can do is to go somewhere and hide themselves. The place where *avidyā* (ignorance) hides has naturally to be unclean, and swine are the most unclean of all animals. The evil spirits (*avidyā*) along with its effects find a safe hiding place in the large herd of swine that was then feeding near the mountains. Therefore they pray to the Son of the Most High God, "Send us to the swine that we may enter them." Jesus readily allows them to do so. The unclean spirits thus enter the swine that numbered about two thousand. That means, on the rising of the sun of wisdom, the darkness of ignorance and its numerous evil effects find their own way to disappear. What ultimately happens to those who are under the spell of *avidyā* is a virtual perishing. The swine haunted by the evil spirits also "ran violently down the steep place into the sea and drowned in the sea."

Verses 14-20 of chapter 5 read as follows:

> Now those who fed the swine fled, and they told it to the city and in the country. And they went out to see what it was that had happened.
>
> Then they came to Jesus, and saw the one who had been demon-possessed and had the legion, sitting and clothed and in his right mind. And they were afraid.
>
> And those who saw it told them how it happened to him who had been demon-possessed, and about the swine.
>
> Then they began to plead with Him to depart from their region.
>
> And when He got into the boat, he who had been demon-possessed begged Him that he might be with Him.
>
> However Jesus did not permit Him, but said to him, "Go home to your friends, and tell them what great things the Lord has done for you, and how He has had compassion on you."
>
> And he departed and began to proclaim in Decapolis all that Jesus had done for him; and men marvelled.

All of that area happened to know of what Jesus did there. Such a person of divine gifts ordinarily is accepted and honoured by the local people. But here the opposite happened; the people asked Jesus to leave their region. This shows more clearly that the demon that possessed the man was *avidyā* (ignorance) itself. Everything done by those who are haunted by *avidyā* is perceived by a wise one to only be meaningless misdeeds. The man is rescued here from such a state and is made into one of balanced state of mind.

Many are the local groups of people who enjoy living in the world of *avidyā*, not even knowing that they are in such a world. They naturally do not wish to leave that world. Even many who are interested in spiritual matters are of this type. They become frightened when they see one among them becoming free of the demon of *avidyā* and attaining enlightenment. They search for the person who caused this transformation in him, because the presene of this one person in their society is enough to turn their present state of existence upside down. Therefore, instead of gaining wisdom from that *guru*, they chase him out of their region. Even individual persons may behave like this. Suppose a person lives happily engrossed in his household and social affairs, thinking that such a happiness is what makes his life meaningful. If he is told by a wise person that a higher wisdom is there that ensures ultimate and eternal Happiness in life, then his response will most probably be, "Do not disturb me with this wisdom of yours. I am living happily without any such." The reaction of the people in the locality Jesus has now reached is similar. The only thing a wise person can do in such situations is to leave the place as soon as possible. Jesus also does so.

The man who was rescued from the unclean spirits, i.e., the man who found freedom from *avidyā*, preferred to leave his own countrymen who were of the above-mentioned type, and to follow Jesus as a disciple. But Jesus did not allow him to do so. He must have thought: "Though the local people refused to accept me, they would not do so with a local man. For him to remain may turn out to be beneficial to them."

Besides, what Jesus asked the man to do was to go home to his friends and tell them what great things God the Lord had done to him, and how He had compassion on him. Jesus intended the man to tell the people that all that had happened were not his doings, but were of God. Those who are fully enlightened see all the actions (*karmas*) as taking place in the one ultimate Reality or God. But the followers or devotees who do not have this perception may think that all such deeds were performed by the particular saint or *guru*. The same was the case also with the man who became freed from unclean spirits. He declared to the people of Decapolis that all this was done by Jesus. Such wrong ways of evaluating and honouring a *guru* by his followers and devotees are what very often result in the development of personality cults within religions. This is one of the ways in which a pure and living wisdom degenerates into a closed and inert religious movement.

We have just reviewed a scene in which those who do not have belief in Jesus and his new gospel chase him away from their locality. This scene has its natural opposite in the very next scene, commencing with verse 21 of chapter 5. This is even suggested by verse 21 which says that Jesus had again crossed to the other side of the lake in the boat. At this new place, even one of the rulers of the synagogue came and begged Jesus earnestly to heal his little daughter that lay at the point of death. Normally, the members of the synagogue are not expected to have any belief in the new gospel that revises the existing Jewish religious customs. Jesus's graceful and prayerful words "Little girl, I say to you, arise" makes the dead girl arise and walk. On his way to the girls house, a sick woman touched Jesus's garments without his knowledge, and immediately she was healed. Both these events show how important is one's belief, whether the presumed healer is aware of it or not.

2.3

A Jñānin at His Home Town

VERSES 1-6 of chapter 6 read as follows:

> Then He went out from there and came to His own country, and His disciples followed Him.
>
> And when the Sabbath had come, He began to teach in the synagogue. And many hearing Him were astonished, saying, "Where did this Man get these things? And what wisdom is this which is given to Him, that such mighty works are performed by His hands?
>
> Is this not the carpenter, the Son of Mary, and the brother of James, Joses, Judas and Simon? And are not His sisters here with us?" And they were offended at Him.
>
> But Jesus said to them, "A prophet is not without honour except in his own country, among his own relatives, and in his own house."
>
> Now He could do no mighty work there, except that He laid His hands on a few sick people and healed them.
>
> And He marvelled because of their unbelief. Then He went about the villages in a circuit, teaching.

When Jesus went to his own home town and taught the new gospel in the synagogue, the people could not accept him as an enlightened *guru,* but only as one among them. Jesus, for that very reason, could not perform there the highest miracle of revealing the kingdom of God or the wisdom secret. He only performed the healing of certain sick people, a miracle merely of worldly value. It is common everywhere in the world that a prophet (*jñānin*) is scarcely honoured in his native place, the fact of which Jesus also proclaims to those people. *Saṁnyāsin*s of India, therefore, customarily leave their native place.

Jesus here is neither among the people who do not believe in him and chase him away, nor among those who fully believe in him, but among those who look at him as one related to them in a worldly context. Among such people, he could only do somethings of a bodily value, represented by his healing a few sick. What a *guru* is capable of depends on the need, quality and competence of those who are to be benefited.

It was uninvited that Jesus went to his native place. And he taught in the synagogue, without making sure that the people there were interested in that wisdom. Had they been so, they would have invited him to teach them. The lesson is that wisdom should not be offered through the act of approaching people, even be they one's own countrymen, but is to be taught only to those who approach with a seeking heart. This lesson is implict in this incident.

Verses 14-29 of chapter 6 portray the episode where John the Baptist is beheaded by the King Herod. This king evidently was corrupted by political ambitions and greed for power on the one side. On the other, he was vitiated by an unrestrained lust for women. Such kings might treat innocent people, even spiritual dignitaries, with hard-hearted cruelty, whether or not they intend to do so. This is the lesson taught in this event. Almost a similar picture will be seen at the end when Jesus is crucified as ordered by Pilate, though the lust for women does not come into the scene there.

Verses 30-44 describe the miracle of 5,000 people being fed with five loaves of bread and two fish. Jesus could do so not particularly by his own will, but because of the greatness of God. The lesson of this episode is that the possibility inherent in the one ultimate Reality or God is inconceivable. Human minds may think of certain things as possible and others as impossible. But sometimes humans come across events which they think are impossible. Then they consider such events to be miracles. But on realizing the ultimate Reality it becomes clear that nothing is impossible in It. That Reality itself is the greatest of all mysteries.

The scene in verses 45-52 describes the event where the sea becomes rough as the disciples were crossing it in a boat, and where Jesus reaches there to calm down the sea and save them. Its meaning, having been examined in our comments on the "Gospel According to Matthew," is not repeated here. The sea was seen there as the *saṁsāra-sāgara.* What happens at the other shore of the sea at Gennesaret is detailed in verses 53-56.

> When they came out of the boat, immediately the people recognized Him. — 6.54

There it was as a *jñānin* who has reached the other shore of the *saṁsāra-sāgara* that he was recognized. The main occupation of such *jñānins* is to heal the disease of ignorance. But the people, even after recognizing him as a *jñānin,* were not interested in his wisdom. They asked him to heal their bodily diseases alone, which he did not hesitate to do because the physical body is not outside their being. They were too ignorant to go beyond the realm of bodily existence and to be benefited by his wisdom teaching. Such a phenomenon is seen everywhere in the world at all times.

Verses 31-37 of chapter 7 read as follows:

> And again, departing from the region of Tyre and Sidon, He came through the midst of the region of Decapolis to the Sea of Galilee.
>
> Then they brought to Him one who was deaf and had an impediment in his speech, and they begged Him to put His hand on him.
>
> And He took him aside from the multitude, and put His fingers in his ears, and He spat and touched his tongue.
>
> Then, looking up to heaven, He sighed, and said to him, "Ephphatha", that is, "Be opened."
>
> Immediately his ears were opened, and the impediment of his tongue was loosed, and he spoke plainly.
>
> Then He commanded them that they should tell no one, but the more He commanded them, the more widely they proclaimed it.
>
> And they were astonished beyond measure, saying, "He has done all things well. He makes both the deaf to hear and the mute to speak."

This section, at first sight, may look like it's about another of the miraculous deeds of Jesus. But, examined as a symbolic event, it could be seen to hide a principle of wisdom significance. The ears of those who live in the world of ignorance, in the usual course, remain closed against the words of wisdom of enlightened *guru*s, not to mention that their speech remains impeded to say anything about wisdom. The two activities that go on in the world of wisdom are to attentively hear the words of a *guru* and to tell others what is thus understood. The man who was brought to Jesus could perform neither of these, because he was ignorant. But, in one respect, he stands apart from other ignorant people — he was fully aware of his inability to listen to the words of wisdom and to talk about their content that would make his life meaningful, though he might have been capable of doing the same in respect of worldly matters. This peculiarity is indicated by the fact that Jesus took him aside from the multitude (7.33). Jesus put his fingers in his ears, and he spat and touched his tongue. This indicates his infusing into the man his own hearing and speaking capabilities. And then, upon his uttering "Be opened," both the disabilities of the man disappeared. In other words, it is with the blessings of a *guru* that an ignorant person gains the ability to acquire wisdom. This miracle story also demonstrates this principle.

2.4

The Essence of the Teaching

VERSES 14-29 of chapter 9 narrate an event in which the disciples of Jesus could not cure the epilepsy of a boy. The boy then was brought to Jesus, and the spirit that was haunting the boy left him immediately. The disciples then asked, "Why could we not cast him out?" Jesus said to them, "This kind can come out by nothing but prayer and fasting." The same event was seen in the Gospel According to Matthew also. The answer given by Jesus to the same question of the disciples then was:

> Because of your unbelief, for assuredly I say to you, if you have faith as a mustard seed, you will say to this mountain, "Move from here to there," and it will move and nothing will be impossible for you.
>
> — Matthew 17.20

Jesus had already given to his disciples the authority to perform all the miracles ranging from those of worldly value like healing the sick, to that of the highest value of expounding the secret of the kingdom of God to the world. Yet they did not have the full faith that would make them capable of doing these things. That is the reason why Jesus admonishes them, "O the faithless generation!" (9.19, see also Matthew 17.17 and Luke 9.19). The above mentioned capability is not attained simply when a disciple fully believes, "It is possible for me." The essential content of this faith rather is the state in which the disciple constantly experiences his complete identity or inseparable oneness with the ultimate Reality or God. His will, in such a state, becomes one with the will of God, every word of his becomes the word of God. There is no power which can transgress it. How is this spiritual experience of being one with God attained? Jesus says, "By nothing but prayer and fasting." A prayer reaches its culmination when the supplicant feels his oneness with the God prayed to. Expounding this truth. Narayana Guru says:

> O God, I have no other desire
> Than attaining the state, now itself,
> Of you and me becoming one.
>
> — *Sadāśiva Darśanam,* verse 5

Verses 30-31 of chapter 9 read as follows:

> Then they departed from there and passed through Galilee, and He did not want anyone to know it.
>
> He taught His disciples and said to them, "The Son of Man is being delivered into the hands of men, and they will kill Him. And after He is killed, He will rise the third day.

The disciples, as was detailed in the last section, could not heal the sick boy brought to them, but Jesus could. The reason for this was sought by the disciples privately when they reached home. And Jesus answered, "This kind can come out by nothing but prayer and fasting" (9.29). Jesus evidently did not want anyone of the public know of this answer. The reason must be that this answer was meant only for his disciples, not for the public. Certain teachings given by a *guru* will be properly understood by only a disciple or sometimes a few disciples who are very close to him, and who have established an intimate bipolarity with him. The *guru* never likes to disclose certain wisdom secrets to the general public. It could also be presumed that Jesus does not feel the need of satisfying the public with such words, because he knows that his days are already numbered.

Jesus has already stated in the Gospel that what he, as a *guru*, wanted to teach his disciples, has already been taught. But we have seen nowhere in his words, what that final teaching is. But a rough idea of that conclusive teaching could be found in verses 33-37 which read as follows:

> And when He was in the house He asked them, "What was it you disputed among yourselves on the road?"
>
> But they kept silent, for on the road they had disputed among themselves who would be the greatest.
>
> And He sat down, called the twelve, and said to them, "If anyone desires to be first, he shall be the last of all and servant of all."
>
> Then He took a little child and set him in the midst of them. And when he had taken him in His arms, He said to them,
>
> Whoever receives one of these little children in My name receives Me; and whoever receives Me, receives not Me but Him who sent Me.

The contents of verses 33-36 of this section have already been examined by us while commenting on the "Gospel According to

Matthew" (18.1-5). The dispute among the disciples was as to who was the greatest among themselves. Jesus says, "Whoever receives one of these little children in My name receives Me; and whoever receives Me, receives not Me but Him who sent Me" (9.37). Jesus is to be understood here as pure wisdom incarnate. His loving and sympathetic identification with children is expressed here so that the disciples may reflect back upon what they will need to inherit the kingdom of God. When he says, "Whoever receives one of these little children in My name receives Me," he means that whoever is capable of perceiving a living *guru* without any social status whatsoever, and divinely innocent as a small child, is the one who knows the *guru*. The one who perceives thus, and finds his identity with such a *guru* with all childlike humility, is the greatest. The essential content of wisdom of which Jesus is an incarnate form, as we know, is the Absolute or God. Therefore, receiving Jesus means receiving God. Put conversely, a real *guru* is the one who always lives with the feeling that all that is perceived here, including himself, are but the fleeting manifest forms of the one Reality or God. This is the sense in which Jesus is the Son of God. And this means that knowing a *guru* perfectly, in principle, means knowing God perfectly. Such is the way the words, "Whoever receives Me, receives not Me but Him who sent Me" are to be understood.

If the "I" in the words "in My name" and "receives Me" is interpreted as referring to the "I" in each of us rather than referring to Jesus alone, then we feel that they gain a new dimension of meaning. The "I" in each of us, in Vedānta, is called *Ātmā* (Self). *Ātmā*, in essential content, is pure Consciousness untouched by any conditioning factor. This Consciousness itself is what exists as the essential content not only in everything but in all the worlds also, and in that context it is called *Brahman*. Therefore, when one receives *Ātmā* or when one acknowledges oneself to be that *Ātmā*, what one realizes is not merely what is real in oneself, but what is *Brahman* itself. This non-dualistic perception of Vedānta, put in terms familiar to the ear of Semitic religions, is what we see in the above words of Jesus. The same Truth is more clearly stated in the Gospel according to John, where Jesus says:

> If you had known Me, you would have known My Father also
> — 8.19

and

> I and My Father are one. — 10.30

The same Truth is simply suggested here in a subtle way, as the solution to a problem regarding the seniority among the disciples.

Another aspect could also be seen to be implicit in these words of Jesus. The essence of his teaching in this context is thus: If anyone desires to be the first, he should learn to be the last and to be the servant of all. An extended version of this teaching could be understood thus, "You are nothing; God alone is great. In order to know the secret of that God, you should know Me. In order to know Me, you should become like a child, as an innocent mind, like a clean slate. You people seem not as such. That is the reason why there is a dispute among you as to who is the greatest."

This context could also be evaluated differently when pertaining to a deeper level of intuitive perception. An innocent child has no social status and lives simply in a down-to-earth way, with no concern for any of life's problems. If this is seen as marking the lowest limit of a vertical axis, then its highest limit is to be seen marked by the Most High God. Jesus as a *guru* comes in between these two limits. An uncontaminated mind, a *guru* who represents the fullness of wisdom as well as the Absolute, and the Absolute itself or God that forms the essential content of wisdom — these three could thus be seen to be positioned at three levels of a vertically conceived range. There is something common in these three levels that unites them to a single context. This common ground is to be intuitively perceived. And this perception indicates the attainment of non-duality, which also is the attainment of the final goal of life, called *parama-puruṣārtha* or *mokṣa.*

It is not any social consideration, but rather the attainment of the highest sublimity of wisdom, that makes one great in the context of spirituality. And upon becoming enlightened as to the wisdom secret, what becomes evident is not one's greatness, but one's insignificance. This results in a deep humility. A person of such an awareness prefers to be the servant of all rather than the master of all. This characteristic of the enlightened person could also be seen clarified by the above words of Jesus.

Verses 38-41 are as follows:

> Now John answered Him, saying, "Teacher, we saw someone who does not follow us casting out demons in Your name, and we forbade him because he does not follow us."

> But Jesus said, "Do not forbid him, for no one who works a miracle in My name can soon afterward speak evil of Me.
>
> For he who is not against us is on our side.
>
> For whoever gives you a cup of water to drink in My name, because you belong to Christ, assuredly, I say to you, he will by no means lose his reward."

The disciples of Jesus happened to witness the event of a person who was casting out evil spirits from a sick person in Jesus's name. But this person did not belong to the official group of disciples of Jesus; still he had full faith in him. The disciples apparently had the idea that only those who were recognized by Jesus as followers should do so in his name. But we saw at the beginning of this chapter (9) itself that even the disciples who had the authority given by Jesus could not drive away the evil spirit from the epileptic boy who was brought to them. Jesus has just pointed out to them that this happened merely because of their lack of faith. Here, on the other hand, a person outside the group performed the same kind of miracle in His name merely on the strength of his faith. The lesson this episode teaches is thus: The deciding factor for one to become capable of performing miracles is not whether one is officially in the group of disciples or not, nor whether one is authorized by a *guru* or not. On the other hand, full faith in the *guru* and the wisdom he teaches alone is what makes one efficient to work miracles. The indication is that, being officially accepted by a *guru* as his disciple, or being authorized by him to possess wisdom, does not make one competent to enter the kingdom of God. Rather it is the full faith in the *guru*, and the indefatigable thirst for wisdom that leads one to the enlightened state. And there is no miracle attainable in life higher than becoming enlightened and making someone else enlightened, or healing someone of the sickness of ignorance. Jesus says, even the one who gives a cup of water in His name will by no means lose his reward. Then how great would be the reward for healing the sick, or even for entering the kingdom of heaven and helping others to enter it by healing their sickness of ignorance? In short, you become acceptable to a *guru* when you understand his basic teaching and live fully in accordance with that teaching, and not because you have once been formally acknowledged as a follower. Jesus therefore says, "He who is not against us is on our side."

The next section is a sort of elaboration on the principle explicated in the present section. Jesus says:

> Salt is good, but if the salt loses its flavour, how will you season it? Have salt in yourselves, and have peace with one another. — 9.50

The analogy of salt is relevant with respect to the dispute among the disciples about superiority as well as to the event of an outsider casting out evil spirits in Jesus's name. Just as the flavour of salt seasons food, full faith in their *guru*'s teachings accompanied by a spiritual insight should flavour the life of the disciples. Such is the wish of Jesus.

Verse 49 of chapter 9 says:

> Everyone will be seasoned with fire, and every sacrifice will be seasoned with salt.

The "fire" referred to in the words "everyone will be seasoned with fire," as is to be assumed, is the sacrificial fire. Fire sacrifice is not something that forms part of India's Vedic culture alone, it was acceptable to the Semitic religions as well. Many are the references to burnt offerings and sacrifices in the Old Testament of the Bible.

The origin of the concept of burnt-sacrifice, a ritual acceptable to almost all religions, is worth searching for. It becomes evident as each individual properly tries to know oneself, that one's existence is inseparable from the total existence of nature. One's separate existence as an individual, then appears to be quite insignificant. The realization of one's own nothingness could well be poetically imagined as a sort of burning out of the individual in the sacrificial fire of the total being. This perception could be what originated the religious ritual of fire sacrifice. In other words, life is only felt to be fully meaningful and filled with Supreme Happiness when the seeker of Happiness burns himself up in the all-inclusive Reality, with the fire of wisdom as the means. This experience in which life itself is a sort of fire sacrifice is the source of a *jñānin*'s greatness, which is derived from his humility. Salt is what makes food flavourable. Similarly, life is rendered fully happy by the present salt of sacrifice. Jesus, in this sense, says, "Everyone will be seasoned with fire."

A fire sacrifice, whatever be its religious background and nature, becomes fully meaningful when it is performed with a clear understanding of its above-mentioned wisdom significance. The salt that flavours a fire sacrifice or any other sacrifice, as intended by Jesus, must be the awareness of the above-mentioned wisdom significance with which it is performed. This wisdom is attained only by those who have full faith in the one all-underlying Reality or God, as well as in the *guru* who has realized and reveals It. Just as salt seasons food, this wisdom, which implies that oneself become lost in the total Being or God, makes every sacrifice meaningful and beneficial in the true sense. Such are the implications of the words "Sacrifice will be seasoned with salt."

The faith as understood here is not merely meant to be some blind belief in any religious dogma. It is rather a belief one will naturally have in the one Reality upon realizing Its nature and content, and also the *jñānin* who has realized It.

2.5

The Fire Sacrifices
The Two Commandments

VERSES 17-18 of chapter 10 read as follows:

> Now as He was going out of the road, one came running, knelt before Him, and asked Him, "Good Teacher, what shall I do that I may inherit eternal life?"
>
> So Jesus said to him, "Why do you call Me good? No one is good but one, that is, God."

This picture is just the reverse side of the one we saw in chapter 9, where the disciples disputed about the superiority among themselves. Jesus, in response to the dispute, said, "If anyone desires to be the first, he shall be last of all and servant of all." Jesus, the *guru* of these disputing disciples, does not consider himself as good. Therefore, when he was called by a devotee, "Good Teacher", he asks him, "Why do you call me good? No one is good but One, that is, God." This means, no human being is perfectly good; perfect goodness belongs to God alone.

All the religions, particularly the Semitic religions, maintain the notion that God is the perfection of goodness. We may, at first sight, think that this means God is perfect in respect to all the goodnesses we know of. The same religions, at the same time, admit that everything is created by God. If so, are not the things we call evil also the creation of God? How then did evil arise in this world, as created by God, the perfection of goodness? This problem, well known to theology as the problem of evil, so far has not been satisfactorily resolved by the theologians of Semitic religions.

The reason why they fail is to be found in the mixing up of two realms of goodness — the absolute goodness of God and the relative goodness commonly known to all of us. The goodness we are familiar with is the creation of our own imagination, and its nature varies depending on circumstances. Therefore it is relative. Even then, the goodness of God remains unchanged. We evaluate certain things to be good and certain others to be evil (in each circumstance) based on our own value notions. All that we evaluate as either good or as bad has one originating source alone. That source-Reality, in Vedānta, is called *Brahman*, and in religions, God. This Reality necessarily has to be beyond both what we call good and evil, because It is the source of both. Being so is God's absolute goodness. Therefore, Jesus, as the Son of Man, representing the relative notion of good and evil, says, "Why do you call Me good? No one is good but One, that is, God."

Though the event narrated in verses 28-34 of chapter 12 has been examined earlier, it is being quoted and examined once again here, because in this context it varies in certain vital details:

> Then one of the scribes came, and having heard them reasoning together, perceiving that He had answered them well, asked Him, "Which is the first commandment of all?"
>
> Jesus answered him,"The first of all the commandments is: 'Hear, O Israel, the Lord our God, the Lord is one.
>
> And you shall love the Lord your God with all your heart, with all your soul, with all your mind, and with all your strength.' This is the first commandment.
>
> And the second, like it, is this: 'You shall love your neighbour as yourself.' There is no other commandment greater than these."
>
> So the scribe said to Him, "Well said, Teacher. You have spoken the truth, for there is one God, and there is no other but He.
>
> And to love Him with all the heart, with all the understanding, with all the soul, and with all the strength, and to love one's neighbour as oneself, is more than all the whole burnt offerings and sacrifices."
>
> So when Jesus saw that he answered wisely, He said to him, "You are not far from the kingdom of God." And after that no one dared to question Him.

The entire structure of Christianity has these two commandments for its corner stone. And these commandments have for their inspiring source, the utterance, "Hear, O Israel, the Lord our God, the Lord is one." The scribe who questioned Jesus also acknowledged the correctness of his answer, when he said, "You have spoken the truth, for there is one God, and there is no other God."

In Vedānta, what is equivalent to God is *Brahman* or *Ātman*. Vedānta also leads us to the final conclusion that no other Reality exists, other than *Brahman*. Furthermore, the two commandments of Jesus, as the scribes also admit, come as corollaries to the doctrine of the oneness of God. They also concede that adhering to these two commandments is higher in value than performing the rituals, burnt offerings and sacrifices. In the Vedic culture of India two trends are also present. The first is ritualism (*karma-mārga*), where it is thought that performing all rituals enjoined in the Vedas is what makes life meritorious. The second is the path of wisdom (*jñāna-mārga*). The ultimate goal of this latter path is realizing the one all-underlying Reality in oneself. Perceiving oneself and all the worlds as part of the eternal flux of the manifest forms of *Brahman* or *Ātman*, finally releases one from all bondage, and this release is what is known in Vedānta as *mukti* or *mokṣa.* That this wisdom surpasses all the rituals in their value is well-acknowledged in India. The present passage of the Gospel shows that the same is the basic stand of Semitic religions as well, whether it is Judaism represented by the scribes or Christianity by Jesus.

We have already covered a detailed examination of these two commandments in our comments on The Gospel According to Matthew. Though well known as the words of Jesus, these two actually appear in different contexts of the Old Testament. What Jesus did was trace these out as the most valuable commandments and re-introduce them in a systematic and sequential order. The former appears as verses 6.4-5 of Deuteronomy, and the latter in Leviticus as verse 19.18.

A scene described in *Bṛhadāraṇyaka Upaniṣad* (chapter III) details how the scholars assembled in the court of King Janaka, one after another, to question the Ṛṣi Yājñavalkya and test his depth of understanding of the all-inclusive Reality. Yājñavalkya answers all of them perfectly true to the basic stand of Vedānta, i.e., the oneness of Reality. Finally comes the well-known lady scholar Gārgī to question him. When she is also silenced by his answer, all of them decide not to question him anymore. Similarly, many Pharisees, Herodians and Sadducees have already questioned Jesus, trying to catch him in his words. This is narrated from the beginning of chapter 12. He has answered all of them satisfactorily. It is after all this that the scribes come forward to question him. The answer Jesus gave not only fully satisfied them, but also convinced them to acknowledge the wisdom of Jesus. Those who intuitively perceive the philosophical implications in these two sequential commandments are to be considered as capable of realizing that the one ultimate Reality is what makes their own life really meaningful. Or, only such a capable person can acknowledge the comprehensiveness of vision enshrined in these words of Jesus. This is the reason why Jesus tells the scribe, "You are not far from the kingdom of God." In the last scene of the Yājñavalkya episode of *Bṛhadāraṇyaka Upaniṣad* it is also said, "Those brāhmaṇas did not dare to say anything" (3.5.28).

2.6

The Resurrection

CHAPTER 16 of the Gospel concentrates on the events related to the Resurrection of Jesus. The body of Jesus, kept within a tomb covered with a heavy stone, disappeared on the third day. Then Jesus reappeared, first to Mary Magdalene. Though she went and told the others who had been with Jesus about him, they did not believe her. The rest of the section reads as follows:

> Afterward He appeared to the eleven as they sat at the table; and He rebuked their unbelief and hardness of heart, because they did not believe those who have seen Him after He had risen.
>
> And He said to them, "Go into all the world and teach the gospel to every creature.
>
> He who believes and is baptized will be saved; but he who does not believe will be condemned.
>
> And these signs will follow those who believe: In My name they will cast out demons; they will speak with new tongues;
>
> they will take up serpents; and if they drink anything deadly, it will by no means hurt them; they will lay hands on the sick, and they will recover. — 16.14-18

The Resurrection of Jesus, from the Vedāntic point of view, is not seen merely as a historical event, but as a symbolic myth. Many of the Upaniṣads, the main source-books on Vedānta, conceive that the ultimate benefit of becoming enlightened is that the knower of the Self attains the world of *Brahman* (*brahma-loka*) (see *Bṛhadāraṇyaka Upaniṣad* 6.2.15 and *Kaṭha Upaniṣad* 2.17). At first sight this may look like it teaches that such a knower (*jñānin*), upon leaving this world, reaches another higher world known as *brahma-loka.* The Upaniṣads also declare: "If known here itself, then it is the Truth, and if not known here itself, it is a great loss." (*Kena Upaniṣad* II.5). "To know" here means "realizing the Self" These two apparently opposite Upaniṣadic utterances need to be perceived unitively. As one remains an ignorant one (*ajñānin*), the apparent world is perceived to be real in itself. On becoming a *jñānin,* one ceases to perceive the world in this way, and instead sees it as the beginningless and endless flow of fleeting manifest forms of *Brahman*. That means the world is seen as *Brahman* itself, no longer as the world. Just by perceiving thus, one has already reached the world of *Brahman* (*brahma-loka*). In other words, the world of the here and now itself becomes transformed into *brahma-loka* for such a one. Such an enlightenment can only be considered meaningful in the context of actual life. This is the sense in which the Upaniṣad says, "If known here itself, then it is the Truth."

As long as one remains ignorant (*ajñānin*), one thinks oneself to be so and so, and to have such and such characteristics. Upon becoming enlightened, on the other hand, one perceives oneself simply as a tiny and fleeting phenomenon that forms part of the boundless body of apparent forms that manifest in the one *Brahman*. That means, the *jñānin* sees himself as one with *Brahman*. This experiential awareness is what in Vedānta is known as *brahma-sākṣātkāra* or *ātma-sākṣātkāra*. A *jñānin* of such an attainment forgoes any bodily-based identity as an individual and experiences identity with *Brahman*. This transformation of identity, in principle, is the resurrection. This philosophically sound, intuitive vision of the resurrection is portrayed in the Gospels as the story where Jesus actually dies, is entombed, and rises to leave the tomb on the third day. Such a method of presentation may have been preferable in view of the people for whom the Gospels were immediately intended.

Many were simple shepherds and peasants, perhaps not yet capable of pure philosophical speculation. A philosophically perfect Resurrection, thus, means that a *jñānin* forgoes his identity as an individual, and realizes his oneness with what ultimately exists.

The psychological phenomenon in which a deceased person is perceived again by some who were deeply attached mentally to the departed is not uncommon. The nature of such a vision depends mainly on the gravity of attachment the perceiver had with the deceased, and also on his mental state. Such visions need not be treated as a sign of any divine nature, either of the perceived or the perceiver. With regard to the present Gospel episode as well, it was to Mary Magdalene that Jesus appeared first. The attachment she had developed towards him is well acknowledged by all biblical scholars. Jesus next appears to two of those who were with him, and the form in which he appeared to them was different from the one Mary saw. This appearance, it is to be noticed, did not occur with all those who were with Jesus, but only to two who were most intimate to him; of course, their names are not mentioned. He later did appear to all the eleven disciples, but it was yet in another form. The attachment these disciples had towards Jesus is a well-known fact. These various forms of Jesus seen by various people with different levels of attachment and of different mental constitutions, indicate that the nature of such visions depends mainly on the mental state of the one who perceives. When the others were informed of the visions these people had, they did not believe them. This usually is what happens with most cases where such apparitions are seen. That others do not believe it does not necessarily render the vision invalid.

Though the eleven disciples also perceived Jesus, it is not clear whether they saw him in the same form or in eleven different forms. When we see something even in our day-to-day life, because perceptual experience is purely subjective, we are not sure whether the form in which it is seen by one is exactly the same as perceived by another. Besides, the size, colour and other peculiarities of the object so perceived by each perceiver vary according to the visual power of the eyes, whether the eyes are colour-blind or not, whether one is short-sighted, long-sighted or has a normal sight, and the like. No exact criterion is available to decide which is really the normal state in these respects. In short, the form and all other qualities of an object seen by one person has necessarily to be different from what another perceives, despite the fact that everyone agrees to give a common name to what they perceive. Because of this common name we agree upon, we think that we are seeing one and the same form. What we are concerned with, in considering this scene, is not something perceived with our external eyes, but with what was mentally perceived by three different grades of viewers. Some may see a mental projection as if through their own eyes, and some may not. Here also, Jesus appears only to a few who had been closest to him. And it is quite clear from the statements in the Gospel that the forms in which Jesus appeared to them differed.

Furthermore, the resurrected form of Jesus, as seen by the disciples also spoke to them. He seemed to tell them, "Go into all the world and preach the gospel to every creature." It simply means that he seemed to call them to bring the good news (gospel) of wisdom to the attention of everyone who lives in ignorance, which is easily attainable as taught by Jesus. Though the disciples felt that Jesus bid them to do so, this wisdom which never loses its novelty, will not be attained by everyone, even if it is offered to everyone. Full faith in the ultimate Reality or God, and in the words of instruction of a *guru*, and virtual initiation from the *guru* are essential prerequisites for its attainment. This truth is well recognized in Vedānta also. *Bhagavad-Gītā*, for example, says:

> Only one endowed with full faith and interest (*śraddhā*) obtains wisdom, — IV.39

and

> The ignorant, the faithless and the doubt-embodied, end up perishing. — IV.40

Jesus also, as heard by the disciples, says in almost the same tone:

> He who believes and is baptized will be saved; but he who does not believe will be condemned. — 16.16

Jesus then appears to tell them of the external signs seen in a person who attains wisdom in such a way. The first among those signs is, "They will cast out demons." The existence of demons is a result of ignorance (*ajñāna*), and the demons are seen by the ignorant (*ajñānin*) to exist. The enlightened do not see demons, and they are well aware that others see demons merely because of their ignorance. Upon reaching the presence of an enlightened *guru* as seekers, such people find that demons disappear in the broad daylight of wisdom the *guru* teaches. What is important in such a context is also the full faith of the one who approaches the *guru*. Such must be the way that the enlightened disciples should cast out demons.

That "they will speak with new tongues" is another of the distinguishing marks of the enlightened disciples. The words of a *jñānin* as well as his language mostly sound strange to an ignorant person, because each live in a different level of understanding. The ignorant, for this reason, may even keep themselves away from where a *jñānin* teaches wisdom. The ignorant would feel that such words would be of a tongue quite strange to them.

The next sign is that "they will take up serpents." The essential content of wisdom, as we know, is one always experiencing one's identity with everything. Those who feel this oneness do not see anything as something "other," and for this reason no being is an enemy to them. The biographies of many enlightened *guru*s like Narayana Guru tell of many stories about how they always remained friendly with serpents and ferocious animals like leopards. The hatred the Jews have for serpents is part of their religion. The present words of Jesus indicate that such a hatred also would be found meaningless.

Another sign is "if they drink anything deadly, it will by no means hurt them." A *jñānin* lives unaffected by all phenomenal changes such as birth and death. He perceives the perishing of his body not as his own death, but simply as his individuated manifest form merging with the Total Being. As far as such a *jñānin* is concerned, drinking something deadly, or even dying, by no means does any harm to his real being. *Brahman* always remains unaffected by any phenomenal change, just as gold remains so feven when assuming various forms of ornaments one after another. The same is true also with those who live in full identity with *Brahman*. The significance of the external sign "they will lay hands on the sick, and they will recover" has already been made clear earlier.

Jesus departs the world, thus, with the greatest expectation that his disciples would become *jñānin*s like him.

Part III

The Gospel According to Luke

Introduction

THE Gospel According to Luke begins thus:

> Inasmuch as many have taken in hand to set in order a narrative of those things which are most surely believed among us,
>
> just as those who from the beginning were eyewitnesses and ministers of the word delivered them to us,
>
> it seemed good to me also, having had perfect understanding of all things from the very first, to write to you an orderly account, most excellent Theophilus,
>
> that you may know the certainty of those things in which you were instructed. — 1.1-4

The commencing words of this Gospel point towards the circumstances in which it was written. The life and teachings given shape to in this Gospel, as we notice at the outset itself, did not originate from any direct relationship the author Luke had with Jesus.

Many stories about Jesus were popular then as narrated by eyewitnesses as well as the ministers of the word. Clear indications of this can be seen in the beginning sentences of the Gospel According to Luke quoted above. Each story-teller must have narrated, in an oral or written form, in his own way. All such stories were known as Gospels, and that of Luke is one among such. Of these many Gospels, those written by Matthew, Mark, Luke and John alone were officially to be included in the Bible, and all the others were rejected by the Nicene Council held by the Church. Among those probably rejected was the Gospel of Thomas, which was recovered in the middle of the twentieth century in Egypt.

The historical fact is that these Gospels were given final shape nearly four centuries after the crucifixion of Jesus. Therefore, it is but natural that it is difficult to conclusively decide which stories were original and which stories contained exaggerations added during the gap of the four centuries by over-enthusiastic believers. The presence of such exaggerations can be felt by anyone who closely studies these Gospel stories with an open and critical mind. As is clearly stated in the present Gospel, what Luke attempted to do was to collect all the reliable information available in the prevailing stories and present them in an orderly fashion. This is written as a letter to Theophilus, who must have been a friend of Luke, and a person who believed in Jesus as a true prophet and saviour.

3.1

Divine and Demonic Traits

THE narratives in chapters 1-3 do not deserve any elucidation in relation to the wisdom context. Verses 1-13 of chapter 4 portray how the temptations of the devil were overcome by Jesus, an event already described in the Gospel According to Matthew. But we see here some additions in the devil's tempting words, which are of vital importance for us. The devil says:

> All this authority I will give you, and their glory; for this has been delivered to me, and I give it to whomever I wish.
>
> Therefore, if you will worship before me, all will be yours. — 4.6-7

To be greedy for wealth is a human trait common among many. The intention of the devil here is to trap Jesus in his net. The devil's claim that all the authority and all the glory have been delivered to him indicates the truth that possessing such *desirables* is what transforms men into devils. *Bhagavad-Gītā* too, in chapter XVI, classifies human traits as divine and demonic (*daivī* and *āsurī*). The divine traits are described as follows:

> Fearlessness, a transparent vision of the Real and the ensuing purity of mind, being well stabilized specifically in *jñāna-yoga,* offering free gifts to the deserving, self-restraint, performing fire-sacrifices properly, studying scriptures on one's own, straight-forwardness;
>
> Non-hurting, honesty, being free from anger, willingness to renounce, calmness, aversion to slander, compassion to living beings, being uninterested in sense-pleasures, gentleness, modesty, absence of fickleness;
>
> Alertness natural to brightness, forgiveness, fortitude, cleanliness, absence of malice, absence of self-esteem — all these are signs seen in those born with divine traits. — XVI.1-3

A part of the description of the demonic traits (*āsurī-sampat*) is given below:

> This much I could gain today. The other wish I will fulfil shortly. This much wealth do I possess now, and much more will be mine before long.

> That enemy has been slain by me; the others will also be done away with by me. I do enjoy everything. I satisfy my ambitions. I am powerful. I am happy.
>
> I am rich and high-born. Who is there equal to me? I will perform fire-sacrifices; I will give gifts; I will enjoy life. Deluded by ignorance are they. — XVI.13-15

As the *Gītā* thus categorically clarifies, the insatiable greed for wealth, fame and power is normal with people of demonic traits. And the devil of the biblical context, who says, "all this has been delivered to me," is but the embodiment of such demonic traits understood in the *Gītā*.

Verses 43-45 of chapter 6 read as follows:

> For a good tree does not bear bad fruit, nor does a bad tree bear good fruit.
>
> For every tree is known by its own fruit. For men do not gather figs from thorns, nor do they gather grapes from a bramble bush.
>
> A good man out of the good treasure of his heart brings forth good, and an evil man out of the evil treasure of his heart brings forth evil. For out of the abundance of the heart his mouth speaks.

A similar section also appears in the Gospel According to Matthew in chapter 7. The difference is that, the comparison made in that context is of true prophets and false prophets, whereas this verse differentiates good people from evil ones. The words of Jesus are so clear that they require no elucidation.

3.2

John the Baptist and Jesus

VERSES 18-23 of chapter 7 are as follows:

> Then the disciples of John reported to him concerning all these things.
>
> And John, calling two of his disciples to him, sent them to Jesus, saying, "Are You the Coming One, or do we look for another?"
>
> When the men had come to Him, they said, "John the Baptist has sent us to You, saying, 'Are You the Coming One, or do we look for another?'."
>
> And that very hour He cured many people of their infirmities, afflictions, and evil spirits; and to many who were blind He gave sight.
>
> Then Jesus answered and said to them,"Go and tell John the things you have seen and heard: That the blind see, the lame walk, the lepers are cleansed, the deaf hear, the dead are raised, the poor have the gospel preached to them."
>
> And blessed is he who is not offended because of Me.

The Jews were always waiting, and are still waiting, for the prophesied coming of the Messiah to save them. John the Baptist sent his disciples in order to ascertain from Jesus himself whether he was the Messiah. Asked by those disciples, Jesus does not give them a direct answer because enlightened seers do not directly claim to be so. Instead, he says "Go and tell John the things you have seen and heard." What they saw and heard is stated afterwards. Miracles ranging from the blind seeing and the dead being raised are what they saw. What was heard is the gospel preached to the poor.

Whatever one sees relates to the events of this world. What is heard, on the other hand, relates to the wisdom-teaching of a *guru*, as the word *śravaṇa* (hearing) of the Vedāntic context denotes. And such teachings do not concern the day-to-day affairs of the world. This wisdom secret itself is what the kingdom of God in the biblical context signifies. The good news or gospel preached by Jesus concerns this kingdom of God. In other words, what Jesus teaches is the wisdom secret. Those who take it in are the poor — not poor because they do not find the means to feed themselves, but in the sense that they are the "poor in spirit," who are the blessed, as was seen in the Gospel According to Matthew (5.3).

In short, what is *seen* in Jesus are miracles related to worldly values, and what is *heard* are of wisdom-value. These two worlds of values come together in the *guru* Jesus, as if from two opposite poles and become non-dually one, each validating the other. This non-duality that a *guru* embodies would be perceived with the inner eyes of only those who have developed an intimacy with the *guru*, known in Vedānta as *guru–śiṣya-pārasparya.* This rapport should not be ruptured by anything. Those who develop such a rapport with their own *guru*s are the blessed. It is in this sense Jesus says: "Blessed is he who is not offended because of Me."

Verses 24-28 of chapter 7 are as follows:

> When the messengers of John had departed, He began to speak to the multitudes concerning John: "What did you go out into the wilderness to see? A reed shaken by the wind?
>
> But what did you go out to see? A man clothed in soft garments? Indeed those who are gorgeously apparelled and live in luxury are in the kings' courts.
>
> But what did you go out to see? A prophet? Yes, I say to you, and more than a prophet.
>
> This is he of whom it is written: 'Behold, I send My messenger before your face, who will prepare Your way before You.'
>
> For I say to you, among those born of women there is not a greater prophet than John the Baptist, but he who is least in the kingdom of God is greater than he."

This section helps us to know Jesus in contrast to John the Baptist who, as admitted by Jesus himself, came to prepare the way before him. Prophets (*guru*s), as first indicated by Jesus here, are not to be distinguished by the good apparel they wear, but from the words of wisdom they speak. John the Baptist, in this respect, is seen by Jesus as someone greater than ordinary prophets (*guru*s). As a prophet, he needs to be considered different from others. The strength of the words he used to teach people must be the reason why this is so. For example, he calls the multitudes who came to him, "Broods of wipers" (3.7). He warns them:

> Every tree that does not bear good fruit is cut down and thrown into the fire.
> — 3.9

Scared by these words the people ask him: "What shall we do then?" He answered:

> He who has two tunics, let him give one to him who has none; and he who has food, let him do likewise.
>
> Then the tax collectors also came to be baptized and said to him, "Teacher, what shall we do?"
>
> And he said to them, "Collect no more than what is appointed for you."
>
> Likewise the soldiers asked him, saying, "And what shall we do?" So he said to them, "Do not intimidate anyone or accuse falsely, and be content with your wages." — 3.11-14

It is his moral instructions, given in such a powerful language, that differentiate him from other prophets. Jesus therefore says, "Among those born of women there is not a greater prophet than John the Baptist." Still, such moral instructions in themselves do not enable you to enter the kingdom of God or to enlighten you. For this reason Jesus reminds us, "He who is least in the kingdom of God is greater than he." That means, even the lowest among those who have entered the realm of wisdom are given a place much higher than the realm of simple morals in which John the Baptist finds himself. Put otherwise, the instructions given by John the Baptist, though strongly worded, have a value related only to the worldly affairs of a horizontal significance, whereas the wisdom taught by Jesus reveals the ultimate Reality or the kingdom of God that has a vertical dimension. What John the Baptist did thus was to prepare the worldly life for the coming of Jesus who was to teach the higher wisdom.

John the Baptist's preparation of the path before the coming of Jesus could be understood on a subtler level in yet another way: A person who listens to the strongly worded moral teachings of John, if he is truly inquisitive, may ask himself, "Why should I be a person who follows such rules?" He cannot expect to get an answer to this question from a *guru* like John the Baptist, but from the one like Jesus. John thus was trying to arouse the inquisitiveness in the people so that they could seek real wisdom from Jesus.

Verses 31-35 of chapter 7 read as follows:

> And the Lord said, "To what then shall I liken the men of this generation, and what are they like?
>
> They are like children sitting in the marketplace and calling to one another, saying 'We played the flute for you, and you did not dance; we mourned to you, and you did not weep.'
>
> For John the Baptist came neither eating bread nor drinking wine, and you say, 'He has a demon.'

> The Son of the Man has come eating and drinking, and you say, 'Look, a glutton and a winebibber, a friend of tax collectors and sinners!.'
>
> But wisdom is justified by all her children."

It is to the multitudes gathered around him that Jesus speaks now. He, by means of the analogy of the children sitting in the marketplace, points towards a peculiar nature generally seen in idling common men. They mostly have no thinking habit of their own and no firm stand of their own, nor their own well-considered decisions. At the same time, they are prone to find faults with others profusely. By habit they begin to dance on hearing a flute played, and to weep on hearing some mourning songs. They feel guilty if they do not do so. The indication is that, they, on hearing the commands of someone who is wilful and has a commanding power, just obey them and act accordingly. They do not care for making sure whether the command is worth obeying, whether the person who commanded is honest and knowledgeable. They, in a sense, could be considered to behave as if they had completely sold their thinking habit to those who command them. Those who idle away in marketplaces need no thinking habit, all the more so if they are children or childlike. The non-thinking followers of modern politicians are almost like these children. Comparable to the faults spoken of by such idlers are the wrongs the ordinary people find in John the Baptist as well as Jesus.

John the Baptist, eating locusts and wild honey by habit, was not a *jñānin*. His mission was preparing the path for the coming of Jesus, the real *jñānin*. This John was accused by the ignorant of being possessed by a demon, perhaps because he appeared to be a gruff person. Jesus, on the other hand, used to eat bread and drink wine as everyone else; then he was accused of being a glutton and winebibber, a friend of the tax collectors and sinners. Thus, ordinary people do not need sufficient reason for accusing prophets of wrongdoing. Those who thus accuse others are like children who do not know how to think before doing so. They do not feel the necessity of possessing any thinking habit. But what transformed both John the Baptist and Jesus into prophets was their thinking habit, an aptitude for intuitive perception, and wisdom — Jesus as a real *jñānin* and John the Baptist as one who prepared the path for the coming of the *jñānin* Jesus.

The higher realm of wisdom does not consider whether the eating habit and other such qualities of one who enters it agree with others or not. Eating and drinking have their place in life only as its lowest level of bodily existence. Its value in life is rather of a horizontal nature. Each person may have a different nature in such respects. These differences are of no relevance in the plenitude of wisdom. Wisdom is one alone, and in its oneness merge all that appear as many at the worldly level. The value of wisdom is thus of a vertical order. A *jñānin* and the one who prepares the path of the *jñānin,* both have their respective places in this vertical order — the former at a higher level and the latter at a lower one. The authenticity and value of wisdom are to be measured by the contentment (*ānanda*) felt by the children of that wisdom who live fully dedicated to it and who live as the same wisdom having assumed external forms. Jesus, in this sense, says, "But wisdom is justified by all her children."

Verses 36-50 narrate the events when Jesus visited the house of a Pharisee named Simon. A woman who was a sinner came to Jesus, washed his feet with her own tears, and wiped them with the hair of her head. Then she kissed his feet and anointed them with the fragrant oil she had brought with her. The Pharisee then spoke to himself:

> This man, if He were a prophet, would know who and what manner of woman this is who is touching Him, for she is a sinner. — 7.39

Jesus read his thoughts and answered:

> There was a certain creditor who had two debtors. One owned five hundred denarii, and the other fifty.
>
> And when they had nothing with which to repay, he freely forgave them both. Tell Me, therefore, which of them will love him more?
>
> — 7.41-42

Simon answered and said: "I suppose the one whom he forgave more." And He said to him, "You have rightly judged" (7.43).

Likewise, if one of many sins and another of a few sins are both forgiven, it will be the former who loves more. Therefore, Jesus tells the Pharisee about the woman, "I say to you, her sins, which are many, are forgiven, for she loved much. But to whom little is forgiven, the same loves little" (7.47).

And then Jesus tells the woman, "Your sins are forgiven."

These words were also counted as blasphemy by those who were present there, for according to them, God alone can forgive sins. Upon reading their thoughts, Jesus tells the woman, "Your faith has saved you. Go in peace." That means, it is not the religious authority of Jesus, but the woman's faith, that saved her. No blasphemy can thus be attributed to Jesus.

3.3

The Unenlightened Disciples and the Uncommon Wisdom

VERSES 17-20 of chapter 10 read as follows:

> Then the seventy returned with joy, saying, "Lord, even the demons are subject to us in Your name."
>
> And He said to them, "I saw satan fall like lightning from heaven.
>
> Behold, I gave you the authority to trample on serpents and scorpions, and over all the power of the enemy, and nothing shall by any means hurt you.
>
> Nevertheless do not rejoice in this, that the spirits are subject to you, but rather rejoice because your names are written in heaven."

Jesus sent his disciples out to the people with the aim of cleansing them of the evil spirits and diseases that have possessed them, and also to speak to them of the kingdom of God. Many are the evil spirits and diseases that plague each of us, even as we remain ignorant of it. Our minds very often become easily vitiated by many unhealthy ideas, imaginations, ideals and desires. Such mental conditionings and attachments are to be treated as the real devils or evil spirits and diseases that possess us in our actual life. Many bodily illnesses, as admitted by modern medicine, are caused by mental maladies. One of the basic source-books of Āyurveda, the Indian system of medicine, begins with the words *rāgādi-rogān* (diseases such as attachment). Only in a mind, cleansed of all such filth, does pure wisdom shine. This wisdom is what the kingdom of God of Bible signifies. This must be the reason why Jesus authorized his disciples both to cleanse the people of all evil spirits and diseases, and also to speak to them of the kingdom of God.

The disciples went around the country, as authorized by Jesus, and came back to him. They then were found rejoicing in their ability to drive away demons in Jesus's name. The rejoicing they experienced in their capability to work miracles clearly shows that they did not grasp the real spirit of the authorization Jesus gave them. Upon hearing from them of their joy, Jesus tells them, "I saw satan fall like lightning from heaven." The indication is that those disciples' minds were filled, not with the spirit of the wisdom he taught them, but with a satanic inclination. Jesus feels this disgrace of his own disciples, as if satan were falling upon them as a lightning bolt from heaven. They really should have felt joy, not in their ability to work such miracle, but in their having been able to convey to the people, the secret of the kingdom of God or of the wisdom they were expected to have realized themselves. Jesus therefore asks them, "Rejoice because your names are written in heaven." That means, rejoicing in their capability to make demons subject to them is satanic. The biblical terms "names written in heaven," in the Vedāntic view, means that one becomes properly enlightened.

Verses 21-22 of chapter 10 are as follows:

> In that hour Jesus rejoiced in the Spirit and said, "I praise You, Father, Lord of heaven and earth, that You have hidden these things from the wise and prudent and revealed them to babes. Even so, Father, for so it seemed good in Your sight.
>
> All things have been delivered to Me by My Father, and no one knows who the Son is but the Father, and who the Father is but the Son, and the one whom the Son wills to reveal Him."

Jesus utters these words in an ecstatic mood. In the light of the events narrated just before in verses 17-20, these words reveal a peculiarity of human nature in relation to the gaining of wisdom. They also reveal the bipolar secret implicit in the context of realizing the ultimate Reality. Jesus refers to this peculiarity of human nature among the so-called wise and learned in his words addressed to God, thus, "Father You have hidden these things from the wise and prudent and revealed them to babes." The wise referred to here must be simply those who think of themselves as educated, and are proud of being wise and knowledgeable. Those of such nature, in India, are called *svayam-dhīrāḥ*. To such people, the secret of the kingdom of God does not become revealed because their minds are already conditioned in many respects. At the same time, the very same secret becomes transparent with ease to those who have innocent minds like those of babes. It may be asked why is it so. Jesus himself answers, "Father, so it seemed good in your sight." That means, the human mind is like this as part of the overall system of life, and no other reason is to be sought for it.

Jesus then says, "All things have been delivered to Me by My Father." These words make it clear that the wisdom, which remains unattainable to the wise and prudent, has become clear to Jesus, with nothing hidden. There is also an indication of the sense of responsibility Jesus feels concerning the imparting of this wisdom to the real seekers (who naturally have innocent minds like those of babes).

To become a *jñānin* (enlightened person) means to realize that it is the one ultimate Reality which has assumed one's own form, and that one is that Reality in essence. This realization, in biblical terms, is the awareness, "I am the Son of that one Father." It is the father, even in the worldly context, who can recognize his son, and it is the son who can recognize his father. The same is true in the context of wisdom also. The essential context of wisdom is the realization of the oneness of the Father and the Son, the oneness of *Brahman* and oneself.

Who can identify a realized *jñānin?* The worldly-minded cannot do so. It is the one ultimate Reality, Pure Consciousness, that makes a *jñānin* of one. And it is this very Reality that the title "Father" signifies in Bible. This is the reason why it is said, "No one knows who the Son is but the Father." Likewise, the Reality is truly known only to those who have realized It as themselves. In this sense it is said, "No one knows the Father but the Son." In short, a bipolarity between the Father and the Son, that culminates in the realization of their oneness, is thus the content of one becoming enlightened.

A seeker also, upon being properly taught by an enlightened *guru* finally realizes the same oneness. If we place the seeker, the enlightened *jñānin* and the Father one above the other in an ascending order, then we can meditatively perceive a unitive context to which the three pertain, as well as the unitive content of the three. Perceiving this unitiveness or non-duality is where all the multiplicities, even of these three, vanish.

Verses 23-24 are as follows:

> And He turned to His disciples and said privately, "Blessed are the eyes which see the things you see;
>
> for I tell you that many prophets and kings have desired to see what you see, and have not seen it, and to hear what you hear, but have not heard it."

The first thing we notice here is that Jesus turned to his disciples and said these words privately. That means, what he intends to say is not meant for the public, but is the secret teaching meant for his disciples alone. The nature of this secret is made explicit by Jesus himself. When the philosophical perception of Reality touches its very core, that perception attains the dimension of a secret wisdom.

As is apparent from the words of Jesus, the disciples directly perceive something secret. Yet he does not make it specifically clear what that secret is. In fact, whatever that can be stated specifically would not be a secret. That Jesus also here directly visualizes something mysterious is evident from the words of verse 21, "Jesus rejoiced in the Spirit and said."

The secret seen both by Jesus and his disciples is really nothing other than what is implied in the words, "No one knows who the Son is but the Father, and who the Father is but the Son, and the one to whom the Son wills to reveal Him." As Jesus rejoices in the revealed secret within himself, so it is expected by him that the disciples also have the same experiential awareness and joy.

Initially Jesus says, "Blessed are the eyes which see the things you see." In other words, everyone does not get an opportunity or luck to have the inner vision they were enjoying. The uncommonness of this vision is underscored by Narayana Guru also when he says:

> Who is there to perceive this supreme secret of the man of enlightenment? — *Ātmopadeśa Śatakam* 63

It has to be understood that knowledge is of two kinds. One, the knowledge we gain through our sense perceptions and the thinking that we do which is based upon these perceptions. Such knowledge is countless, and the objects known thus are also so. Such knowledge, endlessly spread out, is termed "the other" (*anya*) by Narayana Guru in his analysis of the knowing process in his *Ātmopadeśa Śatakam* (One Hundred Verses of Self-instruction) (see verses 36-42). He defines this kind of knowledge thus:

> That knowledge by which reality is perceived
>
> As many and varied, is to be understood as *anya*.

Yet there is another kind of knowledge. It perceives one alone as real. That is to say, all the various items of knowledge are perceived as different functional modes of one Consciousness alone. This kind of knowledge is called *sama* (the same) by the Guru. The definition he gives it is thus: The knowledge that sees one Reality alone manifesting is *sama*.

There is yet an inner experiential vision of non-duality in which the *anya–sama* duality, the duality of the one and the many, just disappears into the oneness of Pure Consciousness. Narayana Guru points to this intuitive vision in these words:

> To wake to and become lost
> In the crystal clarity of
> The unitiveness in which *anya* merges
> In *sama* and vice versa has to be one's goal.
> — *Ātmopadeśa Śatakam,* verse 36

No clear definition of this unitive vision is given by the Guru either. This non-duality is the secret that unites together the Father, the Son and the seeker in the bibical context here, as was already seen in verse 22 above. Nothing more is mentioned about the secret. Really this secret is not expressible through words. For this reason we need not expect Jesus, or any other *guru,* to give more details of it. It is when the bipolarity called *pārasparya* between the *guru* and his disciple reaches its zenith, where the *guru*–disciple duality also vanishes, that the spirit which fills the being of the *guru* and makes him rejoice, becomes the spirit that fills the being of the disciple, causing him to rejoice also.

The words "Many prophets and kings have desired to see what you see, and have not seen it, and to hear what you hear, but have not heard it" indicate that the above-mentioned secret has not been accessible even to many of the prophets of the past, John the Baptist among them. Neither can it be intuitively known just because one is a ruler of the state. The nature of the secret implicit in these words of Jesus is put in another way by *Kena Upaniṣad* (I.3-4) as follows:

> There the eye goes not, speech goes not, nor the mind. We know not That. We know not either how it could be taught. Indeed it is other than the known, and also it is above the unknown. Thus we have heard from the ancient ones who have explained it to us.

As all the enlightened *r̥ṣis* admit, perfect attainment of wisdom is not marked by spoken words, but by a silence from which overflows an intensity of meaning. Such are the implications of these words of Jesus.

Jesus's reference here to the two knowing functions of "seeing" and "hearing" is also of a deeper significance. Attaining a philosophical vision involves two aspects. One is hearing attentively the words of instruction of an enlightened *guru*. This aspect is known as *śravaṇa* (hearing). It is to be followed by intense cogitation (*manana*) on what is heard thus, and meditation (*nididhyāsana*) upon it, resulting finally in the transparent vision of what the *guru* intended to convey through his words. This final stage, strictly speaking, is to be treated as *darśana* (vision), though the word stands for philosophy in general. Such a *darśana* is attained only by a true disciple of a true *guru*. Though prophets and kings were aspirants of this *darśana*, they could not attain it. They failed even to listen properly to the words of a *guru*, the primary stage. Being either a prophet or a king does not qualify one to be a true disciple. Proper *śravaṇa* and *darśana*, both happen only in true disciples (*sacchiṣya*s).

The famous parable of the good Samaritan is narrated in verses 29-37. The moral lesson this parable gives is this: The one who loves with all kindness another, by treating him simply as a human being with no intervention of notions like race, religion, caste or nationality, is the ideal neighbour.

Verses 38-42 read as follows:

> Now it happened as they went that He entered a certain village, and a certain woman named Martha welcomed Him into her house.
>
> And she had a sister called Mary, who also sat at Jesus's feet and heard His word.
>
> But Martha was distracted with much serving, and she approached Him and said, "Lord, do you not care that my sister has left me to serve alone? Therefore tell her to help me."
>
> And Jesus answered and said to her, "Martha, Martha, you are worried and troubled about many things.
>
> But one thing is needed, and Mary has chosen that good part, which will not be taken away from her."

A *guru*'s visit to a home makes everyone living there incredibly joyful. The housewife will then be very busy preparing delicious food for a feast in honour of the guest. But a *guru* is not an ordinary guest; what gives a *guru* satisfaction greater than feasting, and what is of lasting value to those in the house, is to sit near the *guru* and listen attentively to his words of wisdom. But many are not mindful of this. Moreover, to lend an ear to a *guru* requires a certain inborn inclination for wisdom. Martha and Mary, though sisters, are very different in respect of such an inclination. Mary prefers to sit at the feet of Jesus and to listen attentively to his words, whereas Martha finds satisfaction in feeding him. It is Mary's love of wisdom that Jesus values more, rather than Martha's desire to prepare feast for him. Jesus points out the difference in value between these two human trends. Whatever be the delicious dishes that Martha prepares, once these are served and eaten, they become lost to her. On the other hand, Mary's way of treating Jesus, by listening to his words, enables her to imbibe a knowledge of great value that never leaves her.

The same character-difference between Martha and Mary could be seen portrayed in *Bṛhadāraṇyaka Upaniṣad* as between Kātyāyanī and Maitreyī, the two wives of the saint Yājñavalkya. Kātyāyanī is wife to Yājñavalkya as any woman is to her husband in this world. Maitreyī, on the other hand, became a wife of Yājñavalkya in order to be near to him as a disciple, to learn from him without hindrance.

3.4

The Fulfilment of Prayer

THE significance of the prayer cited in verses 1-4 of chapter 11 has been examined by us earlier. Verses 5-13 depict, in the form of a parable, how a prayer of petition finds fulfilment.

In verses 5-8 Jesus says:

> Which of you shall have a friend, and go to him at midnight and say to him, "Friend lend me three loaves;
>
> for a friend of mine has come to me on his journey, and I have nothing to set before him;
>
> and he will answer from within and say, "Do not trouble me; the door is now shut, and my children are with me in bed; I cannot rise and give to you?"
>
> I say to you, though he will not rise and give to him because he is his friend, yet because of his persistence he will rise and give him as many as he needs.

Just as the neighbour-friend rising up from his bed at midnight and giving the man what he needs, depends on his insistence, so too the fulfilment of prayer made by a supplicant to God, or by a disciple to a *guru,* depends on the intensity and persistence of his asking or the quest for wisdom. The highest favour the God in heaven or a *guru* here on the earth can grant to a seeker is enabling him the attainment of the Holy Spirit or the wisdom secret. The higher the intensity and persistence and more fundamental in nature one's search for Reality are, the more will be the clarity of wisdom one attains. The present narration is simply an expanded version of what *Bhagavad-Gītā* (IV.39) says: *śraddhāvān labhate jñānam* (one endowed with full faith and interest alone attains wisdom). Jesus's words, "Ask, and it will be given to you; seek, and you will find; knock, and it will be opened to you," also confirm this.

3.5

Demons and Priests

THE event narrated in verses 14-23 and its philosophical significance, have already been examined by us. As Jesus cast out a demon that was mute, and as the mute began to speak, some commented on it, saying, "He casts out demons by Beelzebub, the ruler of demons." The response of Jesus to this remark was,

> "If I cast out demons with the finger of God, surely the kingdom of God has come upon you."

The demon here symbolizes ignorance, and God wisdom. Ignorance can never be removed with ignorance itself as a means. A gigantic ignorance is never capable of removing an ignorance of lesser magnitude. This is the sense in which the ruler of demons is incapable of casting out ordinary demons. Besides, it is because of ignorance that one thinks the ruler of demons casts out demons. Wisdom alone can remove ignorance, or God alone can cast out demons. Moreover, those, who are well aware that only wisdom removes ignorance, by that very knowledge, are entering the realm of wisdom. In this sense Jesus says: "If I cast out demons with the finger of God, surely the kingdom of God has come upon you."

A demon casting out another demon means there is discord among demons, leading naturally to the destruction of their kingdom. Jesus, therefore, says:

> Every kingdom divided against itself is brought to desolation, and a house divided against itself falls. — 11.17

Though Jesus casts out demons here, these sort of healing miracles were commonly practised then by the priests of the Jewish community. It is the elders among such priests who now accuse Jesus of casting out demons by the power of Beelzebub. Jesus, in effect, is asking the elders: "You accuse me now of driving away demons by the ruler of demons. Then, do you admit that the priests who are your own followers (your own sons) also do the same by the ruler of demons?"

They will never admit it, because the priests claim to cast out demons by God's authority, the force opposite to that of the demons.

This is the way the following words of Jesus are to be interpreted in this context:

> And if I cast out demons by Beelzebub, by whom do your sons cast them out? Therefore, they will be your judges. — 11.19

If the priest who drives away demons in the name of God is like a fully armed man who guards his own palace, then Jesus could be likened to a stronger man who comes upon him and overcomes him. Such is the way the pure wisdom of Jesus makes insignificant the banal priestcraft of the Jews that bases itself on the ignorance of what is ultimately Real or is God, though the priests claim to represent God. Not only ignorance but demons are driven away by pure wisdom.

Jesus, in this context, finally says:

> He who is not with Me is against Me, and he who does not gather with Me scatters. — 11.23

That means, whoever does not respect unconditioned pure wisdom, is against that wisdom. Put otherwise, those who find themselves incapable of, or do not feel the necessity of, harmonizing themselves with the unconditioned eternal Reality are to be considered the haters of that Reality. Those who love and respect that Reality, on the other hand, perceive themselves as inseparable from It, as gathered with It. And those, who do not perceive the one ultimate Reality, see many realities, which is only a sign of their ignorance. Such is the way the above words (11.23) of Jesus would be construed from the Vedāntic perspective.

Verses 24-26 are as follows:

> When an unclean spirit goes out of a man, he goes through dry places, seeking rest, and finding none, he says, "I will return to my house from which I came.
>
> And when he comes, he finds it swept and put in order.
>
> Then he goes and takes with him seven other spirits more wicked than himself, and they enter and dwell there; and the last state of that man is worse than the first."

The previous section consisting of verses 14-23 underscored the difference between priests casting out evil spirits by their rituals and Jesus casting out them by his wisdom. Here in the present section, the evil spirits thus driven away by the priests, after wandering around in search of an abode, and finding none, are imagined to come back to the same man from whom they departed. But upon coming back they see that the man has already become enlightened, perhaps as taught by a *guru* like Jesus, and thus he has become inaccessible to them.

Priestcraft is always associated with ignorance, and so evil spirits always have access there. But the inner being, that is fully cleansed of ignorance and has become bright with wisdom, provides no room for evil spirits to stay. But if the person thus enlightened does not stand firmly by that wisdom, more forceful worldly interests are likely to tempt him and mislead him, resulting in an eventual and an even more dangerous downfall. This is the indication given by the words: "He goes out and takes with him seven other spirits more wicked than himself and they enter and dwell there; and the last state of that man is worse than the first."

A person who remains in complete ignorance does not realize that he lives in ignorance, and therefore he is not worried about it. It is not so with the person who once has tasted wisdom and then falls into the temptations of ignorance. The intensity of remorse he feels will be severe.

Verses 27-28 read thus:

> And it happened, as He spoke these things, that a certain woman from the crowd raised her voice and said to Him, "Blessed is the womb that bore You, and the breasts which nursed You."
>
> But He said, "More than that, blessed are those who hear the words of God and keep it!"

The woman raises her voice and utters words that are impelled by wordly instincts. Yet her words of praise are of a higher spiritual value. In other words, the woman, by standing at a lower level of worldly values, praises the wisdom and its proponent, both of a higher value. Much better than such praise is to raise oneself up to that higher, praiseworthy realm. Such is the indication we see in the response of Jesus.

We read in verses 33-36 as follows:

> No one, when he has lit a lamp, puts it in a secret place or under a basket, but on a lamp stand, that those who come in may see the light.
>
> The lamp of the body is the eye. Therefore when your eye is good, your whole body also is full of light. But when your eye is bad, your body also is full of darkness.

> Therefore take heed that the light which is in you is not darkness.
>
> If then your whole body is full of light, having no part dark, the whole body will be full of light, as when the bright shining of a lamp gives you light.

Though we have examined the parable of the lighted lamp earlier, the philosophical principle brought out here by this parable is different.

There are two kinds of eyes that are mentioned here: One, the external eye, and the other, the internal eye. When your external eye is fully sighted, you perceive your own body fully and distinctly, and you see the world fully and distinctly. But if the external eye is blind, even your own body is seen by you as a dark entity, and the world also appears to be fully dark to you. Likewise, when your mind is filled with the darkness of ignorance, you perceive yourself wrongly, and the world is also seen wrongly. But when your inside becomes fully bright with the lamp of wisdom, you perceive yourself as brightness in essence, and the world also as brightness in essence. The Vedāntic notion that *Ātmā*, the Reality that underlies the being of oneself as well as of the world, is effulgence in essence, is hinted at in these words of Jesus.

3.6

The Ignorant Lawmakers

In verses 45-52, Jesus derides a group of lawyers. It is very difficult to say definitely when laws, both of the state and religions, began to find place in human life. Religious laws are enforced by priests, and state laws by governments. Both these law-enforcement machineries have, from the very beginning, remained vitiated by the tendency seen in the law-enforcers themselves. They may behave as though they are not bound to abide by the very laws they enjoin upon others. This is the reason why Jesus ridicules the lawyers, saying:

> Woe to you also, you lawyers? For you load men with burdens hard to bear, and you yourselves do not touch the burdens with one of your fingers. — 11.46

Even in modern times this same phenomenon admittedly still degenerates both the entire realms of politics and religion.

Greed for power and wealth mainly is what motivates the lawmakers and law-enforcers to behave in such a manner. Not to mention that statecraft and religion are controlled from behind by these greeds, only because of the ignorance of those who are at the helm of affairs. The enlightened *guru*s and prophets who uncompromisingly stick to truth, alone dare to question the activities of such lawmakers and law-enforcers. Such *guru*s and prophets have only the power of wisdom, but no muscle power or money power to support them. The lawmakers and law-enforcers, on the other hand, are supported by manpower, money power and also the power of authority. For this reason, they have always found it easy to do away with such trouble-making *guru*s and prophets.

Nevertheless, all the religious laws gain their authority from the very wisdom taught by such *guru*s and prophets. For this reason, politicians and religionists alike, feel bound to convince the people that they are the upholders of *guru*s and prophets, as well as their traditions. And for this purpose, they may erect tombs over the graves of *guru*s and prophets who were actually killed by their kind, their predecessors or fathers. They are sure that a dead *guru* or prophet will not come up to question them. It is common almost everywhere in the world that a living *guru* is ignored, whereas a dead *guru* is honoured by worshipping his tomb, statue or picture. Pointing towards this typical human tendency, Jesus says:

> Woe to you! For you build the tombs of prophets, and your fathers killed them.
>
> In fact, you bear witness that you approve the deeds of your fathers; for they indeed killed them, and you build their tombs. — 11.47-48

In both religion and politics, peoples' right to think is thus taken over by priests and politicians. Anyone found thinking freely on religious matters is often dubbed heretic, and anyone who does so in politics is dubbed an anti-party worker or even as one who commits treason, depending on the political set-up of the country concerned. And those who have taken over this monopoly of thinking for the people, as was stated earlier, neither interpret nor practise religion or politics truthfully. In short, priests and politicians, while they monopolize peoples' right to think, in their turn are prone to think in a way not based on truth, and thus wrongly. This happens basically because they are ignorant. Indicating this pitiful state, Jesus says,

> Woe to you lawyers! for you have taken away the key of knowledge. You did not enter in yourselves, and those who were entering in you hindered. — 11.52

All laws, whether religious or of the state, are meant to make human life orderly. Human life being part of the total nature, all those laws should agree with the overall laws of nature. Such laws must be applicable to the ruler and the ruled alike. Laws are not meant for the rulers, but for humans, and both the rulers and the ruled are humans.

3.7

Religion and Man

THE whole of chapter 12 contains the teachings given by Jesus to the multitude gathered around him. Among them were also his disciples. Therefore, certain teachings meant only for the disciples also find a place in this chapter.

Verses 1-7 read as follows:

> In the meantime, when an innumerable multitude of people had gathered together, so that they trampled one another, He began to say to His disciples first of all, "Beware of the leaven of the Pharisees, which is hypocrisy.
>
> For there is nothing covered that will not be revealed, nor hidden that will not be known.
>
> Therefore whatever you have spoken in the dark will be heard in the light, and what you have spoken in the ear in the inner rooms will be proclaimed on the housetops.
>
> And I say to you, My friends, do not be afraid of those who kill the body, and after that have no more that they can do.
>
> But I will show you whom you should fear. Fear Him who, after He has killed, has power to cast into hell; yes, I say to you, fear Him!
>
> Are not five sparrows sold for two copper coins? And not one of them is forgotten before God.
>
> But the very hairs of your head are all numbered. Do not fear therefore; you are of more value than many sparrows.

The Pharisees were the religious leaders of the Jewish community. Many of the leaders of institutionalized religions around the world have always had the evil habit of exploiting the innocent laymen to ensure their own self-interest. This happens in modern times just as it did among the Jewish community prior to the advent of Christianity. Commendable moral lessons are taught by such leaders when they face the laymen from pulpits and public platforms. But they privately conspire with co-leaders on the means to ensure their personal interests. Aimed at such leaders, Jesus proclaims, "There is nothing covered that will not be revealed." When a bit of leaven is added to a large quantity of dough kept in a big vessel, the sourness of the leaven spreads throughout the dough. Likewise, the evil thoughts that hide within the religious leaders, who openly give good moral lessons to the public, seep through their words and deeds and come to light and can also be read between the lines of their otherwise good moral lessons. Jesus, therefore, warns the people, in verses 1-3, to be beware of such religious leaders.

For someone to come and kill us is the most frightening thing in the world for many of us. But what is thus killed is merely the body, and not the Reality, called *Ātmā*, that has assumed the form of this body. This fact is really known only to a *jñāṇin.* More terrible than killing the body is keeping another person completely under one's spell, or infusing another person with wrong notions of life and life's goal, by making his naturally pure mind sullied. Such transgressions are done by wilful people on the strength of their commanding power, and sometimes because of their own mistaken or partial understanding. Those who hurt thus are killed, not in body, but in their spirit. The killers of the spirit, therefore, as Jesus warns us here, are to be considered more dangerous than the killers of the body. The hypocritical religious leaders are really the killers of the spirit (*Ātmā*).

There are some people who find joy in catching small birds like sparrows and parrots, and caging them. They may also sell them to those who are interested in them. Similar is the way religious leaders or cult leaders, who trap innocent people and keep them within the cage of dogmas and laws, and sell them to the cause of safeguarding their vested interests. Jesus warns against them thus, "Not one of them is forgotten before God." That means, nothing that happens within the ultimate Reality or *Brahman* is not known to the very same Reality. Jesus tells the people, "You are of more value than many sparrows." Birds, caught by hunters, lose their freedom and can even be sold. Likewise, caught in the trap of the hypocrisy of the leaders of religions or cults, you lose your freedom and you are likely to be sold out as stated above. It is not the institutionalized religions or cults and their proponents that you should rely on in life, but on God alone. Such is the message Jesus gives here.

Verses 13-21 of chapter 12 read as follows:

> Then one from the crowd said to Him, "Teacher, tell my brother to divide the inheritance with me."
>
> But He said to him, "Man, who made Me a judge or an arbitrator over you?"

> And He said to them, "Take heed and beware of covetousness, for one's life does not consist in the abundance of the things he possesses."
>
> Then he spoke a parable to them, saying, "The ground of a certain rich man yielded plentifully.
>
> And he thought within himself, saying, "What shall I do, since I have no room to store my crops?"
>
> So he said, "I will do this: I will pull down my barns and build greater, and there I will store all my crops and my goods.
>
> And I will say to my soul, "Soul, you have many goods laid up for many years; take your ease; eat, drink, and be merry."
>
> But God said to him, "You fool! This night your soul will be required of you; then whose will those things be which you have provided?"
>
> So is he who lays up treasure for himself, and is not rich toward God."

There are many basic principles brought to light in this section. First, the function of a *guru* is not that of being a mediator in such purely worldly affairs like the partitioning of family inheritances. Ignorant of this fact, many happen to approach *guru*s to settle such matters. Those people need not be expected to become interested in the wisdom teachings of those *guru*s. Of course, some priests could be seen interfering in such worldly disputes; still such activities do not come under the properly functioning domain of priests.

The second principle is that the meaning of human life does not consist in accumulating worldly possessions, and that such possessions turn out to be of no value if their possessor is not rich with the ultimate Reality or God.

The rich man of the parable, upon possessing too many crops as a bounty of nature or God, tells his own soul, the divine element within him, "Soul, you have many goods laid up for many years; take your ease; eat, drink, and be merry."

Eating, drinking and merrymaking are meant for one's bodily well-being, and it is to ensure this that the rich man thinks of storing all the produce and worldly things by building a new storehouse. What everyone really aims at is one's own well-being, not merely the body's well-being. Striving merely for bodily well-being has behind it the wrong notion that oneself is constituted simply of the body. The body is merely one's apparent form; what is really the essence of oneself is the substance that assumes all forms, including the bodily one. That substance is nothing other than *Brahman* (God). This awareness makes one rich with God. The one who is thus rich with God neither grieves on the occurrence of a crop failure, nor becomes overjoyed upon getting an abundant crop. He, on the other hand, shares that over-abundant yield produced by nature, with his fellow humans whom are also part of nature.

The goal of life for a person who thinks, "I am this body" naturally is to eat and drink. That means, he lives for eating and drinking, instead of eating and drinking for the sake of living. The one who lives with the latter understanding, even when in possession of abundant natural produce and wealth, finds happiness in being rich with God, not in mere eating and drinking.

Many live with the assumption that they will be living for a long time, as they do now, and with this notion they accumulate wealth for their secure life in the future. They sometimes say, "I amass this wealth to make sure that my children live with no hardships in life." Those who work hard for this purpose do not take into account the fact that those children are also born in this world with the capability to do hard work like themselves.

3.8

Disciples and the Public

PETER, in verse 41, asks Jesus "Lord, do You speak this parable only to us, or to all people?" The parable Jesus had just spoken is about the blessed servant whom his master finds watching for him even at night, not knowing the time of his arrival. Likewise, no disciple knows in advance exactly when the final wisdom secret is gained from the *guru*. He should therefore always wait for it watchfully as it could occur at any time. This is the message contained in the parable told by Jesus. Peter's question now regards whether this message was meant for the disciples or for the public. Jesus's answer is thus:

> For everyone to whom much is given, from him much will be required; and to whom much has been committed, of him they will ask the more. — 12.48

His close disciples as well as the general public could be around when a *guru* teaches. In the present case, the teaching given by Jesus is to the innumerable multitude of people who have gathered there trampling over one another (12.1). What a *guru* teaches in such situations, though meant for all, would be understood by the disciples and the general public differently. A disciple would delve into the deeper significance of those words, while the public would grasp something general about it. Therefore, what a *guru* expects of his close disciples and of the general public to understand from what he teaches would not be the same. Likewise, the benefits the disciples gain in their life from those words would also be different from what the general public achieves.

3.9

A Guru's Anguish

VERSES 49-50 read as follows:

> I came to send fire on the earth, and how I wish it were already kindled!
>
> But I have a baptism to be baptized with, and how distressed I am till it is accomplished!

Jesus tells the people, "I have a baptism to be baptized with." This cannot be an ordinary baptism. It is so important for him that it is what fulfils his life's mission. He makes it clear in his own words thus: "How distressed I am till it is accomplished!"

Earlier John the Baptist declared to the people:

> I indeed baptize you with the water; but one mightier than I is coming. . . . He will baptize you with the Holy Spirit, and with fire.
>
> — 3.16

That means, the baptism that Jesus receives and gives others is not of the ordinary kind, but is a baptism in which one becomes immersed in pure wisdom or Holy Spirit.

A *guru* is already baptized with such wisdom. But his baptism, as far as he is concerned, becomes complete only when his true disciples, at least one, are also baptized by him with the same wisdom. And this is the true life mission of a *guru*. Jesus's distressful longing to fulfil this mission is what the words "But I have a baptism to be baptized" indicate.

A *guru* remains restless within until this consummating stage of his baptism is reached. Therefore Jesus says, "How distressed I am till it is accomplished!" The same restless state of mind of a *guru* is reflected in these words of *Taittirīya Upaniṣad* (I.4.2) which we quote once more:

> Hail! May seekers of Truth approach me!
> Hail! May seekers of Truth approach me variously!
> Hail! May seekers of Truth approach me properly!
> Hail! May seekers of Truth approach me undisturbed by external influences!
> Hail! May seekers of Truth approach me with mental self-control!

What happens to those who thus become baptized with wisdom? What they value most, as we have already seen, is not any kind of wealth in this world. Rather, they prefer to be rich in God. That is to say, this world, as far as they are concerned, is already burned down. Besides, on becoming a *jñānin*, one does not see the world as real on its own, but as unreal on its own, for what is Real is God (*Brahman*) alone. The world as reality thus ceases to exist for him. *Bhagavad-Gītā* (IV.37) also says categorically, "The fire of wisdom reduces to ashes all *karma*s." This world is a world of *karma*s (actions). Jesus also wishes, how great it would be if those who follow him also become baptized with the wisdom that results in the experience where the world becomes burnt down! The words, "I came to send fire on the earth, and how I wish it were already kindled!" are to be understood in this light.

Verses 54-56 are as follows:

> Then he also said to the multitudes, "When you see a cloud rising out of the west, immediately you say, 'A shower is coming' and so it is.
>
> And when you see the south wind blow, you say, 'There will be hot weather,' and there is.
>
> Hypocrites! you can discern the face of the sky and of the earth, but how is it you do not discern this time?

In order to clarify the message contained in this section, the analogy of those who go to a magistrate is given in verses 57-59 that follow. It is better for both the contending parties to settle matters between themselves before going to the court of law. Reaching such a settlement requires a certain discriminative states of mind, which also must be there before going to the magistrate. Likewise, humans should acquire a discriminative state of mind to gain what is ultimately and urgently to be gained in life before it goes to ruin and becomes hellish. How pitiable is it that humans, though capable of analysing the changes in nature, are incapable of discerning what makes their own lives really meaningful and worth living! This is the reason Jesus asks, "How is it you do not discern this time?"

3.10

Sin, Merit and the Greatness of Wisdom

VERSES 1-5 of chapter 13 read as follows:

> There were present at that season some who told Him about the Galileans whose blood Pilate had mingled with their sacrifices.
>
> And Jesus answered and said to them, "Do you suppose that these Galileans were worse sinners than all other Galileans, because they suffered such things?
>
> I tell you, no; but unless you repent, you will all likewise perish.
>
> Or those eighteen on whom the tower in Siloan fell and killed them, do you think that they were worse sinners than all other men who dwelt in Jerusalem?
>
> I tell you, no; but unless you repent you will all likewise perish."

This section, at first look, stresses the importance of repenting for having done something evil. When does one feel necessitated to repent? When one realizes that what one had done is totally wrong. To realize thus means that one becomes a more knowledgeable person. The ultimate limit of this progression in knowledge is to know the secret of the kingdom of God.

To do wrong things chronically is caused by a lack of knowledge or wrong knowledge. Even those who are wise sometimes happen to necessarily do things that are normally counted as bad, in certain unavoidable circumstances. Being the knowers of Reality, they consider such actions merely as necessary evils unavoidable in the overall flow of the nature's events, and therefore they do not count such seemingly wrong actions as sinful, nor as things to be repented over. In common practice, the differentiation between good and evil is based not on the basic understanding of the overall nature of life or the ultimate Reality, but on certain customary value notions and social conventions.

Those who are enlightened perceive all actions, including theirs, as taking place in the one ultimate Reality by virtue of Its creative urge. As they perform only those actions which nature unfolds as part of life, they do not count those actions either as sinful or meritorious. No action really belongs to an individual. Even wilful actions do not really belong to individuals, because it is nature that made the phenomenon of free will a part of human beings. Free will is not a man-made phenomenon. That means, it is the overall nature that functions in humans, in the form of acts like thinking freely, taking free decisions and acting accordingly. Those who have this understanding naturally become free of all sins in life, or rather they are beyond the bounds of the sin–merit duality.

Living completely ignorant of the overall nature of life is as evil as human blood being offered as oblation in fire-sacrifices. In short, it is not whether one actually does evil deeds or not, but it is one's ignorance, that makes one really vile. This secret of *karma* is elaborated in detail in *Bhagavad-Gītā,* particularly in chapter III.

The parable narrated in verses 6-9 is of an exegetic nature, and stresses the importance of being fully aware of reality. The equilvalent of such a section in Indian scriputres is known as Arthavāda. Such sections coming as they are after giving an important teaching, say how valuable that teaching is, and what would be the ill-effect of ignoring it in life. In doing so, it tells some story to substantiate the lesson.

A certain man, after planting a fig tree in his garden, waited three years for it to bear fruit, but it failed. He then asked the gardener to cut it down. The gardener being more prudent, told the master, "Sir, let it alone for this year also, until I dig around it and fertilize it. And if it bears fruit, well. But if not, after that you can cut it down." The master was tempted by his ignorance as to why the tree did not bear fruit, and so ordered the servant to cut it down. But the keeper removed the master's ignorance. He thus was functioning almost like a *guru.*

Verses 22-30 of chapter 13 are as follows:

> And He went through the cities and villages, teaching, and journeying toward Jerusalem.
>
> Then one said to Him, "Lord, are there few who are saved?" And He said to them,
>
> "Strive to enter through the narrow gate' for many, I say to you, will seek to enter and will not be able.
>
> When once the Master of the house has risen up and shut the door, and you begin to stand outside and knock at the door, saying, 'Lord, Lord, open for us;' and He will answer and say to you, "I do not know you, where you are from,"

> then you will begin to say, "We ate and drank in Your presence, and You taught in our streets."
>
> But He will say, "I tell you, I do not know you, where you are from. Depart from Me, all you workers of inequity."
>
> There will be weeping and gnashing of teeth. When you see Abraham and Isaac and Jacob and all the prophets in the kingdom of God, and you yourselves thrust out.
>
> They will come from the east and the west, from the north and the south, and sit down in the kingdom of God.
>
> And indeed there are last who will be first, and there are first who will be last."

The context here is that of Jesus travelling through cities and villages to teach. Some *guru*s take to this way of instructing people. In India, the traditionally accepted way of life of *saṁnyāsin*s is to be wandering mendicants (*parivrājaka*s). They move from village to village teaching people, and are supported by the villagers. Jesus also apparently does the same. Some learned *saṁnyāsins* of modern times move from city to city and lecture to organized gatherings. This practice could also be considered an extension of this way of life. Listening to such talks, whether given to a large gathering, or simply in the street, may enable one to get a general idea of certain aspects about the nature of wisdom; but it never saves one or makes one enlightened. Such is the message contained in the present words of Jesus.

One man, upon eating with Jesus and listening to his words as he was lecturing in some street of the city, asks him, "Are there few who are saved?" What the man intends to know is, "Do people like me also become saved?"

The path that leads to wisdom is not an easy one. Many are the ways to know of worldly things and affairs. But the way to the kingdom of wisdom is one alone. And that too, too narrow to be noticed as a path at all for most. That path is of interiorizing one's perception and seeing what is real within oneself. Jesus therefore says, "Strive to enter through the narrow path."

The talks of scholars or *guru*s on the subject one happens to listen to in the city halls or village streets do not alone make for this narrow path. Such talks perhaps enable one to know of the existence of such a narrower path to wisdom, and that, if one finds it out and treads through it, one may enter the kingdom of wisdom. But, no one just on the strength of listening to such talks, will find himself on the narrow path or treading through it. This narrow path really is within oneself. Only a very few become blessed with the opportunity to discover that path, to enter the inner secrets of the Self, and to realize the kingdom of God within themselves. In this sense Jesus says, "Many will seek to enter, and will not be able."

Only those who are endowed with willing minds, favourable personal traits, ability to think penetratingly and embody the confluence of all these factors at the opportune moment, along with being fortunate enough to get the proper guidance of an enlightened *guru,* really enter the kingdom of God. Many who are desirous of entering it, find themselves ousted. Some may think, because the *guru* has come to their town and visited their houses, as well as eaten with them, as they have also listened to his words, that for this reason they are qualified to gain wisdom. They are totally wrong. The context of gaining wisdom is like a master letting a few inside his room and then shutting the door. The master here represents the *guru* or Jesus. Having personal relationship with a *guru,* having had the chance to listen to his words, or any such thing, does not make one qualified to attain wisdom. If they consider these as qualifying factors for wisdom, then they would have to weep and repent, feeling an intense inner affliction. Yet the opportunity to enter the master's room, to enter the kingdom of God, is not denied to anyone. It is left open to all who come from any direction of the compass, from any country, from any cultural background. And if fully competent, they indeed enter it. Jesus therefore says, "They will come from the east and the west, from the north and the south, and sit down in the kingdom of God."

The personal relationship one has with a *guru,* the help one may have rendered to a *guru,* the status one has acquired in the society, one's economic position and all such matters do not count in the context of gaining wisdom. Those who are first in all these respects may find themselves to be the last to reach the doorsteps of wisdom. And those who are considered last in all these matters could be seen occupying the front row of those entering the kingdom of wisdom. This happens simply because they are competent, they have full faith in and pay full attention to the word of the *guru;* they are endowed with a penetrative eye to see into those words; and above all, they are fully dedicated to the cause of wisdom. Jesus therefore says, "And indeed there are last who will be first, and there are first who will be last."

Verses 31-35 of chapter 13 read as follows:

> On that very day some Pharisees came, saying to Him, "Get out and depart from here, for Herod wants to kill you."
>
> And He said to them, "Go, tell that fox, 'Behold, I cast out demons and perform cures today and tomorrow, and the third day I shall be perfected.'
>
> Nevertheless I must journey today, tomorrow, and the day following; for it cannot be that a prophet would perish outside of Jerusalem.
>
> "O Jerusalem, Jerusalem, the one who kills the prophets and stones those who are sent to her! How often I wanted to gather your children together, as a hen gathers her brood under her wings, but you were not willing!
>
> See! your house is left to you desolate; and assuredly, I say to you, you shall not see Me until the time comes when you say, "Blessed is He who comes in the name of the Lord!"

Herod is the ruler of Jerusalem, as a representative of the Roman Emperor. The basic duty of a ruler or king (*rājā*) is to keep the people pleased (*rājati*). But, as we learn from the history of Jerusalem, as well as of the world, political authority alone can never keep the people pleased. Herod, as Jesus admits here, has the political authority to kill him, yet the very authority is likened by Jesus to a fox that is on the prowl to catch a hen. As we gather from many of his stories, Herod was not at all a just ruler.

There is only one power in this world that is capable of keeping all the people under its wings, just as a hen keeps all its brood under its wings at the moment danger comes. And that power is of wisdom, not of any political authority. It, in essence, is the awareness that all beings are but the children of one God who is in heaven. To put the same in Vedāntic terms, it is the enlightenment that:

> What are known as "this man" or "that man",
> Contemplatively visualized,
> Are in essence all one primordial
> Ātmā assuming various forms."
>
> — *Ātmopadeśa śatakam* 24

Prophets (*jñānins*) are those who consider it their life's mission to keep all people safely under the wings of this awareness. Nevertheless, the history of Jerusalem has been one of killing such prophets. And for this reason, the divisiveness that prevailed in Jerusalem at the time of Jesus continues even now. Furthermore, this divisiveness has attained even more momentum. The Palestinians and the Jews, even today, fight one another for Jerusalem, each to their own detriment.

The overall message that Jesus gives here is this: The state of a country ruled by one who ignores, disgraces or even kills a prophet who brings in the wisdom that unites people together and leads them to a happy and peaceful life, will be woeful. In other words, the ruler, as well as the people, should have the discriminating power to identify a true prophet (*guru*). How is one to identify such a *guru*? The one who totally relies on God alone and perceives everything in that perspective is a true prophet. The same put in Vedāntic terms, the one who perceives that one ultimate Reality (*Brahman*) has assumed the form of oneself as well as of everything in all the worlds, who lives as an embodiment of *Brahman,* and who teaches this Reality to people, is the true *guru.* Such *gurus* (prophets) are to be always honoured, and never dishonoured. Until this truth is understood, Jesus will be taken merely to be the son of Joseph the carpenter, and never as a *guru*. Jesus, in this sense, says, "Assuredly, I say to you, you shall not see Me until the time comes when you say, 'Blessed is He who comes in the name of the Lord!' Such a *guru* that Jesus is, is not recognized by the Pharisees nor by Herod, their ruler. In short, no political authority or military power can bring in peace among people nor into the world as a whole, the enlightened *gurus* and prophets alone can do that. Though such is the nature of *gurus* and prophets, they are dishonoured or even killed by the political authorities.

Verses 7-11 of chapter 14 give a moral instruction that relates to the human longing for fame. Reputation is considered a noble value by almost all scriptures and spiritual masters. But making a concerted effort with this end in view often appears awkward, and sometimes ends up in causing infamy. Jesus here depicts the analogy of the man who occupies the best seat in a wedding feast. Such a person would have to vacate the seat, much to his discomfort and shame, when the more important guest for whom the seat was intended arrives. Therefore Jesus says:

> When you are invited go and sit down in the lowest place, so that when he who invited you comes, he may say to you, "Friend go up higher." Then you will have glory at the presence of those who sit at the table with you.
> — 14.10

Wealthy people, in modern times, can be seen spending huge amounts of money to publicize their pictures, names and biographies.

But such attempts to become famous are counted by those who are wise simply as sign of their meanness and pettiness.

Despite all such publicity, those wealthy people do not get the honour wise people get, in spite of the fact that such wise ones are often economically poor in status. Such wise ones never run after fame; they simply remain in their spontaneous humility that results from their wisdom. As most people have great respect for wisdom, such wise men are always honoured everywhere and are seated accordingly in gatherings. Jesus, therefore, says:

> Whoever exalts himself will be abased, and he who humbles himself will be exalted. — 7.11

Verses 12-14 of chapter 14, that contain a moral lesson, read as follows:

> Then He also said to him who invited him, "When you give a dinner or a supper, do not ask your friends, your brothers, your relatives nor your rich neighbours, lest they also invite you back, and you be repaid."
>
> But when you give a feast, invite the poor, the maimed, the lame, the blind.
>
> And you will be blessed, because they cannot repay you; for you shall be repaid at the resurrection of the just.

This section contains yet another moral teaching, that the good deeds you perform should not be motivated by the returns that could be expected from them. The hope Jesus gives to the doers of such deeds is, "You shall be repaid at the resurrection of the just."

Even the religious gifts given by some rich people in modern times sometimes have behind them the expectation of an indirect return-benefit. Apparently so are the donations given to political parties that form part of the modern democratic mode of governance. All such benefits are of worldly value, and the good deeds performed are also of a worldly nature. But some perform good deeds motivated by no desire at all. Such actions (*karmas*), in Vedānta, are called *niṣkāma karmas* (desireless actions). Concerning such *karmas*, *Bhagavad-Gītā* (II.47) says:

> Doing actions as such alone is appropriate for you; never being concerned with their benefits. Do not (therefore) be benefit-motivated in actions; be not attached to inaction either.

Such *karmas* also do yield results, but not as one desires or asks. The teaching of Jesus here is similar. The results of desireless actions could be either worldly or spiritual. If worldly, those results benefit one and all; and if spiritual, they ensure one's eternal happiness while also making others happy. It is such benefits that are referred to here as, "You shall be repaid at the resurrection of the just." A sort of benefit that could be expected to be enjoyed at least upon resurrection is indicated here. In such an expectation could also lurk a desire, though not worldly. Such an expectation should also be absent in a strictly desireless *karma* admissible to Vedānta.

3.11

The Kingdom of God Within and Its King

VERSES 1-9 of chapter 16 narrate the parable of a rich man and his steward who was a trickster. This lesson, as is stated at the very beginning, is given by Jesus and is intended for his disciples alone. On learning of his fraudulence, the master decides to dismiss the steward. But on hearing of it, shrewd as he was, the steward conspires with the debtors to the master, and rewrites their loan deeds, reducing their debts by half. His hope, in doing so, was that, when expelled by the master, he would be acceptable to the debtors, and they would help him survive. Though not trustworthy, this steward was commended by the master because of the shrewdness with which he dealt with the situation. And Jesus comments on it thus:

> The sons of this world are more shrewd in their generation than the sons of light. — 16.8

The steward really was cheating his master. Fully aware of it, the master acclaims him on account of the shrewdness he showed in dealing with a very difficult worldly situation. The steward was familiar only with worldly matters, and he is an expert in that. The master's interest is also not in the honesty of the steward, but in his shrewdness in worldly matters. Both the master and the servant are thus the sons of the world, and not the sons of light. Those who are considered wise need not show such a shrewdness on worldly affairs which is the reason why Jesus says, "The sons of this world are more shrewd in their generation than the sons of light."

What the steward who gains unrighteously, does is, pick-up new friends hoping that they will support him in the future. Jesus says:

> I say to you, make friends for yourselves by unrighteous mammon, that when you fail, they may receive you into everlasting habitations. — 16.9

The steward gains new friends by fraudulent means, in the hope that he would be welcomed by them in the future. But the unrighteously gained comforts will surely perish on their own. Will these new friends of the steward welcome him even in such a perilous condition? No. That means, he will not be a welcome guest to them forever. When he, already dismissed by the master, thus is not welcomed by his new friends either, he will begin to think, whom should he rely on in life. There is one Reality that is always reliable to all and accepts all. It is the everlasting habitation in the kingdom of God. His attention will finally turn to that abode. Such a turn in life for him actually is led to by his own unrighteously gained wealth and friends. If one happens to be incapable of entering the kingdom of God through the front door by way of longing for it, then, when one's own expertise in worldly matters fails one, one begins to think whether there is something beyond all this that makes life meaningful. One's attention may then turn to the everlasting habitation and one may enter it through the back door as it were. Jesus, in this sense, says, "Make friends for yourselves by unrighteous mammons, that when you fail, they may receive you into everlasting habitation."

Verses 10-13 of chapter 16 clarify, as inferred from the above parable, how valuing the kingdom of God and valuing worldly wealth are not possible together in life, a point we have already discussed.

Verses 7-10 of chapter 17, through yet another parable, show how we are intended to live as the "unprofitable servants" of God, with the clear awareness that "we have done what was our duty to do" as desired by God. This is comparable to a true servant serving his master with all obedience, expecting no returns.

Verses 20-21 of chapter 17 read as follows:

> Now when He was asked by the Pharisees when the kingdom of God would come, He answered them and said, "The kingdom of God does not come with observation;
>
> nor will they say, 'see here!' or 'see there!' For indeed the kingdom of God is within you."

The questions raised here are, "When will the kingdom of God come?" and "Where does the kingdom of God exist?" Translated into terminology familiar to Vedānta, the questions would be like these: "When will we know the Self?" and "Where does the Self exist?" The Self does not come from somewhere. Its existence is not at any specifiable location either. Like the gold substance in all the ornament forms, the Self or God exists as the Substance that fills the being of everything that appears to be, including ourselves. Therefore, the Self's or God's coming is not from somewhere, nor at some noticeable point of time. On the other hand, the Self alone is what exists in the form of everything. If asked, "Where does God exist?" the only answer is, "Everything we see here and now is God become manifest." Asked whether you have seen God, the answer would be, "I see God alone and nothing else. The kingdom of God is our own being."

Verses 1-10 of chapter 19 describe the event in which Jesus stays as a guest with Zachaeus, the chief tax collector and also a rich man. Though an unjust tax collector, Zachaeus was fully devoted to Jesus and repented for all the wrongs he had done. There was a murmuring of protest among those around, for according to them, "He has gone to be a guest with a man who is a sinner" (19.7). Jesus answered to them, "The Son of Man has come to save that which was lost." (19.10).

Jesus, in another context, said, "Those who are well have no need of a physician, but those who are sick" (Matthew 9.12). The present words of Jesus convey almost the same message. The primary function of all the *guru*s is to save the ignorant who are groping in darkness, by shedding onto them the light of wisdom.

In the present context, Zachaeus is the ignorant who desires to be saved. His official duty, as the representative of the Roman Emperor, is collecting taxes from Judea and sending the money to Rome. The tax collectors, including Zachaeus, used to collect taxes in unjust ways, coercing people. For this reason, the Jews despised the tax collectors and even treated them as sinners. But his devotion to Jesus prompted him, as he was a short man, to climb up a tree in order to see Jesus properly as he passed through the road.

It is not the job one does that makes one eligible to approach a *guru* to seek wisdom. It is the awareness of being ignorant and of having committed errors owing to the very same ignorance, as well as the willingness to repent and correct oneself, while at the same time having a full rapport with a *guru,* that make one eligible to approach a *guru* to seek wisdom. Those who live in ignorance are referred to here by Jesus as "that which was lost."

Though a "sinner", Zachaeus realized the wrongs he had done, was willing to correct himself and also to make amends for the wrongs already done. And along with it, he had full faith in Jesus and his words. Noticing this state of mind of Zachaeus, Jesus says, "Today salvation has come to this house" (19.9). That means, the kingdom of God, as far as Zachaeus is concerned, is already at hand.

It is in the form of one's realization of the ultimate Reality or God through wisdom, and the experience of peace that ensues, that the kingdom of God comes. Unaware of this truth, many think of the kingdom of God as similar to a political kingdom, and that its coming will bring about a new political and social order. Those who think so will have to wait forever with a religious fervour for the coming of such a kingdom. Jesus makes clear to such people how mistaken they are, through the parable of the minas in verses 11-27 of chapter 19.

Like all kingdoms, the kingdom of God also needs a king. That king is the *guru* himself. Jesus stands here before everyone as such a *guru* or king. The words of this *guru* should be properly listened to; their inner meaning should be intuitively perceived; and this meaning should be enriched and fostered within. Only by this does one experience the coming of the kingdom of God within, and perceive the *guru* as its king. But this kingdom does not become realized by those who wait for its coming as a new social and political system. Nor will they see the *guru,* the king of that kingdom. For this reason, even as the king is just before them, they find themselves incapable of acknowledging him as king. This fact is indicated in the parable by the words, "But his citizens hated him" (19.14).

Whether or not a disciple realizes the wisdom secret depends upon his level of competence. In Vedānta, these levels are divided into three grades — the fully competent (*uttama-adhikārin*), the mediocre in competentce (*madhyama-adhikārin*) and the least competent (*manda-adhikārin*). The three servants of the parable, entrusted with ten minas, five minas and one mina, respectively, stand for these three grades of disciples. The fully competent one, on becoming enlightened of the secret of the kingdom of God or wisdom, feels the happiness of having gained everything that is to be gained in life. And the ignorant one remains as if having lost everything, even what he possesses. Jesus, therefore, says:

> For I say to you, that to everyone who has will be given; and from him who does not have, even what he has will be taken away from him.
> — 19.26

It is wisdom that makes human life really meaningful and worth living; and the ultimate limit of this wisdom is marked by knowing the secret of the kingdom of God. Those who lack this wisdom are as if already dead; whereas the enlightened live by finding themselves to be immortal. This principle could be seen implied here in an exaggerated tone in the following words of the master who returned as a king:

> But bring here those enemies of mine, who did not want me to reign over them, and slay them before me. — 19.27

The charge brought against Jesus was that he claimed himself to be the king of Israel. But what was the nature of the kingdom of which he was king? This was clarified in our comments on the parable narrated in verses 11-27. The event depicted in verses 28-35 shows how humble was Jesus's kingship. He, as a king followed by his disciples and devotees who form his retinue, rides "royally", mounted on a donkey (or a colt) to Jerusalem. We have already discussed the symbolic meaning of this picture (see chapter 24 of our commentary on Matthew).

As Jesus was travelling royally, mounted on a donkey or a colt, he drew near Jerusalem and saw the city at a distance. Jerusalem was the capital of Judea and the focal point of the Jewish culture. This culture, then, was led by the Pharisees and scribes. Through Jesus cleared the path for universal peace by proclaiming the coming of the kingdom of God, these leaders were unable to perceive it and thus to admit it. Jesus, on seeing Jerusalem, therefore, spontaneously wept for the cultural degeneration this city had undergone, thus:

> If you had known, even you, especially in this your day, the things that make for your peace! But how they are hidden from your eyes.
>
> For the day will come upon you when your enemies will build an embankment around you and close you in on every side,
>
> and level you, and your children within you, to the ground; and they will not leave in you one stone upon another, because you did not know the time of your visitation. — 19.42-44

It is wisdom or the kingdom of God that brings about lasting peace in human life, whether of the individual or of a society or of a nation. And Jesus's coming to the world was as the messenger of this kingdom. But the people of Judea lacked the vision to see the nature of this kingdom of God and to recognize its messenger. They, in one sense, were living in ignorance, blinded by religious dogmatism. This very ignorance, Jesus warns, may become a sort of fortress around Jerusalem that makes it estranged from the rest of the world, and thus naturally subject to many kinds of pressurizations, eventually resulting in the total destruction of the culture, people and city. In such an eventuality, it becomes of no relevance whether such a Judaic culture exists or not. The occurrence of all this happens basically because of the ignorance of the people regarding what kind of person the Messiah they are all waiting for would be, and when he would come. For this reason, even as Jesus lives among them and teaches them as the Christ the Messiah, they fail to recognize him, and do not care to listen to and understand his words that declared the gospel of the kingdom of God. Instead, what they do is level charges against him and lie in wait to catch him and punish him. The reason for all this is stated by Jesus himself, thus, "You did not know the time of your visitation". By "your visitation" Jesus means, the event of the Christ visiting Jerusalem.

Before long, the city of Jerusalem fell and was destroyed, and the Jews became scattered all over the world. A sort of premonition of this historical event of the future could be seen in the above words of Jesus as well.

3.12

Disciples Vary in Kind

CHAPTER 22 describes the scene of the Last Supper. Of the words spoken by Jesus then to his disciples, the following do not find place in either of the gospels we have gone through:

> And the Lord said, "Simon, Simon! Indeed satan has asked for you, that he may sift you as wheat."
>
> But I have prayed for you, that your faith should not fail, and when you have returned to Me, strengthen your brethren. — 22.31-32

There were twelve immediate disciples of Jesus. So far all of them had been seen as equals. But now the scene is about to change. Judas is going to betray his *guru*. Peter, whom Jesus lovingly calls "Simon," is going to deny him three times. Once Jesus was arrested and brought into the house of the high priest, Peter, followed him at a distance. It was then that Peter was constrained to say about Jesus, "I do not know Him." The twelve disciples are going to be proved to be of twelve different types. Peter happened to deny Jesus, and Judas betrayed him, as impelled by satan who entered them. Put otherwise, in a manner that is beyond their control, they became dominated by the demonic nature that was already in them. Satan, in this way, is going to enter all the disciples in different ways, enabling us to decide who is the true disciple and who is not. Jesus, in this sense, tells Peter, "Satan has asked for you, that he may sift you as wheat."

Peter might have denied Jesus merely because he was afraid that he would also be arrested, and in that case, he would not be able to fulfil the mission that Jesus had entrusted him with. And Jesus too prays here for his faith not to fail. Jesus's hope was to build up a church meant to disseminate the gospel of the kingdom of God, on the rock of Peter.

Jesus then says, "When you have returned to Me, strengthen your brethren." It is not immediately clear from these words, from where Peter would be returning to Jesus. The scene where Peter returns after Jesus is put into custody, is about to come. A situation then arises in which the disciples must fulfil their mission in the physical absence of Jesus. He thus could be presumed to be assigning to Peter the responsibility of taking care of the other disciples, as well as those who enter the fold of the new gospel from all over the world. Peter is here expected to return to the eternal presence of Jesus from his physical presence, which merely is transient.

These twelve disciples, before joining up with Jesus as his disciples, were living an ordinary life, each having his own life-interest. Becoming the disciples of Jesus made all of them of one interest in life. Now, with the same interest uniting them, they are destined to show the way of salvation to the people, in the absence of Jesus. It must be the leadership of such a mission that Jesus gave to Peter with these words. Put otherwise, the disciples now have to return to the world as messengers of wisdom without the physical presence of their *guru* to guide them, instead, being guided by feeling his spiritual presence. It must have been as a sort of training for this purpose that Jesus sent them out to the people even while he was living as their *guru*, as is indicated in the next section by Jesus himself.

Verses 35-36 read as follows:

> And He said to them, "When I sent you without money bag, sack and sandals, did you lack anything?" So they said, "Nothing."
>
> Then He said to them, "But now, he who has a money bag, let him take it, and likewise a sack; and he who has no sword, let him sell his garment and buy one."

All these twelve disciples had been residing with Jesus and comprehending the wisdom taught by him. And now the final stage of such a life has come. Along with it, the *guru* is also going to leave the scene. The disciples, from now on, have to go to the world, active as the messengers of the new gospel or wisdom. As Jesus had to suffer himself, so the disciples in their new mission, would also have to face many hindrances and oppositions. They must be well-prepared to face all of such things boldly and wisely, just as Jesus himself did. The war-like preparations to be done on the part of the disciples suggested by Jesus, must refer to such a context. As is to be presumed from the lessons already given by him, and from his character, Jesus would never want his disciples to be engaged in any actual fight using swords.

So long as Jesus was living among them, the disciples were seekers, but from now onwards they are to enter the world as enlightened messengers of wisdom. There is a story very popular in China about a Zen *guru*. A *guru* was walking along a road, carrying a heavy sack on his back. A man who met him asked, "What is the way to liberation?" The *guru* just dropped the sack on the ground and smiled. The man asked again, "How is one to realize it?" The *guru* put the sack back on his back and went on his way.

As part of the means of his search for Reality it is necessary for a seeker to cultivate a sense of detachment towards the world and its affairs. Put otherwise, one has to learn to discriminate the Self from the non-Self, and perceive the former as the Real and the latter as unreal. But upon becoming enlightened, one realizes that it is the Self, which alone has existence, that appears to be the non-Self, as Its fleeting manifest forms. Then, as the manifest forms of the Real, the existence of the world becomes acceptable. Nothing then is to be dismissed as an illusory vision, because every such apparent vision is a manifestation of the Self. While it was discovered as unreal when one was a seeker, it has thus to be re-admitted back as not different from the Real. Jesus also asks his disciples here, as his enlightened apostles, to re-possess whatever had been asked to be given up when they were merely disciples.

Verses 37-38 read as follows:

> For I say to you that this which is written must still be accomplished for Me: "And He was numbered with the transgressors." For the things concerning Me have an end.
>
> Then they said, "Lord, look here are two swords. And He said to them, "It is enough."

The section ends with the words of Jesus, "It is enough." Which are the two swords that are enough for everything? It is not clarified here; so we can only assume.

What happens here is a conflict between two value worlds — one pertaining to spirituality of which Jesus is the king, and the other of the worldly order headed by the governor. The former has a vertical dimension whereas the latter is of a horizontal order. Jesus is about to be arrested by the state authorities who represent the Roman Emperor, on the charge that he claimed himself to be the king of the Jews, which amounts to treason. That means, the conflict is between the kings of two value worlds. The two swords mentioned above could be taken as representing these two worlds. The king of the worldly state has the support of the military. How humble, on the other hand, is the king of the spiritual kingdom has just been seen in the scene of Jesus riding royally on a colt or donkey. Now Jesus is going to prove once more the humility of the world he represents, by submitting himself to the other power. Really the charge against Jesus has value only in the worldly view. And this is the only realm with transgressors. What Jesus says here about himself is, that which is written in the holy scriptures about him necessarily has to be fulfilled (Isiah 52.12), "He was to be numbered with the transgressors." And this will actually take place soon. That means, Jesus's life is going to end, given to worldly powers by being charged with the worldly crime of treason; and so he will be numbered as one among the worldly people. Looked at thus, the passage in Isiah, "And He was to be numbered with the transgressors" yeilds its deeper meaning.

Though the world of spiritual values surrenders here before the worldly ones, Jesus leaves the scene only after entrusting his twelve disciples with the responsibility of taking the spiritual values to the realm of worldly affairs in order to normalize them, and ensure that the duality between the two vanishes in the broad daylight of the non-dual vision of the ultimate Reality. The simple reason is that the ultimate Reality that underlies both the spiritual and worldly aspects of life is one and the same. He expected his disciples would achieve what he could not achieve for them. This achievement is possible only by those who have realized the real content of real wisdom — the spiritual wisdom that subsumes all the value worlds within it. An indication of it could be seen in the words of Jesus, "But now, he who has a money-bag, let him take it, and likewise a sack: and he who has no sword, let him sell his garment and buy one."

In these words Jesus does not accept any defeat of spirituality or any compromise with the worldly values. He intended his disciples, by giving up all worldly possessions, should arm themselves with wisdom and advance as fighters for the cause of real spirituality. But what happened later often indicated otherwise. Admittedly, Christianity became adopted as the state religion by the Roman emperors who acknowledged the Gospels of Jesus as true. But this was not the result of the final victory of wisdom as envisaged by Jesus. It was simply an outcome of a compromise between the two value worlds, as necessitated by some political exigencies on both sides. But Jesus really taught that the worldly values should become surrendered and subservient to the world of spiritual values or to God.

These two value worlds could be thought of yet in another way. The spiritual quest of a seeker-disciple has two simultaneous facets. And for this reason, it is often compared to a sword that has two cutting edges. Here, instead of that, the two edges are simply thought of as two separate swords. One sword is the inner firmness to stand against the temptations of wealth, political power, social status and the like, including what in India are known as *eṣaṇā-traya* (three attractions of life). These latter three are *vitteṣaṇā* (attraction of wealth) *dāreṣanā* (attraction of husband or wife), *putreṣaṇā* (attraction of one's children). The other sword then is the seeker's positive effort to realize the ultimate Reality through disciplined spiritual practices. Upon becoming a *jñānin* (a realized person), what one sees is that whatever one fought against and gave up in the beginning as tempting factors in life, are nothing but the various manifest forms (*vibhūti*s) of the one absolute Reality, i.e., *Brahman* (God). Then one feels, there is nothing to be given up as unreal. It is in such an enlightened awareness that the coming together and becoming one, of the two value worlds becomes actualized.

These two value worlds, in India, are known as *preyas* (happiness derived from worldly possessions) and *śreyas* (highest happiness that derives from wisdom). Naciketas, the disciple-seeker of *Kaṭha Upaniṣad*, is extoled by his *guru* Yama, for his firmness to stand against worldly temptations and his indefatigable quest for knowing the ultimate meaning of life. This episode depicts the differentiation of these two value worlds. *Taittirīya Upaniṣad*, on the other hand, declares:

> He who knows thuswise, becomes well-stabilized in life. He will have enough food. He will become the one who eats food. He will become a great man with good children, enough wealth, the brilliance that goes with the enlightenment of *Brahman*, and also of great fame.
>
> — III.6

This latter Upaniṣadic passage shows how these two value worlds become non-dually one in the man of enlightenment. Such a future attainment by his apostles must have been what was in the mind of Jesus.

Many such interpretations of the two swords are possible. Yet all the human values conceivable as represented by the swords would have a place within the two extreme limits marked by *preyas* and *śreyas*. This must be the reason why Jesus said about the two swords, "It is enough."

Verses 47-53 describe how, as Jesus was praying at the Mount of Olives, Judas, accompanied by the chief priests, the captains of the temple and the elders, drew near to kiss him. They then describe how he (Jesus) reacted to this by asking:

> Judas, are you betraying the Son of Man with a kiss? — 22.48

A disciple kissing his *guru* is a sign of the spiritual rapport between them. We have already noticed that disciples fall into various levels of competence for the attainment of wisdom. It is traditionally accepted in Indian spirituality that the wisdom secret should not be imparted to a disciple who is not fully competent. After completing the wisdom teaching of *Bhagavad-Gītā,* the Guru Kṛṣṇa tells Arjuna:

> This wisdom should in no case be divulged to anyone who is not endowed with austere self-discipline (*tapas*), who is not fully devoted, who is not willing to do service to his *guru,* and who has envy towards Me. — XVIII.67

Similar warnings can be seen given at the end of almost all the Upaniṣads.

Here also Jesus had said in advance that satan would enter each one of the twelve disciples in a different way, and would separate the wheat from the chaff. Judas was the disciple whom satan haunted in the worst way. That means, he was the least competent of all the twelve disciples. The present instance is a glaring example of the treacherous acts that such disciples are likely to carry out. The act of kissing one's *guru,* a sign of the disciples' spiritual rapport with him, is made use of here by the disciple to betray the very same *guru.* And Jesus here indicates that he understands what is happening.

Jesus said earlier in verse 36, "But now, he who has a money-bag, let him take it, and likewise a sack; and he who has no sword, let him sell his garment and buy one." But here, as one of the disciples struck the servant of the high priest and cut-off his right ear with a sword, Jesus says, "Permit even this." He then touches the ear of the servant and heals him. It is clear thus that the swords mentioned earlier are not the literal ones.

3.13

The Crucifixion and Resurrection

THE morning after being arrested, Jesus was led into the council of the elders, consisting of both chief priests and scribes. They asked him, "If you are the Christ, tell us." But he said to them:

> If I tell you, you will by no means believe Me.
>
> And if I ask you, you will by no means answer Me or let Me go.
>
> — 22.67-68

The question of the elders was, "Are you the Christ?" As we have discussed, they represent the Jews who always expect the coming of the Christ. But they are completely ignorant of the way a Christ is to be distinguished. And as long as they remain so, even in case a Christ is born among them, they will never recognize him as the Christ.

The word "Christ" means "the anointed one". Anointed with what? We have seen at the very beginning the picture that Jesus becomes anointed with the Holy Spirit. The Holy Spirit in the biblical context stands for pure wisdom. And what the nature of this pure wisdom is, also has been discussed by us more than once already. This secret of wisdom is not comprehended and realized by all, but only by the real seekers. The elders of the Jews here, and the Jews in general, are not at all seekers. No Master can teach the wisdom secret to any non-seeker. Jesus therefore says, "If I tell you, you will by no means believe."

Suppose Jesus asks them back, What do you mean by "Christ" when you ask me "Are you the Christ?" They will, naturally be unable to answer because they do not know who a Christ is. Therefore Jesus says, "And if I ask you, you will by no means answer Me or let Me go."

Jesus says in verse 31 of chapter 23,

> "If they do these things to the green wood, what will be done in the dry?"

It is wisdom that is likened here to wood. Wisdom could well be thought of as having two kinds of expressable forms. One, as the *guru* who lives as wisdom incarnate, inclusive of his words; and the other, the words of wisdom inherited from the *guru*s of the past. If the former is comparable to green wood or even a living tree, the latter is almost like dry wood. Though the two, in external appearance, may look alike, the former is a living teaching about the living Reality, and the latter were dead letters about the living Reality. Jesus even then continued to be green wood, a living *guru*. It was simply because the Pharisees and the elders lacked the ability to drink in the essential content of wisdom and its liveliness of which Jesus is an embodiment, that they now have trapped him and are about to kill him.

The highest of all values, which makes of a man a real human being, is wisdom. Unfortunately the enemies of that wisdom are also humans. These enemies are none other than those who boast about being the inheritors of the teachings of the ancient *guru*s or prophets, while being unable to drink in the living wisdom content of those teachings. But a living *guru* imbibes his own inner vision of Reality in all Its liveliness, and gives expression to it through words either spoken or written.

It is the *guru*'s words that the seeker must make use of by contemplating on them until he attains the same living Reality that the *guru*'s words were born of. By making use of the *guru*'s words in this way, the seeker imbibes the *guru*'s wisdom, making it his own experience. Unless and until this lively experience is attained, what the seeker gains from those words would only be their literal sense, still dead in nature. Jesus must have felt this eventuality with his words also. Whatever it be, the Jews of those days were a body of people who understood the teachings of the earlier *guru* Moses, in their dead, literal sense, while being proud that they strictly followed his teachings or commandments. And the Pharisees, scribes and elders were their leaders. Their sterile religiosity and hyprocrisy form one of the blatant instances in history of how the green wood, represented by the living teachings of the living *guru*s like Moses, became dry wood.

"Am I not also going to become one such dry wood? To what extent will my teachings also be vitiated by the ignorance of those who follow me?" Such could have been the thoughts of Jesus at that very moment. Actually, Christianity did happen to grow into an official religion that often has little place for the living teachings of the living Christ, but is filled with dead dogmas, rituals and separatism, all derived from the dead letters of the words of Jesus.

At the moment of being crucified Jesus utters:

> Father, forgive them, for they do not know what they do. — 23.34

This is one of the well-known utterances of Jesus. The authorities committed this injustice just because of their ignorance, as was made sufficiently clear in our comment on verse 31. Such acts of ignorance usually have the backing of political authority. The same is true here also. The charge against Jesus, as we know, is that, while the actual ruler of Judea was the Roman Emperor, he claimed himself to be the king of the Jews. No *guru* can teach anyone who not only remains ignorant, but is also ignorant of being ignorant. What all the *guru*s do towards such people is bear with them. It is not any military power, but their spiritual firmness, always accompanied by humility and patience, that forms the strength of all the *guru*s and prophets. Jesus, the Son of Man, is crucified here, but the Son of God in Jesus has no death.

Verses 39-43 of chapter 23 read as follows:

> Then one of the criminals who were hanged blasphemed Him, saying, "If you are the Christ, save yourself and us."
>
> But the other, answering, rebuked him, saying, "Do you not even fear God, seeing you are under the same condemnation?
>
> And we indeed justly, for we receive the due reward for our deeds; but this Man has done nothing wrong."
>
> Then he said to Jesus, "Lord, remember me when You come into Your kingdom."
>
> And Jesus said to him, "Assuredly, I say to you, today you will be with Me in Paradise."

The two criminals who were to be crucified on either side of Jesus were of two different characters. One, like the Pharisees, elders and the general public, mocked Jesus. The second, on the other hand, recognized the guruhood in Jesus. He rebuked the first criminal and glorified Jesus. Interestingly enough, both the criminals demand the same thing: To be saved. One asks him so mockingly to be saved in this world, and the other earnestly to be saved in the kingdom of God. Jesus's response to the latter, it seems, could be elaborated as follows: "You and I alike are going to be killed here; you may be a criminal or an innocent person as I am. Still both of us are to the punished according to certain man-made laws. Yet you know about the truth, and I am the one who visualizes the ultimate Truth. And thus we are almost equals. The greatness of a man is not to be judged with any mere state law as a criterion, but by his wisdom. While everyone — the rulers, priests, scribes, Pharisees, military men, local people, and finally one of the co-condemned criminals — mock me, you, though allegedly a criminal, recognize the greatness of guruhood and therefore honour me.

The last words uttered by Jesus just before breathing his last are thus:

> Father, into Your hands I commend My spirit. — 23.41

The Spirit of Jesus, the real content of his guruhood, is the wisdom to which he became enlightened, that he taught tirelessly to the people, as well as his disciples, and that he lived as an exemplar of. It is this wisdom that Jesus now dedicates to God. It is God (*Brahman*), through self-manifestation, that assumes the form of all the worlds (see the Viśvarūpadarśama Yoga — The Yoga of Cosmic Form of the Absolute — in *Bhagavad-Gītā*, chapter XI). Then the above words of Jesus could also be interpreted thus: "Now I dedicate the wisdom secret I have realized, for the benefit of the entire world and the entire human race."

Verses 1-5 of chapter 24 read as follows:

> Now on the first day of the week, very early in the morning, they, and certain other women with them, came to the tomb bringing the spices which they had prepared.
>
> But they found the stone rolled away from the tomb.
>
> Then they went in and did not find the body of the Lord Jesus.
>
> And it happened as they were greatly perplexed about this, that behold, two men stood by them in shining garments.
>
> Then, as they were afraid and bowed their faces to the earth, they said to them, "Why do you seek the living among the dead?"

A real *guru* is to be seen as having two facets. One is that of an ordinary human being who, like everyone else, lives here, and who teaches those who approach him seeking wisdom, in accordance with the competence of each seeker. This first face also includes his geographical, historical, cultural, educational, linguistic and other background aspects. This person, like every other being, dies and disappears from this world. The other facet is that he is of the eternal wisdom incarnate. The former facet, in the case of Jesus, is signified by his being the Son of Man, and the latter the Son of God. The one that is delivered into the hands of sinful men and crucified is the Son of Man (24.7). The Son of Man ceases to be at the time of the physical death of Jesus, and he then resurrects as the Son of God. All the worldly aspects of the existence of Jesus have come to an end. Now what remains is only the eternal *guru* that has resurrected. And that guruhood has no birth and has no death. To put it in Narayana Guru's words:

> He, having given up the body that really was not his own, has attained, the *Brahman*-body that really is his own.
>
> — verse 2, Obituary to Chattambi Swami

It is in this sense, the men in shining garments ask the women: "Why do you seek the living among the dead?" In an actual *guru* who lives and teaches amongst us, these two facets find non-dual oneness.

The same day two of them were travelling to a village called Emmaus, which was about seven miles from Jerusalem. As they conversed and reasoned about what happened,

> Jesus Himself drew near and went with them.
>
> But their eyes were restrained, so that they did not know Him.
>
> — 24.15-16

We have already seen that the resurrection of Jesus was from non-eternality to eternality, from mortality to immortality. Though the eternal guruhood is as real as someone standing before our eyes, many lack the ability to distinguish that guruhood. Why are they so blind? Simply because ignorance or nescience (*avidyā*) puts a veil over their eyes. Therefore it is said about them, "But their eyes were restrained, so that they did not know Him."

Then they drew near to the village where they were going, and Jesus agreed to spend the night with them as it was too late to proceed further.

> Now it came to pass, as He sat at the table with them, that He took bread, blessed and broke it, and gave it to them.
>
> Then their eyes were opened and they knew Him; and He vanished from their sight. — 24.30-31

As we recognize the immortal *guru* in the mortal person, who lives amongst us as a *guru*, the transient worldly aspects in him become of no relevance. The one who perceives the eternal *guru* in the actually living *guru*, no longer sees the transient *guru* as real. A scene almost similar is portrayed in *Kena Upaniṣad* thus: *Brahman* appeared in the sky in the form of a *yakṣa* (a mysterious being). The gods Fire (Agni) and Air (Vāyu) were deputed by the other gods (*deva*s) to go and find out who or what that *yakṣa* was. Both failed in their mission. Finally Indra approached the *yakṣa*. Just at that moment the *yakṣa* disappeared from the sky and in its place was seen the beautiful Umā, the daughter of the Himalayas. She told Indra that what appeared before him as *yakṣa* was really *Brahman*. Indra thus became the first among the gods (*devas*) to know *Brahman* clearly, and it is for this reason, from the wisdom point of view, that Indra became the chief among gods.

This world undergoes incessant change while existing beginninglessly and endlessly. It is almost like a *yakṣa,* because its secret never becomes known to humans, whatever be the effort they make. But upon realizing that one ultimate Reality, *Brahman,* alone is what appears as the world, one perceives *Brahman* alone as existing and the world of appearance and its mysteriousness become insignificant, as though not existing at all. That is the meaning of the disappearance of the *yakṣa* from Indra's view. Likewise, here the two men or disciples are about to perceive the resurrected eternal *guru* in Jesus, and as soon as their eyes were opened, the apparent, transient perceptible form of Jesus disappears. This episode is portrayed in detail in verses 13-35 of chapter 24.

Verses from 36 up to the end of the Gospel describe the scene of Jesus, after the resurrection, appearing before his disciples and teaching them. "Peace to you" are the words with which he approaches them. But they could not believe him to be the real Jesus because he was already dead, and so they took him to be some spirit. Jesus then asks, "Why are you troubled? And why do doubts arise in your hearts?" (24.38). And then he asks them, "have you any food here?" Then he ate the broiled fish and honeycomb they gave him. By now they could not but believe him. This event also shows that it is not in any spirit form, but with the ordinary body of flesh and bones that he appeared there (24.39). Finally, after winning their belief, Jesus opened their understanding, that they might comprehend the scriptures (24.45). He then spoke to them:

> Repentence and remission of sins should be preached in His name to all nations, beginning at Jerusalem.
>
> And you are the witnesses of these things.
>
> Behold, I send the promise of My Father upon you; but tarry in the city of Jerusalem until you are endued with power from on high.
>
> — 24.47-49

These words of Jesus after his resurrection, when pieced together, could be seen to contain the essential content of the entire teaching given in the Gospel, put in a nutshell. In short, it is for the purpose of condensing the teachings spread through the entire Gospel that this scene in which Jesus re-appears in his ordinary body is reintroduced.

Part IV
The Gospel According to John

4.1

The Word and the World

> In the beginning was the Word, and the Word was with God, and the Word was God. — 1.1

Of all the Gospels, from the philosophical point of view, the one according to John is the most profound. One fundamental problem dealt with in all scriptures concerns the origin of the world. The Holy Bible also begins with the well-known passage of the Genesis, "In the beginning God created the heavens and the earth." Of similar nature are Upaniṣadic passages such as:

> This world in the beginning verily was non-existent. Therefrom indeed was the existent born. — *Taittirīya Upaniṣad* II.7.1

and

> In the beginning, my dear, all this was existence (*sat*), the one only without a second. Some people say, all this in the beginning was non-existence (*asat*), the one without a second, and from that non-existence, emerged the existence of the world.
> — *Chāndogya Upaniṣad* VI.2.1

Narayana Guru also begins his *Darśana-Mālā* (Garland of Visions) with the words:

> All this world, in the beginning, was non-existent indeed. — I.1

The present Gospel also begins with the words "In the beginning." Apparently the "beginning" referred to here is that of the world. That means, a state preceding the coming into being of this world is considered. But such a concept would represent a temporal beginning. Time also should have a beginning. So too should space. It is difficult indeed to think of a state before the beginning of time as well as space. In short, the "beginning" understood here is an unthinkable one, a mystical one, that transcends all temporality and spatiality.

Is it possible to admit such a beginning? The most modern theoretical physics admits this possibility, when it acknowledges that the world began to emerge with a "Big Bang." And it was after this explosion that matter as well as time and space came into being. The explosion, thus, took place neither in time nor in space, nor was there anything to explode. That is to say, modern physics *believes* that it was from pure nothingness that the physical world emerged. The word "believes" is to be emphasized here, for this concept of physics is a mere "belief." Though admitted by modern theoretical physics, doing so goes against the spirit as well as the method recognized to be "scientific." The "beginning" conceived by modern science, thus, is rather a philosophical one rather than a scientific one. It could be said, it is more akin to a religious belief.

This Gospel begins with stating emphatically the philosophical stand, "In the beginning was the Word." The term "Word" used here is the English version of the Greek term "Logos." As everyone familiar with the history of philosophy is well aware, almost all the philosophical terms are given different connotations by each philosopher. So is the case with the word "Logos." The introduction of this word is often credited to the ancient Greek philosopher Heraclitus. According to him, it signifies the cosmic reason that fills and controls the entire cosmos. Similarly, the Upaniṣads of India hold the basic stand that the one all-underlying Supreme Reality (*Brahman*) is pure Consciousness (*cit*) in essence. This *cit* could very well be what "the Word" that was "in the beginning" of the Gospel connotes. This universal Consciousness, in the Semitic religions, is termed "God," and its existence, in the Upaniṣads, is referred to as *sat* (Existence), as we have just seen in the passage quoted above from *Chāndogya Upaniṣad*. Narayana Guru also, at the very middle of his most important work, *Ātmopadeśa Śatakam* (One Hundred Verses of Self-Instruction), says:

> Earth, water, air, fire and space,
> And likewise the I-sense, knowledge, mind,
> Along with waves and ocean,
> And more, all the worlds,
> Become sublimated and attain the state
> Of being pure Consciousness.
>
> — verse 50

Again in the same work, he refers to the actualities of life and the world as:

> A divine sport going on beginningless
> In the one pure, unconditioned Consciousness
> Indeed is all this,
> Thus is it to be understood. — verse 34

These utterences of the seers are not merely some dogmas imposed on us to be believed in blindly. Rather, these are the expressions of the definite conclusions the seers arrived at through their methodic thinking, and confirmed by their direct intuitive experience. The same Reality is revealed in the beginning verse of the Gospel by the Apostle John who was also an outright philosopher.

A "word," in common practice, is rather used as a linguistic expression of some kind of particular knowledge than as signifying pure Consciousness. As some new knowledge, idea, concept or percept gets formulated in our mind, we immediately seek the aid of a linguistic sign we are familiar with in order to express it, and sometimes we even coin new signs for this purpose. All such linguistic signs are known as "words." But "the Word" understood here does not signify any such particular knowledge; it points, on the other hand, to the universal Consciousness that controls the entire cosmos, as well as that which becomes manifest as a specific knowledge. Perhaps it is because English and many other languages lack a proper word to signify this universal Consciousness that the term "the Word" with a capital W is adopted here to give it an expression. But in the Sanskrit language there is a term to signify this one universal Consciousness — the well-known *AUṀ*, pronounced *OṀ*. The entire text of *Māṇḍūkya Upaniṣad* tries to clarify how this Word contains such a connotation. In short, "the Word" with which this Gospel begins could well be treated as equivalent to the word *AUṀ* of the Vedāntic context.

Auṁ is a word formed of one syllable. A syllable, in Sanskrit, is known as *akṣara,* which also means "that which is imperishable." All the specific bits of knowledge that we acquire from time to time are perishable. All such fleeting knowledges get formulated in one Consciousness, as modes of its manifestation. That one Consciousness does not cease to be. And move, this one Consciousness is what controls all the worlds by assuming the form of those worlds. We do not wish here to enter the problem of how it does so. But there should be a linguistic sign to denote that imperishable Consciousness, and that sign also should be imperishable (*akṣara*). *Auṁ* is that imperishable (*akṣara*) sign formed of a single syllable (*akṣara*) that denotes the one indestructible (*akṣara*) Reality or Consciousness.

The Gospel then says, "The Word was with God, and the Word was God." It is but natural with the Semitic religions to conceive the idea of a personal God seated on High, creating and controlling the world. As related to such a context, it could well be said, the Word we have just conceived, was with God, because the universal

Consciousness can abide only in God, the creator and controller of the universe, as is the case with individual consciousnesses abiding and functioning in each individual. But this togetherness of God and Consciousness attains perfection only when the distinction between the two as substance and attribute vanishes, and the two become non-dually one; that means, God is realized as Consciousness in essence, and Consciousness is experientially perceived as God. It is in this profound sense that the cryptical statement "The Word was with God" is to be meditated upon. This non-duality is made more explicit in the statement that follows immediately, "The Word was God." This latter statement totally wipes out any lingering duality between the Word and God. In India, when *AUṀ* is conceived as *īśvara-vācakaḥ* (the word that designates God), *AUṀ* is thought of not merely as a characteristic feature that abides in God, but is conceived and worshipped as God Himself. The words of the Gospel, "The Word was God" thus can be understood and appreciated from the Vedāntic perspective, in this non-dual sense.

The second verse reads as follows:

"He was in the beginning with God."

Two questions could be thought to arise from this verse. One, it was stated in the first verse itself, "The Word was with God." Then, why is it repeated here with the words "in the beginning" added? And two, the Word, in many of the world languages (Sanskrit is an exception in this respect) is not treated as of masculine gender. Then why is "the Word" referred to here as "He?"

The first doubt could be cleared thus: Verse 1 stated merely a pure metaphysical stand, and what was discredited then was the duality of the Word (Consciousness) and God. It is going to be followed by showing how the actual world emerged from the Word that was God. That means, the present context is that of the transition from showing the metaphysical Reality to revealing the process of creative self-unfoldment of that Reality, resulting in the emergence of the apparent world. The words "in the beginning" of verse 2 thus refer to the initial stage of the self-expression of the Word or God. Put otherwise, the actuality of the world is now about to emerge from the one metaphysical Reality. The statement "He was in the beginning with God" indicates that the potentials for the emergence of the world were originally one with God. The Word, in other words, assumes here the role of being the Creator of the world. The same is portrayed in *Īśa Upaniṣad* as follows:

> He assigns throughout endless years various objects according to their natures. — Stanza 8

The words "He assigns . . . various objects according to their natures", imply that the apparent world, in its entire structural perfection, remained as unactualized potentials in God or the Word, and that these potentials became actualized as willed by the same Word.

Now let us think of why "the Word" is referred to as "He." Though God can be neither male nor female, referring to God as "He" is a common practice. That "the Word was God" we have already conceded. Whatever then is true with God should be true with "the Word" also. If God could be treated, at least in linguistic usage, as masculine, then the same could be done with "the Word" also.

Verse 3 of chapter 1 reads as follows:

> All things were made through Him, and without Him nothing was made that was made.

What is signified by "Him", as we have just seen, is nothing other than the one ultimate Reality that could on the one hand be called "the Word" and on the other "God." How the world originated from this one Reality, is one of the major problems dealt with in all the basic scriptures. The same is true with modern physics. According to science, as we have already seen, a big explosion named the "Big Bang" took place in nothingness. Before this explosion there was no matter; there was no time; there was no space. The expansion of the universe that began with that big explosion continues even now. No one knows when it will end.

As a result of this expansion, the evolution of matter occurred, resulting in the formation of the physical world. If an explosion should happen in a mysterious nothingness, and if a fully systematized world should emerge as the result of this evolution, we should admit the existence and functioning of a knowledge that properly directs this process of evolution, resulting even in the emergence of the human mind.

Where does, or did, that knowledge exist? It can only be in the causal nothingness. One Reality alone is there that can exist in nothingness; it is Consciousness. Therefore we have to concede, even though modern physics cannot admit, that what existed as nothingness in the perception of physics, was the beingness of Consciousness. We must acknowledge that the progress of scientific enquiry is also guided by the function of Consciousness. That means, without Consciousness existing, even to think that Consciousness emerged from matter would not be possible. For all these reasons, the *ṛṣis* of ancient India intuitively perceived the ultimate Reality as pure and unconditioned Consciousness (*cit*) in essence, and they called it *Ātman* (*Brahman*). The Apostle John also, as the present passage testifies, had the same perception of Reality and the world.

Everything, from the total cosmic system to the minutest of all individual entities, as treated both in science and philosophy, has emerged or been created. In this sense these are termed "effects." That from which or because of which this emergence or creation of "effects" happens is known as "cause." For example, the emergence of a pot is from clay. The pot then is the effect and clay the cause. Apart from clay, the potter also has to be there to effect the emergence of the pot. Therefore, the potter here is called the "efficient cause" and the clay the "material cause." The former is called *nimitta-kāraṇa* and the latter *upādāna-kāraṇa* in Vedānta.

The world also needs both these causes in order for it to emerge. These two causes, in the case of the world, is the one *Ātmā* alone, one *Brahman* alone, one "Word" alone, for no other Reality existed in the beginning. In the case of the pot, these two causes exist separately. But the causal Reality of the world is one alone, and cannot be two. The Gospel, therefore, says here:, "All things were made through Him, and without Him, nothing was made that was made."

This "Him" is none other than the "Word" that was God, the one alone that was in the beginning. The very first *mantra* of *Aitareya Upaniṣad* also categorically says, "*Ātmā* alone was verily the one that existed here in the beginning." That one God alone is the cause of everything is the basic tenet of all the major religions, except perhaps Buddhism. This one cause, which is at the same time both the efficient cause and material cause of the world, in the context of causality, in Vedānta, is termed *abhinna-nimitta upādāna-kāraṇa* (the material-cum-efficient cause). In short, "the Word" or pure Consciousness is the material cause as well as the efficient cause of the world. The world's apparent existence, therefore, is only as a manifest form of "the Word" or Consciousness and has no existence separate from it. Narayana Guru corroborates this stand as follows:

From the one pure and unconditined Consciousness
Arise countless sparks creating the impression
Of the existent and the non-existent alike,
Which together constitute the world.

And thus, it is to be realized,
Nothing has being apart from the beingness
Of one pure Consciousness or Ātmā.
This enlightenment would reveal
The unitiveness of Truth.
— *Ātmopadeśa Śatakam,* verse 89

The above words of the Gospel also reveal the same reality.

Verses 4-5 read as follows:

> In Him was life, and the life was the light of men.
>
> And the light shines in the darkness, and the darkness did not comprehend it.

The exceptional peculiarity of planet Earth is the countless living species in it. Whether life exists on any other orbiting objects in the endlessly expanding universe is a problem that the human mind remains yet incapable of resolving. It is true that the search for the possibility of life on Mars, the planet nearest to Earth, is going on among astrophysicists. Still, finding out for sure about the existence of life, if any, in the farthest limits of the boundless cosmos may always remain something inaccessible to human effort.

Be that as it may, how the phenomenon of life originated on the earth still remains a mystery. Scientists are continuing their search and sometimes we see press reports indicating that they have taken one step more towards the final answer. All such searches are fundamentally based upon the notion that everything originates from matter, and so they think, life's origin also must be so. No one seems to have asked, "Is this notion scientific?" Nor is it asked, "Is it not a belief just like any religious belief?" As long it is not a scientifically proven truth, it has to remain a belief. Nevertheless, it is with this notion as its foundation that the entire edifice of current scientific thinking is erected.

Thus scientists search for the origin of life in the physically material proteins, by analysing their subtle sub-atomic structures. Protein, at the sub-atomic level, is merely an aggregate of the physical particles of energy or of the physical waves of energy. Out of such physical entities, how does the non-physical aspect of life awaken so that it can control the physical body itself? This problem still remains unresolved. As long as the scientific enquiry is made based on the notion that life emerged from matter, it seems, the problem how material proteins and the non-material aspect of life are related, will remain a mystery.

This problem is approached by scriptures differently. First of all, they accept one ultimate Reality to be the material cause as well as the efficient cause of the world (*prapañca*). And the world conceived thus is inclusive of both mind and matter, both the non-physical animating principle and physical matter. Mind and matter, thus, are not seen to be related together as cause and effect, but as two self-unfolded forms, opposite in nature, of the one ultimate Reality. The life principle, called *cetanā* in Sanskrit, and referred to as soul in many religions, is thus perceived in scriptures as undifferentiated from the one ultimate Reality, as is physical matter. This Reality, when closely examined, would be found to be unconditioned Consciousness in essential content, called *cit* or *saṁvit* in Sanskrit. This is the basic teaching of the Upaniṣads as well. Consciousness is the well-acknowledged external sign of what is called "life" in the Gospel here. The words of the Gospel "In Him was life" are thus to be understood as signifying the inseparable oneness of the ultimate Reality or "the Word" and the life-principle.

This one ultimate Reality, pure Consciousness in essence, by assuming the forms of the thinking mind and its search for Reality, thus appears also as the distinguishing feature of the phenomenon called human life. This is the reason why the human species is counted to be of the highest order. In this sense, it is said here, "The life was the light of man." Consciousness, the most apparent distinguishing feature of life, as everyone experiences directly, is brightness in essence; it is never felt as darkness.

For brightness to stand out as brightness, there should exist darkness for its background. Bringing a lit lamp to a place already brightly lit would not be of much significance. But the same lamp brought to a dark place makes it shine brightly. The same is true with the brightness that we call consciousness or "life." As we have discussed, the life principle in Vedānta is termed *cit*, meaning consciousness. The opposite of *cit* is *acit* (non-consciousness) or *jaḍa* (inert matter). As related to the internal function of consciousness, brightness signifies wisdom and darkness ignorance. It is where ignorance dominates that wisdom should shine. There is no need of wisdom shining where wisdom already reigns. The words of the Gospel "The brightness shines in darkness" are to be evaluated and understood in the light of all this. Ignorance is to be perceived also as forming the opposite pole of wisdom. This is one of the reasons why *Bhagavad-Gītā* along with portraying the self (*Ātmā*) as "The effulgence of all that shines," states also, "It is beyond darkness" (XIII.17).

Matter could be perceived to form the dark pole, opposite of the brightness that consciousness is, and likewise *jaḍa* as that of *cit,* and ignorance as that of wisdom. Yet, the dark pole never has control over the bright pole. Ignorance never controls wisdom. *Jaḍa* never controls *cit.* Darkness really is not an existent entity. It merely is the absence of light. The non-existent darkness can never be in control of the existent brightness. Ignorance (*ajñāna*) likewise is the absence of wisdom (*jñāna*). So too is the *jaḍa* the absence of *cit,* and matter the absence of consciousness. *Jaḍa* (inert matter), therefore, has no existence of its own; its existence is only as an experience formed in *cit* (consciousness). That means, the apparent existence of *jaḍa* happens in consciousness, and hence has no existence of its own. Matter, in other words, does not control mind; on the contrary, it is consciousness that controls the existence of matter. Put otherwise, it is brightness that controls darkness. Perceiving intuitively all these nuances, John says, "The darkness did not comprehend it." The suggestion is that ignorance has never been in control of wisdom. In our day-to-day life also, we do not see ignorance giving shape to our life or knowledge. It is knowledge, on the contrary, that guides our life. We could even say that it is consciousness that functions as any lack of knowledge, with full control over it.

So far we have been examining in detail the first five verses of the Gospel According to John. These initial verses could be considered the most important ones of the Gospel, as they condense the philosophical vision of the Apostle. We repeat these verses here:

> In the beginning was the Word, the Word was with God, and the Word was God.
>
> He was in the beginning with God.
>
> All things were made through Him, and without Him nothing was made that was made.
>
> In Him was life, and the life was the light of men.
>
> And the light shines in the darkness, and the darkness did not comprehend it.

Those who are familiar with Vedānta would find these sentences to portray the creation picture given throughout the Upaniṣads, but presented here in terms more familiar to the Semitic religions. This picture could be summarized as follows:

One *Ātmā* (conceived in the Gospel here as "the Word") alone existed in the beginning; *Ātmā* alone exists now in the form of the world; *Ātmā* alone will continue to exist forever. This *Ātmā* is unconditioned Consciousness (*cit*) in essence. It thus is a functional living Reality, because Consciousness never remains functionless. Infinite are such functional potentials latent in *Ātmā*. Being conscious of Itself, *Ātmā* desires to perceive for Itself, what are such possibilities. This desire arises simply for the joy of perceiving Its own hidden possibilities, just as a child gives shape to many things, and then destroys them, simply for the sheer joy of bringing out the possibilities hidden within himself. This self-unfoldment of *Ātmā* is a process that continues forever, because the possibilities hidden in *Ātmā* are infinite.

This process means that *Ātmā* must assume the form of the subjective aspect (again called *cit*) on the one side, and the objective aspect (*jaḍa*) on the other. Of these two manifest aspects of *Ātmā*, the *jaḍa* or the inert and gross matter-aspect is of the nature of darkness; whereas the *cit* or the subtle mind-aspect is of the nature of brightness. How does the Self, in essence pure effulgence, give birth to darkness? And by remaining in that darkness, how does it also function as the light of men? These questions are answered by Vedāntins thus: It is all owing to the indefinable creative urge called *māyā* inherent in *Ātmā*. A vivid picture of how the non-dual Consciousness (the Word), because of Its own *māyā*, assumes the forms of both *avidyā* (ignorance or nescience) and *vidyā* (knowledge or wisdom) is portrayed by Narayana Guru as follows:

> Seen from one side, there are various activities;
> These seem to be real because of nescience (*avidyā*).
> Seen from the other, there is perceived
> Pure and unconditioned Consciousness alone,
> And this is what constitutes
> The realm of true knowledge (*vidyā*).
> It is *māyā* that makes the real
> Appear always thus as two-sided.
> The enlightened awakening that transcends this duality
> Alone assures the turīya state. — *Ātmopadeśa Śatakam*, verse 72

Avidyā has never comprehended *vidyā; jaḍa* has never comprehended *cit;* ignorance has never comprehended knowledge or wisdom; darkness has never comprehended brightness. Inspired by Its own *māyā*, the Word, God, pure Consciousness or *Ātmā*, unfolds Itself, and assumes the forms of opposites like brightness and darkness, mind and matter, subject and object, *cit* and *jaḍa*, the internal and the external, the subtle and the gross, cause and effect, and the like. The aggregate of all such dualities constitutes the apparent world.

Even when such a mysterious self-expression occurs in It, *Ātmā* remains unaffected in its essential content, even as gold remains gold itself when, over time, it assumes the forms of various kinds of ornaments. That is to say, God remains unaffected even when the world is created by Him from Himself; so too "the Word" remains unaffected; Consciousness Reality remains unaffected; brightness remains unaffected.

Thus a creation picture, given in terms of cause and effect, is evidently brought to relief in these first five verses of the Gospel. Even while doing so, the inseparable oneness of cause and effect is retained perfectly. Such is the clear philosophical or rather mystical vision that these five verses render intuitively perceptible to the meditative eyes of a contemplative seeker.

4.2

The Mission of Jesus

VERSES 6-8 of chapter 1 are as follows:

> There was a man sent from God, whose name was John.
>
> This man came for a witness, to bear witness of the Light, that all through him might believe.
>
> He was not that Light, but was sent to bear witness of that Light.

The Missions of John and Jesus

These verses summarily indicate the nature of the birth of John the Baptist, the nature of his life's mission, and the nature of the relationship he had with the one Light. All this concerning Jesus will also be stated in verses 9-13 to follow. A comparison of these two sections would be an interesting study in this context, and before entering it we quote below the verses 9-13 also:

> That was the true Light, which gives light to every man who comes into the world.
>
> He was in the world, and the world was made through Him, and the world did not know Him.
>
> He came to His own, and His own did not receive Him.
>
> But as many as received Him, to them He gave the right to become children of God, even to those who believe in His name:
>
> who were born, not of blood, nor of the will of the flesh, nor of the will of men, but of God.

That everything that was made through the Word that was God, the Light not comprehended by any darkness, we have just seen in verses 1-5 above. In its light is to be understood the coming into being of John the Baptist as well as Jesus. Just as everything was created of the Word, John and Jesus were also incarnate forms of the same Light that was the Word or God. But different were the ways in which the two functioned, and thus the ways in which the two were related to God, their source-Light. John not only was originated from God "the Light" but also was "sent from God." What was the purpose of sending him to this world? "To bear witness to the Light" as is stated clearly in verse 8. Which "Light" is it? It could be the Light that God is, and could also be the "true Light" that Jesus was (verse 9). What John the Baptist could do was simply exhort to the world, "Repent, for the kingdom of heaven is at hand" (Matthew 3.2). This was just a call or warning, and nothing more. He really was bearing witness to the world that the one (Jesus) to follow him was truly capable of teaching the world. Jesus would teach how to become one with the Light, after people repented. John was capable of baptizing people with mere water unto repentence, so that the one who was to follow him would baptize them with the Holy Spirit and fire. He admitted that he was not worthy even to loosen the sandal strap of the one mightier than him to follow.

If John the Baptist was a man sent into the world by the true Light of God, then Jesus could be considered that very Light Itself, having come down to the world in the form of a man. It is true that everything emerges from God; but in the usual course many remain unaware of this reality. They, called the ignorant, do not have the occasion to live as that true Light even when being that Light. Given that oneself is true Light Itself, to know that everything emerges from the true Light and to perceive that everything emerges from oneself are equally true. Evidently this latter perception also remains beyond the reach of the ignorant. The words of the Gospel, "He was in the world, and the world was made through Him, and the world did not know Him" are to be understood as related to this context.

The Immortal Man

God had no origin, and will not cease to exist either. Upon realizing oneself to be that God in essential context, one does not perceive oneself as a person born on a particular day, but to exist beginninglessly and endlessly. In this sense it is here said, "He was in the world"(1.10).

God and the World

How are God and the world related? It is like the relation between gold and the forms of ornaments it assumes. Gold's existence is expressed in the form of ornaments, or in some such given shapes. That means, such forms are the real abode of gold. Likewise, the world is the real abode of God or of the Word. Given that Jesus is that Word become incarnate, his coming could well be spoken of as, "He came to His own" (1.11). Such is the way Jesus and the world are related — just as God and the world are related.

The Light Shines in the Darkness

Nevertheless, it is not with the awareness that the one Light or God is what fills their being, by which people usually live. In that respect, they live in darkness. Even when they thus are in darkness, the true Light or God always exists in them as their essential context and shines in them as their apparent existence, as well as their various kinds of knowledge. This is also the sense in which it was said earlier in verse 5 above, "The Light shines in the darkness."

But as we fully believe in the truthfulness of the words of an enlightened *guru,* and as we, with that belief as our firm basis, direct our search for Reality inwardly towards our own being, then we realize ourselves to be the children of God. Therefore it says here, "But as many as received Him, to them He gave the right to become children of God, even to those who believe in His name."

The Birth of Jesus

In the three Gospels already examined, the birth stories of both John and Jesus are described summarily or in detail, and in more actual terms. But the present Gospel adopts a different way in this respect, as in other respects also. The nature of the births of both men are merely suggested poetically and in a symbolic way, as clothing for a subtle philosophy. Concerning John's birth, it says only that he "was a man sent from God" and that "He was not the Light, but was sent to bear witness of that Light." Jesus's birth, on the other hand, is indicated by saying, "That was the true Light which gives light to any man who comes into the world," and that he was "born not of blood, nor of the will of the flesh, nor of the will of man, but of God."

In some translations of the Bible, the above verse (1.13) is preceded by the words "who was." Such a rendering would mean that it is Jesus who is "the one born, not of blood." But according to the translation given here, the verse above is preceded by the words "who were." This alternate rendering would mean that it is those who believe in Jesus's name who "are born, not of blood." From the Vedāntic perception, both meanings yielded from the different translations are perfectly acceptable.

In the former sense, the verse here concerns the birth of Jesus as the Son of God. Though Jesus was the son of Mary, the wife of Joseph, he was not the son of Joseph, but was begotten by God. And this is one of the basic tenets of Christianity. We have already discussed in detail, while commenting on the Gospel According to Matthew, the way this tenet is understandable from the Vedāntic perspective.

Let us now see how the same text is to be understood if it is taken in the latter sense of "who were."

The God of the biblical context, as we have already seen, stands for what in Vedānta is called *Brahman* (*Ātman*). This one ultimate Reality, as causal to all beings and all the worlds, is portrayed in *Taittirīya Upaniṣad* (3.1) as follows:

> That verily from which beings are born, that by which those that are born live, into which they finally reach and merge — seek to know That. That is *Brahman*.

The birth of beings, according to our understanding, happens as a result of the sexual union between males and females. But, when the *Praśna Upaniṣad*, in its first chapter, upon pondering on this phenomenon of reproduction, advances the idea that there exists a Consciousness or Knowldege that systematizes life and its unbroken continuance through the union of males and females. This Consciousness is considered the original cause of the birth of everything. That means, a male begetting an offspring with a female forms part of the life system structured by that one causal Consciousness. This emergence of beings, including humans, happens not as willed by man, nor as willed by carnal desire; it simply happens as willed by Consciousness–Reality Itself. The present passage of the Gospel, "Who were born, not of blood, nor of the will of the flesh, nor of the will of man, but of God" is thus highly reminiscent of what the first chapter of *Praśna Upaniṣad* pictures.

The Word Became Flesh

Verses 14 reads thus:

> And the Word became flesh and dwelt among us, and we behold His glory, the glory as of the only begotten of the Father, full of grace and truth.

By "the Word became flesh" we mean the one eternal and abstract Reality or Consciousness as It assumes all fleeting, apparently concrete forms. We have already seen how the one *Ātmā* (pure Consciousness), according to the Upaniṣadic concept, desired, "Let me become many" (*Chāndogya Upaniṣad* 6.2.3; *Taittirīya Upaniṣad* 2.6.3), and how that desire resulted in the emergence of the world from that very same

Consciousness. Many are the individuated forms that emerged thus, and Jesus was one among such. But others live in ignorance of their real source, thinking they originated from their parents. Jesus, on the other hand, who knew the reality concerning the origin of everything, saw his own origin in "the Word that was God." And this wisdom raised him to the status of a *guru*. In the context of guruhood, the dialectical unity of the eternal and abstract *guru*-principle, and the transient human *guru* who lives in flesh and blood, is also relevant. It is when the eternal *guru*-principle assumes the form of an actual *guru* who lives among the people teaching them, that the eternal guruhood really becomes of value in the context of actual human life. In this sense it is said here "And the Word became flesh and dwelt among us, and we beheld His glory, the glory as of the only begotten of the Father, full of grace and truth."

Full of Grace and Truth

When an actual *guru* thus lives among us, approachable by everyone and available to anyone, two postitive aspects could be thought to come together and blend in him. One is truth and the other grace. Truth is indicative of the eternal ultimate Reality, and it is to be properly understood. Its opposite, untruth, will never be present in a *guru*. Grace, on the other hand, is not an eternal principle to be understood, but is a positive value that ensures happiness to oneself and others, and also makes life graceful. This is something to be practised. Its opposite also will not be present in a *guru*'s life. If truth is considered to have a vertical dimension, then grace has a horizontal dimension. Just as a vertical axis and a horizontal axis meet at a neutral point, when these two (truth and grace) non-dually meet in the actual life of a person, one complementing the other, he could be counted to have attained the highest glory of a perfect *guru*.

The Only Begotten of the Father

A *guru* is the embodiment of the perfection of wisdom. The luminous clarity and brightness of wisdom is always found in a *guru*. This personal luminosity of wisdom is called *brahma-varcas* in the Upaniṣads. The same luminosity is now seen in Jesus also, termed here as "the glory as of the only begotten of the Father." That the "Father" of the biblical context is equivalent to the one all-underlying Consciousness or *Brahman*, we have already noticed.

In what sense is Jesus to be understood as the only begotten of the Father? The Reality causal to everything phenomenal is one, the phenomenal world that emerged from that Reality is one; and the phenomenon of life in that world is also one. The unity of the apparent world and the phenomenon of life, admittedly, is the enigma before us that makes us think philosophically. Put conversely, the world and the phenomenon of life in it form an integral whole; the Reality that controls it is one; and the wisdom we have of that Reality is also one. The *guru* who lives as the embodiment of that wisdom and who reveals that wisdom is also one. For this reason only one eternal *guru* is in all the numerous actual *guru*s who live in flesh and blood, whatever be the temporal and spatial gaps between them. We have already seen, how that one *guru* is the Son of God. Therefore each such *guru,* that has emerged at any time or clime, is the one begotten of God. Put otherwise, each living *guru* is the one begotten of God in the sense that he is the embodied form of the one abstract and eternal *guru*-principle. Therefore, the part of the verse 14 "We beheld His glory, the glory of the only begotten of the Father," proclaims that we are witnessing the presence of that glory in Jesus. What we are witnessing here perceptually in Jesus was previously witnessed by John as the one *guru* prophesied in scriptures, as indicated in verse 15 which reads as follows:

> John bore witness to Him and cried out, saying, "This was He of whom I said, 'He who comes after me is preferred before me, for He was before me'."

The sentence "We behold His glory, the glory of the only begotten of the Father" clearly demonstrates that we are now perceptually feeling the presence of Christ's glory. The same glory was previously confirmed by John as being the *guru*'s glory that is prophesied in the scriptures. In Indian thought, the former kind of knowing is called *pratyakṣa-jñāna* or *yukti,* and the latter kind of knowing *śabda-jñāna* or *stuti.* In modern Western thought, they might be considered as a posteriori and a priori respectively. So this verse means that what we directly witness (*pratyakṣa-jñāna*) as Christ's glory is confirmed by scriptural evidence (*śabda-jñāna*). Thus, the two means of knowledge validate each other to become one non-dual intuitive perception.

He Was Before Me

The words "He was before me" of John the Baptist, in verse 15 quoted above, deserves our special attention. To claim that one who is to follow existed before the one who is followed, from the ordinary perspective, makes no sense. But when the word "He," as was stated earlier, is understood as signifying the eternal *guru*, this claim becomes fully meaningful. Jesus will also say, in the very Gospel (verse 8.58), "Most assuredly, I say to you, before Abraham was I Am."

Guru's Grace

What we saw in verse 15 is the indubitability of Jesus's guruhood (*sad-guru*). The presence of such a *guru* is experienced by those around him as a feeling of intense grace streaming towards them for no apparent reason. And they will feel that this *guru* is the very fullness of grace. He is experienced so simply because he is indeed the embodiment of full and perfect grace, which is the Father in heaven, the one Absolute Self. Thus, when the grace of God fills the being of a living *guru*, and when this grace in him streams forth into a seeker or certain seekers, then the life's mission of a living *guru* could be considered fulfilled. This fulfilment is admitted in regards to Jesus, as verse 16 reads thus:

> And of His fullness we have all received, and grace for grace.

Revaluation of Judaism

Verse 17 reads as follows:

> For the Law was given through Moses, but grace and truth came through Jesus Christ.

Jesus, the fullness of grace, happened to be born among the Jews. The religion and life of the Jews had then taken a rigid shape by a mechanistic following of the ten commandments of God as given by Moses. But God is not merely a law-giver; He is also the fullness of grace, the grace-giver as well as a giver of the Truth that underlies this grace. When the laws of Moses were imbued with Truth and grace by Jesus as the representative of God, those laws became molten down and reshaped as these two laws:

> You shall love the Lord your God with all your heart, with all your soul, with all your mind, and with all your strength.
>
> You shall love your neighbour as yourself. — Mark 12.30-31

In the place of certain laws that are to be followed as commanded by formal religion, Jesus here brings back to life two even more ancient laws (Leviticus 19.18). These are to be willingly followed, for they are imbued with the values that make life meaningful. This is the sort of revaluation effected by Jesus in the realm of human law.

God is Invisible

Verse 18 reads as follows:

> No one has seen God at any time. The only begotten Son, who is in the bosom of the Father, He has declared Him.

We have already examined in what sense the invisibility of God is to be understood. The one ultimate Reality as such is abstract. No one perceives directly anything abstract, for it has no form of its own. It is similar to the invisibility of the gold-reality pure and simple, the indestructible substance in all the destructible ornaments; ornaments alone are visible. All such fleeting ornamental forms are assumed by the indestructible and formless gold-substance. Without this gold's existence, no ornamental form could appear. Likewise, without the existence of the invisible and indestructible Reality known as God, and without His grace, I cannot appear to be, you cannot appear to be, the world as a whole cannot appear to be. Just as if an ornament becomes aware, "I am really Gold," each one of us should become aware "I am really that eternal God." A *guru* is a person who is well aware of this reality. If an ornament could perceive its being in gold, similar would be the way an enlightened person perceives his being in God. Put in terms familiar to the Semitic religions, one perceives oneself in the bosom of God. Only a *guru* of such a perception can lead the ignorant towards the enlightenment, "I too am God."

The Gospel Is Summarized

The first eighteen verses of this Gospel could well be treated as containing the essential content of the philosophy of the Apostle John, given expression to in a summary fashion, with Jesus as the symbolic instrument. The rest of the Gospel, then, can be seen merely as an elaborated version of the same philosophy, expounded in the form of the actual words of Jesus, the living *guru*.

This Gospel begins by introducing the Word as God. And the present section (verses 1-18) ends by saying that the only begotten Son of that Word declared the secret of the very same Word. In other words, it ends where it began. *Chāndogya Upaniṣad* begins by enunciating a new meaning, of wisdom significance, of the monosyllable *AUṀ*, which otherwise was of a ritualistic import forming part of the ritual *udgītha*. It ends with the realization of the very same meaning of *AUṀ* to be one's own self-content. The present context in the Gospel is similar. The Word or God, in the Upaniṣads, is called *Brahman* (*Ātman*). The one who knows the secret of *Brahman*, equivalent to the only begotten Son, is known in Vedānta as *Brahmavit*. The Upaniṣads give emphasis to the reality that a *Brahmavit* is *Brahman* indeed (e.g., *Muṇḍaka Upaniṣad* 3.2.9) because knowing *Brahman* means realizing oneself to be *Brahman* in essence. Put in biblical terms, the one who knows the secret of "the Word" is the Word Itself in essence; or the one who knows the secret of God is God Himself in essence. And he always spontaneously declares that very secret to the world.

4.3

The First Disciples

THIS section of the Gospel comprising verses 35-42 describes how two disciples of John the Baptist followed Jesus and how one of them found the Messiah in Jesus. It then describes how Simon Peter, upon being brought to Jesus by Andrew, is acknowledged by Jesus as his first disciple, later to be called Cephas (a Stone). These verses read as follows:

> Again the next day, John stood with two of his disciples.
>
> And looking at Jesus as He walked, he said, "Behold the lamb of God!"
>
> The two disciples heard him speak, and they followed Jesus.
>
> Then Jesus turned, and seeing them following, said to them, "What do you seek?" They said to Him "Rabbi, where are You staying?"
>
> He said to them, "Come and see." They came and saw where He was staying, and remained with Him that day (now it was about the tenth hour).
>
> One of the two who heard John speak, and followed Him, was Andrew, Simon Peter's brother.
>
> He first found his own brother Simon, and said to him, "We have found the Messiah" (the Christ).
>
> And he brought him to Jesus. Now when Jesus looked at him, He said, " You are Simon, the son of Jonah. You shall be called Cephas."

John the Baptist never claimed himself to be a prophet, though others acclaimed him as one. The true prophet, according to John, was Jesus, the lamb of God. Having recognized him as such, John's simple mission, as was stated earlier, was to cry in the wilderness, "Make straight the way of the Lord." There is really a sort of inconsistency in "crying in the wilderness" and "making straight the way of the Lord." "To make straight the way of the Lord" admittedly means making the path of the real prophet who was to follow, as easy as possible. But the ease for this was made by John in the wilderness. Who is there to listen to it? These aspects could well be seen to come together in the actual life of Jesus. A great multitude was there to believe in him and also to follow him. Still he was being hounded all through his life. The Pharisees and scribes were constantly pursuing him, and finally they did trap and crucify him. The straightening of his path that John the Baptist intended to ensure had thus remained a cry in the wilderness. Earlier scriptures also had prophesied what would happen to Jesus at the end of his life, though born as the Son of God. All this is to be kept in mind as we correlate the parts, "The voice of the one crying in the wilderness", and "To make straight the way of the Lord" of verse 1.23, as related to the life of Jesus. In other words, the nature of the Jesus's life can be seen hinted in these words of his harbinger.

Seekers Find Their Guru

It is well-recognized in the Vedāntic context that a true seeker finds a true *guru* who corresponds to all his personal traits only by chance, or as decided by God. In this scene also, Andrew and another man were already disciples of John the Baptist. But John had already made it clear that he was not the true *guru* or Christ; yet he knew who really was.

John looked at Jesus as he was walking along that path and said to his disciples, "Behold the lamb of God!" That means, he shows to his own disciples who the real *guru* is. And so two of his disciples follow Jesus immediately. Thus, instead of the disciple finding the true *guru* by chance or by God's grace, here the true *guru* is shown to the disciples by the one who was sent by God as his predecessor, to make straight his path.

A Seeker's Goal

Jesus, on seeing the two following him, asks them, "What do you seek?" A *guru* is always followed by those seeking something. *Bhagavad-Gītā* (VII.16) says, four types of people usually seek a *guru*'s guidance. It says:

> Arjuna, of four types are the virtuous who adore Me meditatively: the distressed, the knowledge-seeker, the aspirant of wealth and the wise.

As is clear from these words, people with various interests, ranging from the desire for worldly wealth to the highest kind of wealth — wisdom — may approach a *guru* seeking guidance. Jesus here in effect asks the men who follow him, "What is the goal that prompts you to follow me?"

The two men ask in return, "Rabbi, where are you staying?" This response might look like a part of their informal greeting each other; but it is more than that. It indicates, on the other hand, that the two are willing to find out the real abode or Reality wherein Jesus finds his being.

As was stated earlier in verses 33-35, John the Baptist bore witness to "The spirit descending from heaven like a dove and He remained upon Him." Thus becoming enlightened, Jesus finds his being in the Spirit, called *Brahman* in Vedānta. Making this point very clear, Narayana Guru in his *Municaryā Pañcakam* (Five Verses on the Way of Sages) says:

> An abode owned by him,
> Forest areas, river banks,
> Or even uninhabited places,
> Wherever be he lives,
> The yogī's mind resides
> Always in Brahman.
>
> — verse 5

Jesus's reply to their enquiry is: "Come and see." A real *jñānin* neither states nor claims himself to be residing in *Brahman* as *Brahman*. Nor is his state something that can be clarified and made convincing to someone else. It can only be directly perceived in him and his life, by a fully competent disciple.

Andrew and his friend did follow Jesus to see where he was staying. Furthermore, they remained with Jesus that day. No one then thought whether there would be enough room for two more to stay where Jesus was. The simple reason is that in *Brahman,* the real abode of a *guru,* everyone has room to exist. The only thing needed is the mind and ability to discriminate that abode, and to find it out.

It is stated here that, "It was about the tenth hour." The indication could be that this moment was the most auspicious as far as those seekers were concerned. It was thus at a singular moment when all the favourable factors conspired together so that they could recognize the real *guru* in Jesus. Andrew immediately found his own brother Simon Peter and declared to him, "We have found the Messiah." Admitting their discovery, Jesus tells Simon Peter, "You are Simon the Son of Jonah. You shall be called Cephas." The Aramaic word *kita* or "Cephas" (Peter or Petros) means "stone" or "rock." It was upon the firm rock that was Peter that the Church was built, so that the new gospel could reach throughout the world.

A Guileless Seeker

Verses 43-51 read as follows:

> The following day Jesus wanted to go to Galilee, and He found Philip and said to him, "Follow Me."
>
> Now Philip was from Bethsaida, the city of Andrew and Peter.
>
> Philip found Nathanael and said to him, "We have found Him of whom Moses in the Law, and also the prophets wrote — Jesus of Nazareth, the Son of Joseph."
>
> And Nathanael said to him, "Can anything good come out of Nazareth?" Philip said to him, "Come and see."
>
> Jesus saw Nathanael coming towards Him, and said to him, "Behold, an Israelite indeed, in whom there is no guile!"
>
> Nathanael said to Him, "How do You know me?" Jesus answered and said to him, "Before Philip called you, when you were under the fig tree, I saw you."
>
> Nathanael answered and said to Him, "Rabbi, You are the Son of God! You are the King of Israel!"
>
> Jesus answered and said to him, "Because I said to you, 'I saw you under the fig tree', do you believe? You will see greater things than these."
>
> And He said to him, "Most assuredly, I say to you, hereafter you shall see heaven open, and the angels of God ascending and descending upon the Son of Man."

This section narrates how Philip and Nathanael became the disciples of Jesus. Philip was from Bethsaida, the native place of Andrew and Simon Peter, already disciples of Jesus. Nathanael might have been a friend of Philip. Andrew and Peter could have described to Philip their experiences regarding Jesus. It could have been based on this information that Philip tells Nathanael, "We have found Him of whom Moses in the Law, and also the prophets, wrote — Jesus of Nazareth, the Son of Joseph." But the friend Nathanael was not willing to accept straight away the truth of what Philip told him. He asks Philip, "Can anything good come out of Nazareth?" Nazareth was a small village in a remote area. How can the Messiah, the fullness of goodness, emerge from such a place? This was his doubt.

Nathanael's question has implicit in it two things — one, his tendency to evaluate everything critically, and two, his outspokenness. The only possible response to such a critical enquiry concerning spiritual attainment, as was in the case in the previous section, would be, "Come and see." Philip responds in the same way. As Nathanael, still doubting, approaches him, Jesus simply says, "Behold, an Israelite indeed, in whom there is no guile!"

Jesus is represented throughout the Gospels as the King of Israel. Moreover, the words of Nathanael "You are the King of Israel" follow. Jesus here sees a guileless subject of the kingdom in which he is the king. The kingship of Jesus, as we have already noticed, is not of any political significance. He really is the spiritual king of the spiritual kingdom that could be designated as Israel. The king of a spiritual kingdom admittedly is none other than a *guru*. The guileless subject of that kingdom is a sincere disciple-seeker (*sacchiṣya*). The present context, thus, is that of a true *guru* meeting a true disciple.

It must be in the sense, "How did you recognize me as a seeker?" that Nathanael asked Jesus, "How do you know me?" The reply given by Jesus here is highly suggestive, interesting and thought-provoking. He says, "Before Philip called you, when you were under the fig tree, I saw you." Before Philip tells his friend Nathanael about Jesus, and invites him to go and see him, Jesus had noticed him sitting under the fig tree. The picture of a genuine seeker going away from the maddening crowd to sit absorbed in meditation under a tree, preferably a banyan tree, is very familiar to the spiritual tradition of India. Here also Jesus had recognized Nathanael as a contemplative seeker sitting alone beneath a fig tree. Nathanael's feeling of exaltation in Jesus having recognized him as such a seeker, could be seen resounding in his words, "Rabbi, You are the Son of God. You are the King of Israel."

The Guru–Disciple Duality Vanishes

What happens when a *guru* and a disciple come together with full rapport between them? The wisdom secret becomes transferred from the former to the latter. That this rare event is about to happen is declared by Jesus in an exalted mood, when he says, "Most assuredly, I say to you, hereafter you shall see heaven open, and the angels of God ascending and descending upon the Son of Man."

A person enlightened as to the wisdom secret always appears to have a special kind of radiance in his person. In Vedānta this is known as *brahma-varcas.* The same radiance is cited here in a more pronounced manner by Jesus in terms familiar to the Semitic religions, by bringing into the picture the angels of God that ascend and descend upon the Son of Man. Who really is the Son of Man that Jesus refers to here? He usually refers to himself as the Son of Man. But here Nathanael has already acknowledged him as the Son of God. Therefore, the Son of Man referred to by Jesus here must be Nathanael himself. Thus the indication could be of the experience in which Jesus and Nathanael are seen as non-dual. Even the *guru*–disciple duality vanishes when the disciple becomes enlightened with the grace of his *guru*, as is well acknowledged in the Vedāntic tradition.

4.4

Miracles

VERSES 1-11 of chapter 2 narrate the event where Jesus miraculously changes the water filled in pots, into wine, at a marriage feast in Cana, when they ran out of wine. The symbolism and significance of this event has already been discussed by us earlier. It is his mother who informs Jesus, "They have no wine"(1.3). This shows she had already taken congnizance of the greatness of her son.

But Jesus's response to her, as though harshly retorting was, "Woman, what does your concern have to do with Me?" (1.4). Though given birth to by Mary, Jesus was made a *guru* by God. It is thus as an external sign of the realization of the intrinsic oneness of God and himself that Jesus could do all the miraculous acts, ranging from transforming water into wine that pleases one's palate and stomach, to revealing the secret of the kingdom of God, the greatest of all miracles, that ensures ultimate spiritual happiness. The relationship between a mother and son pertains merely to the worldly level, which is of no relevance and value in the context of the above-said realization that pertains to a purely spiritual level. The response of Jesus to his mother cited above could therefore be considered a warning against the promiscuous mixing of these two value worlds.

At this time Jesus also said, "My hour has not yet come." Though already having four close disciples, he was yet to come to the attention of the people as a prophet. The present miraculous episode actually marks the beginning of this recognition. A lighted lamp, as was stated earlier, is never kept under a bushel. Likewise, an enlightened person never remains unnoticed by the public. All the *guru*s and prophets of the past have had in their life some event by which they came to the notice of the public. No such event had yet happened in the life of Jesus. At this juncture he might have thought, let this be the occasion for the same.

Jesus's act of changing water into wine, at the first sight, sounds like an impressive miracle. But is it not normally water itself that becomes transformed into wine? The water content of the soil is drawn up by the roots of the grapevine, and passes through the vine where it becomes transformed into grapes, and finally ends up in becoming wine after fermentation. This really is a miracle that incessantly goes on in nature. Not only wine, but everything we eat and drink is a transformation from the constituent elements of soil and atmosphere. The Indian philosophers perceive such basic elements as five in number, namely, space (*ākāśa*), air (*vāyu*), fire (*agni*), water (*ap*) and earth (*pṛthivī*). No one knows exactly why and how these elements undergo the transformation mentioned above. Modern science relegates the activity by simply saying that it takes place in nature. It is really the creative power of nature that not only transforms water into wine, but creates from itself the great prophets like Jesus. So too are all of us created. A *jñānin* who becomes fully enlightened of the secret behind this, so to speak, becomes transformed as the very same secret. In the light of all this, the event where water gets changed into wine by a *jñānin* becomes perfectly meaningful.

His Mother and Brothers Become Disciples

Verse 12 of chapter 2 reads as follows:

> After this He went down to Capernaum, He, His mother, His brothers, and His disciples; and they did not stay there many days.

We have just seen that, when Mary in the capacity of being his mother, said to him, "They have no wine," the retort from Jesus was, "Woman, what does your concern have to do with me?" In apparent contrast to this attitude, here we see Jesus going to Capernaum followed by his mother, brothers and disciples where they go to spend a few days. Mary has forgone her status as the mother of Jesus, as is to be assumed from her words to the servants, "Whatever He says to you, do it" (1.15). This shows that, it is as disciples, not as blood relations, that his mother and brothers accompanied him as camp followers. Jesus, thus, does not deny the opportunity to the close relatives to become his disciples on the grounds that they are so.

The King of Israel

Verses 13-22 describe the event of Jesus, just before the Passover of the Jews, going to Jerusalem and cleansing the temple of God, by driving away all those who converted it into a marketplace. According to the other three Gospels, this event happened just before the crucifixion of Jesus, when he reached the Jerusalem Temple royally as a king by riding a donkey, and followed by a retinue. Here the same event is portrayed to have taken place at the beginning stage of his life's mission. Nevertheless, an opportune moment to do so is brought in this scene as well. Though Jesus was not yet charged with claiming himself to be the king of Israel, at least his disciple Nathanael had already proclaimed him to be so. Even after Nathanael does so, we see Jesus saying, "My hour has not yet come." His act thereafter of miraculously changing water into wine at Cana was also shown as if to indicate, "My hour has come." The next sign that shows "My hour has come," or as the demonstration of his authority as king of Israel, is when he drives away the merchants and money changers from the abode of God. It was over the temple of God that he applied his kingly authority, not over the political region of Israel. The duty of the Son of God is to apply his God-given authority over the abode of God, the temple (Nathanael has also already admitted that Jesus is the Son of God). The kingship of Jesus derives from the spiritual awakening of his oneness with God; and its authority is to be applied wherever anyone has a spiritual relationship with God. This kingship has no political colouration. The other things of wisdom significance implied in this event have been discussed earlier.

The Knower of Human Nature

Verses 23-25 read as follows:

> Now when He was in Jerusalem at the Passover, during the feast, many believed in His name when they saw the signs which He did.
>
> But Jesus did not commit Himself to them, because he knew all men,
>
> and had no need that anyone should testify of man, for He knew what was in man.

Jesus, using his authority as the king of Israel, drove away all those who were occupying the temple precincts defiling that abode of God. Those who disliked this, asked him, "What sign do you show to us, since you do these things?"(2.18). The guruhood of a *guru* really has no external sign. Though some textbooks of Vedānta delineate how real *gurus* appear, the essential content of real guruhood is beyond the bounds of all definitions and external signs, its fullness being hidden in the realm of a Silence to be written with a capital "S." Nevertheless, there were a few in the temple precincts to believe in his name (not in Jesus himself), by taking what he did there as the real sign of a holy man. What really is the "name" they believed in? It could be the name "Messiah," the awaited king of the Jews. And this, as we know, is a name deeply rooted in the Jewish culture. In short, those who believed in his "name" were willing to do so only by confining themselves to the already existing religious beliefs and traditions of the Jews. These belief patterns and traditions admittedly are of a relativistic and conditioned nature. The guruhood of a *guru,* on the other hand, is of an absolutist nature and is not conditioned by any factor whatsoever. It is doubtful whether anyone present there was capable to understand and appreciate Jesus as such a *guru.* Those, who are ready to believe in someone on seeing some external sign, are likely to shift their belief to someone else upon seeing a more attractive sign in that other person. Then, in such cases, it becomes impossible to recognize who the real Messiah is. Jesus here is looking for those who can comprehend and believe in the absolute and unconditioned Reality and Its proponent, a real *guru,* with all their heart, with all their soul, with all their mind, and with all their strength, without looking outward for external signs. People endowed with such a penetrating vision are very rare, as was well known to Jesus. He, therefore, was not inclined to take seriously those who considered him to be the Messiah simply by seeing what he had done at the temple.

The part of the verse "He had no need that anyone should testify of man" could be interpreted in two ways. The state of being God-like is there when the state of being human attains its perfection. A man of such a state never aspires that he be so recognized by the world. He, in other words, is a person who has completely given up persuing worldly ways and worldly recognition. If he pursues anything at all, it would be the way of God.

It could also be taken to mean that Jesus needed no one's testimony in respect to his knowledge of human nature. He was well aware, to what extent human nature is made to deviate from Reality by man's own interest in the prevailing religion with its belief patterns and traditions, in race considerations, in loyalty to one's nation, in geographical and historical exegencies, and above all in one's longing for power and wealth. We see in the life of Jesus himself the instances where one of his own close disciples betrays him, and another denies him three times during one and the same night. Jesus was not ignorant of all such human frailties. Therefore, whether the world acknowledges him or not, was not a matter of any concern for him.

4.5

The Second Birth

VERSES 1-15 of chapter 3 read as follows:

> There was a man of the Pharisees named Nicodemus, a ruler of the Jews.
>
> This man came to Jesus by night and said to Him, "Rabbi, we know that You are a teacher come from God, for no one can do these signs that You do unless God is with him."
>
> Jesus answered and said to him, "Most assuredly, I say to you, unless one is born again, he cannot see the kingdom of God."
>
> Nicodemus said to Him, "How can a man be born when he is old? Can he enter a second time into the mother's womb and be born?"
>
> Jesus answered, "Most assuredly, I say to you, unless one is born of water and the Spirit, he cannot enter the kingdom of God.
>
> That which is born of the flesh is flesh, and that which is born of the Spirit is spirit.
>
> Do not marvel that I said to you, 'You must be born again.'
>
> The wind blows where it wishes, and you hear the sound of it, but cannot tell where it comes from and where it goes. So is everyone who is born of the Spirit."
>
> Nicodemus answered and said to Him, "How can these things be?"
>
> Jesus answered and said to him, "Are you the teacher of Israel, and do not know these things?
>
> Most assuredly, I say to you, We speak what We know and testify what We have seen, and you do not receive Our witness.
>
> If I have told you earthly things and you do not believe, how will you believe if I tell you heavenly things?
>
> No one has ascended to heaven but He who came down from heaven, that is, the Son of Man who is in heaven.
>
> And as Moses lifted up the serpent in the wilderness, even so must the Son of Man be lifted up,
>
> that whoever believes in Him should not perish but have eternal life.

The Pharisees, as we know, are the scholars among the orthodox Jews. They are all waiting for the coming of a Messiah, but they do not acknowledge Jesus, who has already come, as the prophesied Messiah. Furthermore, the Jews not only hated Jesus, but finally they crucified him as well, simply for the reasons that he spoke about the kingdom of heaven and eternal life (*mokṣa*) in the tone of a person of authority, and because he was considered as the king of Israel. Nicodemus was one among those Pharisees, yet he saw Jesus as a God-sent teacher. Afraid of being noticed by the other Jews, he chose to meet Jesus by night.

Nicodemus openly tells Jesus, "Rabbi, we know that You are a teacher come from God; for no one can do these signs that You do unless God is with him."

The Secret of "Signs"

Jesus never claims himself to do any unworldly "sign;" he even derides those who ask him to show "signs." Still others perceive such "signs" in him; they are aware also that no one can do such "signs" unless God is with him.

Put in Vedāntic terms, Jesus is a knower of *Brahman* (*brahma-jñānin*). That means, he is enlightened of the reality that *Brahman,* called God in Semitic religions, is what manifests as all the worlds and every phenomenon in them. Such an enlightened person perceives *Brahman* (God) alone in the being of everything as well as of himself. It is in this sense that the Upaniṣads proclaim, The knower of *Brahman* becomes *Brahman* indeed:

brahma-veda brahmaiva bhavati — *Muṇḍaka Upaniṣad* 3.2.9

There is no end to the possibilities inherent in *Brahman,* and no one can definitely assess what is impossible in *Brahman* (God). In the case of a knower of *Brahman,* whatever is possible in *Brahman* could be seen manifest in him also. Such phenomena seen in the knowers of *Brahman,* and not seen in others who are ignorant, are what the term "signs" denote here.

Jesus, instead of showing any "sign," simply answers, "Unless one is born again, he cannot see the kingdom of God." The connotation of being born again has already been examined by us. The birth from the womb of one's mother is the first one. The second birth is that of being born as "I am *Brahman*" from being "I am so and so." In other words, becoming a *jñānin* is the second birth. Becoming so, in the biblical context, is conceived as becoming baptized in the Spirit. The one who is born a second time in this sense is known as *dvija* (twice-born) in India. Unable to understand this secret, Nicodemus asks,

"Can he enter a second time into the mother's womb and be born?" Jesus then answers, "Most assuredly, I say to you, unless one is born of water and the Spirit, he cannot enter the kingdom of God. That which is born of the flesh is flesh, and that which is born of the Spirit is spirit." Being born of water signifies, to be born of the womb of a mother. A child in the womb is surrounded by water. Modern science also acknowledges that the emergence of life is not possible in the absence of water. As is made more explicit by Jesus himself here, what is born of the physical body is the physical body alone. And this body admittedly is inert by nature. What glorifies human life is not the inert aspect of his being, but is the Spirit aspect, or the Consciousness aspect. One being reborn into the identity with Spirit or Consciousness, is what by being "born of the Spirit" signifies (3.6). Implying all this, Jesus says, Do not marvel that I said to you, "You must be born again."

Jesus reminds Nicodemus, how free is the life a person who is well aware, "I am *Ātmā*" or "I am simply a minute part of God's self-manifestation," and how unforeseen are the events in the life of such a person. No one can predict what, how and where anything will unfold from the infinite possibilities inherent in God or the one ultimate Reality. Whatever is relevant with the total being or God is relevant with the individual being of the person who has realized, "I am *Brahman*." Therefore Jesus says, "The wind blows where it wishes, and you hear the sound of it, but cannot tell where it comes from and where it goes. So is everyone who is born of the Spirit."

In short, it is like hearing the sound of the blowing of the unpredictable wind, that people see as "signs" in the life of the twice born. As suggested by the words "So is everyone who is born of the Spirit," the so-called signs are what others see in the life of a person who is thus born a second time.

The Mystery

Nicodemus, still remaining doubtful, asks again, "How can these things be?." Even after being taught by a *guru* that everything in all the worlds emerges from the one ultimate Reality as the unfoldment of the infinite potentials hiding in the very same Reality, and that everything merges back into the same Reality, the listener may continue to doubt, "How can all this happen?" Nicodemus was such a listener. The arising of such questions also indicates the limit of what can be taught through written or spoken words. Such questions can be seen asked by disciples in the Upaniṣads also. The immediate response from the *guru* on such occasions is, "The question you are asking transgresses the limits" (*Praśna Upaniṣad* 3.2). Or else the answer given would be that all these happen because of the *māyā* of *Ātmā*. To say so means only that there hides a magic-like mystery in It, which makes it impossible to explain it to someone else. That is to say, even though a new word like *māyā* is introduced, it does not serve the purpose of solving the basic problem. For this reason, Jesus tells Nicodemus, "Are you the teacher of Israel, and do not know these things?" It thus means, there remains in It a secret aspect that becomes fully transparent to the enlightened, but is even for them inexpressible through words.

The Liberated Ones or Muktas

Jesus refers Nicodemus as a teacher because he is one of the religious scholars among the Jews. Despite being a teacher, Nicodemus, as is clear from the present instance, is fully ignorant of what a real *guru* should know. Those who thus continue to ask questions like this on the one side, and those who have realized the Reality in their own being and live as having merged in the aloneness of that Reality — the experience known as *kaivalya* in India — on the other, are differentiated by Jesus "you" and "We" with a capital "W." The implications of the words of Jesus are thus: the answer to the question you ask me is not to be found in the words "We" speak; "Our" life itself is its answer. Jesus yet complains, "You do not receive Our witness." That is to say, "you" remain incapable of perceiving "Our" own life as the answer to "your" question. Therefore "you" continue to ask, "How can these things be?"

Who is capable of being a living answer to the question, instead of speaking about it? Only he who has come down from heaven (3.13). The concepts heaven, the Son of God and the Son of Man have all already been examined by us in detail, and so we do not need to repeat them here. Jesus here emphatically states, "that whoever believes in Him should not perish but have eternal life" (3.15). The words "whoever believes in Him" must be taken to denote the one who understands and believes in the Reality in himself. He, in other words, is the enlightened person who has realized the unthinkable and unknowable Reality that underlies the being of himself as well as of everything, and who lives as that Reality embodied. It is not finding a definite answer to the above-said question that these enlightened ones gain. Rather, they attain a state that makes them totally free of all such questions. These questions become totally irrelevant in that experiential awareness. Those who exist totally immersed in this experiential awareness are to be termed "the liberated ones" (*mukta*s). This attainment in biblical terms, is known as "to have eternal life." Jesus therefore proclaims, "so must the Son of Man be lifted up, that whoever believes in Him, should not perish but have eternal life." To where must the Son of Man be lifted up? To the status of being one who has come down from heaven. That means, an ordinary man, through enlightenment, must become uplifted as the extraordinary man that a *jñānin* is.

4.6

Deeds Done in God

VERSES 16-21 of chapter 3 read as follows:

> For God so loved the world that He gave His only begotten Son, that whoever believes in Him should not perish but have everlasting life.
>
> For God did not send His Son into the world to condemn the world, but that the world through Him might be saved.
>
> He who believes in Him is not condemned; but he who does not believe is condemned already, because he has not believed in the name of the only begotten Son of God.
>
> And this is the condemnation, that the light has come into the world, and men loved darkness rather than light, because their deeds were evil.
>
> For everyone practising evil hates the light and does not come to the light, lest his deeds should be exposed.
>
> But he who does the truth comes to the light, that his deeds may be clearly seen, that they have been done in God.

God Gave His only Begotten Son

The sense in which we understand "the only begotten Son of God" has already been clarified. This Son is none other than an enlightened *guru*. "Eternal life" or *mokṣa* (liberation) is the ultimate goal attainable, but only to those who fully take the words of instruction of a *guru* in full faith. Such *guru*s, capable of guiding seekers to this eternal life, have always emerged in the world at critical junctures when the fulfilment of such a mission was a historical necessity. Historians have not found a way to explain how this phenomenon happens. As part of some unknowable activity that takes place in nature, exactly when the world is badly in need of guidance, an enlightened one appears. The religiously minded say, this happens as willed by God, or that this happens because God loved this world so much. The same phenomenon is portrayed in *Bhagavad-Gītā* (IV.17) thus:

> Whenever laxity with regard to *dharma* (righteousness) comes about, *adharma* (unrighteousness) asserting itself, O Arjuna, then I myself come forth.

The world created by God, the world that has emerged as the self-unfoldment of God Himself, can only be loved by God, for He loves Himself, as all of us love ourselves.

So it is said here also, "For God so loved the world that He gave His only begotten Son, that whoever believes in Him should not perish but have everlasting life" (3.16). It means, those who accept the *guru*'s teaching as true, and subject it to *manana* (cogitation) and *nididhyāsana,* (meditation), realize themselves in essential content to be the one Reality that has no birth or death. This attainment is what "to have eternal life" signifies.

A Guru's Role

Gurus (prophets) emerge in this world thus in an inexplicable way, as it were willed by God, because of His love for the world. They lead people who face crises in life to the wisdom that enables them to cross over all crises and problems in life. They, in a sense, with all kindness, usher disciples to the realm of the brightness of wisdom from the darkness of ignorance, the source of all problems.

People thus led find themselves in a safe harbour where no problem — not even that of death — agonizes them. Put otherwise, the role of a *guru* is not to judge the rights and wrongs of people, nor punish the wrong-doers and reward the doers of good. Imparting no punishment on anyone, good or evil, a real *guru* saves everyone who is a seeker. Therefore it is said here, "For God did not send His Son into the world to condemn the world, but that the world through Him might be saved" (3.17).

Is Condemned Already

It is said in verse 18, "He who believes in Him is not condemned; but he who does not believe is condemned already, because he has not believed in the name of the only begotten Son of God." The words, "He who does not believe is condemned already," after saying, "He who believes in Him is not condemned," imply that the condemnation is not invoked by the *guru*. The "condemnation" neither necessarily means a sort of punishment one gets in another world, after death and the final judgement, like having to go to hell. Those who turn a deaf ear to the words of wisdom of the enlightened masters, and those who do not have any respect for the bright world of wisdom, do turn their life here itself into a hell. Really, wisdom shines in one's being in the form of the awareness that could be expressed thus:

What are known as "this man" or "that man",
Contemplatively visualized,
Are in essence all one primordial
Ātmā assuming various forms.
— *Ātmopadeśa Śatakam*, verse 24

In the case of the one who lives as the apparent manifestation of this wisdom, he always sticks to the ideal,

Whatever one does for one's own happiness,
Should be conducive to
The happiness of others as well. — Ibid.

Such is the way of life that agrees with the oneness of the all-underlying Reality (*Ātmā*).

On the contrary, there are those who live with no respect for this ideal and the wisdom behind it. They perform actions intended to ensure their own happiness at the cost of the happiness of others. By doing so, they have already turned their lives into a fiery ocean of hell, and they really suffer in that hell, as is warned by Narayana Guru in verse 25 of *Ātmopadeśa Śatakam*. What *gurus* do is not to push such evil-doers into the fire of hell, but to also help them to save themselves if possible by turning their attention to the wisdom about the ultimate Reality (God). Those who do not care for their guidance have already made a hell of their lives. Here the Gospel does not say, "He who does not believe *will be condemned;*" rather it says, "He who does not believe *is condemned already*."

The Condemnation

The rest of the section continues to clarify the nature of the condemnation meant here. The truth is that it is the one ultimate Reality called *Ātmā, Brahman* (God), Pure Effulgence or Unconditioned Consciousness in essence, that assumes the fleeting apparent forms of all of us and all the worlds. The life of the one who lives in the realization of this Truth would always be in full accord with "the light that has thus come into the world." But if, instead of knowing the Reality and thus perceiving one's own life as a manifest form of that Reality, and thereby making life fully meaningful, one is tempted to be guided by one's personal interests alone and indulge in pleasures and sense gratifications, then such a person loves darkness rather than brightness. For the same reason, the activities of such would turn out to be corrupt. Such persons of corrupt activities naturally distance themselves from the bright world of wisdom; they like darkness, and they hide themselves in darkness, because they live in the darkness of ignorance. They cover their evil actions with the darkness of their own ignorance.

But there are those who "do the truth," i.e., those who live as the embodiment of the one Reality and act accordingly. They perceive the brightness of Consciousness (*Ātmā*) or God as what is real in them. They do not see the deeds they do really as theirs, but as God's creativity finding self-expression. As stated in verse 21 here, as far as such a person is concerned, "his deeds may be clearly seen, that they have been done in God."

Karma-Yoga

How are one's deeds to be seen as done in God? God, *Brahman* or the one ultimate Reality alone is what really exists. What appear to be many are simply Its fleeting manifest forms. These forms emerge because that Reality has inherent in It a boundless creative urge that incessantly finds expression. This creative urge that effects the emergence of everything that has come into being, is called *karma* (action) in *Bhagavad- Gītā* (VIII.3). All the activities that take place everywhere in all the worlds are nothing but this creative urge finding expression. Our own deeds, including our mental activities and free will, are no exception. The one ultimate Reality, when in a self-activated creative state, is called nature (*prakṛti*). The word *prakṛti* is the combination of the prefix *pra* standing for "to be proper" and the word *kṛti* meaning "action," another word for *karma.* That means, the word *prakṛti* as well as the reality of *prakṛti* have *kṛti* (activity) as inseparable from it. We, forming part of that *prakṛti,* have the same creative urge in us also. Those who live in the bright world of wisdom realize that no actions, including those of their seeming free will, are really their own. In fact, none has the capability to create in himself the ability to act; it must be in us as part of *prakṛti* (God's creative self-expression). Therefore, when we remain active, the actions really are of *prakṛti.* Those who remain engaged in their normal activities with this awareness, neither think that the deeds they do are their own *karmas*, nor that the fruits of those deeds should belong to themselves. Such deeds done in life with no sense of attachment are known as *niṣkāma-karmas* (actions performed unmotivated by desires). What such doers of actions really attain in life is to realize their inseparable oneness with the creative Reality or *prakṛti* or God, by performing those deeds as a means. They thus become *karma-yogī*s. Such is the way the passage "His deeds may be clearly seen, that they have been done in God," is understood and appreciated by a Vedāntin.

Jesus and John the Baptist

Verses 22-30 portray a scene where both Jesus and John the Baptist are baptizing people on either bank of the same river in Judea, yet where more people come to Jesus for baptism. When this is pointed out by some of his disputing disciples, John's response was thus:

> A man can receive nothing unless it has been given to him from heaven.
>
> You yourselves bear me witness, that I said, 'I am not the Christ', but "I have been sent before Him?"
>
> He who has the bride is the bridegroom, but the friend of the bridegroom, who stands and hears, rejoices greatly because of the bridegroom's voice. Therefore this joy of mine is fulfilled.
>
> He must increase, but I must decrease. — 3.27-30

Though Jesus and John are both prophets, they are not of the same grade. Each prophet would have, as though decided by God, a special capability of his own. He can do only what he is thus capable of. It is in this sense John says, "A man can receive nothing unless it has been given to him from heaven."

John has himself made it clear earlier to the Jews that he was not the Christ, but was only the one sent before the Christ by God, to prepare His way. John has admitted also that he was not worthy even of loosening the sandal strap of the one who was to follow him.

The difference between himself and Jesus is poetically depicted by John thus: Jesus is the bridegroom who has a bride; I am merely a friend of him. At the time of wedding, the attention of all naturally would be upon the bride and the bridegroom. The friends of the groom would crack jokes about him, and they would rejoice in his responses. Similarly, I am the friend of the bridegroom Jesus, waiting to rejoice upon hearing his words of wisdom. Furthermore, the following words of John show clearly how sincere he was in declaring, "Therefore this joy of mine is fulfilled. He must increase, but I must decrease." These words really are as bright and spirited as a burning fire.

The Witnessing One in Action

Verses 31-36 of chapter 3 read as follows:

> He who comes from above is above all; he who is of the earth is earthly and speaks of the earth. He who comes from heaven is above all.
>
> And what He has seen and heard, that He testifies, and no one receives His testimony.
>
> He who has received His testimony has certified that God is true.
>
> For He whom God has sent speaks the words of God, for God does not give the Spirit by measure.
>
> The Father loves the Son, and has given all things into His hand.
>
> He who believes in the Son has everlasting life; and he who does not believe the Son shall not see life, but the wrath of God abides on him.

Humans, first of all, are seen here to belong to either of two categories: "he who is of the earth," and "he who comes from heaven." By "he who is of the earth" is meant, those who think that life is made meaningful by the enjoyable objects they amass from this world. What they always think of and what they always speak of are matters of such a value world. But there are a few who "come from above." That means, those who visualize the one ultimate Reality that forms the meaning content of their own existence, and that makes their life meaningful. They are "above all," or they are far above all those who are always involved in worldly matters. This higher realm of values, in Vedānta, is known as *śreyas* and the lower one *preyas.*

"He who comes from heaven" is known in India as a *jñānin.* His life is not of the kind that remains immersed in earthliness, but "what He has seen and heard, that He testifies." Put otherwise, a *jñānin* remains a witness to all that goes on in himself as well as around him. This witnesshood liberates him from all attachments towards everything that he sees and hears. This liberated state, in Vedānta, is called *mukti* or *mokṣa.* Such a liberated *jñānin* lives in the world of the here and now, by perceiving himself and everything "he sees and hears" as one ultimate Reality (God) alone, variously manifest. He may also be seen externally engaged in activities just as those of the earth. But his attitude towards such activities is different. He perceives even his own actions as pertaining to the one Transcendental Reality. His goal in doing actions (*karmas*) is to uphold the total world order of which he is an integral part, and not to enjoy their fruits. He simply plays his role in the upkeep of the overall system of life, called *loka-saṁgraha* in *Bhagavad-Gītā* (III.28).

But "no one receives his testimony." That means, no one of earthly interest is capable of understanding the greatness of a *jñānin*'s wisdom. And for this reason, none of them acknowledges such a *jñānin* either. The difference between those of the earth and those of heaven is portrayed in *Kaṭha Upaniṣad* (2.1.1) as follows:

> The self-existent (Creator) cut the sense-organs open outward-looking; one, therefore, looks outward, not within himself. Certain wise ones, nevertheless, seeking immortality with eyes interiorized, have seen the undwelling Self.

The "wise one" of the Upaniṣad is none other than "He who has received His testimony" indicated here in the Gospel. It is also emphasized, "He has certified that God is true." The implicit meaning is that the life of the wise one itself testifies that the Supreme Self or God is the one ultimate Reality.

The *gurus* who have thus realized the one ultimate Reality or God and who live as that Reality embodied, have nothing to speak about other than that Reality, no matter how far-reaching their words are. Their final word really would be their Silence that brims with an ineffable meaning content, "for God does not give the Spirit by measure." That means, immeasurable and boundless is the wisdom attained upon enlightenment. The knowledge that pertains to the earth is not so; it is always given definiteness by measurement and calculation.

Father and Son

That "The Father loves the Son, and has given all things into His hand" is a phenomenon common among those of the earth as well. Rearing a good son and finally entrusting him with all the responsibilities is what makes a father feel fulfilled in life. But such a father does not feel the fulfilment which is not of the earth. The same phenomenon of inheritance could be perceived to be true with the heavenly Father also. That Father also loves all His children — all the living beings. But this love of God remains inaccessible to those who live ignorant of being the children of that heavenly Father. *Jñānins* or *gurus*, on the other hand, are those who are fully aware of this secret. They live with the knowledge that God loves everyone, and by experiencing the love of God at every moment in life. Such a *jñānin* lives filled with the feeling, "O! what a wonder! God has endowed me with this wisdom secret." Such a Son of God, no doubt, experiences eternal life (*mukti*) every moment during His life. The one who believes in this Son of God or *guru* also would follow the same path of God, and will eventually attain eternal life. Those who do not discern such *gurus* and turn a deaf ear to their words, never find the path of God, nor do they attain eternal life. On the contrary, they eventually end up turning their life into a hell in this world. Such a hellish experience is what is termed here as "the wrath of God that abides in him."

4.7

Unrelenting Action

Two Patterns of Worship

THE whole of chapter 4 of the Gospel According to John describes the scene where Jesus asks a woman of Samaria "Give Me a drink," while at the Jacob's well, when he was weary from a journey from Judea to Galilee via Samaria. This event we have examined earlier. On perceiving him to be a prophet, the woman says:

> Our fathers worshipped on this mountain, and you Jews say that in Jerusalem is the place where one ought to worship. — 4.20

Jesus then tells her in response:

> Woman, believe Me, the hour is coming when you will neither on this mountain, nor in Jerusalem, worship the Father.
>
> You worship what you do not know; we know what we worship. . . .
>
> But the hour is coming, and now is, when the true worshippers will worship the Father in spirit and truth; for the Father is seeking such to worship Him.
>
> God is Spirit, and those who worship Him must worship in spirit and truth. — 4.21-24

Each tribe or clan has its own traditional concept of God or of a worshippable deity. As an apparent example of this phenomenon, the woman of Samaria tells Jesus here, "Our fathers worshipped on this mountain, and you Jews say that in Jerusalem is the place where one ought to worship." Her word "our" refers here to the Samaritans and "you" to Galileans. Jesus is a prophet who transcends all such parochial and clanish religious concepts and practices, and who reveals the magnificence of knowing the one God or ultimate Reality, and adoring that God in a way untainted by any relativistic notion. Those of the former type of religiousness always prefer to go to a particular place and worship the deity that supposedly presides over that region, and to perform that worship in a particular traditional way. Such people are referred to by Jesus as "you." And by "we" he means those who are capable like him, of perceiving the one Father as the all-pervading and formless Reality that assumes the form of all that appears to be, instead of seeing God as an idol located somewhere or in some temple or other places of worship.

What Jesus indicates here is that his life's mission is to endow the people with the inner clarity to intuitively perceive and worship God as the formless Reality that pervades the being of everything. The difference between "you" and "we" in this case is that, "You worship what you do not know; we know what we worship" (4.22). With regard to the ultimate Reality, what is more important is knowing It, or rather realizing It, than worshipping It. And what happens to the one who really knows that one Reality? The grandeur of that Reality is such that one can do nothing but worship It. Above all, one's worship always will then be fully in line with what one knows of the Reality. Worshipping what one does not know is not only inferior, but in all likelihood, it goes wrong and also creates wrong notions and dogmas in the believers' minds.

God Works Non-stop

Chapter 5 of the Gospel is centred around the event where Jesus, on a Sabbath day, heals a man who had an infirmity for thirty-eight years, and how he faces the Jews who questioned his labouring so on the Sabbath. Jesus responds:

> My Father has been working until now, and I have been working.
> — 5.17

That this world was created by God, is a concept accepted by all religions. Instead of thinking that this creation took place at a particular point of time long long ago, it would be more scientific to admit that God's creation of the world is going on incessantly, and is happening even now. New entities are always being created in nature everywhere. For the reason that the creation of a new apparent form implies the dissolution of some already existing form or forms, dissolution has also to be admitted to be constantly taking place spontaneously along with creation. The Upaniṣads perceive this phenomenon to be the absolute Reality, also called *Ātman* (*Brahman*), giving expression, by Its own wilful imagination, to the creative urge already inherent in Itself. As a result, the never-ending flow of the world, called in philosophy "the eternal flux," becomes apparent. No moment is there when this Reality remains inactive. Should it remain so, the appearance of the world would cease to be. This one Reality, as we know, is what Bible calls "the Father in heaven" or "God." The words of Jesus, "My Father has been working until now" thus become fully meaningful.

God thus remains active without intermission. Sabbath has no place in it. The Genesis of Bible, it is true, clearly states:

> Thus the heaven and the earth, and all the host of them were finished.
>
> And on the seventh day God ended His work which He had done, and He rested on the seventh day from all His work which He had done. — 2.1-2

It is this seventh day that is observed by the Jews as the Sabbath. But it would be found, when closely observed, that God's resting on the seventh day is also an integral part of God remaining ever active. As part of the onward flow, actions occur in both an uphill and downhill manner, both *pravṛtti* and *nivṛtti* — being both positively active and restful. The picture of total actions (*karma*s) becomes complete only when this restfulness or non-action is given its due place, just as a painting gains perfection through both light and shade. Concerning the nature of this action (*karma*) of God, *Bhagavad-Gītā* says:

> What is action and what is non-action, even the wise seemingly are confused in this regard. — IV.16

Again *Gītā* says:

> Elusive indeed is the course of actions. — IV.17

And

> He who sees non-action in action and action in non-action, is wise, he is a *yogī*, he is the doer of all actions. — IV.18

A person who remains externally inactive and fully restful is perceived by such a *yogī* as also forming an inseparable part of nature's overall flow of action. All actions, in the *yogī*'s perception, take place in the one Reality which one realizes as oneself, and thus in effect take place in oneself. This is the sense in which it is said in the above *Gītā* passage, "He is the doer of all actions."

A visualizer of Reality (*satya-darśin*) is not a person who merely perceives or even conceives Reality; such a person really is one who lives as that Reality. In that person's vision, all the actions that take place in his own life are not his actions, but are actions of the *Ātmā*, the one Substance in the being of all the worlds. No intermission, nor Sabbath, is there in the actions that take place in *Ātmā* (God). In the case of the *yogī* who lives as *Ātmā* also, there is no break of action or Sabbath.

Jesus here goes beyond the realm of the religious observance of Sabbath, and perceives the creativity of the one ultimate Reality or God in his own being. And it is with this intuitive vision of his identity with God that Jesus heals the man of his infirmity and openly declares, "My Father has been working until now, and I have been working."

Nevertheless, the Jews about him were not living as a people with the penetrative eye to see the Father-secret that Jesus sees. They could never bear any violation of the rules of Sabbath. The crux of the matter for them was not to properly understand or live by true religious principles, but was instead to strictly adhere to the religious rules. Therefore, they treated it as a crime for Jesus to even think of "God as His Father," thus "making Himself equal with God" (5.18). Jesus's response at this juncture also is to be understood and evaluated in view of the secret of the *karma* (action) – principle we have tried to indicate above. This is reflected in the words of Jesus:

> Most assuredly, I say to you, the Son can do nothing of Himself, but what He sees the Father do; for whatever He does, the Son also does in like manner. — 5.19

The Son Judges

Jesus says in sequel to this:

> The Father judges no one, but has committed all judgement to the Son. — 5.22

God or the ultimate Reality is not something concrete. It is the abstract Substance that fills the being of everything concrete everywhere. This abstract Reality, or God, never teaches humans, a part of the concrete world. It is prophets and *guru*s who do it. Having realized that everyone and everything, themselves included, are all but the one abstract Reality become variously manifest, they teach this wisdom to those who are ignorant of it. Their teachings normally consist of the disclosure of the above secret, as well as the instructions on the manner by which people should live fully in accord with that wisdom. All the scriptures have these two sections in them, either as mingled or given separately. The latter is the way the *guru*s of India preferred. In view of this fact we should understand the words of Jesus:

> The Father judges no one, but has committed all judgement to the Son.

Immortality

In continuation of this Jesus says:

> Most assuredly, I say to you, he who hears My word and believes in Him who sent Me has everlasting life, and shall not come into judgement, but has passed from death into life. — 5.24

Listening with all attention to the wisdom teachings of one's *guru*, pondering continuously on what was thus taught by the *guru*, and finally realizing through meditation the vision behind that teaching, make one reach the state of final liberation called *mukti*. The ultimate Reality thus realized is admittedly birthless and deathless. Therefore the one who realizes, "I am that Reality" also becomes liberated from birth and death. This state of liberation, as we have already noticed, is what Bible calls "eternal life."

All manifest forms originate from the one Reality and belong to the realm of relativity. Nothing in this realm is eternal or absolute in itself. Man, as a thinking animal with a sense of value, is one among such forms. Hence all existing moralities that arise of man's sense of value also belong to what is relative. The duality of righteousness and unrighteousness, which originate from the one Reality as part of man's value sense, strictly speaking, belongs to the realm of relativity. The one who realizes "I am that Reality" also thereby is beyond this duality. Only where this duality has relevance does any sort of judgement becomes meaningful. Jesus therefore says, "Most assuredly, I say to you, he who hears My word and believes in Him who sent Me has everlasting life, and shall not come iñto judgement, but has passed from death into life."

The Guru Śrī Kr̥ṣṇa of *Bhagavad-Gītā* also, just before concluding his teaching, asks his disciple Arjuna:

> Abandon all *dharma*s and take refuge in Me alone, I will liberate you from all sins. You don't have to grieve. — XVIII.66

Such a *jñānin* lives by finding oneness with the ultimate Reality that is immortal and ever-living, in this sense, has passed from death into life.

4.8

Jesus Testifies About Himself

VERSES 30-47 of chapter 5 read as follows:

> I can of Myself do nothing. As I hear, I judge; and My judgement is righteous, because I do not seek My own will but the will of the Father who sent Me.
>
> If I bear witness of Myself, My witness is not true.
>
> There is another who bears witness of Me, and I know that the witness which He witnesses of Me is true.
>
> You have sent to John, and he has borne witness to the truth.
>
> Yet I do not receive testimony from man, but I say these things that you may be saved.
>
> He was the burning and shining lamp, and you were willing for a time to rejoice in his light.
>
> But I have a greater witness than John's; for the works which the Father has given Me to finish — the very works that I do — bear witness of Me, that the Father has sent Me.
>
> And the Father Himself, who sent Me, has testifed of Me. You have neither heard His voice at any time, nor seen His form.
>
> But you do not have His word abiding in you, because whom He sent, Him you do not believe.
>
> You search the Scriptures, for in them you think you have eternal life; and these are they which testify of Me.
>
> But you are not willing to come to Me that you may have life.
>
> I do not receive honour from men.
>
> But I know you, that you do not have the love of God in you.
>
> I have come in My Father's name, and you do not receive Me; if another comes in his own name, him you will receive.
>
> How can you believe, who receive honour from one another, and do not seek the honour that comes from the only God?
>
> Do not think that I shall accuse you to the Father; there is one who accuses you — Moses, in whom you trust.

For if you believed Moses, you would believe Me, for he wrote about Me.

But if you do not believe his witness, how will you believe My words?

The Jews, as we have already seen, asked Jesus, when he reached the Jerusalem Temple and drove the merchants and money changers out of the temple, "What sign do You show to us, since You do these things?" (2.18). Jesus did not answer them straightaway. The present context could be treated as Jesus's response to that question, as he continues to speak to the Jews.

Whatever all the *gurus* say and do, not to speak of what they think, in a sense, would be a sort of external gleaming of what they realize within. It is the Reality they have realized that is called *Brahman* in Vedānta and God in Bible. That means, their action in life is to simply give expression to their God-vision, through word and deed. In this sense Jesus says, "I can of Myself do nothing" (5.30).

Jesus then says, "As I hear, I judge." "To hear", in the Vedāntic context, means to listen attentively to the words of wisdom of one's *guru*, or to learn such recorded words of the *gurus* of the past. Those recorded words are what we consider as scriptures. A *guru* is a *jñānin* who has realized the ultimate Reality or God as the Substance in his own being. As far as he is concerned, expressing what he experiences within and hearing the words of God from the Most High, in essence, are not two. Prophets usually teach not only what the nature and content of the one Reality or God is, but they instruct also on how to live properly as guided by that Reality. To put this in Indian terminology, the teachings of all prophets have the nature of both Śrutis and Smr̥tis. The Śrutis contain the teachings about what is Real in life, and these teachings are of eternal value. Smr̥tis, on the other hand, consist of injunctions (*vidhis*), and along with these come taboos (*niṣedhas*). The term *vidhi* means the instructions on what should be done in life by a person, and *niṣedha* is the term for what should not be done. Neither of these are of everlasting value. Yet both originate from one's conviction about the eternal Reality; as learned from one's *guru* or as heard from God. Hence the words of Jesus, "As I hear, I judge".

Two Kinds of Laws

Jesus then makes clear how righteous his judgement is. Common laws may get shaped as willed by certain persons of authority, as made by the current states, in order to enforce certain healthy regulations in the society, or as the injunctions of religions. All such laws are relativistic in nature. That means, these are subject to alteration depending on the exigencies of changing circumstances. All such regulations *in toto* are referred to by Jesus here as "My own will" (5.30). But there exists another set of laws that derive their value from the ultimate Reality, God, or the overall system of life. Not limited by spatial or temporal considerations, such laws are absolutist in nature. "The will of the Father who sent Me" (5.30) are the words with which Jesus indicates such laws. Such an absolutist order of righteousness may accommodate within what we in the usual course count to be unrighteous also, because such acts happen to be unavoidable as part of the overall creative flow of nature. Such a non-relative sense of righteousness transcends the bounds of the sense of justice commonly known to us and of all man-made laws. The inner meanings contained in the words of Jesus: "I do not seek My own will but the will of the Father who sent Me" (5.30) are to be contemplated in the light of all this.

Two Kinds of Witnessing

Now Jesus tells the Jews of his right to teach and correct them. Two kinds of testifying of that right are possible — one from man and the other from God.

Suppose one bears witness to one's own truthfulness, such a witnessing is never acknowledged either by the ordinary laws or by the traditional conventions of human societies. Jesus therefore needed someone else to bear witness to him simply because it was the world that was to be benefitted by him. This need was fulfilled by John the Baptist as a historical necessity. Acknowledging this fact, Jesus says, "You have sent to John and he has borne witness to the truth" (5.33).

A *guru* really needs no testifying from someone. Therefore Jesus says, "Yet I do not receive testimony from man, but I say these things that you may be saved" (5.34). It is the concern for the people around him, who needed to be saved from their ignorance, that made Jesus acknowledge a worldly witnessing, which occurred as though willed by God. John, as that witness, was a bright burning lamp. But his words that announced the coming of the real saviour turned out to be just a cry in the wilderness. John's testifying of Jesus thus was not heeded by the Jews.

The other kind of witnessing is of God, and it is a witness greater than John's (5.36). The connotation is that it is beyond the bounds of all worldliness. Jesus performs acts that are external signs of his perception of the one Father or Reality within himself. Such actions, bodily, mental or verbal, themselves serve the purpose of witnessing or testifying that he is an enlightened *guru.* In this sense, Jesus says, "for the works which the Father has given Me to finish — the very works that I do — bear witness to Me, that the Father has sent Me" (5.36). The Jews did not have the penetrating eye to see this witnessing given by God, for the reason disclosed here by Jesus himself when he says: "And the Father Himself who sent Me, has testified of Me. You have neither heard His voice at any time, nor seen His form. But you do not have His word abiding in you, because whom He sent, Him you do not believe" (5.37-38). Only in the *jñānin*s who live as the embodiment of the God-Reality are found such actions of Godliness that testify of themselves. To those who are incapable of perceiving and acknowledging such *jñānin*s this witnessing always remains concealed, and the Jews here were such.

The Need of a Guru

The Jews, in their life, ideally and strictly follow the Ten Commandments of Moses as well as the teachings in the Old Testament. The most acceptable spiritual authority for them is Moses. They hold in high esteem the Ten Commandments of Moses, as containing everything that helps them ensure happy life in this world, as well as salvation in the hereafter. Acknowledging this sort of religiousness in the Jews around him, Jesus says, "You search the Scriptures, for in them you think you have eternal life; and these are they which testify of Me" (5.39). Despite the fact that the very same Moses and the scriptures they rely on also allude to Jesus as a future prophet and the Christ, the Jews were unwilling to acknowledge Jesus as the Christ, and so they continued awaiting for the coming of the Christ. This waiting continues even now. They, for this reason, not only did not approach Jesus in search of eternal life, but some even despised him. Jesus therefore says, "But you are not willing to come to Me that you may have life."

The lives of those who live simply to eat, drink and make merry, with no aspiration to know the Reality concerning life, and with no desire to lead their lives in accordance with that Reality, are virtually empty of meaning and inert by nature. Such a life could be transformed into a meaningful one only if one's attention turns to the teachings of enlightened *guru*s or prophets. Such are the meanings implied in the above words of Jesus.

Two Kinds of Greatness

Greatness could be acquired in human life, as was already stated, as attributed by others as well as given by God. Jesus's complaint about the Jews is that they do not have the eye to see his God-given greatness. What they see in men as greatness is the honour given by other men. But Jesus says, "I do not receive honour from men" (5.41). He thus makes clear that the worth of a *guru* is not to be measured with the honour he receives from the society as the norm. His value solely depends upon his living as the one ultimate Reality, or God, become incarnate. This is visible only to those who love God or those who thirst for knowing the Reality. But the Jews here do not have in them such a quality. Jesus says, "But I know you, that you do not have the love of God in you" (5.42).

Jesus's greatness is as the one who has come in the name of the Father in heaven. But the Jews do not acknowledge that greatness of Jesus (5.43).

Honour in soceity is ordinarily gained somewhat like this: One man presents himself as an honourable person, and someone else publicizes the greatness of the first. He in return glorifies the man who publicized his greatness, as an honourable person or even a prophet. They thus glorify one another, not at all caring for the real greatness that comes from God (see verse 5.44).

4.9

The Bread of Two Types

JESUS, as we have noticed earlier, fed a great multitude of around 5,000 people, with five barley loaves and two small fish. The leftovers of it filled twelve baskets (6.13). On seeing this miracle, people said:

> This is truly the prophet who is to come into the world. — 6.14

The glorification given by these people need not be taken to be a recognition of the real greatness of Jesus. They did so simply because they got enough food at a place where there was nothing to eat, and thus they felt exulted. This probably was the reason why they praised Jesus. He was not unaware of this, as is evident from his words:

> Do not labour for the food which perishes, but for the food which endures to everlasting life. — 6.27

People will not hesitate even to make the man who feeds them sumptuously in a miraculous way their king. Such a kingship has validity only on the worldly level. Jesus's kingship of which he was well aware, was not of that kind:

> Therefore when Jesus perceived that they were about to come and take Him by force to make Him king, He daparted again to a mountain by Himself alone. — 6.15

After this the disciples went down to the sea, and tried to cross the sea towards Capernaum in a boat. Then the sea arose because of a great wind, and so Jesus walked across the sea to save them (6.16-21).

Attracted by Jesus's miraculous act of feeding 5,000 people with five loaves and two fish, the people reached Capernaum to seek out Jesus. They wondered how he had reached there. They therefore asked him, "Rabbi, when did you come here?" Jesus replies them thus:

> Most assuredly, I say to you, you seek Me, not because you saw the signs, but because you ate of the loaves and were filled.
>
> Do not labour for the food which perishes, but for the food which endures to everlasting life, which the Son of Man will give you, because God the Father has set His seal on Him. — 6.26-27

The Food for Everlasting Life

The people reached Capernaum, not on knowing the *guru* in Jesus, but in the exhilaration that they had eaten their fill, miraculously with five loaves of bread and two fish. This happened when Jesus took the loaves, glorified God and distributed them to the people. The loaves increased in quantity enough to feed all the 5,000 people present. This became possible because of the total identity Jesus had with God or the ultimate Reality. Whatever is possible with God happens as a natural course in the life of such a person also. In other words, this happened as an external sign of the internal oneness with God, that Jesus was constantly experiencing. This Grace of God, as far as Jesus is concerned, is his everlasting food. But the people gathered there are incapable of seeing this Grace of God, and of understanding what it is. To them Jesus says, "Do not labour for the food which perishes, but for the food which endures to everlasting life" (6.27). This latter kind of food, as we have already noticed, is nothing but the highest wisdom. Those who live in that wisdom never have to seek the worldly food they need; it reaches them unasked for. All the worldly necessities, in their case, come and minister to them, instead of having to seek them out. This is openly admitted by the Upaniṣads, as it is actually experienced by the enlightened *guru*s. In short, those who eat the food that satisfies the hunger for everlasting life, do not have to go, in search of the food for the bodily hunger. This happens miraculously. All this can be seen as suggested in the present miracle of Jesus.

Now, what should one do in order to be in possession of the food for everlasting life? Jesus answers, "Which the son of Man will give you, because God the Father has set His seal on Him" (6.27). Jesus here does not disclose the wisdom secret to those people who do not have concern for anything higher than getting enough to eat. He instead asks them simply to believe in the words of the *guru*. In his own words:

> This is the work of God, that you believe in Him whom He sent.
> — 6.29

Not understanding him, people again ask him:

> What sign will You perform then, that we may see it and believe You?
> — 6.30

They are quite unable to realize that the bread they have just eaten come from the Father in heaven, and therefore are looking for some other sign from Jesus so as to believe him. They thus remind him of the signs recorded in the scriptures. They say:

> Our fathers ate the manna in the desert; as it is written, "He gave them bread from heaven to eat." — 6.31

They, as orthodox Jews, believe in the story that their fathers survived in the desert by eating the manna that came from heaven, even as they remain ignorant that the bread they have just eaten was a similar gift of God.

Jesus then tells them,

> "Most assuredly, I say to you, Moses did not give you the bread from heaven." — 6.32

Put otherwise, it is not because of Moses who lived long long ago that they could eat the bread from heaven and feel satisfied just then, or when their ancestors roamed in the wilderness for forty years, but because of the ever-living Father in heaven. Therefore Jesus continues:

> My Father gives you the true bread from heaven.
>
> For the bread of God is He who comes down from heaven and gives life to the world. — 6.32-33

This means that those who take refuge in God, or in the ultimate Reality, do get the bread they need for survival along with getting the eternal bread of wisdom that ensures everlasting life. Only bodily hunger is needed to receive the food that ensures bodily survival. But a spiritual hunger to know the Truth and thus to make life fully meaningful, is necessary to feel satisfied with getting the kind of food that ensures eternal life.

Jesus Discloses His Life's Mission

Verses 35-40 read thus:

> And Jesus said to them, "I am the bread of life." He who comes to Me shall never hunger, and he who believes in Me shall never thirst.
>
> But I said to you that you have seen Me and yet do not believe.
>
> All that the Father gives Me will come to Me, and the one who comes to Me I will by no means cast out.
>
> For I have come down from heaven, not to do My own will, but the will of Him who sent Me.
>
> This is the will of the Father who sent Me, that of all He has given Me I should lose nothing, but should raise it up at the last day.

> And this is the will of Him who sent Me, that everyone who sees the Son and believes in Him may have everlasting life, and I will raise him up at the last day.

Jesus happened to lecture to the people, as we know, subsequent to the event of feeding 5,000 of them with five loaves and two fish. It is also to be noticed that Jesus's words here are centred round bread, by treating it as a symbol. With this as a base, Jesus now tells the people what his real mission in life is. Most of the people who listen to him, apparently, do not have much sympathy for Jesus. It is to such a mob that he discloses his mission and the importance of having belief in him as a *guru.*

The Bread of Life

Jesus, as a *guru,* is to be considered the representative or messenger of God, or of the one ultimate Reality, who has been born in this world owing to the Grace of God. Pure wisdom, an absolutely abstract, inner vision in nature, is to be counted as the most high. No higher value is attainable in human life. Bread's value, on the other hand, pertains to the earthly, here and now aspect of life as was just exemplified.

A messenger of God must be a person who lives in this world. In such an earthly life, he would be compelled to bring down the highest wisdom to the realm of the here and now, so that it would be of value and applicable in human life. Therefore Jesus perceives himself as the other-worldly wisdom having come down as "the bread of life" (6.35) in the here and now. When the words "of life" are understood in relation to the earthly level, then the word "bread" would mean that which is essential for the survival of that life. This was the bread by which 5,000 people were fed. But when understood as standing for the eternal life (*mukti*), the word "bread" would signify Jesus himself as the highest wisdom become incarnate.

Anyone who approaches such a Jesus with full belief "shall never hunger" in both of these senses. What is needed to satisfy the believer's ordinary hunger will come to him as provided by God Himself, and his thirst for wisdom will find the satisfaction of having attained the highest of all wisdom attainable. Jesus, therefore, says, "He who comes to Me shall never hunger, and he who believes in Me shall never thirst" (6.35).

A Two-sided Covenant

Nevertheless, the Jews gathered there did not have the inquisitiveness and firm belief to approach him in search of wisdom and thus to attain eternal life. Therefore Jesus had to tell them openly that what he offers is meant only for those who believe in him. Three constituent factors are involved in this context and are to be differentiated — the Father who sent Jesus, Jesus himself, and the believers who approach Jesus. Jesus first of all says, "All that the Father gives Me will come to Me." What Jesus gained, which is given by God, as we have already noticed, is the inner secret of the highest wisdom, as signified by the event of his baptism by the Holy Spirit. It could then be said that the above words of Jesus mean that God has given him the wisdom secret in its entirety.

The event whereby true seekers or disciples approach a *guru* with full faith in him as an enlightened one, also must happen equally by the Grace of God. Such genuine seekers are treated by a *guru* to be God-given. In this sense it also could well be said, "All that the Father gives Me will come to Me." This sense becomes all the more meaningful when the above line is read along with the words that follow, "The one who comes to Me I will by no means cast out" (6.37).

The reason for this is also disclosed by Jesus thus, "For I have come down from heaven, not to do My own will, but the will of Him who sent Me" (6.38). A *guru* considers teaching the highest wisdom secret to the seeking minds of the people, as his only natural duty in life; and this, according to him, is the will of the one who sent him also. This will of God is seen by Jesus to pertain to two levels. One is indicated by the words "that of all He has given Me I should lose nothing, but should also raise it up at the last day" (6.39). That means, the wholeness and integrity of the wisdom secret given to him by God should be kept in tact and transmitted to the world in all its purity and liveliness, and that his whole life, till its last moment, will be transformed into a means for this purpose. The second level of God's will is denoted by these self-explanatory words, "And this is the will of Him who sent Me, that everyone who sees the Son and believes in Him may have everlasting life; and I will raise him up at the last day" (6.40).

The first level evidently is a sort of covenant between God and Jesus, and the second a similar one between Jesus and believers. These two covenants are of such a nature that one is complementary to the other, one is meaningless without the other. The two thus could be treated as the dialectical counterparts or the obverse and reverse of a unitive covenant.

Those who get a transparent perception of this context in its entirety, who believe in Jesus and make it their own experience, will realize, "I am the bread of life," just as Jesus himself did.

Moses and Jesus

It is not to his disciples, but to the Jews who do not believe in him that Jesus speaks now. And here Jesus emphasizes the necessity of believing in the *guru* and his words. This belief, as we have already noticed, is not different from the *śraddhā* of the Vedāntic context. Incapable of understanding the deeper significance of Jesus's words, the Jews take his words, "I am the bread that came down from heaven" (6.41) in their literal sense, and begin to say among themselves:

> Is not this Jesus, the son of Joseph, whose father and mother we know? How is it then that He says, "I have come down from heaven?"
> — 6.42

Having become used to sticking to the sterile old articles of faith, the Jews neither are able to nor do they feel the necessity to raise themselves up to the sublime realm of higher wisdom, and thus reach the one all-inclusive Reality. To have the chance and ability for this also requires the Grace of God. Only those who are so blessed try to come closer to *gurus* like Jesus. He therefore says:

> No one can come to Me unless the Father who sent Me draws him; and I will raise him up at the last day. — 6.44

What do those who, by the Grace of God, happen to approach a *guru* and are taught by him, gain in life? They gain what is called *mukti* or *mokṣa* (liberation) or being raised to eternal life, also called *amr̥tatva* (immortality) in Vedānta. In this sense Jesus says, "I will raise him up at the last day." The words "at the last day" mean that this gain will mark the last stage of one's spiritual attainment. The same idea of liberation is repeated by Jesus when he says, "He has seen the Father" (6.46).

The most authoritative scriptural teachings for the Jews are the words of Moses. He and his followers, while lost in the desert, were able to survive on the manna that came down from heaven. Though a heavenly food, everyone who ate it survived but eventually died later. Yet the bread that came down from heaven to Jesus, and was now being offered to the people, is what ensures immortality. He is an incarnate form of that bread, the highest wisdom, and he assures, "One may eat of it and not die" (6.50). That means, those who gain this wisdom realize that they, in essence, are the one birthless and deathless Reality. Being that Reality, they become liberated from the phenomena of birth and death. The phenomena like birth and death are meaningful only in the realm of appearance where change is the norm. Wherever change occurs, the disappearance of old forms (death) and appearance of new forms (birth) are also inevitable. Jesus, in the above words, indicates the basic difference between two mannas — the one that came down from heaven to Moses, and the bread of wisdom that came down to Jesus from heaven. That is to say, those who ate of the first kind of manna died; but those who ate the bread of wisdom attained eternal life. This difference is somewhat like the one between Vedas and Vedānta in the Indian context. Those who take to Vedic rituals can expect to reach heaven in the hereafter, which is only a transitory gain. On the other hand, the liberation (*mukti*) that one attains here itself through the Vedāntic wisdom, is everlasting, because through wisdom one realizes oneself to be immortal. *Bhagavad-Gītā* (II.46) portrays this difference by comparing the Vedas to small pools that would become inundated by the flood waters of Vedānta.

To Eat His Flesh and to Drink His Blood

Jesus continues:

> The bread that I shall give is My flesh, which I shall give for the life of the world — 6.51

Now we have already seen in what sense Jesus is the bread that came down from heaven. To put it summarily, Jesus is pure wisdom that has assumed human form. Therefore, for him to impart that wisdom to real seekers, in principle, means, to share his own body with them, as the bread they can eat. But the Jews lacked the intuitive eye to see this subtle philosophical truth. Hence they questioned among themselves:

> How can this Man give us His flesh to eat? — 6.52

Understanding what they are disputing about, Jesus tells them again:

> Most assuredly, I say to you, unless you eat the flesh of the Son of Man and drink His blood, you have no life in you.
>
> Whoever eats My flesh and drinks My blood has eternal life, and I will raise him up at the last day. — 6.53-54

The most important promise that Jesus offers those who believe in him is this:

He who eats My flesh and drinks My blood abides in Me, and I in him. — 6.56

In recognition of this principle, the sacrement of Holy Communion became an indispensable part of church ritual in Christianity which is a reiteration of what Jesus did during his Last Supper.

Since Jesus is an enlightened *guru,* one who has attained identity with God or the ultimate Reality, his body is not to be considered a mere physical entity. The ultimate Reality is Pure Consciousness in essence. He who experiences identity with that Reality also is Pure Consciousness in essence; his physical body is also not excluded from that Reality. This is the reason why all *guru*s are always honoured or even worshipped as the embodiment of God. Indeed, those who receive the wisdom teaching from such a genuine *guru* cannot help doing so. In the above passage Jesus refers to the case in which a disciple may eat of his wisdom-body, and thus transform his own being into the embodiment of the very same wisdom. This is made clear by Jesus's words, "He who eats My flesh and drinks My blood abides in Me, and I in him" (6.56). The suggestion is that even the duality of *guru* and disciple vanishes when the latter gains the wisdom secret from the former.

We consume drinks or water along with solid food. In the case of the wisdom-meal also, if the flesh is treated as bread, then the blood that forms part of the body is counted as the drink.

The Teaching Turns Enigmatic

These words, spoken by Jesus to the Jews who did not believe in him, pass from one stage to another, and seemingly become more and more enigmatic. Finally they appear so mysterious that even his own disciples, who have full belief in him, find them very difficult to understand. Those disciples, therefore, say among themselves:

This is a hard saying; who can understand it? — 6.60

Having understood what they were talking about, Jesus asks them:

Does this offend you?

What then if you see the Son of Man ascend where He was before? — 6.62

We have noticed that, as Jesus was talking to the Jews, his words impulsively gained an enigmatic nature. It is but common that there would be a difference of opinion among the listeners regarding their intended significance. This happens mainly because listeners lack the penetrative eye to see what hides within such words. In the case of Jesus, his words alone are not what is mysterious about him; he himself is a mystery. And the ultimate limit of that mystery lies in the fact that he is the perceptible incarnate form of the imperceptible and abstract supreme Reality. Equally mysterious is the event in which the perceptible form of Jesus merges back into the imperceptible Reality, from where he emerged. This event is much more mysterious than the words he speaks. Jesus therefore wonders, what would be the state of these disciples when they directly witness that event. Really this emergence and mergence of Jesus symbolizes the mystery behind our own emergence from the one Reality and our mergence back into that Reality. There is no mystery greater than this phenomenon.

The Spirit and Life

Jesus continues to his disciples:

> It is the Spirit who gives life; the flesh profits nothing. The words that I speak to you are spirit and they are life. — 6.63

Jesus uses here two keywords — the Spirit and life. These words ordinarily are treated as synonyms. But it is evident that their usage here is not so, because of the statement, "It is the Spirit who gives life." We are already familiar with the Holy Spirit that descended like a dove upon Jesus from heaven that was opened (Luke 3.21-22). This happened when Jesus was baptized by John. As we have already seen, the Holy Spirit is none other than the ultimate Reality that became fully revealed to Jesus at that very moment. That "Holy Spirit" must be what the Spirit signifies here. This Holy Spirit, in Vedānta, is called *Ātman* (*Brahman*). And the "life" mentioned here, then, has to be the individuated aspect of the very same Spirit, which we call the life principle in all beings, and is called the soul in religion. This "life" is to be perceived to have a functional domain with two extreme poles. The lowest pole is the animating principle in living beings that is sustained by the ordinary bread, as we have already seen. The highest pole is that aspect in human beings which eats the bread of wisdom and thus attains eternal life. It is the one Spirit (*Ātman*) that becomes conditioned as both these aspects of the "life." As admitted here in the Gospel, this principle is acceptable to Vedānta also, where one unconditioned Consciousness-Reality (*cid-vastu*) is perceived as manifesting as all that appears to be, both mental and material. But this Reality becomes crystal clear only to the one with an intuitive eye, which can only be granted by God. Jesus therefore reminds his disciples:

> No one can come to Me unless it has been granted to him by My Father.
> — 6.65

The words, "No one can come to Me" do not mean that no one can approach Jesus physically. It only means, no one can approach the real message that the life and words of Jesus impart, unless granted so by God. Even some of the disciples who are physically near to Jesus, as we have noticed earlier, do not understand his words and the message they impart. Some of them even betray or deny him. They thus were not close to Jesus, even though they were always physically near. This point could also be construed in his words "The flesh profits nothing."

4.10

The Authority that Jesus Has

NOW the Jews' Feast of Tabernacles was at hand (7.2). About the middle of the feast, Jesus went up into the temple and taught. And the Jews marvelled, saying:

> How does this man know letters, having never studied?
>
> Jesus answered them and said, "My doctrine is not Mine, but His who sent Me.
>
> If anyone wants to do His will, he shall know concerning the doctrine, whether it is from God or whether I speak on My own authority."
> — 7.15-17

Jesus was not educated formally, but this was no hindrance to his becoming a *jñānin* anointed by the Holy Spirit. Almost all the Masters of the world can be seen to have had no formal education. Historically speaking, hardly anyone who had a high formal education and had occupied a high position in the society can be seen to have risen to the level of such Masters. King Janaka of the Upaniṣads and Gautama Buddha were perhaps exceptions to this in ancient India. Despite this fact, the Jews marvel that Jesus has become a *jñānin* who speaks with authority. This is because they live in a society conditioned by the notion that unless formally educated, no one can become a wise person. Jesus's overall response to this is thus, "My doctrine is not Mine, but His who sent Me. If anyone wants to do His will, he shall know concerning the doctrine, whether it is from God or whether I speak on My own authority."

There are those who are well educated, well read, and even familiar with scriptures. When they speak on the strength of the knowledge thus acquired, they depend mainly on their personal eminence. But there are those very rare individuals who have an aspiration to know the ultimate Reality concerning life, and also have the blessing of that very same Reality. They finally attain the exulting experience of the Reality that reveals Itself to them, just like a cow releases milk for its little calf. Whatever such a person speaks regarding that Reality will not be founded on his personal eminence, but upon the glory of that Reality alone. All the *gurus* and prophets are of this type regardless of their education or position. The authoritativeness of their words does not derive from their scholarliness nor from their skill in logical reasoning. The Reality that becomes revealed through their words will be self-evident. Becoming enlightened about this Reality is not possible with those who are familiar with the commonly known patterns of logical thinking alone. At the same time, those who are aspiring to take the Reality in and to live as guided by It, will absorb the words that reveal It. And these seekers will always declare openly and boldly that what they heard thus contains the key to knowing the Truth. In this sense Jesus says, "If anyone wants to do His will, he shall know concerning the doctrine, whether it is from God or whether I speak on My own authority."

How to Judge

The self-evident Truth and whatever is in accord with It is known in religious terms as the will of God. The activities of those who rely completely on this will of God are naturally bound to be in harmony with that will. Whatever agrees with that will need not be appraised as either good or evil, just or unjust. Such activities, so to speak, are beyond the bounds of any sense of justice commonly known to the world of man-made laws and customs. Jesus therefore says,

> "No unrighteousness is in him" (7.18).

When social customs and man-made laws are counted as the criteria for appraising what is right and what is wrong, then all judgements based on that notion are made according to appearance, not according to Reality. Much different is the judgement that has God's will or the self-evident Reality for its norm. Jesus, in this sense, says,

> Do not judge according to appearance. — 7.24

Jesus tells those who are hatching plans to capture him:

> You will seek Me and not find Me, and where I am you cannot come.
> — 7.34

A *jñānin* remains always residing in the absolute Reality, that is, *Brahman* (God). But this state of being one with the Reality remains alien to those who treat the one who exists in that state as an enemy. Such is the sense in which Jesus utters these words. But this is completely infathomable to the Jews who are around him. The *jñānin* remains unmindful of whether he is captured or not, or whether he is even killed or not, by those who hold appearance to be the highest value.

The Light of the World

Jesus tells the Pharisees again in chapter 8 of the Gospel:

> I am the light of the world. He who follows Me shall not walk in darkness, but have the light of life. — 8.12

Jesus is not merely a prophet who is well aware of the non-dual oneness of the ultimate Reality. He is also a *guru* who lives as that Reality. The resonance of this experiential oneness can be heard all through chapter 8 of this Gospel.

Advaita Vedānta of India, as well as the mysticism of the West, equally hold that the one ultimate Reality is pure and unconditioned Consciousness (*cit*) in essence. That Consciousness is in essence effulgence is self-evident. This light is not merely one that leads the world through the right path in life; it is not merely a light that reveals the nature of the world; more than all this, it is the effulgence that assumes the form of the world also. It is as the incarnate form of that effulgence that such a *guru* speaks with authority. In other words, that effulgence and Jesus are not two. Such is the broader sense in which he says, "I am the light of the world."

When one faithfully follows such a *guru*, one becomes transformed into that light. Whether one finds oneself in the external darkness of night, or among those who live in the internal darkness of ignorance, one does not have to be in darkness, because one is the light of eternal life, and the embodiment of the light that the ultimate Reality is. This is the reason why Jesus says, "He who follows Me shall not walk in darkness, but have the light of life."

Jesus Testifies to Himself

Jesus here, in a way, is giving testimony to himself, or he is presenting himself as the evidence regarding the truthfulness of what he says. Such a testimony never becomes acceptable against any existing worldly law. Therefore the Pharisees accuse him thus:

> You bear witness of Yourself; Your witness is not true. — 8.13

Jesus's reply to this charge is also founded on his certain realization of the Reality concerning life. For a *jñānin* is a person who lives in full certainty of the Reality from which everything including himself emerges, into which everything merges back, and as a manifest form of which everything exists. So the words of *jñānin*s always have an authoritativeness of their own. But this does not become evident to those who live ignorant of that Reality, like the Pharisees in the present case. Jesus therefore tells them:

> Even if I bear witness of Myself, My witness is true, for I know where I came from and where I am going; but you do not know where I come from and where I am going. — 8.14

In fact, what everyone should know in order to make their life meaningful is, from whence one has emerged and to where they are to disappear. The certitude and authoritativeness of an enlightened person who has resolved this conundrum, and has realized the Reality, was seen in the previous event described in this chapter. A woman who was caught in adultery was brought before Jesus by the scribes and Pharisees, and they asked him:

> Teacher, this woman was caught in adultery, in the very act.
>
> Now Moses, in the law, commanded us that such should be stoned. But what do you say? — 8.4-5

Jesus's studied but calm reply was thus:

> He who is without sin among you, let him throw a stone at her first — 8.7

Jesus did not judge anyone there. But those words of Jesus, forceful and incontrovertible, yet calm, contained more than a mere passing of judgement. Here also, Jesus, implicitly tells the Pharisees, "I judge no one" (8.15).

But Jesus did not remain without passing a judgement on that adulteress. He said to her "Neither do I condemn you, go and sin no more" (8.11). This is not a judgement as per any human law. But what the scribes and Pharisees are familiar with are only the human laws or the judgements according to the flesh (8.15). Nevertheless, the very same Jesus who said, "I judge no one", continues:

> And yet if I do judge, My judgement is true; for I am not alone, but I am with the Father who sent Me. — 8.16

That is to say, if any judgement comes from Jesus, it would always have its source in the oneness he experiences with God or the ultimate Reality. Though no such judgement is known to human law, Jesus reminds the Pharisees that they are bound to accept his judgement even according to the Jewish law they follow. For according to that law, when two men bear witness to something, it is to be accepted as true (8.17). Here also two are there to testify to Jesus — one himself, and the other God (8.18).

Jesus is fully confident of the indisputability of his words, which is why he says, "I am One who bears witness of Myself" (8.18). Really, over and above this self-witnessing is the witnessing of God also, for he is a *jñānin* who perceives God as the Reality in himself. Therefore he adds, "And the Father who sent Me bears witness of Me" (8.18). The Pharisees then ask, "Where is Your Father?" (8.19). Jesus answers simply:

> You know neither Me nor My Father. If you had known Me, you would have known My Father also. — 8.19

4.11

The Secret of Non-duality

No ignorant person realizes the greatness of a *guru*. Likewise, the one God or the ultimate Reality that the *guru* realizes as what is real in him is also not understood by the ignorant person. Put otherwise, no such person knows who he really is. Had he known himself properly, he would have known the Father who sent him, for it is that Father who has come down Himself in his form. It is in such a sense that the above-cited words of Jesus "You know neither Me nor My Father" can be interpreted from the Vedāntic perspective.

The other side of the same picture is also made explicit by Jesus thus, "If you had known Me, you would have known My Father also." The implicit meaning is that, had they recognized the real *guru* in Jesus, they would have realized the Reality in their own being as the Father in heaven. In other words, a proper knowldege of themselves would have become a proper knowledge of God also. What we hear resonating in the above words of Jesus is nothing other than the secret contained in the *mahāvākya*s (great dicta) like *tat tvam asi* (That thou art) and *aham brahma asmi* (I am the Absolute) of Vedānta. Such *mahāvākya*s contain the crux of Vedānta.

The words of Jesus in verse 19, as is made clear in the next verse, were spoken by him in the treasury as he taught in the temple. It could be to underscore the worth of those words, which reveal the secret of non-dual wisdom, that it is here specifically stated that Jesus spoke those words while he was teaching at the most worthy place, in the holiest temple as far as the Jews are concerned. Additionally, the indication here is that, though the Jews intended to catch Jesus, they did not dare to do so at such a public and holy place as the treasury of the temple. There is no other reason for no one laying hands on him is stated here other than

> "His hour had not yet come" (8.20).

Those who happen to come to this world with the noblest mission of revealing the highest secret of wisdom do not usually disappear from this world before satisfactorily fulfilling their mission even if their lifespans are not lengthy. The only reason we could give for this fact is that such is the way things are systematized in this world by the very Reality which is revealed through the *guru*'s words. This truth is revealed here by these words.

Immortality

Jesus said to them:

> I am going away, and you will seek Me, and will die in your sin. Where I go you cannot come. — 8.21

Jesus notices that those who intend to catch him do not do so even when he is near them. What prompts their failure is their own inability to comprehend the real significance of his words. This virtually is their sin. As they allow Jesus to be killed because of this sin, it is not Jesus who really dies, but they themselves. Jesus does not hesitate to remind them of this reality.

As a person who is well aware that he, in essential content, is the one birthless and deathless Reality, Jesus never sees the disappearance of his present visible form as the cessation of his being, because what is real in him never ceases to be. The Jews who are looking for an opportune moment to catch him, on the other hand, are totally ignorant of their own immortality. In their world of ignorance, therefore, both birth and death are real. The warning given by Jesus to the Jews, for this reason, could be interpreted thus: You live in the world of ignorance and thus of sin. Therefore, what you attain in your life is death. I, whom you intend to catch and kill, am immortal.

Jesus is fully convinced of himself being immortal, whether living with the present body or not. Even as the present visible form perishes, the deathless and birthless Substance that has assumed this form continues to exist. The ignorant do not attain this immortality, either here or hereafter. In this sense, Jesus says, "Where I go you cannot come."

"I Am He"

Totally incapable of understanding Jesus, the Jews thought he was intending to commit suicide as a means of avoiding being caught by them (8.22).

Disappointed though he was on noticing his valuable words were wasted because no one was there to understand him, he says:

> You are from beneath; I am from above. You are of the world; I am not of the world. — 8.23

Jesus points out to them the only way to save themselves from all sin and thus from death. He says:

> If you do not believe that I am He, you will die in your sins. — 8.24

The essential content of realizing the ultimate Reality is to have the direct experience that the one Reality or God (referred to here as "He") is what has assumed the form of everything in all the worlds and of oneself. With those who have this realization, to say "that Reality alone exists" and "I alone exist" mean the same. The final conviction we should have therefore is "I am He", or "Everything emerges from Me", as *Chāndogya Upaniṣad* (VII.26.1) prefers to express this experiential awareness (*ātmata evedam sarvam*). Jesus also says, "I am He."

Jesus's warning to the Jews is in effect this: unless and until you experience directly your oneness with the ultimate Reality or God, you will remain in ignorance; you will remain as sinners; you will attain death. Immortality or eternal life will then remain unattainble by you. The Upaniṣadic dictum, *mr̥tyoḥ sa mr̥tyum āpnoti ya iha nāneva paśyati* (whoever perceives many [as real] here goes from death to death), could be heard echoing here in these words of Jesus:

> Therefore I say to you that you will die in your sins; for if you do not believe that I am He, you will die in your sins. — 8.24

I Do Things that Please Him

Jesus tells them again,

> And He who sent Me is with Me. The Father has not left Me alone, for I always do things that please Him. — 8.29

There is really no difference in connotation between saying, "The one ultimate Reality is what has assumed the form of everything," and "Everything is sent by Him." The former statement is more in line with the terminology of Vedānta and the latter with Semitic religions. On feeling that one Reality is what fills the being of oneself, one also perceives that that Reality does not leave one alone. It is comparable to an ornament form that emerged from gold which always feels, "Gold does not leave me alone." The actual life of a person who experiences his inseparable oneness with the Reality or God, would always be as a specific form in which God finds expression. Everything that happens in life of that person, and everything that he does in life, naturally becomes agreeable to God. Such is the sense in which Jesus says, "I always do things that please Him."

The Truth Shall Make You Free

Though these enigmatic words of Jesus were not understood clearly, there were a few there who glimpsed something precious in them. A few, for this reason without understanding him, began to believe in him. Addressing such new believers, Jesus says:

> If you abide in My word, you are My disciples indeed.
>
> And you shall know the truth, and the truth shall make you free.
> — 8.31-32

There are many who become attracted to a *guru* (spiritual master) immediately on listening to him once or twice, but thereafter they simply forget or ignore it. Such persons do not achieve the ultimate benefit that the *guru*'s words aim at, which is nothing other than the attainment of *mukti* (liberation). What in Vedānta is known as *mukti,* in common parlance, is termed 'freedom;' and the same is the word Jesus also uses here.

How does one become truly free? By knowing the truth or what is ultimately Real. It is simply because people lack any knowledge of such an eternal Reality that they attach themselves to fleeting entities that simply appear to be, and so totally bind themselves unto them. They live without even knowing that they are in a state of bondage. Therefore, even someone else's good advice about how they may make themselves free goes unheeded. It is only, so to say, by the Grace of God one happens to ponder upon the eternal Reality, finally realizing that oneself is that Reality, and so experiences the blissful liberation this realization results in. Only this experience allows one to realize that, until then one remained in darkness, totally bound to the unreal. In the present case also, the real significance of Jesus's assurance to the new believers "You shall know the truth, and the truth shall make you free" is still not grasped by them. Having never lived as slaves, they do not understand that they have yet to become free. Therefore, they say:

> We are Abraham's descendants, and have never been in bondage to anyone. How can you say, "You will be made free?" — 8.33

Nature of Bondage

Jesus then replies:

> Most assuredly, I say to you, whoever commits sin is a slave of sin.
> — 8.34

The Vedāntic term nearest to sin is *avidyā* (nescience). It consists of the mental function by which the Real remains unknown and the unreal is wrongly taken to be the real. It is but natural that those who live in *avidyā*, ignorant of the Real, develop strong attachments towards what is unreal, causing their bondage in life. Thus the words "whoever commits sin is a slave of sin" becomes perfectly meaningful according to Vedānta.

The Living Truth and the Dead Letters

The Jews are a people who cling to the ancient tradition that began with Abraham, and they are proud to be so. That tradition is strictly adhered to by them, true to the letter, and to the instructions given by Abraham, as well as by the later prophets like Moses. Jesus, while fully respecting that tradition, is a *guru* who has become enlightened about the secret concerning God, the Father even of those prophets. And he lives as an embodiment of that secret. Yet those who simply live by mechanically following the instructions of the ancient prophets, remain ignorant of the real wisdom content hidden in the very words they follow. They thus happen to live by repeating and learning by heart all those words which are rather like the dead bodies of the prophets who lived in the ancient past. By sticking alone to those instructions in life, they really grope in darkness for guidance while living. Jesus, on the other hand, is a *guru* who has realized in his life the living Reality of God, and who lives as guided by the light of that realization. The words of instruction of such a *guru* also naturally would be vibrant with life's energy, which is really that of God. Intending to point out this difference, Jesus tells them:

> I speak what I have seen with My Father, and you do what you have seen with your father. — 8.38

He Sent Me

The Jews answered, "Abraham is our father." Jesus said to them:

> If you were Abraham's children, you would do the works of Abraham.
>
> But now you seek to kill Me, a Man who has told you the truth which I heard from God. Abraham did not do this.
>
> You do the deeds of your father. — 8.39-41

Jesus, by the words, "You do the deeds of your father" does not mean that they do as their real Father God himself does, or as their clan father Abraham did in his life, but that they are repeating what their unreal fathers did. The Jews really did understand what Jesus meant, and so they retort, "We were not born of fornication; we have one Father — God" (8.41). Jesus immediately comes back to his point thus:

> If God were your Father, you would love Me, for I proceeded forth and come from God, nor have I come of Myself but He sent Me.
>
> — 8.42

One who is fully aware that God or the ultimate Reality is one's real Father, realizes also that one came to this world not by one's own will, but as sent by God or by that Reality. Everything and everyone come into being as wilfully imagined by that one Reality. But most of the people live ignorant of this basic reality concerning themselves. Only the enlightened ones like Jesus live fully aware of it; and such are loved by all of unprejudiced mind, and even by wild animals, for no known reason. Jesus therefore says, "If God were your Father, you would love Me."

4.12

Competence to Gain Wisdom

THE Jews here, who listen to Jesus's words, also honestly proclaim that God is their Father; yet they remain ignorant of the inner meaning of this concept. For them, it is an article of faith. They lack the capability either to think of or to know the philosophical significance of what they believe in their religion. Jesus therefore says:

> Why do you not understand My speech? Because you are not able to listen to My word. — 8.43

Those who are endowed with an eagerness to know, along with faith, one complementing the other, alone can delve into the inner meanings of the words uttered by the *gurus*. The Jews here, who are the new believers of Jesus, and are whom he faces now, do not really possess such qualities. Something veils them from the sense in which they are the children of God. This veil, in Vedānta, is called *māyā*, which here is termed "the devil," expressed when Jesus says:

> You are of your father the devil, and the desires of your father you want to do. — 8.44

It is here that Jesus makes clear who their "father" is, when he said just prior, "You do the deeds of your father" (8.41). The place of devil in Bible is similar to that of *māyā* in Vedānta. Those who come from this devil hear the words of the devil alone; they never hear the words of God. And those who are of God hear God's words, and never the words of the devil (see 8.47).

The Vicious Circle of Ignorance

The above words of Jesus were not understandable to the Jews who were around. They therefore thought he was haunted by a demon (8.48). Denying and correcting them, Jesus says:

> I do not have a demon; but I honour My Father, and you dishonour Me.
>
> And I do not seek My own glory; there is One who seeks and judges.
>
> Most assuredly, I say to you, if anyone keeps My word he shall never see death. — 8.49-51

Those who believe in the existence of demons or evil spirits, and in the likelihood of these haunting them, as we have seen on a previous occasion, are ignorant of what ultimately exists. Thus they remain ignorant. What the ignorant consider as real, they do perceive as real; thus they see the existence and workings of evil spirits. The enlightened, on the other hand, perceive one Reality, God (*Brahman*) alone, as existing and working. They do not see any evil spirit anywhere, because it is what people believe in that they see. The most powerful evil spirit that haunts man is his own ignorance of himself. Being haunted by this demon of ignorance the Jews now think Jesus is haunted by some demon. This is a glaring example clearly showing the nature of the vicious circle created by ignorance (*ajñāna*). But Jesus is not an ignorant person in the least; he is an enlightened one, a *jñānin.* He is not only fully aware that he is not haunted by any demon, but also that even the idea of the existence of demons is a creation of ignorance. Therefore he says unhesitatingly, "I do not have demon."

Is one's own testimony as to whether or not one is haunted by an evil spirit enough? Seen from the worldly point of view, such a judgement would not be considered valid. But the words of Jesus come from another kind of authority, which transcends all worldly perspectives. His words derive, on the other hand, from his direct experience of the being of the ultimate Reality or God in himself, and from honouring It fully. By indicating that authority, Jesus says, "I honour My Father."

A *jñānin* never thinks of his own greatness, neither does he blow his own trumpet. He does not consider himself as a person of eminence, but merely as an insignificant and humbly fleeting fragment of the great Reality, God. Therefore, it is not to be considered that Jesus took seriously being dishonoured by the Jews. He himself says:

> You dishonour Me.
>
> I do not seek My own glory. — 8.49-50

Nevertheless, there is one who watches over what His own Son does, he who was sent to the world. God's wish is that His Son should reveal the greatness of His kingdom or the wisdom secret to the world. He must always watch His son and judge whether he carries out his assignment gloriously or not.

Therefore Jesus cannot pull himself back just because the Jews do not acknowledge him as the Son of God. He says, "There is One who seeks and judges."

Jesus then reminds them how valuable are the words he utters as ordained by God Himself, thus, "Most assuredly I say to you, if anyone keeps My word he shall never see death."

Jesus's words here are a replete expression of his inseparable oneness with God, as well as everyone else's. Listening to those words, cogitating on them, and meditating on them, allow one to realize that it is the one birthless and deathless Reality that has assumed one's own fleeting form. By realizing this reality, one finds one's identity with that Reality and so becomes deathless, though the form (individual) that Reality has assumed for the time being vanishes. The disappearance and appearance of these fleeting forms do not make the Real content in them non-existent. That content is birthless and deathless. One thus realizes, "I am that deathless Reality." Such is the sense in which the words of Jesus "He shall never taste death" are to be appreciated.

Before Abraham was, I Am

The Jews, on hearing these words of Jesus, begin to suspect all the more strongly that he is possessed by a demon. They say:

> Now we know that you have a demon! Abraham is dead, and the prophets; and you say, "If anyone keeps My word he shall never taste death."
>
> Are you greater than our father Abraham, who is dead? And the prophets are dead. Whom do You make Yourself out to be? — 8.52-53

To these people who speak in such terms, Jesus says:

> If I honour Myself, My honour is nothing. It is My Father who honours Me, of whom you say that He is your God. — 8.54

Even though the Jews repeat the words "our God" with full faith, they are totally ignorant of the God they speak of. And for this reason, they do not know how to live according to the will of God either, other than adhering to the religious laws they are taught. While at the same time, it is the very same "our God" they repeatedly mention, who is the sole witness to the greatness of Jesus. So basically there is a vast difference between the Jews here and Jesus. Pointing it out, Jesus says,

"Yet you have not known Him, but I know Him." — 8.55

Jesus concludes his lecture by clarifying the uniqueness of the great masters like himself, with these mysterious words,

"Before Abraham was, I am." — 8.58

We should perceive in a *guru*, as we have already understood, two distinct aspects: one, the eternal *guru* of which he is an embodiment, and two, the temporal and spatial manifest form of the same guruhood, as a human being who was born, lives and will die. A real *guru* never lives identified with the latter aspect. On the contrary, he lives identified with the ever existing *guru*, not as a person who was born and is destined to die. It is in this sense that Jesus says, "Before Abraham was, I Am." In other words, the guruhood represented by Jesus existed even before Abraham whom the Jews consider as their original father.

A context very similar to this appears in *Bhagavad-Gītā* also. In it, the Guru Śrī Kṛṣṇa tells Arjuna, the disciple:

This unexpending *yoga* I first declared to Vivasvān. He taught it to Manu, who in turn imparted it to Ikṣvāku! — IV.1

The very same age-old *yoga* is again being declared to you now by me. — IV.3

Vivasvān lived long before the time of the *Mahābhārata* story, of which *Gītā* forms a part, whereas Śrī Kṛṣṇa who was presently teaching Arjuna lived during that period. Then how could Śrī Kṛṣṇa teach Vivasvān? Arjuna raises this doubt. Then Kṛṣṇa tells him of the eternality of the guruhood in him. This ever existing *guru*-principle assumes the forms of living *gurus* time and again as and when mankind is badly in need of the guidance of an enlightened one. Only such actual *gurus* in this world can teach. The eternal guruhood as such never teaches directly. Clarifying this aspect, *Gītā* says:

Whenever laxity with regard to *dharma* comes about, *adharma* asserting itself O Arjuna! then I Myself come forth. — IV.7

4.13

The Way God Acts

CHAPTER 9 of John's Gospel narrates the event of a man who was blind from birth, who becomes sighted, and the ensuing happenings. Religiously-minded people, on seeing a man who is handicapped from birth, or who has became so somehow, ordinarily assume that he must have committed some sin to deserve this. If not he in this life, his ancestors must have done so, or else he himself in his previous births must have been a sinner. The disciples of Jesus also, on seeing a man who was blind from birth, ask Jesus:

> Rabbi, who sinned, this man or his parents, that he was born blind?
> — 9.2

Rather than assuming that the bodily impairment of a person was caused as stated above, the more scientific and absolutist stand would yield a view like this: nature incessantly brings forth from itself an infinite variety of new facets of existence, or the one Reality manifests ever new forms. An overall structural perfection, along with certain laws of consistency, could be noticed everywhere in this self-unfoldment of nature. Nevertheless, almost all the laws of nature have exceptions. In fact, to have exceptions to its own rules, as it were, is also part of the law of nature. Then, what we think of as the deformity of a person is also part of nature's self-unfoldment. To put this in religious terms, such is the way God works, or the way God's *karma*s find expression. Therefore, the question, "How did this happen?" is of no relevance. Jesus therefore answers:

> Neither this man nor his parents sinned, but that the works of God should be revealed in him. — 9.3

Day and Night

A sort of principle of day and night is involved here. Daytime represents the wisdom that perceives all the events in nature as the handiworks of God. In that daytime all the events, from a man being born blind, to everything that takes place in the entire cosmic system, are visualized as the work of God that goes on everywhere unceasingly. No one, upon visualizing this, would feel like asking how such and such a thing happened in nature. In that broad daylight, whatever one happens to do as a natural course, also turns out to have the noble character of God's work. Jesus, therefore, says:

> I must work the works of Him who sent Me while it is day. — 9.4

This daytime is something that dawns within, mostly when the graceful blessings of a *guru* envelop one. Even when one feels this daytime within, others who are nearby need not feel it. One's transparency of vision, in all its purity, need not necessarily be transmitted to the next generation either. The daytime of wisdom thus eventually makes way for the night that follows. In that darkness of ignorance, all the works one performs in life are taken to be one's own actions (*karma*s). Then one performs action with the sense of being their doer, and so attached to their fruits. Thus, in effect, those works cease to be the actions of God. Any action performed in life becomes true to Reality only when seen as God's work. Therefore Jesus says,

> The night is coming where no one can work — 9.4

Jesus perceives what he does also pertain to this context. His acts, then, do not take place in the darkness of ignorance, as if not the works of God; they take place, on the other hand, as the actions of God in the broad daylight of wisdom. This is the way Jesus reveals this reality in his own way:

> As long as I am in the world, I am the light of the world. — 9.5

Put otherwise, as long as he lives, the daytime that Jesus represents also will continue. The mysterious action that heals the blindness of a man also, in his perception, is something that happens as willed by God, and not as something worked out by him as a person of unworldly attainments.

> When He had said these things, He spat on the ground and made clay with the saliva; and He anointed the eyes of the blind man with the clay. — 9.6

But it was not when he did this that the blind man was healed. In order to make clear that this healing happens as willed by God, not as worked out by himself, Jesus, after anointing the eyes of the man with the clay, asks him, "Go, wash in the pond of Siloan" (9.7). Now, Siloan means "Sent." That means the healing of the man was "sent" by God. In short, he became blind as willed by God, and his healing also takes place in the same way.

Then why could not God have kept him sighted even from birth? We ask such questions by making use of the human intelligence we possess. Yet the will of God always remains inestimable to the human mind. It is better we do not ask this question.

Actions and Sinful Actions

Jesus goes on talking to the Pharisees on the same topic of blindness, and as a result the meaning of "blindness" gains a new dimension. Now the Pharisees begin to suspect, "Are we blind also?" (9.40). Jesus says to them:

> If you were blind, you would have no sin; but now you say "We see." Therefore your sin remains. — 9.41

There are beings in this world, blind in respect to the idea of the real and the unreal, with no worry about good and evil. The actions of these beings are neither sinful nor meritorious; such are mere actions (*karma*s). For example, the "cruel" killings done by animals, particularly ferocious animals, can never be considered sinful actions, but merely are actions natural to them. It is so because such animals live in a sort of blindness. But humans are not so, particularly the Pharisees who now try to judge Jesus. They are proud that they discriminate the good from the evil, and the real from the unreal. They, in that sense, think, "We see." When such people do something that goes against their own notion of the good, such actions become naturally sinful. The Pharisees, by not recognizing Jesus as the Christ, and by judging and finally killing him, are committing the sin of violating the very doctrines they believe in. Such are the implications of Jesus's words, "If you were blind, you would have no sin; but now you say, 'we see.' Therefore yours sin remains."

4.14

One World, One Religion

Jesus says:

> "Most assuredly, I say to you, he who does not enter the sheepfold by the door, but climbs up some other way, the same is a thief and a robber.
>
> But he who enters by the door is the shepherd of the sheep.
>
> To him the doorkeeper opens, and the sheep hear his voice; and he calls his own sheep by name and leads them out.
>
> And when he brings out his own sheep, he goes before them; and the sheep follow him, for they know his voice.
>
> Yet they will by no means follow a stranger, but will flee from him, for they do not know the voice of strangers."
>
> Jesus used this illustration, but they did not understand the things which He spoke to them. — 10.1-6

Jesus again speaks to clarify what he meant by these puzzling words. It then becomes clear that he compares the people to sheep, and himself to the shepherd, as the *guru*, who directs them to have a proper goal in life, as well as a befitting means to attain it. He says:

> Most assuredly, I say to you, I am the door of the sheep.
>
> All who came before Me are the thieves and robbers, but the sheep did not hear them. — 10.7-8

An important livelihood of the people of Judea in those days was the rearing of sheep. Jesus, therefore, chose this as an analogy to tell the listeners who he really was. The common practice of shepherds was to pen the sheep in their fold at night and to let them out in the morning to lead them to the grazing ground. Jesus says, the safe door for the sheep to enter their pen is himself. The purport is that he is the *guru* who leads them to the safest abode of wisdom and thus to make them really happy and peaceful in life. The authority that Jesus has to declare this derives from his realization of the kingdom of God within himself. Until the time of Jesus, these Jews only had the leadership of the scribes, Pharisees and the like. What they knew was not the secret of the kingdom of heaven, but only certain commandments given in the scriptures. Therefore, these leaders could only compel the people to live abiding by those commandments. Not having become enlightened, they were not the safe and direct door for the sheep to enter their pen and to get out. They are, therefore, to be treated as thieves and robbers who enter the pen through some other devious way (see 10.8).

Those true seekers who listen to the words of wisdom of an enlightened *guru* easily differentiate him from the religious scholars who are only learned in scriptures. Naturally their attention turns from the scholars to the enlightened one. Jesus, in this sense, says, "I am the door of the sheep. All who came before Me are thieves and robbers, but the sheep did not hear them."

The Door and the Good Shepherd

Jesus, in verse 11, says,

> "I am the good shepherd."

Just now we have seen Jesus himself saying, "I am the door" (10.7). His claim thus is that the door through which the sheep (people) are let into the pen, and the good shephered who leads the sheep in and out of the pen are himself. Such a claim is not understandable when logically looked at. The door through which seekers enter the domain of wisdom is the word of the enlightened *guru.* A *guru* and his word cannot be seen as separate, for a *guru* becomes a *guru* only when he teaches wisdom. A *guru* does not remain satisfied with teaching wisdom to the people, he also leads their lives along the path of wisdom. It is not merely from his words that people get guidance. His very life serves as a torch for them. Such is the implicit meaning of the earlier words of Jesus, "He goes before them; and the sheep follow him" (10.4). Guruhood finds expression through words in order to teach wisdom, as well as through the *guru*'s life in order to teach how to live in full accord with wisdom. He is thus the door as well as the shepherd.

A Teaching of Universal Value

Jesus continues:

> I am the good shepherd; and I know My sheep, and am known by My own.
>
> As the Father knows Me, even so I know the Father. — 10.14-15

We have seen in another context, which qualities are found together in a *guru* as a good shepherd. The Son knowing the Father well, and He in turn functioning as a good shepherd for the sheep, together comprise the essential content of this context. As there is a rapport as well as a covenant between the Father and the Son, so there is developed a rapport and agreement beetween the Son and the people. How the one becomes contentless and meaningless without the other was also noticed by us earlier. Fully dedicated to God or the ultimate Reality is the life of a genuine *guru.* On the other side of it, like the reverse side of a coin, comes his life which is fully dedicated to the cause of the Happiness of mankind as a whole or of the total life system. A *guru* could thus be seen as a link between *Brahman* (God) and everything in all the worlds. The former side of this covenant was seen in the part of verse 10.15 quoted above. Indicating the latter side of it, Jesus continues:

> I lay My life for the sheep — 10.15

A *guru*'s words always brim with the visualization of the one Reality, with the realization of his own oneness with that Reality. Such words are felt to be meaningful by any seeking person, anywhere in the world, not merely by the people who hear him first hand. All seekers would feel the Reality-content in those words to be meaningful in their own lives. The significance of the words of Jesus, thus, is not only relevant to the Jewish community whom he addresses here. There could be people anywhere in the world attracted to those words. His words are not only meant for the Christian community that acknowledges him as the only saviour. Visualizing mankind as one unit is natural with all *guru*s. Mankind can be considered to have attained Peace in life when they live as guided by the one Reality underlying their own being, about which all *guru*s teach. Men cross the barriers between separate religions and live as one human family once they realize that what all *guru*s reveal is but one Truth alone, and that it is that Truth which makes them free in the true sense. And they cross those barriers when they forgo the notion that people who follow the teachings of one *guru* are of one religion, and those of another *guru* are of another religion. Jesus, therefore, says:

> And other sheep I have which are not of this fold; them also I must bring, and they will hear My voice; and there will be one flock and one shepherd. — 10.16

There is a safe door for the sheep to enter the pen. It, in effect, serves as the pointer for the sheep as to which direction they should enter and which they should not. This door, in Indian religion, is known as *dharma* (righteousness). That which is not righteous is called *adharma*. There are two ways ordinarily available for men to decide what is righteous and what is not. One is that of the moral codes that form part of the scriptural teachings. Such kind of scriptures in India are known as Dharma-Śāstras. The scribes and Pharisees in the present case are familiar with such lawful codes. The other way is to adhere to the wisdom teachings of the *guru*s, where people naturally find themselves living according to Truth without necessarily strictly following any social moral codes as such. The first makes one bound to many relativistic considerations, while the latter is the absolutist way free of all such thoughts, even of the duality of *dharma* and *adharma.* Though to be entered with care, with the guidance of a shepherd, the latter way leads one to absolute freedom. As such a *guru,* Jesus says, "I am that door."

Jesus, a Satya-dharman

Thus a pattern of behaviour in life, that transcends the bounds of *dharma* and *adharma,* gets shaped from pure wisdom, as though willed by the Reality or God. A *guru* is the embodiment of that Reality. That means, such a way of life issues forth from the *guru* himself. Jesus in this sense says, "I am the good shepherd." Put otherwise, both Reality (*satya*) and the righteous way of life (*dharma*) become non-dually one in a true *guru* (*sad-guru*). Such a person is distinguished as a *satya-dharman* in *Īśa Upaniṣad* (*mantra* 15). Jesus thus is a *satya-dharman.*

Despite all these words spoken out by him, the Jews who were listening to him, were not of a mindset to acknowledge Jesus as a true *guru* or the Christ. Still full of doubts, they again ask him:

> How long do You keep us in doubt? If You are the Christ, tell us plainly. — 10.24

No *guru* openly declares that he is a true *guru* or the Christ. But words that evidently show that he is an enlightened person have already profusely come forth from him. And miracles merely of worldly value, like giving sight to the blind man, also were seen in him by the Jews. They still prefer not to believe in him. Jesus therefore finally says:

> I told you, you do not believe. The works that I do in My Father's name, they bear witness for Me.

But you do not believe, because you are not My sheep. — 10.25-26

"The works I do in My Father's name" mentioned by Jesus, range from the miracle of giving external sight to the blind man, to speaking the words of highest wisdom that remove the inner blindness of men. Seeing all such works of Jesus, sadly enough, did not arouse any spiritual rapport with him in the minds of the Jews here. For this reason, Jesus tells them straightaway "You are not My sheep", though they were around him and hearing him.

Were they disciples having any spiritual aspiration as well as a spiritual rapport with him, they would have drunk in the non-dual secret with which his words are filled and would have experienced the rapture of it. That non-dual secret, which did not find its way into the minds of the Jews here, is once again affirmed by Jesus, in a very cryptic form, in a tone with a touch of emotion, thus,

"I and My Father are one" — 10.30

4.15

One with the Selfhood of God

CHAPTER 11 describes the event where Jesus raised Lazarus from the dead and what followed. Mary and Martha, the sisters of Lazarus, were close devotees of Jesus. Even after they sent word to him of the sickness of Lazarus, Jesus stayed two more days at the place where he was. Even after that, instead of going to visit the sick man, Jesus told his disciples, "Let us go to Judea again" (11.7). Now Judea was a place where people were seeking to stone him, a fact which the disciples reminded him of. Then Jesus responded thus:

> Are there not twelve hours in a day? If anyone walks in the day, he does not stumble, because he sees the light of this world.
>
> But if one walks in the night, he stumbles, because the light is not in him.
>
> — 11.9-10

Wisdom Does not Fear Ignorance

As everyone knows, it is easy to walk in the daytime without stumbling. But it is not so at night. There is a real possibility of falling or faltering if one walks in the darkness of night. The day and night mentioned here by Jesus are not of the ordinary kind. Day here stands for the brightness of wisdom, and night for the darkness of ignorance. It has become clear by now that the Jews here live in the night time of ignorance, and for this reason they stumble upon their life's journey. In the course of their stumbling comes their intention to stone Jesus. He, on the other hand, is a *guru* who lives in the broad daylight of wisdom where there is no room for any stumbling. Day does not fear night, and wisdom has no fear of ignorance. For this reason, Jesus has no hesitation to go into the midst of those Jews who are ignorant. As long as wisdom shines with all its glory, fearlessness will be there in life. Jesus still lives in the bright daylight of wisdom. Therefore he asks his disciples, "Are there not twelve hours in a day?"

A *guru* is an enlightened person, and thus is the Son of God. But in this world he has actually to live as the son of Man. As the Son of God, he always walks in the broad daylight of wisdom. But in actual life, in unavoidable situations, as the son of Man, his life may have to yield to the ignorance that prevails in worldly life. It is only there where he stumbles, as symbolized by those who stumble when walking at night.

I Am the Resurrection and the Life

Finally when Jesus decided to visit the house of Martha and Mary in Bethany to see Lazarus, it was too late; it had already been four days since Lazarus had been laid in the tomb. Martha then tells Jesus:

> Lord, if You had been here, my brother, would not have died.
>
> But even now I know that whatever You ask God, God will give You.
> — 11.21-22

What Martha means is that, had he visited them before the death of Lazarus, Jesus could have saved him. Jesus then says, "Your brother will rise again" (11.23). The dead, according to the belief of the Jews, may resurrect according to the last judgement of God. But Jesus adds:

> I am the resurrection and the life. He who believes in Me though he may die, he shall live.
>
> And whoever lives and believes in Me shall never die. — 11.25-26

The resurrection that Jesus refers to is not to happen after death. It should occur even as one lives. This resurrection really is none other than becoming twice born (*dvija*), as we have seen earlier. In essence, it is to become one with the Selfhood of God. One attains it by becoming resurrected from the state of being a mortal individual being, having birth and death, to the state of being the birthless and deathless *Ātmā* (Self) or God. This is attained by realizing, while living, what is the real content in the being of oneself. Such a state of attainment in Vedānta, is known as *jīvan-mukti* (to be liberated while living). The emergence and remergence of bodies are perceived in that state to be but fleeting manifestations that occur in the one Reality (*Ātmā*), and which in no way affect the oneness and immutability of the *Ātmā* (God). It is comparable to the rising and subsiding of the waves that do not affect the oneness and eternality of the ocean. Therefore, the perishing of the body, as far as the enlightened ones are concerned, is no death at all.

The oneness with the Selfhood of God, in its turn, is attained most often with the graceful imparting of wisdom by a *guru* to a seeking disciple who fully believes in the truthfulness of his words. For a person who is thus enlightened, the *guru*, resurrection and life are all undifferentiable, which is why Jesus says, "I am the resurrection and the life."

A person of such a resurrection considers the falling of perishable body not as marking the end of life, but as merely one of the numerous phenomena that appear as a part of the eternal flow of apparent manifestations. The eternality of life becomes actualized through the emergence and remergence of manifest forms. What we call death, then, is but part of the eternality of life. As this wisdom is attained only through a *guru,* Jesus says, "He who believes in Me, though he may die, he shall live" (11.25). The purport is that, he who attains wisdom as taught by a true *guru* in whom he fully believes, realizes his immortality. Death no longer is of any concern for him. The appearance and disappearance of bodily forms are not considered by him as the birth and death of what he really is. Jesus therefore says, "Whoever lives and believes in Me shall not die."

Raising Lazarus: A Symbol

Lazarus who had been laid to rest in a tomb four days before, finally came back to life and rose up from the tomb. The greatness of God, and the belief of both Martha and Mary in Jesus as the Son of God, are the only causes attributable to this miraculous occurrence. Jesus said earlier, "He who believes in Me, though he may die, he shall live." Lazarus's coming back to life could be seen as a sort of exaggerated visual exposition of the wisdom content in these words of Jesus. Very similar is the way how chapters X and XI of *Bhagavad-Gītā* are related. Chapter X teaches the philosophical truth that everything in all the worlds, including all the inevitable specific events in human life, is nothing but the manifest form (*vibhūti*) that ceaselessly appears and disappears in the one Reality (*Brahman*). This teaching is presented as an actual vision in the next chapter where *Brahman* is seen with Arjuna's own eyes to have assumed the cosmic system and the life system in it. From the Vedāntic perspective, Lazarus's coming back to life is to be taken rather as a symbol than as a mere event.

In order for the one *Ātmā*-Reality in one to become self-evident, the inert aspect in the being of oneself has to be removed first. Lazarus rising up symbolizes one becoming free of death and attaining immortality by means of wisdom. The stone that was covering the tomb of Lazarus represent the inert aspect in ourselves, to be negated first. Jesus therefore asks,

> "Take away the stone." — 11.39

Upon removing that stone of inertness the real resurrection of Lazarus occurs.

Jesus, just before being captured by the Pharisees and scribes, tells his disciples, "The hour has come that the Son of Man should be glorified."

Jesus, A Grain of Wheat

> Most assuredly, I say to you, unless a grain of wheat falls into the ground and dies, it remains alone, but if it dies, it produces much grain. — 12.24

That Jesus is wisdom embodied, we have already noticed. If it should become beneficial to the world, the seed of wisdom should fall into heart of all the people. It is compared here to one grain of wheat or paddy growing a hundredfold after being sown into a proper field. And this hundredfold growth becomes possible only when the seed sown dies and becomes part of the soil. Likewise, the grain of wheat that Jesus as an individual is, has to perish and disappear, to ensure that what he represents grows a hundredfold. Put otherwise, Jesus's acceptance of death virtually means his living a hundredfold in the future.

The philosophical implications of the rest of the chapter 12 have been discussed by us earlier in different contexts. In verse 48 of the chapter, Jesus says:

> He who rejects Me, and does not receive My words, has that which judges him — the word that I have spoken will judge him in the last day.

Those who reject him and do not receive his words apparently are the Pharisees and scribes. They too have their own notion of the last judgement based on a perception of the commandments of Moses; a notion relativistic and conditional in nature. Those who live guided by such a notion, though they think they are happy in life, really have the happiness available in hell alone. Jesus's words, on the contrary, have for their source the realization of the one ultimate Reality or God. And the wisdom contained in those words is purely absolutist in nature. This wisdom has always to be the final criterion for all judgements. The above words of Jesus are to be understood as related to this context.

4.16

The Guru–Disciple Bipolarity

JOHN the Gospel writer, at the beginning of chapter 13, says:

> Jesus knew that His hour had come that He should depart from this world to the Father, having loved His own who were in the world. He loved them to the end. — 13.1

This statement apparently is about the life of Jesus near his final days. All that he wanted to teach his disciples had already been taught. The state of Jesus's mind at that particular time could be heard resounding in the above words of St John.

Loving whatever is one's own and whoever is dear to one, as "These are mine" is natural in human life. The one who loves thus develops a sort of identity with what one loves. As long as this sense of identity exists, the love one feels for oneself is extended to the ones loved also. Who are the ones loved here by Jesus? It could be said, he loved his close disciples whom he taught, or even he loved the people who believed in him. But as a *jñānin,* what Jesus loves is not merely a few disciples or a few believers alone; his love is for the world as a whole. Such is the way the words, "having loved His own who were in the world" become meaningful in the Vedāntic perspective.

Where is the limit of the world he thus loved? The only answer would be, he loved the world to its end. This end could be taken temporally as well as spatially. In this sense John says, "He loved them to the end."

Guru Washing the Disciples' Feet

The chapter then describes the details of the scene where Jesus washes the feet of his disciples and wipes them with the towel with which he was girded. When he came to Simon Peter to wash his feet, he said to Jesus, "Lord, are You washing my feet?" Jesus answered, "What I am doing you do not understand now, but you will know after this." Peter said to him, "You shall never wash my feet." Jesus answered him, "If I do not wash you, you have no part with Me" (13.6-8).

For disciples to wash their *guru*'s feet and sprinkle that water over their own heads — sometimes even drinking it — is an observance familiar to the Indian culture. The present scene in the Gospel shows that this ritual was practised by the Jews also. While remaining a seeker, the disciple performing personal services for his *guru* and washing his feet are but natural markings of the bipolarity between them. But when this intimacy reaches its peak, and when the *guru* has already imparted the wisdom secret to the disciple, the difference between the wisdom of the *guru* and the wisdom of the disciple vanishes, and thus the *guru*–disciple duality also becomes meaningless. Recognizing this principle is what the ritual of the *guru* washing the feet of the disciple in return signifies.

What a *guru* realizes as the real content of his own being, as well as of the whole world, is pure Consciousness or *Ātmā,* and attaining this realization is the essence of wisdom. He imparts this wisdom in its true form to his disciple. Handing it down heirarchically thus from *guru* to disciple through generations is the one and only wish a *guru* has in his life. A *guru* does not merely expect a disciple to know the secret of wisdom; he should also walk on the path of the same wisdom in his life. This must be the implicit meaning of the ritual of a *guru* that washes his disciples' feet, the organs meant for walking.

A New Commandment

Jesus gives his disciples a new commandment in verse 13.34, thus:

> A new commandment I give to you, that you love one another; as I have loved you, that you also love one another.

Though said directly to his disciples, these words, as a commandment, are meant for the entirety of mankind. The love a *guru* has for all is unconditional. So is the love of God for everyone. It could well be said therefore that a *guru*'s love and God's love are equal. Those who experience the love of a *guru* or God realize also that there is nothing to despise in all the worlds. Furthermore, feeling this unconditional love of God or *guru*, then becomes reflected in their life as they love one another unconditionally. This commandment of Jesus, in fact, needs no comment.

4.17

The Way, the Truth, the Life

JESUS says in chapter 14, verse 6:

> "I am the way, the truth, and the life."

The context here is that of Jesus preparing for the end of his life in this world and go back to God from where he came. He invites his disciples also to go back to the same abode of God, from where they also came, as made clear in verse 3. God, thus, is the common source and goal of both Jesus and his disciples, which is but natural, for no Reality other than God (*Brahman*) does exist. Now there should always be a means to reach any goal. As no reality other than God exists, God has to be the means as well. For the very same reason, Jesus is not different from God, and thus is the means. Hence his words:

> No one comes to the Father except through Me. — 14.6

A context almost similar to this appears in *Taittirīya Upaniṣad* in its third *vallī* (chapter). Bhr̥gu, the son and disciple of Āruṇi, approaches his father seeking to be taught in *brahma-vidyā* (Science of *Brahman*). The father gives merely an indication of what *Brahman* is, and then asks his son to go out and to know *Brahman on* his own, by undergoing austere self-discipline (*tapas*). The father immediately reminds him also, "That austere self-discipline (*tapas*) is *Brahman*" (*tapo brahmeti*). Put otherwise, the goal to be attained itself is what functions as the means of attaining it as well. Jesus also in this sense says, "I am the way and the truth."

This truth is to be realized while living here and now. Furthermore, life here becomes fully meaningful only when it becomes a living image of the Truth thus realized. One then feels one's own life to be inseparably one with the Truth or *Brahman*. This is indicated by the words of Jesus, "I am the life."

The Sanskrit equivalent to "I" is *ātmā*. That this *ātmā* is consciousness in essential content is well acknowledged in Vedānta, and the same is the experience that everyone has of themselves. This consciousness is designated by the word *cit* in Sanskrit, a word that forms part of the compound word *sat-cit-ānanda*, which denotes *Brahman* (*Ātmā*). It is well known in Vedānta that the way to know the ultimate Reality is through interiorizing one's search, looking at oneself, and thus perceiving what is the essential content in one's own being. This essential content is finally found to be pure Consciousness. And apparently it is in the very same Consciousness that the search for the Consciousness-Reality also takes place. That is to say, "I am (Consciousness is) the way."

The ultimate Reality in oneself, which is the Reality in everything also, being Consciousness in essence, means "I am (Consciousness is) the Truth."

The world, including the phenomenon of life in it, is perceived by Vedāntins as the beginningless and endless sport that happens within the one Consciousness (*Ātmā*). That means, the mysterious phenomenon called life is part of the innumerable manifest forms of the one and only Reality (*Ātmā*) that is Consciousness in essence. It could thus well be said, "I am (Consciousness is) the life."

Again in verse 6 Jesus says, "No one comes to the Father except through Me."

"To come to the Father" means, to have the direct intuitive perception of the one ultimate Reality which is nothing but pure Consciousness. Not to mention that the effort for this attainment also takes place in the same Consciousness. This Consciousness-Reality or *Ātmā* is what "I" signifies here. Thus the statement "No one comes to the Father except through Me" means, realizing the ultimate Reality is attained only through the efforts, of Consciousness with the guidance of a *guru.*

Jesus again says,

> "If you had known Me, you would have known My Father" — 14.7

"If you had known me" means, "had even one known oneself." One knowing what is Real in oneself, as we have already seen, means knowing God (*Brahman*).

Another Helper

Verses 15-17 of chapter 14 read as follows:

Jesus says:

> If you love me, keep My commandments.
>
> And I will pray the Father, and He will give you another Helper, that He may abide with you forever,

> even the Spirit of truth, whom the world cannot receive, because it neither sees Him nor knows Him; but you know Him, for He dwells with you and will be in you.

Here Jesus also speaks to his disciples and these words form a part of his final words of instruction.

We have noticed earlier, what the commandments of Jesus are. It is better to interpret the words. "Keep My commandments", to mean "You will spontaneously keep My commandments" than "You should keep My commandments." The time for giving positive guidance to his disciples is now over, for these words come from Jesus at the fag end of his life. Their faith and true discipleship will be reflected in their day-to-day life, in the form of their adherence to the commandments of the *guru*. This happens naturally, rather than as a bounden duty.

What Jesus says then is exceedingly obscure. He is about to leave the world, and thus his actual presence, among the disciples will shortly cease. It is in this context that Jesus tells his disciples, "I will pray the Father, and He will give you another Helper, that He may abide with you forever." The Helper meant by Jesus is presumably the wisdom secret he has already taught them, but which is yet to become clear to them. Once it has become transparent, it will abide with them forever. This secret was first seen as the Spirit that descended on Jesus from heaven as he was baptized by John the Baptist. The same is here referred to as the "Spirit of truth." Jesus is to be thought to be praying to God, "Let this Spirit descend on My disciples also." It is to be assumed from the earlier words of Philip to Jesus, "Lord, show us the Father and it is sufficient for us" (14.8), that the Father or the one ultimate Reality remains yet to become evident to them through wisdom. Ordinary people are not expected to feel the presence of the Spirit of truth in guiding their lives. It is felt only by those who have drunk the essence of wisdom taught by their *guru,* which is the reason why Jesus says, "Whom the world cannot receive, because it neither sees Him nor knows Him."

Did Jesus feel that the Spirit of truth was already with his disciples? It is true that he has already taught them whatever he wanted to convey to them. After all this, and especially at the moment of his departure, every true and hopeful *guru* would take it for granted that the disciples are already in possession of the wisdom secret he taught. Therefore Jesus separates them out from the people of the world and says to them, "But you know Him, for He dwells in you and will be in you."

The Spirit of truth that Jesus speaks of as having been known to the disciples, is the one the world has never seen and has never known. In what manner do the disciples know it? They know it as the essential content of their own being, even as an ornament realizes itself to be gold in content. And for this reason Jesus says, "He dwells with you." That means, what is real in them is the Spirit of truth. And it is that Spirit that will always be with them even after Jesus leaves them.

4.18

The Finality of the Teaching

JESUS continues in verses 18-21 of chapter 14 as follows:

> I will not leave you orphans; I will come to you.
>
> A little while longer and the world will see Me no more, but you will see Me. Because I live, you will live also.
>
> At that day you will know that I am in My Father, and you in Me, and I in you.
>
> He who has My commandments and keeps them, it is he who loves Me. And he who loves Me will be loved by My Father, and I will love him and manifest Myself in him.

To feel as if one has become an orphan is one of the worst distresses in human life. The one Master that protects everyone is God or the one ultimate Reality. And this Reality fills each of us as the Substance of our own being. What all the *guru*s really do is to show us this Master already in ourselves, and thus free us from the sense of orphanhood that we wrongly had. Jesus also did the same. In this sense he tells his disciples, "I will not leave you orphans."

It is when this secret becomes opened to us, as revealed by the *guru,* that we really feel the presence of the *guru* in ourselves. Jesus therefore says, "I will come to you."

Differentiating again the people of the world from his disciples, Jesus says, "A little while longer and the world will see Me no more." That means, Jesus, from the worldly point of view, is about to die. But the disciples do not see, or rather are not expected to see, their *guru* Jesus in this way. The real *guru* is to be seen by them not as the perishable body, but as the eternal Reality. It is therefore said, "But you will see Me." The reason for their seeing him is also clarified immediately by Jesus, "Because I live." The purport is that the *guru* Jesus is not to be seen by the disciples as the body that ceases to be, but as the ever-living *Ātmā* within everyone, that neither dies nor was born.

What happens to the disciple upon seeing the *guru* thuswise? He sees himself not in the external form that perishes, but in the invisible and ever-living *Ātmā* that has assumed the present fleeting form. Jesus in this sense says, "you will live also."

We have examined earlier how the Father in heaven, the Son or *guru*, and the faithful disciples, together belong to a vertical order with God at the top, the disciples at the bottom, and the Son coming in the middle. These three are so mutually related that one becomes meaningless without the other two. Underscoring this mutuality, Jesus says, "At that day you will know that I am in My Father, and you in Me, and I in you." By "At that day" is meant, the time when their imagined orphanhood disappears.

Of these three that form a graded order, God and the Son form a pair of a higher level, and the Son and disciples form another pair at a lower level. The depth of the above-said mutuality that becomes an experiential awareness, depends solely on the intensity of the bipolarity between the pair at the lower level. Those who live filled with that experience naturally live in line with the commandments of the *guru*. Such commandments are really not obligatory; on the other hand, these are merely the spontaneous way by which wisdom finds expression in the disciples' actual life, as was seen earlier. Jesus therefore says, "He who has My commandments and keeps them, it is he who loves Me." The words "loves Me" indicate the rapport that develops between Jesus as a *guru* and the disciples. And the growth of this rapport happens mainly because of the interest the seeker has in the Father in heaven and in the *guru* who sees clearly the secret of the Father within himself. Jesus therefore says, "He who loves Me will be loved by My Father." As the seeker's interest in the Father and the bipolarity between the seeker and the Son reach their zenith simultaneously, the reality concerning the Father becomes spontaneously transparent to him. Attaining this transparency is felt by such a seeker as the love the Father has for him. That is the sense in which it is said, "will be loved by My Father."

The wisdom teaching of a *guru* reaches its finality when the *guru* reveals his own self-reality — that he is the Father in essence — to the disciple who develops an intense interest in knowing the Father through his rapport with the *guru*. This revelation of the wisdom secret often takes the form of a Silence that brims with the ineffability of what is meant to be revealed. This is the reason why Jesus says, "I will love him and manifest Myself to him."

4.19

Again on the Importance of the Guru–Disciple Rapport

VERSE 22 of chapter 14 reads as follows:

> Judas (not Iscariot) said to Him, "Lord, how is it that You will manifest Yourself to us, and not to the world?"

We saw just now the zenith of Jesus's revelation of his self-being to the disciples. This happens prior to his departure from the disciples, taking for granted that what he had taught them earlier has been fully imbibed by them. But the present words of Judas indicate that the disciples failed to grasp it. They did not even have the penetrative mind to differentiate the teachings given by a *guru* to the general public and those given to the disciples with an intimate rapport with him.

Jesus's reply to Judas is as follows:

> If anyone loves Me, he will keep My word; and My Father will love him, and We will come to him and make Our home with him.
>
> He who does not love Me does not keep My words; and the word which you hear is not Mine but the Father's who sent Me.
>
> — 14.23-24

The pivotal part of this reply is, "If anyone loves Me, he will keep My word." "If anyone loves Me," as we have already seen, means, "if anyone really has the *guru*–disciple rapport with him." In fact, a sort of disappointment is there on the part of Jesus that even the disciples closest to him do not really have the spiritual rapport with him strong enough to assimilate the inner secret of what he says. This could be seen echoed in his above words.

A disciple with the proper rapport with a *guru* not only assimilates the experiential wisdom content in the *guru*'s words or his meaningful Silence, but also the disciple's life becomes transformed as an expression of that wisdom. That means, everything in his life becomes filled with the spirit of that wisdom. It is in this sense that Jesus says, "If anyone loves Me, he will keep My word."

We have seen earlier how God the Father and the Son (*guru*) are essentially undifferentiable. Therefore, those who love their *gurus*, in the sense we have just seen, are naturally loved by God. Jesus therefore says, "We will come to him and make Our home with him." We have already noticed the oneness of Father, Son and the Spirit of truth. These three, therefore, are referred to together here as "We" with a capital "W." We have already noticed also how the Reality finds home in the one who knows it.

Through the analogy of the true vine in verses 1-15 of chapter 15, Jesus makes clear to the disciples how the rapport they have with him will bear much fruit in their lives, like the bunches of grapes on a vine. This fruition is nothing other than the Self-happiness that fills the being of Jesus, which becomes theirs, as is evident from verse 11 which reads thus:

> These things I have spoken to you, that My joy may remain in you, and that your joy may be full.

Jesus restates the essential content of his commandments in verses 12-17. Furthermore, he makes it clear that no longer would he call the disciples servants, but that they would be treated as friends (verse 15). He also assures them that all he knows concerning the wisdom secret has been taught to them. To quote his own words:

> All things I heard from My Father I have made known to you.
> — 15.15

A sort of equality between *guru* and disciples is attained in such a state, which is the reason why the disciples are elevated from the status of servants to that of friends.

4.20

The Guru Departs to the Advantage of the Disciples

JESUS continues:

> Nevertheless I tell you the truth. It is to your advantage that I go away; for if I do not go away, the Helper will not come to you, but if I depart, I will send Him to you. — 16.7

On listening to the words of wisdom of a *guru,* the core of the teaching does not immediately become transparent to a disciple. One has to ponder over it again and again, perhaps for years without pause. It may so happen that the secret becomes clear only after the lifespan of the *guru.* This final attainment of clarity is traditionally known as enlightenment. The Helper Jesus offers to send to his disciples is this enlightenment itself, which we have already noticed. As long as the *guru* lives among them in the flesh, the disciples may think that their *guru,* the embodiment of wisdom, is with them to teach more, and so they feel they do not have to worry. Mostly it is after the lifetime of the *guru* that a disciple tries his best to delve deep into the inner meanings of what the *guru* taught. We have already noticed that in the present case, the disciples have not yet attained the perfection of wisdom Jesus expected of them. Jesus therefore says, "It is to your advantage that I go away; for if I do not go away, the Helper will not come to you."

Assignments to the Disciple

Jesus says again:

> If I depart, I will send Him to you.
>
> And when He has come, He will convict the world of sin, and of righteousness, and of judgement:
>
> of sin, because they do not believe in Me;
>
> of righteousness, because I go to My Father and you see Me no more;
>
> of judgement, because the ruler of the world is judged. — 16.7-11

The Helper that will be with the disciples in the future apparently refers to their becoming enlightened as to the wisdom secret. On becoming so, they naturally gain the capability to discriminate the sinful from the meritorious, the righteous from the unrighteous, the just from the unjust. The assurance that they would become so is explicit in the words of Jesus, "When He has come, He will convict the world of sin, and of righteousness, and of judgement." Then it is stated in what sense the disciples' enlightenment is expected to convict sin, "of sin, because they do not believe in Me."

Even though Jesus was a true *guru* who lived among the Jews, they did not believe in his words. There is virtually no sin in human life more vile than this. Jesus expects that in the future his disciples will be wise and prudent enough to remind the Jews of the nature of sin they have been committing.

Now Jesus tells his disciples why they should convict the world for righteousness, "Of righteousness, because I go to My Father and you see Me no more."

It is simply because the Jews had the wrong sense of righteousness, that Jesus had to leave this world and return to the Father, which resulted in the unexpected loss and grief for his disciples. This wrong sense of justice in no way was unfavourable to Jesus; on the contrary, it gave him an easily accessible opportunity to return to his Father, the abode of supreme and unconditioned righteousness. But the disciples, at least for the time being, had to swallow the bitter outcome of losing their *guru* forever. Jesus therefore expects his disciples, through becoming enlightened, to be wise and bold enough to teach the Jews how wrong and debased their sense of righteousness was.

Now Jesus tells his disciples why in the future they would have to convict the world or the Jews for their wrong judgement, "Of judgement, because the ruler of the world is judged." The wisdom teaching of a *guru* is not aimed at guiding the life of any particular group of people or race; it is meant for the benefit of the entire world. And a *guru*, in this sense, is the ruler or king of the world. Any judgement, in the normal course, is pronounced by the king or a judge who represents the king. But just the opposite is what will now happen, the king (Jesus) is going to be judged by the people, the wise is going to be judged by the unwise, the enlightened one is going to be judged by the unenlightened. It is on the strength of their ignorance that the unwise are going to judge the wise. Jesus expects his disciples, at least in the future, to attain the insight that enables them to convince the Jews as to how the nature of their judgement was upside down.

Jesus Departs and Comes Back

Jesus say:

> A little while, and you will not see Me, and again a while, you will see Me. — 16.16

The real greatness of the guruhood that Jesus represents, as we have already noticed, is not yet realized by the disciples. And for this reason, they will at first see the bodily departure of Jesus as his death, which will grieve them. Jesus therefore says, "A little while, and you will not see Me."

But later, with their own enlightenment as their Helper, they will re-visualize the eternal guruhood that was in Jews, and in that sense he says, "And again a little while, and you will see Me."

Unaware of the real greatness of a true *guru*, the disciples will grieve over the crucifixion of Jesus. And those Jews who caused it will rejoice. But in the future, after availing themselves of their Helper, the Spirit of truth, then Happiness will occupy the place of grief. It is for this reason Jesus tells them in verse 20:

> Most assuredly, I say to you that you will weep and lament, but the world will rejoice; and you will be sorrowful, but your sorrow will be turned into joy.

4.21

A New Language

JESUS, in verse 16.25 says to his disciples:

> These things I have spoken to you in figurative language; but the time is coming when I will no longer speak to you in figurative language, but I will tell you plainly about the Father.

Jesus taught the essential content of wisdom to his disciples as well as laymen, in a figurative language that profusely made use of parables and analogies. This method could be seen handily applied in philosophical writings since the most ancient of times. Socrates was an expert in it as can be seen in the *Dialogues* of Plato. The epics *Mahābhārata* and *Rāmāyaṇa* of India are saturated with such parables and tales. Scriptures of all religions are no exception. Vedānta is also full of such analogies. This method was used profusely at a time when scientific thinking had not yet developed sufficiently. It is quite possible to make clear the same spiritual or philosophical truth in a scientific way without resorting to parable or analogy. What all the scriptures and serious philosophical works attempt to do is to expound the nature and content of the one all-underlying Reality that is ineffable. This very Reality is termed "the Father" in the Gospels. Jesus prophesies here the coming of a time when the future *guru*s like him will expound the secret of "the Father" in a more precise or even a scientifically conceived language that uses no parable or analogy.

As a more scientific method of revealing the non-dual secret of wisdom is developed, it will clarify now the duality between the seeker and the Reality sought also naturally vanishs, because the seeker and the sought are merely two opposite poles of a unitive situation, one meaningless without the other. The necessity of a mediator between God and the seeker then also does not become an absolute necessity. In this sense Jesus continues:

> In that day you will ask in My name, and I do not say to you that I shall pray the Father for you;
>
> For the Father Himself loves you, because you have loved Me, and have believed that I came forth from God. — 16.26-27

Worldly Instincts Cause Tribulations

Jesus, in verse 33 of chapter 16, says:

> In Me you may have peace. In the world you will have tribulation; but be of good cheer, I have overcome the world.

By "In the world you will have tribulation" it is meant that if the disciples identify themselves with the world or the people, then there is every chance that life will become full of problems. The possibility of facing many difficult situations will always be there when the disciples find themselves among the people, involved in the affairs of the world. Such an identification with the people and the distress this brings arise in them (the disciples) thanks to their own worldly instincts. Once free of these instincts, they find themselves having no such problems. Or else, the difficulties in life are no longer felt to be tribulations. Giving up worldly instincts becomes possible only when they rely on Jesus or the ultimate Reality that he represents. It is therefore said, "In Me you may have peace." Once the identity with the Reality or rapport with the *guru* becomes truly established, no difficulty in life is felt to be distressing. Jesus therefore asks his disciples, "But be of good cheer." Hence, to become free of worldly instincts, in effect, means to gain victory over the world. The worst of all misfortunes, seen under the spell of worldly instincts, is the one Jesus is about to face. But he does not consider it to be a tribulation. On the contrary, in his perception, it is the joyous occasion of returning to his Father. Jesus expects his disciples also to develop such an attitude.

Eternal Life

Eternal life, as has already been clarified, is the sense of immortality arising from the perception that the one ultimate Reality, and the nature of *guru* who reveals that Reality, are not different from oneself. Jesus underscores this point when he prays God:

> And this is eternal life, that they may know You, the only true God, and Jesus Christ whom You have sent. — 17.3

So the realization of one's own inseparable oneness with the ultimate Reality or God, is the essential content of attaining eternal life, which is stated beyond doubt by Jesus thus:

> Holy Father, keep through Your name those whom You have given Me, that they may be one as We are. — 17.11

The same point is clarified by Jesus again thus:

> that they all may be one, as You, Father, are in Me and I in You; that they also may be one with Us. . . . — 17.21

Again Jesus says in the same tone:

> that they may be one just as We are one.
>
> I am in them, and You are in Me; that they may be made perfect in one. . . . — 17.22-23

About the eternal glory of guruhood Jesus says:

> That they may behold My glory which You have given Me; for You loved Me before the foundation of the world. — 17.24

We have already examined the philosophical implications of these words, when we commented on the earlier words of Jesus:

> Before Abraham was, I am. — 8.58

Laws of Two Kinds

Just when he was about to pronounce his judgement after examining Jesus, Pilate asks him:

> Do You not know that I have power to crucify You, and power to release You? — 19.10

Jesus answered:

> You could have no power at all against Me unless it had been given you from above. Therefore the one who delivered Me to you has the greater sin. — 19.11

There are laws made by the human mind, and there are laws that are part of nature, where no human thought avails. The latter kind could be termed God-given laws. Only when harmony between these two sets of laws is lacking, does restlessness appear in society.

Either of these sets of laws could be the basis by which one person can have power over another. The authority of a particular judge in the realm of man-made laws is drived from the laws made by the ruler or the body of rulers. That means, the judge as such has no authority to judge. In this sense, Jesus says, "You could have no power at all against Me unless it had been given you from above."

Now as for the God-given laws, there is no authority above Jesus other than God. The power Pilate has to judge is not derived from

God either. Seen thus, Pilate has no power over Jesus. A person of no authority is thus the one who takes decisions here as if having absolute authority. Therefore Jesus's words, "You could have no power at all against Me unless it had been given to you from above," could be understood also in a figurative antithetical sense in this context, meaning, Pilate was given no authority "from above" by God to apply his judicial power on Jesus.

Seen thus from the worldly point of view as well as from the spiritual point of view, it is to a person who has no power over Jesus that he was delivered to be judged. Those who did so, no doubt, committed a sin worse than the one Pilate is going to commit right now. Therefore Jesus's words, "Therefore the one who delivered Me to you has the greater sin."

The Resurrected Jesus

Jesus, in verses 19-20 of chapter 20, repeats these words to his disciples, "Peace be with you." It is to the disciples who have lost their peace, that the resurrected Jesus now speaks these assuring words. This is the way he brings peace to them:

> He breathed on them, and said to them, "Receive the Holy spirit."
> — 20.22

Going beyond the realm of imparting wisdom or the Holy Spirit verbally, the resurrected Jesus now imbues the disciples with the same Holy Spirit silently in the form of his breath. The same wisdom secret was expounded by him before his crucifixion with the spoken word as medium. In short, a fundamental difference could be noticed between the living Jesus and the resurrected Jesus. The former was a *guru* who taught wisdom by the use of words. The same wisdom secret is transfused into the disciples through the silence of the resurrected Jesus.

4.22

Signature of the Evangelist

AFTER the Resurrection, Jesus appeared three times, according to the present Gospel. First it was to Mary Magdalene to whom he became visible, which happened right at the tomb where his body was lain. Initially the angels, who were found sitting at the head and feet, and then Jesus himself, ask Mary, "Woman why are you weeping?" (20.13, 15). Thus, Mary is reminded that Jesus's departure from this world is not something to be grieved over. No one's death, according to the philosophy of the eternal life taught by Jesus, shall be the cause of any sorrow. Worldly people, ignorant of the reality concerning life, grieve over the death of those who are very dear to them, but they do not do so at the death of everyone. On the other hand, those who are enlightened as to the wisdom secret do not rejoice at the birth nor feel grieved at the death of anyone. Mary, though a woman whose love for Jesus was very intimate, need not be expected to have fully imbibed the wisdom secret he had taught. She therefore weeps over the death of Jesus. The Resurrected Jesus now reminds her that he was a *guru* who taught the secret of eternal life, and so his bodily departure does not mark his cessation, and hence is not to be grieved over. His departure from this world, as we have already seen, was perceived by himself simply as the return to his Father. In India also, the perishing of a *guru*'s body is never considered as death, but is treated as the attainment of *mahā-samādhi* (to find his original abode).

When Jesus appears the second time he breathed upon the disciples and said, "Receive the Holy Spirit" (20.22). "To receive the Holy Spirit" means, to become enlightened about the secret of wisdom. In the life of such an enlightened *jñānin* there can always be seen a sort of absolutism, or a state of being that is not dependent upon anything relative, rather only upon God. The words they speak are also as true as God, and so whatever they wilfully imagine will come true as well. This phenomenon demonstrates that they are in complete identity with God. In other words, whatever is possible with God, becomes also possible with them because of their complete identity with God. That is the reason why Jesus tells his disciples, after breathing the Holy Spirit into them:

> If you forgive sins of any, they are forgiven them; if you retain the sins of any, they are retained. — 20.23

In India also, it is to be remebered, God and *guru* alike are considered *satya-saṅkalpa*s, meaning those whose wilful imaginations come true.

New Fishermen

Jesus showed himself to the disciples the third time, at the Sea of Tiberias, where they were all set for fishing. It was at a similar scene that Simon Peter and his brother in the beginning were asked by Jesus, "Follow Me, I will make you fishers of men." Standing for the other extreme pole of that scene, the fish here evidently denote men. That the disciples have now started fishing indicates, they have already initiated a concerted effort to gather more adherents to the new wisdom movement begun by Jesus. But they did not make any catch.

Jesus, then on the shore, and unrecognized by the disciples, told them:

> Cast the net on the right side of the boat, and you will find some. — 21.6

This advice indicates that they should not try to make everyone a follower of Jesus Christ.

First they should find out the right kind of men with the right openness of mind and competence for wisdom. The net should be cast toward them. The disciples made the effort as directed by Jesus, and then, "they were not able to draw it because of the multitude of fish" (21.6). Now it is not to be expected that the disciples actually started evangelism in the days immediately following the Crucifixion. Still, the Evangelist John gives such a directive, indirectly through this symbolic event, i.e. that the attempts of the disciples in the future should not be to make everyone a follower of Jesus Christ. Upon getting the right kind of direction, the disciples felt no difficulty in recognizing who was giving it to them. They said, "It is our Lord" (21.7). Thereafter they did not ask him, "Who are you?" even when Jesus sat down and had breakfast with them (21.12).

Peter, the Rock

As the Resurrected Jesus was having breakfast with his disciples, he asks Simon Peter three times, "Simon, the son of Jonah, do you love Me?" (21.15-17). It was the same Peter who denied Jesus three times just before the Crucifixion. Therefore the present question of Jesus could be taken as the dialectical counterpart of Peter's denial, in effect neutralizing its ill-effects. Peter also repeatedly says, "Yes, Lord You know that I love You," by way of confirming this neutralization.

Peter is the rock, as we have seen earlier, upon which Jesus intended to build his Church. It is also to be noticed that Peter becomes puzzled when Jesus enters the subtleties of his wisdom teaching. At the same time, Jesus fully trusts Peter. As Jesus has already noticed, Peter's ability is in organizing the movement to propagate the gospel, rather than in delving deeper into the subtle and experiential levels of the wisdom implicit in it. To organize any movement, even a purely spiritual one, needs some sort of worldly instinct, and Peter can be trusted to be good at that.

The Unnamed Disciple

There is yet reference here to another disciple whom Jesus loved, at the end of the Gospel's last chapter. Though his name is not mentioned, it could easily be presumed from the statements about him that he is none other than John the present Evangelist. About this disciple, Jesus tells Peter, "If I will that he remain till I come, what is that to you? You follow Me" (21.22). Such a blessing is not given even to Peter. The present Gospel, as has already become quite clear to us, gives much importance to the clarity and depth of the wisdom teachings of Jesus. The ultimate value of wisdom is nothing other than the realization of one's own immortality, called *amṛtatva* in Vedānta, and eternal life in the Gospels. The statement of Jesus about this particular disciple, "I will that he remain till I come," could well be taken to signify that he enjoys the ultimately sweet fruit of wisdom. The character of this disciple, as is noticed by Jesus the *guru,* is such that he easily grasps the nuances of his wisdom teachings, and as a result straightaway attains immortality. This character could be considered as the reverse side of Peter's character. A spiritual movement thrives only when the organizing power of someone and the clarity of wisdom of someone else support one another.

Right at the end of the Gospel, it is said about this unknown disciple:

> This is the disciple who testifies of these things, and wrote these things. — 21.24

In other words, this disciple is none other than the person who wrote this Gospel. The above verse could thus be treated as a sort of signature by the author placed at the end of his work.

Part V
The Gospel of Thomas

Introductory Remarks

THE New Testament Gospels, as written by Matthew, Mark, Luke and John, are the mainstay of Christianity as a religion. All these four gospels narrate the biography of Jesus of Nazareth. In all these the story ends with the Crucifixion and Resurrection. The wisdom teachings of Jesus are interwoven along with the fabric of these biographical details. The Gospel of Thomas, which did not find a place in Bible, is totally different in nature. It contains only 114 simple sayings of Jesus. In this Gospel he performs no physical miracles, reveals no fulfilment of prophesy, announces no apocalyptic kingdom about to disrupt the world order, and for no one's sins. Instead, Thomas's Jesus dispenses insight from the bubbling spring of wisdom (saying 13), discounts the value of prophecy and its fulfilment (saying 52), criticizes the concept of an actual end of the world (sayings 51, 113), and offers a way of salvation through the wisdom enshrined in his own words.

According to biblical historians, works that incorporate Jesus's life and teachings were written by many. Of these, the four that were found to be the most helpful for the growth of the Christian Church and which portary the personal character of Jesus in the best light, were chosen and included in Bible. The one by Thomas was perhaps among the discarded. A papyrus copy of it was recovered accidentally in 1945 from one of the huge cliffs that flanked the river Nile in Upper Egypt. Let us give a brief account of how this event unfolded.

There is a sort of organic sediment found every year during a particular season underneath the high cliffs along the Nile River. This area is not far from the modern city Nag Hammadi. Once Muhammad Ali and his friends reached this place by camel. They let the camels graze at a nearby ground, and then dug around a large boulder beneath the cliff. Apparently their intention was to collect manure. Much to their surprise they uncovered a big storage jar with a bowl sealed on top of it as a lid. Muhammad Ali hesitated to open it for fear that some *jin* or other evil spirit would come out of it. But the possibility of a treasure being hidden in it also occurred to him. His love for gold overcame his fear of *jin*s, and he smashed the jar with his mattock.

What came out of it was really something golden — the golden papyrus fragments of a precious library. Thirteen such books were in this treasure trove. The Gospel of Thomas was among these.

It was St Thomas, the author of this Gospel, who is believed to have come to India, where he founded four churches in different places of the present-day Kerala state. The Christian Church thus initiated by him is now known as the Mar Thoma Church. It is also believed that St Thomas died at the hillock now known as St Thomas Mount near the modern Chennai City, and that his mortal remains were buried at the Sam Thom Church, Chennai.

Certain thinkers believe, though it is certainly not incontrovertibly proven, that Jesus did not die at the cross, but escaped from it and thereafter, along with a few of his disciples, travelled to India. According to them, he died in Kashmir. St Thomas was one among the disciples who reputedly accompanied Jesus on his travel to India. But based on historical facts, it seems more likely that St Thomas reached India, if at all he did, through the trade relations that the Malabar Coast of India had with the Mediterranean region, which existed ever since the pre-Christian era.

Another ancient Christian denomination known as the Coptic Church exists in Egypt to this day. They traditionally use Coptic language, a derivative of the ancient Egyptian language. They once had a very ancient library. The books unearthed by Muhammad Ali and his friends may well have been the relics of that library. The Coptic original is now safely preserved at the Coptic Museum of Old Cairo, and copies of it are in the Bodleian Library of Oxford University, the British Library of London and the Houton Library of Harvard University.

Mervin Meyer prepared a new edition of the Gospel of Thomas after closely examining the original Coptic text under ultraviolet light, and it was published by Harper San Francisco, New York. The present commentary follows this edition.

As the text of this Gospel is not very popular, we quote here all the 114 sayings of Jesus Christ, but the passages already commented on are left without comment.

5.1

Prologue

These are the hidden sayings that the living Jesus spoke and Judas Thomas the Twin recorded.

THIS opening passage of the Gospel of Thomas indicates that Jesus Christ is not thought of here merely as a prophet who died on the cross, but as a *guru* who eternally lives in the heart of everyone. And as is to be presumed, the meaning content of these sayings of Jesus, attentively and faithfully recorded by the intimate disciple Thomas, is of eternal value.

Whose twin was the Judas Thomas who faithfully recorded these invaluable words of Jesus? He should be the twin of the living Jesus himself, but not a twin in the biological sense. It is rather that Thomas must have established a spiritual rapport with Jesus so intimate that he acquired a status almost equal to that of being a twin of Jesus in regard to spiritual enlightenment.

1. And he said: "Whoever discovers the interpretation of these sayings will not taste death."

However hidden or mystical be the meaning of one's sayings, no one expects that person to live forever in the flesh. The death mentioned here, therefore, is not a bodily one. When a piece of ornament, upon its self-enquiry, finds out, "I am gold," it also realizes, "I have no death," because the gold-substance in the ornament does not cease to exist. Likewise, as one discovers one's own real content through contemplative self-enquiry, and so realizes, "I am *Ātmā*," or "I am the Absolute," one also becomes assured of one's immortality. The words of wisdom of all the *gurus* are aimed at enabling the seeker attain this immortality.

2. Jesus said: "Let one who seeks not stop seeking until one finds. When one finds, one will be troubled. When one is troubled, one will marvel and will rule over all."

We admittedly have the ability to grasp all that is worldly, by observing things and understand them by applying our rational thinking. This also includes the realm of the latest findings in science and technology. All such enquiries and discoveries are externally oriented, and are objective by nature. But discovering what is real within one's own being is totally different than such pursuits. Those who are familiar only with the former type of enquiry may even doubt the possibility and relevance of the latter kind of (subjective) enquiry. Even after becoming convinced of the necessity of self-enquiry, some might find it difficult to proceed with it simply because their minds are too conditioned by the former kind of enquiry. But the interiorized self-enquiry really is so simple and direct that it needs no proceeding with. This search for Reality is like an ornament seeking to know gold, or a wave seeking to know water. In fact, it needs only to be experienced directly that "I really am that Reality." This very simplicity and directness is the reason why those who are familiar only with an exteriorized form of enquiry may find this realization to be something impossible or too transcendental to attain.

But there are a few who feel the necessity for this self-enquiry and stick to it relentlessly. Such people one day will feel how purely simple and direct this enquiry and its answer are. At that very moment, all notions they had about life and nature will become turned upside down. At first this will trouble them. Then their restlessness will make way for quietude, and for a feeling of marvel. Life itself is then felt to be an inexplicable marvel.

As an ornament might realize itself to be the splendid gold in essence, so one might realize oneself to be the absolute Reality in essence. Then one will marvel and, as an ornament might realize that it is the very same gold that assumes all ornamental forms, so one might realize oneself to be the very same absolute Reality that assumes the forms of all things in the universe. Then one will rule over all.

The first saying here states what the ultimate value of wisdom is. Realizing onself to be immortal is the benefit of enlightenment. The second saying describes how the wisdom enquiry is to be made, and also how it terminates.

5.2

The Kingdom Inside and Outside You

> **3.** Jesus said: "If the leaders say to you, 'Look, the kingdom is in heaven,' then the birds of heaven will precede you. If they say to you, 'It is in the sea,' then the fish will precede you. Rather, the kingdom is inside you and it is outside you.
>
> When you know yourselves, then you will be known, and you will understand that you are children of the living father. But if you do not know yourselves, then you dwell in poverty, and you are poverty."

THE belief that the kingdom of God is in heaven, a world even above the skies, is a common feature of Semitic religions. Most believers also agree that this most high place, where God resides, is not reachable by flying as the birds do, or as the aeroplanes do, or even as the modern spacecrafts do.

How then is that world to be reached? That world can be reached only in our imagination. All imagination, as everyone can agree, gets formulated in our consciousness or mind. So too the upper world has to be admitted to exist as ideas in consciousness. Then that most high world has to have a dimension much different from the world we are familiar with.

The world of heaven and the Father in heaven are imagined by believers as the perfection of all good qualities that are imperfect or totally lacking in our world. This perfection of qualities apparently has a value dimension. Seen valuewise, heaven represents the plentitude of all that is good, the world we are living is the abode of both good and evil, and hell is where evil alone prevails. A heirarchy of values ranging from perfect goodness at the topmost level, and that which is totally evil at the bottom, could thus be conceived. This concept gets formulated in consciousness, and all the values are experienced in consciousness. In short, heaven, earth, hell and all such have being in our consciousness as value worlds. This is the reason why the kingdom of heaven can never be reached by the birds.

Should the kingdom of God be above all the worlds? Why can't it be below everything or somewhere else? A solution to this problem can also be found only with our value notion as a reference point. Suppose a very honourable person arrives. He will immediately be offered a seat of honour. In India this is called *agrāsana* (highest seat). Why can't that person be offered a seat at a lower level? How is the respect we have for a person related to the seat offered to him? The only answer is, human nature is such that whatever is considered to be of high value is placed at a higher level. There is nothing higher in value than God in human estimation. Therefore God is imagined to occupy the highest world. Still, that world has relevance only in the realm of values, and all value notions are within us. Hence the words of Jesus, "the kingdom (of God) is inside you."

It is said immediately, "and it is outside you." We have already seen how the kingdom of God is within oneself. It is not only inside me; it is inside you; it is inside everyone; it is inside everything; it is inside the earth and heaven; it is inside all the worlds. That which is outside each of us is what we call "the external world." Thus, this external world is also filled with the kingdom of God. That means, what we think of as "the outside" also is filled with the kingdom of God within us. To put the same in plain modern terminology, the internal and the external, the subjective and the objective, the knower and the known, the mental and the material, are all nothing but the kingdom of God or the one ultimate Reality (*Brahman*) become manifest variously. This kingdom is called *svarājya* (one's own kingdom) in the Upaniṣads (*Chāndogya Upaniṣad* 2.24.12, 3.6.4, 3.7.4, 3.8.4, 3.9.4; 3.10.4; *Taittirīya Upaniṣad* 1.6.2; *Maitrī Upaniṣad* 6.36).

What is the easiest way to know this great kingdom that fills both inside and outside? Since the knower's being also is in essence that very kingdom, the best and straightest course of knowing it is for the knower to know what he is in essential content. On knowing oneself thuswise, one realizes that what is real in oneself is what is real inside everything and outside everything. "I am in everything," or "I am everything" thus becomes a realized actuality. For one to know oneself in this way is the true self-knowledge. Then it becomes clear that the kingdom of God within oneself is what unfolds itself as everything, that everyone is a child of God. Jesus in this sense says, "When you know yourselves, then you will be known, and you will understand that you are the children of the living father."

A lack of self-knowledge means that one does not know what is real in oneself; nor what is real in the world; nor what is real in life; nor what is the meaning of life. Being impoverished in respect of life's meaningfulness smites the lives of such. Therefore Jesus says, "If you do not know yourselves, then you dwell in poverty."

The source of this poverty is nothing other than one's own ignorance. That means, oneself is the cause. Since this ignorance is an ignorance of what is real in oneself, the result is that one is virtually lacking to oneself. Therefore Jesus says, "and you are poverty."

Put otherwise, the wealth of the self, and the poverty of the self, are both self-created, both within the experiential being of the person concerned. A richness of self-knowledge ensures a richness of life, and a poverty of self-knowledge ensures an impoverishment of life.

> **4.** Jesus said: "The person old in days will not hesitate to ask a little child seven days old about the place of life, and that person will live. For many of the first will be last and will become a single one."

The elderly man who asks a child of seven days about the place of life or rather the meaning of life, apparently lived his life with no understanding of its meaning. He, in other words, lived in total poverty, or as poverty embodied, as we have just seen. A seven-day old child, on the other hand, lives with no feeling of poverty, but with the extensiveness of the meaningful life before it, yet without the knowledge of it. The ignorance of the old man is of a totally negative nature; it renders his life meaningless. The ignorance of the child, on the other hand, has inherent in it all the possibility of realizing the meaningfulness of life that lies ahead of it.

If the old man thinks, life ends with when the physical body falls, he knows very little about life. The fall of the body is simply one of the phenomena that form part of the eternal flux of life's process. This process consists of the incessant appearance of manifest forms, their transformation, and their eventual disappearance. This takes place in the one ultimate Reality that alone exists always. Had the old man known this, he would have become like a child. He who perceives life as such, finds no relevance in differentiating childhood and old age. Both are simply two different stages in the transformation that occurs in an individual manifest form. The only difference between the appearances of the old man and the child is that the former happened earlier and the latter happened later. The first becomes one with the last, once the one Reality in both is perceived. It is therefore said, "the first will become the last and will become a single one."

5.3

The Way

> **5.** Jesus said: "Know what is in front of your face, and what is hidden from you will be disclosed to you. For there is nothing hidden that will not be revealed."

KNOWING oneself, as we have already seen in verse 3, is how wisdom is attained. It was also seen that, upon knowing oneself properly, one will see everyone as the children of one living Father. That means, upon knowing the one Reality, one's own self will be perceived to be what appears as everything around. Then everything is seen as the different forms in which but one Reality appears. The words of the present verse, "Know what is in front of your face" are to be understood in this sense of the present context. On attaining this wisdom, one perceives one Reality alone in all that is already known and all that is not yet known. Put otherwise, knowing the Reality concerning what is seen around, reveals the secret concerning all that is not seen as well. Therefore it is said, "and what is hidden from you will be disclosed to you."

With only ordinary sense perception and logical thinking to rely on as the means of knowing in the search for reality, one becomes convinced that what is already known can be but little, and what is yet to be known is endless. But on attaining the wisdom understood here, it is intuitively perceived that the endlessly expanding unknown world also has no existence other than as the manifest forms of the Self-Reality or the Father. Jesus therefore says, "For there is nothing hidden that will not be revealed."

5.4

Religious Observances

> **6.** His followers asked him and said to him: "Do you want us to fast? How should we pray? Should we give to charity? What diet should we observe?"
>
> Jesus said: "Do not lie, and do not do what you hate, because all things are disclosed before heaven. For there is nothing hidden that will not be revealed, and there is nothing covered that will remain undisclosed."

THE words, "Do not lie and do not do what you hate" may sound like an ordinary moral instruction. But the basis of this instruction is the philosopical truth, "all things are disclosed before heaven." That is to say, because nothing is apart from the one ultimate Reality, whatever happens in everything is well known to It, for that Reality is consciousness in essence. The same Reality is what has assumed our own forms — we who are tempted to lie and to do what we hate.

Human actions, in India, are traditionally classified into three — physical, verbal and mental. Of these three, only the physical and verbal actions are cited here. When we go wrong in these actions, it may be possible to hide such actions from others, but these can never be hidden from ourselves, from the Father, the Reality in our being.

Jesus, here, does not answer the questions of his followers directly. The indication may be that, other than adhering to the moral instructions given here by him, along with an understanding of the philosophical reality behind them, no fasting, no prayer, no charity, no strict dietary observance are needed. A hint could also be seen here that a person who is enlightened and who lives accordingly, is not bound to observe religious rituals and vows as such. In short, all that pertains to the realm of actions (*karmas*) is subsumed by wisdom, as *Bhagavad-Gītā* (IV.33) clarifies as follows:

> All *karmas* (actions) in their entirety, terminate, O Arjuna! in wisdom.

5.5

Worldly Traits

> **7.** Jesus said: "Fortunate is the lion that the human will eat, so that the lion becomes human. And foul is the human that the lion will eat, and the lion will become human."

THE lion is an animal that will eat humans if it gets a chance. Therefore, from the human perception, a lion is a ferocious animal. In the realm of spirituality too there is an animal that lies in wait to catch humans and is ready to eat all the human qualities in them. It is nothing other than the worldly traits that arise in human as the result of their attachment to worldly values. Suppose a man eats a lion. Then the ferocious animal becomes assimilated into his body and the harmful animal becomes a harmless part of his being. Likewise, instead of one being subjugated by the worldly traits, if one subjugates those traits, digests them and assimilates them into one's being by means of the burning digestive fluids of wisdom, then such traits do not misguide one any longer. Then those traits remain in them as part of their being under full control. But if the opposite is the case, then man becomes devoured by those traits; he in effect becomes transformed into that ferocious animal. Such a life for humans is loathsome; it is a cursed life.

In short, a real human is the one who wins over the lion of worldly traits.

5.6

Discriminative Power

8. And he said, "Humankind is like a wise fisherman who cast his net into the sea and drew it up from the sea full of little fish. Among them the wise fisherman discovered a fine large fish. He threw all the little fish back into the sea and with no difficulty chose the large fish. Whoever has ears to hear should hear."

THE quest for knowledge and finally for wisdom is natural with humans. Furthermore, it is this quest that makes them really human. Jesus's disciples, as we have already noticed, were mostly fishermen previously. Therefore, the nature of acquiring wisdom is made clear to them by him by making use of fishing as an analogy.

There are two kinds of knowledge open to us to acquire. One is the knowledge about every specific detail of the objective world or of ideas. The possibilities of such knowledge are endless, because the objects to be known are boundless. This kind of knowledge is termed "the other" (*anya*) by Narayana Guru. The other kind of knowledge is a knowledge by which one reality alone is seen in everything. It is the insight that perceives all specific knowledges, all specific experiences, all specific mental activities, as different functional facets of the one and only consciousness. Narayana Guru characterizes this as "the same" (*sama*) kind of knowledge. On having this knowledge or rather wisdom, one realizes that there is nothing outside the bounds of this knowledge and then one feels all the former types of knowledge to be insignificant. This is like a discerning fisherman keeping the one big fish of his catch with him and throwing all the little ones back to the sea. Put in the terminology familiar to Vedānta, upon acquiring the wisdom of *Brahman*, or rather upon realizing *Brahman*, one becomes fully convinced of the insignificance of all kinds of worldly knowledge and the values associated with them.

Disregarding the former type of knowledge does not imply that the actuality of the world and its values are merely to be ignored. On the other hand, the actual world and the multiplicity in it are perceived not to be different from the one Reality. What is really needed is the capability to discriminate these two aspects of knowledge, which are of such a nature that one is meaningless without the other.

> **9.** Jesus said: "Look, the sower went out, took a handfull (of seeds), and scattered (them). Some fell on the road, and the birds came and pecked them up. Others fell on rock, and they did not take root in the soil and did not produce heads of grain. Others fell on thorns, and they chocked the seeds and worms devoured them. And others fell on good soil, and it brought forth a good crop. It yielded sixty per measure and one hundred and twenty per measure."

This parable has been examined by us earlier.

5.7

A Guru's Anguish

> **10.** Jesus said, "I have thrown fire upon the world, and look, I am watching it until it blazes."

THE teaching a *guru* imparts to his disciple is like throwing fire upon the world. As the intense yearning for the wisdom of realizing the ultimate Reality matures in the disciple, he feels that all his interests in worldly affairs are burning away. As the fire of wisdom or the fire of *Brahman* blazes, the entire world and the eternal flow of actions (*karma*s) in it burn up, and the embers of that fire alone remain. *Bhagavad-Gītā* (IV.37) also asserts the same thing as follows: "This fire of wisdom reduces to ashes all the *karma*s." A real *guru,* after teaching the wisdom secret, waits in anguish until this happens within the disciple.

> **11.** Jesus said, "This heaven will pass away and the one above it will pass away.
>
> The dead are not alive, and the living will not die.
>
> During the days when you ate what is dead, and you made it alive. When you are in the light, what will you do?
>
> On the day when you were one, you became two. But when you become two, what will you do?"

The highest of all human aspirations, as held by the Semitic religions, is to finally reach heaven. This heaven is also admittedly a world. All the worlds being subject to destruction, heaven also has to cease to exist some time. If there is a world above heaven, being yet another world, it also will cease to be at some point. What unceasingly exists is one Supreme Reality, which alone assumes the forms of all these worlds. This Reality is called *Brahman* (*Ātman*) in Vedānta, and God in Bible. With all this in mind Jesus says, "This heaven will pass away, and the one above it will pass away."

Just as all the worlds are subject to decay, so too are the inhabitants of all these worlds. But there is a perception of life in which one does not see all these perishable worlds and their inhabitants as real — the perception of seeing only the one Reality that has assumed the forms of all these, as real. On having this perception, it becomes transparent that oneself is but that very same Reality in essential context, or oneself is that Reality that was never born and never dies. To realize "I am the one birthless and deathless Reality" in Vedānta, is known as attaining immortality (*amṛtatva*). On realizing oneself to be the Immortal alone, it is also realized that till that moment one was living in ignorance about oneself, with the mistaken notion that birth and death are real.

A really meaningful life is one in which one constantly experiences one's own immortality. Then it becomes clear that a person is as if dead when clinging to the perception that both birth and dying are real. Jesus therefore says, "The dead are not alive."

Those who have a really meaningful life, who experience their own immortality, do not consider the fall of their physical form to be their death or cessation. This event is also perceived by them to form part of the everlasting flow of life. Therefore it is said, "The living will not die."

It is when an ignorant person (*ajñānin*) becomes enlightened that he is revealed to him as immortal as well. Then what happened to the *ajñānin* who had birth and death? The *jñānin* ate the *ajñānin.* As the ordinary food eaten gets assimilated into the body, so too the *ajñānin* becomes assimilated into the being of the immortal *jñānin.* Such is the nature of the life of those who live in the broad daylight of wisdom. In this sense Jesus says, "During the days when you ate what is dead, you made it alive. When you are in the light, what will you do?" The question "what will you do?" is rhetorical, needing no answer. The enlightened ones simply live as immortals. They are not bound to do any action (*karma*) as such. All the actions in their lives as well as in nature are perceived by them to take place in the one immortal Reality. They live free of all *karma*-related bondages.

Just the opposite side of what was stated here is shown next. Even when the gold and the ornaments are conceived as distinct, the one indestructible reality and the other fleeting apparent forms, these two aspects actually remain inseparably one. The error we commit is that of separating the non-dual entity into two. Likewise is the mistaken separateness of the one ultimate Reality and our being; this separateness has place only in our imagination as ideas, As we think of ourselves as entities existing separate from the one Reality, we find ourselves as mortals also. This is the realm of ignorance (*ajñāna*) where birth and death appear to be real. In short, when what is really one is thought of wrongly to be two, we inadvertently fall into the sufferings natural in the realm of birth and death. The words of Jesus, "On the day when you were one, you became two. But when you become two, what will you do?," it seems, could easily be understood in the light of this Vedāntic vision.

> **12.** The followers said to Jesus, "We know that you are going to leave us. Who will be our leader?"
>
> Jesus said to them, "No matter where you are, you are to go to James the Just, for whose sake heaven and earth came into being."

The present question of the followers was asked earlier in the Gospel of John. But Jesus's answer here is a bit different. That the Spirit of truth will be sent to them as a messenger, was the answer given then. The implication, as we have already noticed, is that what should lead the disciples in the future is the realization of the ultimate Truth, or the awareness of their unity with what is ultimately real, as well as the sense of justice which is the Spirit of truth reflected in their actual life. Here, on the other hand, Jesus says, James the Just is the person whom they should approach for guidance. Who is this James the Just?

Marvin Meyer, in his *The Gospel of Thomas* gives the following note about James the Just:

> James the brother of the master succeeded to (the leadership of) the church with the apostles. He was named Just by all from the times of the master until ours, since many were called James. This one was holy from his mother's womb. He did not drink wine or strong drink, nor did he eat meat; no razor touched his head, he did not anoint himself with oil, and he did not make use of the bath. He alone was allowed to enter into the sanctuary, for he did not wear wool but linen. He used to enter alone into the temple and be found kneeling and praying for forgiveness for the people, so that his knees grew dry like a camel's, because he constantly bowed down on his knees in worship of God and asked forgiveness for the people. So because of the extraordinary character of his righteousness he was called the Just and Oblias, that is, in Greek, rampart of the people and righteousness, as the prophets point out concerning him.
>
> James the Just, thus, was the brother of Jesus and the leader of the church in Jerusalem until his death in CE 62. The Secret Book of James 16.5-11 has James present himself as the person who sends the other followers of Jesus out on their missions. "So, not wishing to give them offence, I sent each one of them to a different place. But

> I myself went up to Jerusalem, praying that I might acquire a share with the beloved ones who will appear."[1]

James the Just could thus be assumed to be a personified form of the Spirit of truth, both in respect the transparency of the vision of truth as well as perfect righteousness.

This world commonly is perceived by many as a storehouse of sufferings. But the perception of the enlightened is much different. They see it merely as the one ultimate Reality become creatively unfolded. That means, heaven and earth and all the other worlds are nothing more than the self-manifestation of the one and only Reality. Without assuming the forms of these worlds, the Reality as such does not exist. It could therefore be said, these worlds emerged for the sake of the one Reality's self-expression. The one who constantly experiences identity with that Reality, really is that Reality. Thus it could also be said, it is for his sake that these worlds exist. It should be in this sense that the expression "for whose sake heaven and earth came into being," became a popular expression in Jewish literature to praise someone.

1. *The Gospel of Thomas*, tr. Marvin Meyer, New York: Harper San Francisco, 1992, pp. 73-74.

5.8

The Ineffability of Wisdom

> **13.** Jesus said to his followers, "Compare me to something and tell me what I am like." Simon Peter said to him, "You are like a just messenger."
>
> Matthew said to him, "You are like a wise philosopher."
>
> Thomas said to him, "Teacher, my mouth is utterly unable to say what you are like."
>
> Jesus said, "I am not your teacher. Because you have drunk, you have become intoxicated from the bubbling spring that I have tended."
>
> And he took him, and withdrew, and spoke three sayings to him.
>
> When Thomas came back to his friends, they asked him, "What did Jesus say to you?"
>
> Thomas said to them, "If I tell you one of the sayings he spoke to me, you will pick up rocks and stone me, and fire will come from the rocks and consume you."

THE question asked by Jesus is answered by his three disciples in three different ways. Simon Peter, as we have already noticed, is an expert in organizing the church of Jesus as a spiritual movement. And for this reason, he sees Jesus with a socially biased mind. The answer he gives also is of such a nature.

Matthew, on the other hand, has in-depth understanding of the philosophy Jesus teaches, and hence his reply reflects his perception of Jesus as a wise philosopher.

But the answer given by Thomas goes beyond both. He visualizes Jesus as the embodiment of the ineffability of the realization of what is ultimately Real, a state known in Vedānta as Self-realization (*ātma-sākṣātkāra*).

Jesus contrasts the nature of the answers given by his three disciples and finds Thomas as the one who has absorbed the real Spirit of his enlightenment and what he intended to teach.

Jesus first tells Thomas, "I am not your teacher." Once a disciple becomes fully enlightened of the full significance of what the *guru* intended to impart to him, the higher–lower order that existed between the two is no longer of any value. Both are equal thereafter. This is the reason why Jesus tells Thomas, who has already become equal to him in wisdom, "I am not your teacher."

The secret of wisdom is something that intoxicates the one who imbibes it. For this reason, some of the enlightened appear to be as if drunk. This state often is known as God-intoxication. One such Indian saint in modern times was Sri Ramakrishna Paramahansa. Almost similar is the state Thomas was in then, as indicated by Jesus.

Thereafter Jesus took him away from the others and spoke to him three secret sayings. The secret sayings are not divulged here. The Evangelist Thomas apparently does not intend to disclose it to the world, as is to be assumed from the words he utters to the others after he came back. Or else, disclosing it is of no benefit, as it would never be appreciated in its real sense by those who are not well prepared to become enlightened through an intense yearning for wisdom that is supported by a austere self-discipline involving a sort of self-heating up, called *tapas* in Vedānta.

A similar scene appears in *Bṛhadāraṇyaka Upaniṣad.* It consists of an assembly of scholars in the court of the King Janaka. The scholars intended to test how enlightened the Sage Yājñavalkya was. Many of them asked him questions from different perspectives, and Yājñavalkya answered all of them to their full satisfaction. Among them was Ārtabhāga who posed the final question when he asked this:

> "Yājñavalkya," said he, "when the speech (voice) of this dead person enters into fire, the breath into air, the eyes into the sun, the mind into the moon, hearing into the waters, the body into the earth, the self into space, the hairs of the body into the herbs, the hairs on the head into the trees, and the blood and the semen are deposited in water, what then becomes of this person?
>
> "Ārtabhāga, my dear, take my hand. We two alone shall know of this, this is not for us two (to speak of) in public."
>
> The two went away and deliberated. What they said was *karma* (action), and what they praised was *karma.*"

The Upaniṣad does not say exactly what they did deliberate about regarding *karma,* and how it was that *karma* was praised, except by giving a very vague indication thus, "Verily one becomes good by good action, bad by bad action. Therefore, Ārtabhāga of the line of Jaratkāru, kept silent."

Just as the Upaniṣad does not reveal what Yājñavalkya and Ārtabhāga conversed about regarding *karma,* the present Gospel also does not disclose the three sayings Jesus spoke to Thomas. Instead, their ineffability alone is indicated by Thomas's statement to his friends.

Before entering it, let us clarify one point by way of digression. Yājñavalkya's words "Ārtabhāga, my dear, take my hand" are not to be taken as an equivalent to the modern practice of shaking hands when two person meet each other. This practice is merely a social one, a part of making friends with one another. But the present context is entirely different. Ārtabhāga's intention was to question the authenticity of the wisdom of Yājñavalkya. But what happens rather is that he unwittingly proves himself to be a fully competent disciple of Yājñavalkya. Yājñavalkya, on his part, compassionately lifts Ārtabhāga up into the higher realms of his own wisdom by offering a helping hand; thus making him (Ārtabhāga) an equal to himself. This is the significance of Ārtabhāga taking Yājñavalkya's hand. In its place, Jesus here tells Thomas, "I am not your teacher."

When asked by his friends, "What did Jesus say to you?" the immediate response of Thomas was, "If I tell you one of the sayings he spoke to me, you will pick up rocks and stone me."

We have already seen how certain *jñānin*s appear as if intoxicated. In this respect too, Jesus and Thomas are almost equals. Yet different are the ways in which both give expression to it. Jesus remains in a serene state, whereas Thomas becomes exulted. The alcohol type of intoxication that ordinary people experience is a sort of induced darkness that veils their consciousness. On the other hand, in a *jñānin* it results from his attaining the perfect transparency of consciousness. There are those who confuse these two types of intoxication, and take the latter for the former. Thomas here simply points at the fact in poetic language when he says, "If I tell you one of the sayings he spoke to me, you will pick up rocks and stone me." But the words that follow are even more enigmatic. He says, "And fire will come from the rocks and consume you."

The rocks that the friends are likely to pelt at Thomas represent the misunderstood wisdom secret. If the wisdom secret is thus misunderstood and thrown back at the one who knows it properly, then the very same secret will turn out to be inimical to those who do so. The basic interest of those who do so would naturally be not in wisdom but in actions (*karma*s). All such *karma*s would be revealed to be of no basic value in life once the wisdom secret has become evident. *Bhagavad-Gītā* (IV.37) also categorically says, "This fire of wisdom reduces to ashes all the *karmas*." Similar instances exalting the value of wisdom appear in the Upaniṣads also, with the difference that in them the positive and negative sides of this value are shown separately. For example, the passage, "Your head would have fallen off had you not come to me" of *Chāndogya Upaniṣad* (5.12.2). And what happens when one becomes fully enlightened of the wisdom secret? *Chāndogya Upaniṣad* (5.2.3) says, "Upon this wisdom being taught, even a dry stump will start sprouting new leaves and growing new branches."

Apart from quoting such parallels, it is not possible to elucidate such statements as the one Thomas makes here to his friends. One thing is definite: it was a wisdom secret which was incommunicable by words, and even if communicated, would not be understandable to anyone unless their competence for it had fully matured. It is so because all verbal communication implies a duality between the words and their meanings, whereas the wisdom secret transcends even this duality. For this reason, the final stage of teaching is imparted by a true *guru* to his dear and fully competent disciple, through a silence that brims with the ineffable wisdom secret, rather than through words uttered. In India, such a *guru*-model can be traditionally seen in Dakṣiṇāmūrti, a name by which Śiva is known as a *guru*. Praising this *guru*-model, the great Śaṅkara says:

> Behold, beneath the banyan tree sit aged disciples and a young *guru*. By his silent instruction their doubts are wholly iradicated.

What is left unstated in the text also cannot be commented on. As everyone knows, any given commentary can only be made upon what is stated in the text. Therefore the unstated secret that Jesus imparted to his dear disciple Thomas has to be realized by the seeker on his own.

5.9

Absolutist Religious Observances

> **14.** Jesus said to them, "If you fast, you will bring sin upon yourselves, and if you pray, you will be condemned, and if you give to charity, you will harm your spirits.
>
> When you go into any region and walk through the countryside, when people receive you, eat what they serve you and heal the sick among them. For what goes into your mouth will not defile you; rather, it is what comes out of your mouth that will defile you."

FASTING, prayer and offering gifts or services as charities are always considered meritorious deeds by pious people, and this practice could be seen in all relgious followers. Such observances are not felt to be obligatory by *jñānin*s, but by *ajñānin*s. Fasting, in this context, is meant for cleansing one's physical body of all accumulated impurities, as well as to make up for the errors committed knowingly or unknowingly. This observance becomes meaningful only when dualities like purity and impurity, merit and sin, right and wrong, prevail. And such dualities persist only so long as one lives in ignorance. An enlightened *jñānin,* on the other hand, perceives in both what is conventionally thought of as sinful and meritorious, only different ways in which the only Reality manifests itself. Instead of strictly following such a socially designed morality, he adheres to the absolutist morality by which one lives fully identified with that Reality. Such is the way he transcends all dualities. In his perception, the worst of all sins is to live ignorant of that Reality. In short, the need for fasting as a religious observance is felt necessary by those who live guided by relativistic norms which originate basically from ignorance. Even after becoming a *jñānin,* if one feels obliged to practise such religious observances as if an *ajñānin,* it is in one sense, equal to bringing sin upon oneself.

Practising prayer, similarly, is felt a necessity only when one sees the duality of the benevolent God and the supplicant. Prayers, especially those for favours, are usually made when one feels that some needs remain unfulfilled, and can be fulfilled by the favours of God. But a *jñānin* perceives himself one with God, and therefore his wishes and God's wishes become identical. He feels no needs unfulfilled in life. He, therefore, does not feel prayer to be an absolute necessity in life. If a person who is thought of as a *jñānin* feels obliged to pray, it indicates that he is not a real *jñānin*.

Certain *jñānin*s, it is true, could also be seen praying. They do so not on feeling it to be an absolute obligation as far as they are concerned, but only to guide others and not to create confusion in the minds of the ignorant around them. *Bhagavad-Gītā* (III.26) also warns:

> Do not create confusion in the minds of the ignorant who live attached to their actions.

Otherwise, it could be done so as to conform to the integrity of community life, the constituent members of which are mostly ignorant. In such circumstances, if a *jñānin* gives up the practice of praying, the *ajñānin*s will also follow suit.

It is also considered meritorious to generously extend a helping hand to the needy, and also offer financial aid to charitable institutions. Offering of gifts or services is always performed by one to another. It becomes meaningful only when the giver feels the existence of a receiver different from himself; that means, when a duality between one and the other exists. A *jñānin* perceives himself alone as the one existing Reality, as we have clarified earlier. Offering any gift with the idea, "I am giving this to somebody else," violates the basic perception of the oneness of the Self. A *jñānin* therefore offers no gift as such to anyone.

This in no way means that an enlightened person is not generous and compassionate. He lives generously and compassionately, but not with a sense of being generous and compassionate. One is so because one sees oneself in every being. One's love for oneself then naturally extends towards everyone. One feels self-happiness in sharing whatever one has with everyone around. The thing one gives to oneself never becomes a gift or donation. A *jñānin*, who sees himself in everyone, sharing with everyone what he possessed is in effect no gift at all.

The significance of the second part of the 14th saying has been examined by us earlier.

5.10

The Birth of a Guru

> **15.** Jesus said, "When you see one who was not born of woman, fall on your faces and worship. That is your father."

THERE is no one in this world who is not born of a woman. Even Jesus, the Son of God, was born of Mary, a woman. Then who is the one Jesus refers to as not born of woman? Is it God himself? The words "When you see one" imply that it is not God either, because no one sees God with his own eyes. "The one who is not born of woman," thus is neither an ordinary human being nor God.

Though all are born of women, a *guru* is not so. A living human being, when fully transformed into the embodiment of the perfection of wisdom, becomes a *guru*. That is to say, it is wisdom that made him a *guru*. The birth of a *guru* is from wisdom, and not of any woman. It is in complete forgetfulness of this reality that people, in the conventional sense, say, such and such a *guru* was born of so and so, and such and such is his birthday. The birthdays of certain *guru*s are even celebrated with much pomp.

A *guru* thus born of wisdom is the one who gives you a second birth by imparting the wisdom secret to you, thus becoming your father. Such are the connotations of the present words of Jesus.

5.11

The Eye of the Eye

16. Jesus said, "Perhaps people think that I have come to impose peace upon the world. They do not know that I have come to impose conflicts upon the earth: fire, sword, war. For there will be fire in a house. There will be three against two and two against three, father against son and son against father, and they will stand alone."

17. Jesus said, "I shall give you what no eye has seen, what no ear has heard, what no hand has touched, what has not arisen in the human heart."

THE *guru* of *Kena Upaniṣad* says the following about the one Reality that functions as the impelling force behind all the faculties in our being:

> The ear even of the ears, the mind even of the mind, the word even of the words, the *prāṇa* (vital force) even of the *prāṇa*s, the eye even of the eyes — the wise one who knows this Reality becomes liberated from this world of becoming and attains immortality. —2

The same *guru,* when further elaborating on this point, says:

> That which the eyes do not see and because of which the eyes see, that indeed is *Brahman,* be aware of. —6

Similarly, *Chāndogya Upaniṣad* says:

> Because of which the unheard becomes heard, the unthought of becomes well thought of, and the unknown becomes well known.
> — 6.13.1

The experiential awareness hidden within such Upaniṣadic passages could be seen echoed here in the 17th saying of Jesus. Some historians think that Jesus was much familiar with Indian philosophy, particularly Vedānta. They might find the present passage to substantiate their stand. But, those who visualize the one ultimate Reality may emerge in any part of the world, and the words they utter to reveal that truth naturally would have many similarities. The present passage could be seen to evince this fact also.

One alone is the Reality that assumes the form of everything and that impels everything to be functional. And this Reality, as we know, is called *Ātman* (*Brahman*) in Vedānta. Thus what appears as the sense-organ called the eye, and what enables it to see objects, is that *Ātman* alone.

How is it possible then for the very same eyes to see that causal *Ātman* behind them? The same is true with the other sense-organs and the other knowing faculties as well. The assurance given by Jesus in verse 17 is that he will reveal the secret of the Reality that underlies the being of all the knowing faculties.

5.12

The Beginning and the End

18. The followers said to Jesus, "Tell us how our end will be?"

Jesus said, "Have you discovered the beginning, then, so that you are seeking the end? For where the beginning is, the end will be. Fortunate is one who stands at the beginning. That one will know the end and will not taste death."

THIS is yet another of Jesus's sayings that sounds much like an Upaniṣadic dictum. The problem dealt with here apparently is of birth and death. The question of what happens after death arises from the ignorant mind of a seeker like Naciketas of *Kaṭha Upaniṣad.* And one who knows the reality concerning birth and death does not ask this question. The question thus arises out of ignorance. If it is answered as to what will happen after death, it will be an answer in accordance with ignorance. Jesus, on the other hand, replies from the standpoint of an enlightened *jñānin.*

This can be further elucidated with a verse of *Taittirīya Upaniṣad.* Bhṛgu, the disciple and son of Varuṇa, requests his father to teach him *brahma-vidyā* (science of *Brahman*). The father just says:

(Understand) food, vital breath (*prāṇa*), sight, hearing, mind, speech (as *Brahman*).

Then he continues:

That verily from which beings are born, that by which those that are born live, into which they finally reach and merge — seek to know that. That is *Brahman.* — 3.1

Brahman, in other words, is the Reality that was causal to the emergence of everything including the seeker, and into which everything finally merges upon dissolution. One who knows, what was in the beginning, thus knows what will be there as one ceases to exist in appearance as well. It could also be said that one who asks about what will happen at one's end does so only because one does not know anything about one's beginning.

The beings thus born of *Brahman* do not become separate from that source-Reality. Instead, *Brahman* Itself is what appears as the worlds and all the beings in them, just as water itself is what appears as waves. Every mortal wave has the immortal water for its essential content. Likewise, every being that has emerged thus has *Brahman* alone for its essential content. This *Brahman* is birthless and deathless. One who just upon realizing "I really am the birthless and deathless *Brahman,*" becomes immortal. This is the reason why Jesus says, "Fortunate is one who stands at the beginning: That one will know the end and will not taste death".

> **19.** Jesus said, "Fortunate is one who came into being before coming into being.
>
> If you become my followers and listen to my sayings, these stones will serve you.
>
> For there are five trees in paradise for you; they do not change, summer or winter, and their leaves do not fall. Whoever knows them will not taste death."

Each individual being gets formulated, as we have seen, in the one all-underlying *Brahman* Reality. The seeker thus finds out that what existed before his emergence and causal to it, really was *Brahman.* One realizes also that in essential content he is that Reality. That essential content in oneself has never come into existence; on the other hand, it has always been existing. That means, one really is *Brahman* that has never come into being. Put otherwise, what existed before one's coming into being was oneself. The seeker who realizes thus is here qualified as "fortunate."

The highest of wisdom secrets the disciples can expect to get from Jesus their *guru* is nothing other than this. The seeker who becomes enlightened of this secret, perceives him self in everything. As one finds oneself as one's own cause, one finds oneself to be the cause of everything as well. One perceives even an inert stone as having emerged from oneself. The nature of an effect is dictated by its cause. This fact is put in rather figurative terms by Jesus thus, "These stones will serve you." Giving stress to the other side of this picture, *Taittirīya Upaniṣad* says:

> He who knows these knows *Brahman.* To him all gods offer tributes.
>
> — I.5

Likewise, *Chāndogya Upaniṣad* says:

> He who knows the *sāman* thus, he really knows all. All quarters bring him offerings. — 6.21.2

Such a world of wisdom itself is to be counted as the paradise of this context. No other reality than *Ātmā* exists in that paradise. And this *Ātmā,* assuming the forms of individual beings, keeps them alive as well. This life principle is called *prāṇa* by Indian thinkers. This *prāṇa* is conceived by them as funcitonally appearing in five different modes known as *prāṇa, apāna, vyāna, udāna* and *samāna.*

Comparing this life principle to an ever-growing tree is a symbol acceptable to almost all religions of the world. This tree is conceived as having roots growing upwards and branches downwards, in *Bhagavad-Gītā* (XV.1) and *Kaṭha Upaniṣad* (6.1).

The five modes of *prāṇa* seen in individual living beings could also be conceived as functioning in the cosmic system as a whole, as visualized in *Praśna Upaniṣad* (chapter III). Vedānta, as we know, perceives the universe as a living entity, as the polar opposite of the living individual being, or life-situation with these two poles. Conceiving the universe as a living entity is not something wholly unfamiliar to modern Western thought, as well as to modern science. For example, "Gaia" is the name given today to a living earth or universe.

One and the same *prāṇa*-principle thus is to be thought of as functioning fivefold, both individually in each being and universally in the cosmic system. This *prāṇa* really is neither individual nor universal, and this non-dual *prāṇa* is equated to *Ātmā* in the *Praśna Upaniṣad.* It is this *prāṇa*-principle that manifests universally as the seasonal changes and individually as the corresponding bodily and mental states in the being of each person. This *prāṇa,* which is causal to the seasonal changes, does not undergo these changes. If this *prāṇa,* with its five facets, is likened to five trees, then the peculiarity with these trees is that their leaves do not fall; they remain evergreen and ever new. One who knows *Ātmā* in the form of this fivefold *prāṇa*-principle, as is to be presumed from the assurance Jesus gives, does not taste death.

5.13

Minuter than the Minutest, Greater than the Greatest

20. The followers said to Jesus, "Tell us what heaven's kingdom is like."

He said to them, "It is like a mustard seed. [It] is the smallest of all seeds, but when it falls on prepared soil, it produces a large plant and becomes a shelter for birds of heaven."

THAT Jesus means by the kingdom of heaven *Ātmā* (Self) or the wisdom of the Self, we have already noticed. *Ātmā* is too subtle to become an object of any sense-organ or even the mind. In that sense it is minuter than the minutest. Being the Reality that unfolds itself as all the worlds, It is greater than the greatest as well, as *Svetāśvatara Upaniṣad* (3.20) prefers to put it. The same is the picture portrayed by Jesus here.

A tiny seed inheres in itself all the potentials to grow into a big tree. Likewise, infinite is the possibility *Ātmā* hides within Itself to manifest as all the worlds and all their details. The prepared soil mentioned here then could be conceived as this possibility becoming actualized.

Conceiving the kingdom of heaven as the wisdom of the Self, its tininess indicates its subtle nature — so subtle that it is not even conceivable to the mind. Then the prepared soil stands for the mind of a disciple well-matured in competence. Such a disciple, upon imbibing this very subtle wisdom secret, intuitively perceives its scope to be so vast that all the disciplines and sciences that we can think of, have their legitimate place within its chambers. Such an enlightened one functions like a shade tree for the entire world, and under its shade every human being can find the solace he seeks in life.

5.14

The Necessity of Being Strong-minded

21. Mary said to Jesus, "What are your followers like?"

He said, "They are like little children living in a field that is not theirs. When the owners of the field come, they will say, 'Give our field back to us.' They take off their clothes in front of them in order to give it back to them, and they return their field to them.

For this reason I say, if the owner of the house knows that a thief is coming, he will be on guard before the thief arrives and will not let the thief break into the house of his estate and steal his possessions. As for you, then, be on guard against the world. Arm yourself with great strength, or the robbers might find a way to get to you, for the trouble you expect will come. Let there be among you a person who understands.

When the crop ripened, the person came quickly with sickle in hand and harvested it. Whoever has ears to hear should hear."

THE context as a whole is compared to a field of crops ripening for a harvest. Jesus, as we have noticed in other Gospels, likens his disciples to harvesters, and those who are willing and open-minded to come to his new wisdom-path, to the crop to be harvested. The disciples who are to serve as harvesters are considered here by Jesus as "Children living in a field that is not theirs." "Children" in the context of wisdom teaching stand for those who are not matured enough and therefore feeble in mind, as they are called so in many contexts of the Upaniṣads. Here also Jesus is afraid, an element of childishness and feebleness still lurks in his disciples.

The crop they are supposed to harvest, new believers in the new way, are spread all over the world. And those who are in the world are most likely controlled by worldly interests, that is traits and instincts called *loka-vāsanā*s. The duty of the disciples, thus, is to bring those who are still under the spell of worldly traits to the new path of wisdom that liberates them from all such conditionings. But these disciples apparently are yet to become well founded in their own understanding of the new wisdom. And for this reason, when the people who are meant to be attracted to its path are pulled away by the force of worldly traits and interests, the strength to counteract this and to firmly bring the people back to their side is found lacking in these disciples. Jesus is well aware of this. Because of this lack of strength to be gained through wisdom, these disciples, instead of keeping the new flock in their possession, are most likely to give up even what they already possess when faced with those who are worldly minded. The clothes they give up represent Jesus, his wisdom and everything related to it that they already possess. Jesus earnestly wishes that his disciples will not give these up. Therefore they must remain fully alert in two respects, as Jesus continues to say.

The disciples have to remain on guard like the owner of a house who knows that a thief will come to break into his house. There are those who decidedly stick to the path of wisdom. But around them the world is always ready to tempt them into the mire of worldliness. A true seeker therefore should be endowed with the inner strength to resist all such enticing forces. A similar directive is also given in *Bhagavad-Gītā* (VI.26) as follows:

> As and when the fickle and unsteady mind strays out, then and there it is to be kept a tight rein on, bringing it back under the sway of one's own Self-content.

The context here is also that of the mind straying. As long as one's mind is fickle, as long as worldly traits in one are forceful, the attack of that enemy will come. Proper discrimination supported by a wilful mind alone will help one confront this attack. Jesus here expresses his wish for at least one disciple who has these qualities. There is also an indication that no one with such qualities is there among the disciples.

Had there been at least one such disciple, instead of giving back the field and the crop, he would determinedly harvest the crop by using the sickle of discrimination (*viveka*) and sense of detachment (*vairāgya*). In other words, he would attract to his side all properly inquisitive and open-minded people.

5.15

Deconditioning the Mind

> **22.** Jesus saw some babies nursing. He said to the followers, "These nursing babies are like those who enter the kingdom." They said to him, "Then shall we enter the kingdom as babies?"
>
> Jesus said to them, "When you make the two into one, and when you make the inner like the outer and the outer like the inner, and the upper like the lower, and when you make male and female into a single one, so that the male will not be male nor the female be female, when you make eyes in place of an eye, a hand in place of a hand, a foot in place of a foot, an image in place of an image, then you will enter [the kingdom].

NURSING babies are in a state of not knowing anything about the outer world, but remain totally filled with the bliss of being suckled by the mother, their source. The babies' identity is then at one with their source reality. Not different is the case of those who have realized the ultimate Reality (*Ātman*). Undisturbed by all that appears and happens externally, they always remain fully merged in the *sat-cit-ānanda* content of the one Reality, the original source of everything.

But the disciples of Jesus are not little infants; they are all grown men. The minds of small children have not become conditioned in any way; but the minds of adults have already become vitiated by all kinds of conditionings through the knowledge they have acquired, experiences gained and traits developed throughout their lives. The nursing children, in one sense, already live in a heaven of innocence. The grown-ups, on the other hand, must find the kingdom of heaven and enter it through a door of some kind. Here Jesus indicates how this is possible for them.

All sense of duality arises because consciousness undergoes different kinds of conditionings. Once all these conditionings are erased from the mind, the one unconditioned consciousness, the essential content of the ultimate Reality, the kingdom of God, naturally shines. Inside–outside, subject–object, male–female, cause–effect, above–below and such dualities are numerous, and all these appear to be real only when the *Ātman*-Reality becomes subject to different kinds of conditioning factors. *Ātman,* as such, really is *sat-cit-ānanda.* Upon realizing oneself to be that *sat-cit-ānanda* in essential content, everything is known to be that *sat-cit-ānanda,* and one merges into that *sat-cit-ānanda.* Such is the mark of attaining the kingdom of heaven.

On entering this kingdom, instead of seeing the eyes and the objects they see as real, one perceives as Real only God, the eye that sees the two together. This experiential aspect is reiterated in the words of Jesus citing the examples of hands, feet, form and the like.

We have quoted earlier, passages similar in nature to this, from *Kena Upaniṣad.*

> **23.** Jesus said, "I shall choose you, one from a thousand and two from ten thousand, and they will stand as a single one."

Not everyone is competent to enter the kingdom of God. *Bhagavad-Gītā* (VII.3) says:

> Among ten thousand men, one perchance strives for the perfection of attainment. Even among those who strive thus and attain the goal, one perchance knows Me right to the core.

In the case of the rare ones who have entered the kingdom thus, their plurality becomes lost in the oneness of the kingdom they have reached.

> **24.** His followers said, "Show us the place where you are, for we must seek it."
>
> He said to them, "Whoever has ears should hear. There is light within a person of light, and it shines on the whole world. If it does not shine, it is dark."

Jesus the *guru* is to be understood, not as a person, but as of the essential content of the effulgence of wisdom. The Reality that shines as a *guru* is what manifests as the world as well. A *guru,* who in essence is effulgence, makes life in this world also shine brightly and meaningfully.

If that Reality or wisdom does not shine, then everything becomes concealed by a darkness — a darkness that conceals even the fact that everything remains concealed by darkness. Life in this world as such is a sort of groping in darkness if there is no *guru*'s guidance readily available. Therefore, Jesus the *guru* is not to be searched for in some particular place, but each seeker should find him as the Self-effulgence within their own being.

5.16

The Way to Enter the Kingdom

25. Jesus said, "Love your brother like your soul, protect that person like the pupil of your eye".

26. Jesus said, "You see the speck that is in your brother's eye, but you do not see the beam that is in your own eye. When you take the beam out of your own eye, then you will see clearly to take the speck out of your brother's eye."

27. If you do not fast from the world, you will not find the kingdom. If you do not observe the sabbath as a sabbath, you will not see the father.

FASTING is one of the religious observances practised in all religious followings, and is a sort of deliberate withdrawal from life's usual routine. Unless the same kind of withdrawal from worldly affairs and worldly interests occurs in one's own life, one will not find the kingdom of God. This kingdom, as we have noticed earlier, is to be found within oneself. Perceiving this kingdom of God within is not possible without one withdrawing oneself from the habit of looking outwards; instead, one has to look inwards. This looking inwards is fasting in the wisdom context. Jesus therefore says, "If you do not fast from the world, you will not find the kingdom."

The world and everything in it, according to the Genesis of the Bible, was created by God in six days and He rested on the seventh day. In remembrance of this rest of God, the seventh day of a week is observed as the sabbath by the Jews. It is an inviolable rule with them that no one should engage in any activity that day. The main element in this religious observance apparently is to rest. The person who runs around feverishly throughout the six days a week and rests upon the seventh day as merely a religious duty, does not find the kingdom of heaven, nor the Father in it. It is not merely a day of bodily rest that follows a feverish week, but is a withdrawal from all such activities in order to calmly look within oneself. This alone helps one find the secret of the Self within. This interiorized search for the self, in India, is known as *nivṛtti-mārga.* This in no way means that all of life's normal activities are to be given up. Instead, one should attain the clarity of vision by which the resting Self alone is constantly perceived in all such activities. This ensures a restful life that is constant. Only those with such a perception possess the kingdom of God.

Saying 27 mentions two disciplines that are to be practised in a revised form. The former involves one's positive attunement to a revalued fasting habit. The other basically involves the negative nature of withdrawal. These positive and negative disciplines could well be conceived as forming the two opposite poles of a dialetical situation in the context of discipline, the result of which we can perceive only meditatively.

5.17

A Guru Grieves

> **28.** Jesus said, "I took my stand in the midst of the world, and in flesh. I appeared to them. I found them all drunk, and I did not find any of them thirsty. My soul ached for the children of humanity, because they are blind in their hearts and do not see, for they came into the world empty, and they also seek to depart from the world empty. But now they are drunk. When they shake off their wine, then they will repent."

THESE words of Jesus resound with the pain an enlightened *guru* feels for the people who live in total ignorance, even as such a *guru* lives amongst them in flesh and blood, always willing to teach them. Not only do they live in ignorance, they also live drunk with the wine of their own ignorance. Every human being is born in this world ignorant. But preparing to die as an enlightened person is what makes life meaningful. Nevertheless, people usually spend their entire lifetime preparing to only die in ignorance. Jesus mentions the case of such people here. A true *guru* feels pained for such peoples' sake, despite that he may be helpless to help them. A *guru* can impart wisdom only to a peson who becomes cleared of ignorance-born-intoxication, and who repents for remaining ignorant so far. Jesus utters these words in regards to those Jews who remain uninterested in, or even resistant to the wisdom teaching or the kingdom of heaven, brought forth to them by himself.

> **29.** Jesus said, "If the flesh came into being because of spirit, it is a marvel, but if spirit came into being because of the body, it is a marvel of marvels. Yet I marvel at how this great wealth has come to dwell in this poverty."

The one ultimate Reality (*Ātmā*) is pure Consciousness (*cit*). It is this non-dual *Ātmā* that unfolds itself both as the gross matter and as the subtle mind. How does it become possible for the extremely subtle *Ātmā* (Reality) to assume the form even of gross physical matter? It is a marvel indeed, and this marvel is what in Vedānta is called *māyā*.

Why can't we think that consciousness arises from matter, as is held by modern science? We can only say that for such a possibility to happen is a marvel of all marvels.

That pure Consciousness or *Ātmā* is what has assumed the forms of all the worlds, is a priceless wisdom. But such a wisdom secret, or Jesus the embodiment of that wisdom, dwells here among a people that do not feel at all the necessity and value of this wisdom; so pitiable is their poverty in spirit. It is a marvel indeed.

5.18

Doctrinal Differences

> **30.** Jesus said, "Where there are three deities, they are divine. Where there are two or one, I am with that one."

It is evidently image worship that is indicated here. Though many are the deities worshipped by idolaters, such deities could be seen in many cultures to have been reduced to three. For example, there is the Indian pantheon of three deities (*trimūrtis*), namely Brahmā (the Creator), Viṣṇu (the Sustainer) and Maheśvara (the Annihilator). Perhaps Jesus had familiarity with other religious cultures, such as the Indian one, in which there are three principal deities.

The later Christian concept of the Trinity — the Father, the Son and the Holy Spirit — is also of the same order. Instead of abnegating such cultural trends common among the religiously minded, Jesus acknowledges these also as having divinity, and thus as not objectionable.

Yet some others are there who give more importance to philosophical speculations. They first bifurcate what fundamentally exists as the subject and the object, or as mind and matter, and then try to solve the problem of, which abides in which. The value of their thinking is also acknowleged by Jesus.

Some others prefer to think that one ultimate Reality (*Ātmā*) alone exists eternally. They do not even have the notion that they are the knowers of that Reality. They simply experience their being lost in that Reality where the notion of being an experiencer also vanishes. Jesus says, "I am with that one." That means, "I and that one are not two." The words of *Bhagavad-Gītā* (VII.18): "Dignified indeed are all of them; but I hold the *jñānin* as Myself" could also be recalled here.

> **31.** Jesus said, "A prophet is not acceptable in the prophet's own town; a doctor does not heal those who know the doctor."
>
> **32.** Jesus said, "A city built upon a high hill and fortified cannot fall, nor can it be hidden."

33. Jesus said, "What you will hear in your ear, in the other ear proclaim from your rooftop. For no one lights a lamp and puts it under a basket, nor does one put it in a hidden place. Rather, one puts it on a stand so that all who come and go will see its light."

34. Jesus said, "If a blind person leads a blind person, both of them will fall into a hole."

5.19

Māyā

> **35.** Jesus said, "You cannot enter the house of the strong and take it by force without tying the person's hands. Then you can loot the person's house."

ONE of the aspects of the final goal attained by any spiritual enquiry is that each seeker must ultimately come fully under his own control. The Upaniṣads conceive this achievement as becoming fully founded (*pratiṣṭhitam*) in the Self.

Are we not now under our own control? In the usual course we think we are so. But as long as we do not know ourselves in the true sense, we really live controlled by ignorace. How did this ignorance get into us without our knowledge? It happens, as held by Vedāntins, because of *māyā.* In other words, we unknowingly live under the spell of *māyā.* It could even be said, *māyā* possesses us. For the reason that this happens without our knowledge, any chance to escape from it is also scarce. In short, *māyā*'s grip on us is very strong. As long as it remains so, our thoughts continue to be directed to the outside world, where our interests are for external objects alone, and the temptations for the pleasures derived from those objects remain forceful. A real seeker therefore should become endowed with an inner clarity and wilfulness to mercilessly cut down this *māyā* and the temptations effected by it. On accomplishing this one realizes, "So far I was possessed by *māyā.*" This is something like a house, though possessed by a storng man, gets looted by a thief once the owner is caught and his hands are tied.

> **36.** Jesus said, "Do not worry, from morning to evening and from evening to morning, about what you will wear."

Those who live by perceiving themselves in the one ultimate Reality or God, do not worry about their daily needs. This point has already been clarified earlier in the other Gospels.

5.20

Become Childlike

> **37.** His followers said, "When will you appear to us and when shall we see you?"
>
> Jesus said, "When you strip without being ashamed and you take your clothes and put them under your feet like little childern and trample them, then (you) will see the child of the living one and you will not be afraid."

THE disciples ask this question apparently to Jesus himself while he is right before them. They must have asked this as prompted by a yearning to intuitively perceive the real *guru* in Jesus. Such a perception in essence is not different from attaining the kingdom of heaven by imbibing in the wisdom secret from the *guru.* We have already seen that one's mind must become innocent and like a clean slate in order to attain the enlightenment of the said wisdom secret. It is not uncommon to see children in public strip and throw down their clothes, even stomping them beneath their feet innocently. Equivalent to this act of children is when the seeker gives up his ego, along with all kinds of conditionings and misguided ideas, and makes his mind clean so that unconditioned wisdom may be freshly imprinted upon it.

> **38.** Jesus said, "Often you have desired to hear these sayings that I am speaking to you, and you have no one else from whom to hear them. There will be days when you will seek me and you will not find."
>
> **39.** Jesus said, "The Pharisees and the scribes have taken the keys of knowledge and have hidden them. They have not entered, nor have they allowed those who want to enter to do so. As for you, be as shrewd as snakes and as innocent as doves."

The wisdom secret is also hidden in the Jewish scriptures. (These form part of the Old Testament of the Holy Bible.) But the right to teach these scriptures is monopolized by the Pharisees and the scribes. They, ignorant as they are of the wisdom secret, know only the apparently literal sense of those words. And those who try to search for that secret are persecuted by them in order to safeguard their monopoly to teach the scriptures. Even Jesus had to suffer this persecution.

To depend on such Pharisees and scribes is of no use for the disciples of Jesus who intend to find out the wisdom secret. On the other hand, if they listen to the words of Jesus with all shrewdness and cogitate incessantly on them in a meditative mood, along with wiping out all the conditionings and their ill-effects that have already tarnished their inner being, they are sure to possess on their own the key to the wisdom treasure. What is this key is not stated by Jesus here. Possibly it is the same "dialectics" that existed among the Greek thinkers before the time of Jesus, and *yoga-buddhi* well known to the Indian context, particularly in the *Bhagavad-Gītā*. Socrates qualified this key as "the coping stone of wisdom." This way of intuitively perceiving the otherwise inconceivable Reality could be seen to be profusely used by Jesus, as we have tried to clarify in these comments.

5.21

Forewarnings

40. Jesus said, "A grapevine has been planted away from the father. Since it is not strong, it will be pulled up by its root and will perish."

WHAT is likened here to a grapevine presumably is our own lives. As we have already noticed, life becomes really happy and meaningful when it is well-rooted in the one ultimate Reality or God, and if it is so, life is felt also to be eternal, with the phenomena of birth and death not affecting its unbroken continuance. But because of our total ignorance of ourselves, we try to make our life stably founded on something other than that Reality, for example, accumulated wealth, social status and the like. However persistent be such attempts, like the seeds that fall on a rock without well-tended soil, their sprouts become destroyed with no opportunity for them to take root and flourish. In order to avoid such an eventuality, we must find the ultimate Reality in our own being and heedfully perceive our lives as emerging from and appearing within that Reality or God. Such is the forewarning that resounds in these words of Jesus.

41. Jesus said, "Whoever has something in hand will be given more, and whoever has nothing will be deprived even of the little that person has."

42. Jesus said, "Be passers-by."

Travellers, on their way through many destinations, may happen to stay one night at a wayside inn, and depart from there the next morning. While at the inn, they would make friends with one another, perhaps never to meet again. Similar is life in this world. We all live here for some time, make different kinds of relationships, many taken very seriously, and then depart from this world. Apart from the enlightened ones, no one exactly knows their own origin. With the unenlightened, their own source remains unknown, and where they reach upon leaving this world, also remains unknown. Still we are prone to make our lives, that merely are insignificant middle parts between some unknown beginning and unknown end, full of problems, instead of thinking we are just passers-by in the travellers' inn named the world. *Bhagavad-Gītā* also says:

Indistinct were all beings in the beginning, distinct in the middle they are all; indistinct they become at dissolution, O Bhārata, what is therein to bemoan? — II.28

43. His followers said to him, "Who are you to say these things to us?"

He said to them, "You do not know who I am from what I say to you. Rather, you have become like the Jewish people, for they love the tree but hate its fruit, or they love the fruit but hate the tree."

The worth of a *guru* is to be evaluated upon the basis of the words of wisdom he speaks. Jesus many a time tried to reveal the secret of wisdom to his followers. But they were not endowed with the clear insight necessary to understand its essential content, nor to appreciate his authoritativeness to speak those words. This is the reason why they ask the present question.

Jesus, in response, compares their lack of proper insight to the state of mind of the Jews. The Jews were then a people who had a great love and respect for the tree of their tradition. But there is a wisdom that gave shape to that tradition, and what Jesus did was re-interpret and re-introduce that very same wisdom. But the Jews were quite incapable of understanding and appreciating it. Furthermore, they hated Jesus who brought a fresh light to the wisdom secret hidden in their own tradition. They, in this regard, are people who love the tree and hate its fruit.

The religious interest of the Jews is to strictly adhere to the traditional commandments like those of Moses. But they forget that such commandments come from only those who are enlightened as to what is ultimately True. If that enlightenment is a tree, the commandments are its fruits. They, in this regard, love the fruit and hate the tree.

44. Jesus said, "Whoever blasphames against the father will be forgiven, and whoever blasphames against the son will be forgiven, but whoever blasphames against the Holy Spirit will not be forgiven, either on earth or in heaven.

The Father, the Son and the Holy Ghost together constitute the trinity that forms part of the fundamental belief pattern of Christianity. As we have already seen, the Father, from the Vedāntic perspective, signifies *Brahman*, the Son, the *jñānin* who is fully aware that he is a minute element of *Brahman*, and the Holy Ghost, the essential content of wisdom. Suppose one speaks disrespectfully of *Brahman;* this in no way affects the purity of that Reality. Suppose one discredits a *jñānin;* this does not affect him in any way. But suppose one desecrates wisdom itself; this is tantamount to having no concern for knowing the meaning of one's own life, and for that matter, of having any respect for it. The one who does not respect himself can never make life happy and meaningful, here or hereafter.

45. Jesus said, "Grapes are not harvested from thorn trees, nor are figs gathered from thistles, for they yield no fruit. A good person brings forth good from the storehouse; a bad person brings forth evil from the corrupt storehouse in the heart and says evil things. For from the abundance of the heart this person brings forth evil things."

46. Jesus said, "From Adam to John the Baptist, among those born of women, no one is so much greater than John the Baptist that the persons eyes should not be averted. But I have said that whoever among you becomes a child will know the kingdom and will become greater than John."

47. Jesus said, "A person cannot mount two horses or bend two bows. And a servant cannot serve two masters, or that servant will honour the one and offend the other. No person drinks aged wine and immediately desires to drink new wine. New wine is not poured into aged wineskins, or they might break, and aged wine is not poured into new wineskin, or it might spoil. An old patch is not sewn onto a new garment, for there would be a tear."

48. Jesus said, "If two make peace with each other in a single house, they will say to the mountain 'Move from here,' and it will move."

5.22

The Nature and Content of Reality

> **49.** Jesus said, "Fortunate are those who are alone and chosen, for you will find the kingdom. For you have come from it, and you will return there again."

JESUS here states with no obscuration, the Vedāntic position, that everything emerges from the one ultimate Reality, everyone lives as a manifest form of that Reality, and everyone finally merges in that Reality. Realizing this wisdom secret is not an accomplishment attained by everyone; this experiential certainty is gained only by a few true seekers. Likewise, such an attainment is not gained through collective efforts either. Making efforts and becoming awakened have to take place in every seeker individually, through their austere self-discipline which is called *tapas* in Vedānta. This is indicated by Jesus in his words, "Fortunate are those who are alone and chosen, for you will find the kingdom."

> **50.** Jesus said, "If they say to you, 'Where have you come from?' say to them, 'We have come from the light, from the place where the light came into being by itself, established [itself], and appeared in their image.' If they say to you, 'Is it you?' say, 'We are its children, and we are the chosen of the living father.' If they ask you, 'What is the evidence of your father in you?' say to them, 'It is motion and rest'."

The idea brought to relief in the last saying is continued here as well. The most basic teaching of Vedānta is that the one all-underlying Reality is pure Consciousness (*cit*) in essence. Everyone has the experience, and hence it is a fact needing no proof, that Consciousness is an experience of effulgence. *Bhagavad-Gītā* says:

> That is the effulgence in all that shines, and, it is said, is beyond all darkness. — XIII.7

Muṇḍaka Upaniṣad says:

> Within the perishable appearances (*śarīras*) is that *Ātmā,* effulgence in essence. — 3.1.5

From the very effulgence–Reality or Father came into being both the present questioner and the answerer. Both, in other words, are the children of the same Father. The difference between the two is that the questioner does not know this truth whereas the answerer does. Such questioners are many, but those who are capable of answering such questions are hardly to be found. The latter therefore are qualified here as "the chosen of the living father."

That "living father" is neither an abstract idea nor a concrete object. He is neither mind nor matter. He, on the other hand, is the one living Reality that transcends the mind–matter duality, and that appears as these dual aspects. He is the Reality that appears as all the worlds, as the blend of mind and matter.

It is again asked, what is the sign of that living Reality. The answer is, "It is motion and rest." In other words, it moves and does not move at the same time. When assuming the form of the world, every minute element of it is in motion. Viewed thus, the ultimate Reality is in a constant state of motion. But as the one omnipresent Reality, it has nowhere to move to, for no place exists where it is not. It is motionless in that sense. The same kind of apparently paradoxical statement about the Reality or God can be seen in *Īśa Upaniṣad* as follows:

> It moves and It moves not; It is far and It is near, It is within all this and It is also outside all this. —5

Innumerable dualities such as subject and object, mind and matter, inside and outside, day and night, light and shade, pleasure and pain, cause and effect, are perceivable in the world and in the phenomenon of life in it, all emerging from one effulgence-Reality or Father. Such emergence of dualities is counted here as the sign of the Father or God.

> **51.** His followers said to him, "When will the rest for the dead take place, and when will the new world come?"
>
> He said to them, "What you look for has come, but you do not know it."

One and only one Reality is what exists. Everyone and everything is a minute manifest form of that Reality. That Reality was never born; it never dies. As every living being is that Reality in essence, the question "When do they rest after death?" does not arise at all. What we call the birth of a being is nothing more than the event in which the eternal Reality assumes a new transient form, and death is the giving up that form. The Reality continues to exist despite the appearance and disappearance of its assumed forms.

This eternal Reality itself is called the kingdom of heaven as it is already there within each of us, and, as we are already that, it is not something yet to come. Knowing it as the Reality within ourselves is itself the coming of the kingdom of heaven.

> **52.** His followers said to him, "Twenty-four prophets have spoken in Israel, and they all spoke of you."
>
> He said to them, "You have disregarded the living one who is in your presence and have spoken of the dead."

Those who follow Jesus, recognizing him as a prophet, still do so without fully understanding the deeper significance of the words he utters. They do so only because they honour the predictions of the earlier prophets that such a prophet would emerge in the future. That means, they are incapable of comprehending the wisdom teachings of a living *guru* that is an embodiment of the one ever-living *guru*-principle, but instead they honour the authoritativeness of the dead ones. This in a way shows the ignorance of their religiosity. It is against this ignoble state of mind of his followers that Jesus speaks here.

> **53.** His followers said to him, "Is circumcision useful or not?"
>
> He said to them, "If it were useful, children's fathers would produce them already circumcised from their mothers. Rather, the true circumcision in spirit has become valuable in every respect."

Circumcision is a religious custom practised by Jews and Muslims alike. It first became a custom among the Jews, and its origin was derived from a covenant that the patriarch Abraham had with God. Initially it was considered a bodily mark that differentiated the males of the Jewish community from others, and as marking the transition stage in the grown-up males' lives as they started to live independently, free of the parent's control. This custom could be considered almost equal to the Indian practice of ceremonially wearing the sacred thread called *upanayana*. Though serving some such social purposes, this custom cannot be counted to form part of the system of life that nature unfolds. Were it so, male bodies would be born naturally circumcised. Nor can it be thought, that this practice has some true spiritual value. Anything of spiritual value cannot be something merely physical, but has to happen within, directing one from the darkness of ignorance to the brightness of wisdom and happiness. Such a spiritual circumcision is what one needs, according to Jesus. These words of Jesus could also be treated as a revaluation of the concept of circumcision, by uplifting it from the realm of blind ritualism to something meaningful in the context of wisdom.

54. Jesus said, "Fortunate are the poor, for yours is heaven's kingdom."

55. Jesus said, "Whoever does not hate father and mother cannot be a follower of me, and whoever does not hate brothers and sisters and bear the cross as I do will not be worthy of me."

5.23

The Knowledge that Is Above Knowledge

> **56.** Jesus said, "Whoever has come to know the world has discovered a carcass, and whoever has discovered a carcass, of that person the world is not worthy."

ALL modern sciences, in the usual course, try to understand the objective physical world. Whatever be the details entailed in these studies, the knowledge we gain from them always concerns the matter-aspect of the world, that is, the inert-aspect of the world. Those who pursue such a study gain more and more clarity about the inert-aspect of the world, or the inert or matter aspect of life. But they never attain the all-inclusive knowledge — the knowledge that does not exclude life or consciousness from its purview, or the knowledge of the Reality which remains undivided into mind and matter.

There is another kind of knowledge that concerns the very same material aspect of Reality. It perceives the material side of the world's appearance merely as the gross aspect of the manifest form of the one absolute Reality. At the other pole of this gross material side comes the subtle aspect, that of the mind. A person, who perceives the material aspect of existence thus, does not exist apart from the one ultimate Reality, does not become primarily interested either in the material aspect or in the mind aspect, but rather in the one Reality that appears as both. Those who knowingly or unknowingly are biased towards either of these aspects, are really to be qualified as the "worldly people." The understanding they have formulated about the living world would also naturally be an inert or non-living one. Those who have discovered this secret of the inert matter, or the "carcass," are not such "worldly people," but are those who think and live in a realm that transcends what could be called "worldly;" such a One is a *jñānin*, who does not belong to this world or who does not care for the worldly. It is in this sense, Jesus says, "Whoever has discovered the carcass, of that person the world is not worthy."

> **57.** Jesus said, "The father's kingdom is like a person who had [good] seed. His enemy came at night and sowed weeds among the good

seed. The person did not let them pull up the weeds, but said to them, 'No, or you might go to pull up the weeds and pull up the wheat along with them.' For on the day of the harvest the weeds will be conspicuous and will be pulled up and burned."

58. Jesus said, "Fortunate is the person who has worked hard and has found life."

The secret concerning life or the ultimate Reality is not found without serious and strenuous effort on the part of the seeker, as could be seen from the stories about the lives of all great masters and prophets. *Taittirīya Upaniṣad* also underlines the importance of intense self-discipline that involves a sort of self-heating up (*tapas*) in order to properly realize *Brahman,* when it says:

Through austere self-enquiry seek to know *Brahman.* — 3.1

59. Jesus said, "Look to the living one as long as you live, or you might die and then try to see the living one, and you will be unable to see it."

The world, seen as a whole, is a living entity. The underlying Reality of it also has to be one. The easiest way to realize that Reality, in the case of ordinary seekers, is to approach an enlightened *guru* who lives as the embodiment of that living Reality. Unless and until that Reality is realized in oneself, life would be felt to be meaningless and aimless. And those who live so are as though already dead. In their frustration they grope for life's meaning in the words of dead *guru*s and prophets. Such virtually dead people gain merely the literal meaning of those words. The living Truth behind those words remains far from them.

There are priests who teach the laity that those who perform good deeds in this world, reach the abode of God after death. The hypocracy in such religious teachings is revealed in the words of Jesus, "Or you might die and then try to see the living one, and you will be unable to see." God realization has to be an attainment while living in this world. Giving the hope of doing so in an unknown world in an unknown state misleads people, doing good deeds in this world having high moral value notwithstanding. *Kena Upaniṣad* also says:

If known here itself, then it is the Truth. If not known here itself, it is a great loss. — 2.5

60. [He saw] a Samaritan carrying a lamb and going to Judea.

He said to his followers, ". . . that person . . . around the lamb."

> They said to him, "So that he may kill it and eat it."
>
> He said to them, "He will not eat it while it is alive, but only after he has killed it and it has become a carcass."
>
> They said, "Otherwise they cannot do it."
>
> He said to them, "So also with you, seek for yourselves a place to rest, or you might become a carcass and be eaten."

The lamb carried by the Samaritan, though a living one, is as if already dead, because it is going to be killed and eaten before long. Likewise is the case of those who live ignorant of the meaning of life. They are being carried only to be consumed by their own ignorance. The lamb is quite unaware that it is going to be killed, so it happily clings to the shoulders of the Samaritan. So too these people also lie in utter ignorance that they are going to be consumed by an ignorance that appears to be their saviour. Though biologically alive, these people are as if already killed, like the present lamb.

The Samaritan has to kill the lamb in order to eat it, for a living lamb cannot be eaten. Likewise, those who are well aware of the secret of life alone do really live; no one can render them dead. They never become struck down by ignorance and conditionings. Jesus, therefore, in effect, tells his followers: "If you intend to make your lives meaningful, find yourselves as being carried by the ultimate Reality or God, by making self-enquiry. Or else, you will also be carried away and eaten up by ignorance and the conditioning factors of relativism. That is to say, your lives also will turn out to be meaningless."

5.24

The Enlightened and the Ignorant

> **61.** Jesus said, "Two will rest on a couch; one will die, one will live."
>
> Salome said, "Who are you, mister? You have climbed on to my couch and eaten from my table as if you are from someone."
>
> Jesus said to her, "I am the one who comes from what is whole. I was given from the things of my father."
>
> "I am your follower."
>
> "For this reason I say, if one is [whole] one will be filled with light, but if one is divided, one will be filled with darkness."

THIS short dialogue shows the difference between the ignorant state and the enlightened state of man, in terms of their values. As two people repose on one couch, both the ignorant and the enlightened live in one and the same world. *Muṇḍaka Upaniṣad* portrays the same difference as between two birds as follows:

> Two birds, companions (who are) always united, cling to the self-same tree. Of these two, the one eats the sweet fruit and the other looks on without eating. —3.1.1

The ignorant one, though biologically living, for the reason that he always lives in fear of birth and death and their sufferings, is as if already dead. But the enlightened one, who lives fully aware of himself being the birthless and deathless Reality, is one who really lives, and such a one thus lives eternally.

Salome apparently is a follower of Jesus. His entrance into her life effected a total change in it. His coming was like someone who was sent by a person of authority. He slept on the couch of her room, and he ate from her table. Such was the influence of Jesus in her life. Still she did not understand properly what kind of person he was, nor comprehend clearly the content of his message. She therefore marvels at it, and asks, "Who are you, mister?"

Jesus's reply in essence is thus: "A Reality that is an undivided whole exists. It is that Reality that sent me to you. That Reality, nothing other than the Father in heaven, entrusted me with certain invaluable things; I am here to share them with you."

Salome expresses her willingness to receive what Jesus has to share, in her words, "I am your follower." In response to these words, Jesus clarifies by saying in essence: "Therefore I say to you, that Reality that is an undivided whole is pure light in essence. The one who knows it becomes filled with that light, or becomes that light in essence. But when what is real is seen as many or divided, one is in the darkness of ignorance, and the one who sees so becomes filled with that darkness, and life becomes filled with darkness."

Regarding the two who rest on a couch: those who perceive Reality as an undivided whole and live as that light are represented as the "One will live," and those who live in the darkness of ignorance and perceive the real as divided are represented as the "One will die?"

These words of Jesus could be seen to be a variant of the Upaniṣadic passage:

> One who perceives many as existing,
> He goes from death to death.
>
> — *Kaṭha Upaniṣad* 2.1.11

At this juncture, where the present Gospel is already half way through, the nature of the rapport between Jesus and Salome as *guru* and disciple has become sufficiently clear. Therefore these words of Jesus in the middle of the work could be considered to touch the core of his wisdom teaching.

5.25

Competence for Wisdom

62. Jesus said, "I disclose my mysteries to those [who are worthy] of [my] mysteries. Do not let your left hand know what your right hand is doing."

Jesus here, brimming with wisdom, reveals its secretive value. We had a glimpse of its experiential content at the end of the last saying. In India too, after revealing the wisdom secret to his closest disciple, an Upaniṣadic *ṛṣi* would advise him to teach it only to his eldest son or closest disciple. Jesus also says, "I disclose my mysteries to those who are worthy of my mysteries."

In Mediterranean culture, as in India, one's right hand is thought of as clean and the left one as unclean. If a *guru* is comparable to the right hand, then the disciple is like the left hand. Even when a *guru* reveals the wisdom secret to a disciple, the latter need not immediately imbibe its wholeness. The words of Jesus: "Do not let your left hand know what your right hand is doing," could be taken as the suggestion that it is better on the part of the disciple not to attempt to grasp that secret in its wholeness.

Lord Buddha was once informed by some of his disciples that what they understood from his teachings was that no self (*ātmā*) existed. The Lord replied, "Look at that tree. How many leaves does it have?" They said,"Innumerable." Then the Lord said, "Of those innumerable leaves, I have shown you only one."

63. Jesus said, "There was a rich person who had a great deal of money. He said, 'I shall invest my money so that I may sow, reap, plant, and fill my storehouses with produce, that I may lack nothing.' These were the things he was thinking in his heart, but that very night he died. Whoever has ears should hear."

64. Jesus said, "A person was receiving guests. When he had prepared the dinner, he sent his servant to invite the guests.

The servant went to the first and said to that one, 'My master invites you.'

That person said, 'Some merchants owe me money; they are coming to me tonight. I must go and give them instructions. Please excuse me from dinner.'

The servant went to another and said to that one, 'My master has invited you.'

That person said to the servant, 'I have bought a house and I have been called away for a day. I shall have no time.'

The servant went to another and said to that one, 'My master invites you.'

That person said to the servant, 'My friend is to be married and I am to arrange the banquet. I shall not be able to come. Please excuse me from dinner.'

The servant went to another and said to that one, 'My master invites you'.

That person said to the servant, 'I have bought an estate and I am going to collect the rent. I shall not be able to come. Please excuse me.'

The servant returned and said to the master, 'The people whom you invited to dinner have asked to be excused.'

The master said to the servant, 'Go out on the streets and bring back whomever you find to have dinner.'

"Buyers and merchants [will] will not enter the places of my father."

This fairly long section of the Gospel brings out the two primary value worlds before us to choose from. One is that of worldly dealings, where what lures man is the opportunity to accumulate more and more wealth, and the worldly pleasure it proffers. The more one becomes lured by this world, the more one becomes distanced from the real happiness (represented in the parable by the dinner), and gets involved in activities that result in unhappiness, by excusing oneself from life's real happiness.

Such a tendency in life results in making life filled with utter unhappiness. The buyers and merchants who excuse themselves from the dinner represent this value world.

The other value world aims at realizing the ultimate meaning of life, and this goal is represented by "my father" here. What is ultimately achieved in this value world is unconditional and unbounded happiness, signified by the dinner.

It is possible to invite people to the former value world; they accept or reject the invitation as they please. But it is not possible to invite just anyone to the latter value world. Even if invited, it often fails, as the present parable taken as a whole signifies. The interest in that value world should naturally well up from within oneself accidentally or by God's grace, and such an interest will eventually bear fruit. The wayfarers in the streets who happened to have the chance to enjoy the good dinner, represent this.

> **65.** He said, "A [. . .] person owned a vineyard and rented it to some farmers, so that they might work on it and he might collect its produce from them. He sent his servant so that the farmers might give the servant the produce of the vineyard. They seized, beat and almost killed his servant, and the servant returned and told the master. His master said, 'Perhaps he did not know them.' He sent another servant, and the farmers beat that one as well. Then the master sent his son and said, 'Perhaps they will show my son some respect.' Since the farmers knew that he was the heir to the vineyard, they seized him and killed him. Whoever has ears should hear."
>
> **66.** Jesus said, "Show me some stone that the builders rejected: That is the cornerstone."

5.26

The One Who Is Utterly Lacking

> **67.** Jesus said, "One who knows all but is lacking in oneself is utterly lacking."

ATTEMPTING to gain knowledge is characteristic of humans. All the branches of science now known and all that is yet to emerge are part of man's quest for knowledge. Suppose one learns all these sciences and branches of knowledge thoroughly and gains an encyclopaedic knowledge of everything. Still his life need not necessarily be happy and peaceful. The simple reason is that though he knows everything else, he is ignorant about himself. Each knowing themselves properly is what is known as self-knowledge (*Ātma-jñāna*). It is upon knowing oneself that one possesses oneself. Then alone one realizes that oneself or the Self is what appears as everything. Possessing oneself, thus, in effect, becomes possessing everything. Upon remaining ignorant about oneself, one remains lacking in oneself as well as in everything.

As long as one remains ignorant about oneself, all the knowledge one has about everything else lacks a firm foundation. A life that is based on such foundationless knowledge will also be lacking in firmness and happiness. This is the reason why many modern educated people live so unhappily and restlessly. On knowing onelself, on the other hand, all the knowledge one has gained becomes well-founded, and life itself becomes well-founded. Then one feels that there is nothing lacking in life.

> **68.** Jesus said, "Fortunate are you when you are hated and persecuted; and no place will be found, wherever you have been persecuted."

The beginning part of this saying appeared earlier in the Sermon on the Mount of the Gospel According to Matthew. But the reason given here for the hated and the persecuted to be fortunate is a bit different. Any hatred and persecution can be committed only to the external apparent aspects like the body and mind of a person. But what is real in a person can neither be hated nor persecuted. This one Reality is what appears as the hater and persecutor as well. There is no place where It is not; It exists eternally; It is totally free of all hatred and persecution. If one feels "I am that Reality," then the very hatred and persecution one is subject to serve as a means for realizing that oneness of Reality.

> **69.** Jesus said, "Fortunate are those who have been persecuted in their hearts: They are the ones who have truly come to know the father. Fortunate are they who are hungry, that the stomach of the person in want may be filled."

The persecution mentioned here is not an external one; it is the intense agony one feels within when in quest for wisdom. This state of agony, a sort of persecution one imposes on oneself, is what in Vedānta is known as *tapas* (heating up). Only those who become subject to such an internal anguish, that could be likened to birth pangs, realize what is ultimately Real, the Father. The parable of the hungry exemplifies this principle, for only those who are hungry can feel the full satisfaction of eating.

> **70.** Jesus said,"If you bring forth what is within you, what you have will save you. If you do not have that within you, what you do not have within you [will] kill you."

Ātmā or God is the one Reality that fills the being of everyone. Aware of this reality, one lives as a manifest flickering of the one Father, and perceives the Father alone in everything. For this reason, nothing causes him suffering. He thus lives saved from all sorrows.

But, as long as one does not realize oneself as the one Reality that assumes the form of everything, one lives as if having lost one's own self. And for the one who lives so, the very loss of self becomes the root cause of all sufferings. It is this loss of the self to oneself that lies at the base of most of the psychological maladies of modern times, originating from the societal bias to educate the mind towards becoming only what appears externally. *Īśāvāsya Upaniṣad* says that those who suffer so live as if they have killed themselves (*mantra* 3).

5.27

The All-inclusiveness of Wisdom

> **71.** Jesus said, "I shall destroy [this] house, and no one will be able to build it [. . .]."

THE scriptures of the Jews, and the vision of life that is based upon these, consider them to be a people chosen by God. Such a perception of life necessarily has to be relative; and that which is relative and conditioned has no eternal existence either.

But the vision of life that Jesus, as a true *guru,* is aimed at benefitting the entire humanity, as it perceives the one Reality to exclude nothing. To use an analogy preferred by *Bhagavad-Gītā,* all the little pools in an area become subsumed beneath an all-inundating flood of pure water.

Similar is the way all narrow and relativistic perceptions of life are subsumed by the all-inclusive and comprehensive absolutist perception. Therefore Jesus in effect says: "I shall destroy the narrow and sectarian perception of life. The vision of Reality I introduce and represent will subsume it, rendering it of no value any longer."

> **72.** A [person said] to him, "Tell my brothers to divide my fathers' possessions with me."
>
> He said to the person, "Mister, who made me a divider?"
>
> He turned to his disciples and said to them, "I am not a divider, am I?"

The infinite possibilities for knowledge could basically be classified into two. One is the knowledge that perceives reality as many. This sort of knowledge is called *anya* (other) by Narayana Guru, and as *avyavasāyātmikā buddhi* (unconvincing and irresolute knowledge) in *Bhagavad-Gītā* (2.41). It is the basis of all worldly affairs and the problems we face in them.

The other kind is the knowledge in which one Reality alone is seen in all that appears as many. Narayana Guru termed it *sama* (same) and *Bhagavad-Gītā* called it *vyavasāyātmikā-buddhi* (fully convincing and resolute knowledge). All *guru*s basically teach the *sama* kind of knowledge.

The person who approaches Jesus here asks him to be a mediator in the dispute between him and his brothers with regard to dividing their father's possessions, an affair that pertains purely to the realm of the *anya* kind of knowledge, purely a worldly dealing. Standing firmly on the *sama* kind of knowledge, Jesus virtually says: "I am not a person who divides anything; my role is to teach you to see the One in the many." It is also implied in this saying that a *guru* should never be dragged into settling worldly dealings.

5.28

Workers Are Few

73. Jesus said, "The harvest is large but the workers are few. So beg the master to send out workers to the harvest."

GOOD-NATURED people yearning to make their lives meaningful are everywhere in the world. They were earlier compared to a crop ready for the harvest. The responsibility of harvesting that crop, in the present case, belongs to the disciples of Jesus. So what they must do is imbibe the wisdom secret from Jesus and teach it to such people. Jesus is well aware of the scarcity of such disciples. As a general rule, people who dedicate themselves to the cause of wisdom are hardly to be found in this world. In short, concerning wisdom, the takers are many but the givers are very few. Even the best *guru* may find himself helpless to create such givers. They can only teach whoever happens to approach them. Those who approach thus become seekers as though willed by God, and their discovery of a true *guru* also happens in the same way. A *guru* in this matter can only pray God to send to this world more seekers who are willing to dedicate themselves to the cause of wisdom.

74. He said, "Master, there are many around the drinking trough, but there is nothing in the well."

Thoroughfares having public wells by their sides for the use of travellers, mostly pedestrians, were very common in olden days. There were also water troughs kept by the side of the wells, meant for the cattle grazing in the locality, as well as for the bullocks that pull carts, to quench their thirst. The well should have had enough water in it if the troughs were to be kept filled.

Many are those who thirst for wisdom. But what will be their plight if enough givers of wisdom and the required basic facilities together are not forthcoming to effect the quenching of their thirst? Here in the parable, the well is available and the water trough is also there; but the water is lacking. Likewise, the basic facilities for teaching wisdom are available; what is absent is the wisdom itself, along with the wisdom-teacher. In the present context of the Jewish culture, their religion and scriptures together form the facilities available. But these facilities now are like a lifeless body, like words that have lost their meanings, in the absence of enlightened teachers. The present saying is suffused with such a sad feeling.

An almost similar situation seems to prevail in modern times. Religions, religious beliefs and ideologies have become as if dead the extent that the act of man killing man is considered a holy act. The only way to save the human race from such peril, in the absence of a living *guru* readily available to give guidance, like Jesus, is to follow the ever-living wisdom teachings of the enlightened *guru*s of the past. Their words help restrain us from violent activities, making us benevolent, compassionate and tolerant in religious matters.

> **75.** Jesus said, "There are many standing at the door, but those who are alone will enter the wedding chamber."

Here the wedding chamber stands for the attainment of the Supreme Happiness by means of wisdom. In a wedding chamber there is the coming together (*yoga*) of two mutually complemantary counterparts, so becoming enlightened is also the coming together (*yoga*) of two aspects — the seeking self and the Self he seeks. All spiritual disciplines are aimed at this attainment, and it happens within each seeker individually as a result of their own spiritual quest. A mass of people together becoming enlightened is not possible. Nor have spiritual practices like mass prayers, meditation and lectures given in a big crowd, ever made anyone enlightened.

> **76.** Jesus said, "The father's kingdom is like a merchant who had a supply of merchandize and then found a pearl. That merchant was prudent; he sold the merchandize and bought the single pearl for himself. So also with you, seek his treasure that is unfailing, that is enduring, where no moth comes to devour and no worm destroys."

The message this saying gives is that those who realize the high value of wisdom ignore all that is of insignificant fleeting value, and live a life that considers wisdom alone to be the prime concern.

5.29

Everything Indeed Is Brahman (sarvam khalvidam brahma)

> **77.** Jesus said, "I am the light that is over all things. I am all: From me all has come forth, and to me all has reached. Split a piece of wood; I am there. Lift up the stone, and you will find me there."

THE basic teaching of *Chāndogya Upaniṣad* (3.14.1) is *sarvam khalvidam brahma* (everything here indeed is *Brahman*). *Taittirīya Upaniṣad* also declares:

> That verily from which beings are born, that by which those that are born live, into which they finally reach and merge — seek to know that. That is *Brahman*. — 3.1.1

The present saying of Jesus is apparently a variant of these Upaniṣadic utterings. Just as Jesus is fully convinced of being the one ultimate Reality, *Brahman* or Father, so too a seeker's goal should be to realize himself to be so. On attaining this goal, he experiences within, "I am the source of everything; I am the Reality to which everything finally reaches." This state of realization is signified by the great dictum (*mahāvākya*) of Vedānta, *aham brahma asmi* (I am *Brahman*).

> **78.** Jesus said, "Why have you come out to the countryside? To see a reed shaken by the wind? And to see a person dressed in soft clothes, [like your] rulers and your powerful ones? They are dressed in soft clothes, and they cannot understand truth."

Wisdom never appeals to those who are after social status, political power and the luxuries of life. Those who live for these things are mostly seen in cities. The inhabitants of the countryside mostly live a simple life. It is for those who lead a simple life, accompanied by high thinking, that the path to wisdom is cleared. And in the case of an enlightened one, such a life is an easily discernible external mark.

> **79.** A woman in the crowd said to him, "Fortunate are the womb that bore you and the breasts that fed you."
>
> He said to [her], "Fortunate are those who have heard the word of the father and have truly kept it. For there will be days when you will say, 'Fortunate are the womb that has not conceived and the

breasts that have not given milk'."

The same event was narrated earlier in another Gospel. But the response of Jesus here is a bit different as it ends.

It is simply in a worldly sense the woman here glorifies Jesus's mother. By giving birth to and feeding a baby that later grew up to become an enlightened person, a woman does not become great. Life really becomes glorious only when one conceives the hidden meanings of the words that reveal the Father or the ultimate Reality and thereafter delivers and nurses it. Only when this takes place in one, does it become clear how inconsiderable is the value of mere physical conception, delivery and nursing. The blessing Jesus gives to the woman virtually is, "The day will come when you go beyond such a world of insignificant values."

80. Jesus said, "Whoever has come to know the world has discovered the body, and whoever has discovered the body, of that person the world is not worthy."

This saying simply repeats the idea in saying 56 upon which we have already commented.

5.30

Renunciation and Enlightenment

> **81.** Jesus said, "Let one who has become wealthy rule, and let one who has power renounce (it)."

PEOPLE as a rule are deludedly lured by powerful positions acquirable on the strength of their wealth. They may even get the chance to rule the state, particularly in the modern democratic system. But the power needed for spiritual attainment is of a different order — the power of an earnest yearning for wisdom and the will to stand by it at any cost. Those who own this power do not aim at a amassing wealth and acquiring powerful positions. Rather, they prefer to renounce these. The spiritual culture of India also recognizes the fact that no gain of spiritual wealth is possible without renouncing worldly wealth and position.

> **82.** Jesus said, "Whoever is near me is near the fire, and whoever is far from me is far from the kingdom."

One goal alone — gaining wisdom — is what takes one to the abode of a *guru.* In the fire of that wisdom the entire realm of values that pertains to the world becomes burned up. *Bhagavad-Gītā* also declares, "This fire of wisdom reduces to ashes all *karma*s" (4.37). Gaining wisdom means also attaining unconditioned Happiness; it is the attainment of immortality as well. With those who live immersed in such an experience of Supreme Happiness, all their interests in what pertains to the world becomes burned away. But there are many who do not feel the necessity of approaching a *guru* or of seeking wisdom. By distancing themselves from a *guru,* or what he teaches, they really are distancing themselves from the attainment of unconditioned Happiness, from immortality, and from the meaning of life itself.

5.31

Reality and Māyā

83. Jesus said, "Images are visible to people, but the light within them is hidden in the image of the father's light. He will be disclosed, but his image is hidden in his light."

THE whole world, as we know, is filled with forms; and each of these forms is visible or knowable. One of such visible forms is the seeing person himself. There is a Reality that underlies the being of all these forms, that keeps these as forms, and that Reality in oneself is realized to be pure light in essential content. This Reality, in the usual course, is not noticed by many, for the reason that it remains hidden from all sense perceptions.

What is it that keeps it hidden from view thus? It is nothing other than the Effulgence-content of the Father, the one ultimate Reality. The one Effulgence-Reality, in other words, Itself acts as a sort of veil that hides from view the effulgence-reality in the individual seeker. This veil, in Vedānta, is known as *māyā.* Once this veil is removed, the Effulgence-Reality of the Father comes to the fore to be intuitively perceived. Then it also becomes revealed that the very same Effulgence-Reality is what appears as the individual seeker also.

What is the real form of that Effulgence-Reality? It has no form other than being pure effulgence. Its visible form, in other words, just vanishes in its own effulgence. Put otherwise, perceiving or knowing that Reality as such is not possible with our knowing faculties. It can be perceived and known only in the form of the world It assumes. A real *jñānin* is the one who perceives the one Reality or Father in the form of all the perceptibles and knowables.

84. Jesus said, "When you see your likeness, you are happy. But when you see your images that came into being before you and that neither die nor become visible, how much you will bear!"

One's own external form is very dear to each, and each enjoys looking at its image in a mirror. Such a form is the visible one. Yet there is an invisible Reality that assumed this visible form. All visible forms perish or die, but that one Reality never dies. It existed even before one was born in the present form, and it will continue to exist even after one's present form perishes. Being invisible, that Reality, as a rule, is not noticed by many as existing. But on happening to hear about it from aknowledgeable person, one may seek it and finally visualize it intuitively. Then one realizes that oneself is not the external fleeting form that was earlier thought of as oneself, and that oneself really is that eternal Reality. If one can enjoy looking at the image of the fleeting form of oneself, what will be the kind of happiness one feels when one realizes oneself to be that Immortal Reality! One may become so overwhelmed as to be unable to bear it! The immortal Reality mentioned here is what in Vedānta is known as *Ātmā* and *Brahman*.

5.32

Ordinary Men and a Guru

85. Jesus said, "Adam came from great power and great wealth, but he was not worthy of you. For, had he been worthy, [he would] not [have tasted] death."

THE one Reality that is the source of everything necessarily has to be a great power, a great wealth. This wealth does not belong to anyone; it is rich with itself. This is the sense in which it is a "great" wealth. That great source of everything is immortal, and whatever issues from it also has to be immortal in essential content. This immortality is directly and constantly experienced by all the *guru*s.

But Adam happened to eat the forbidden fruit and thus was ousted from being immortal. It could well be said, that eating the forbidden fruit was itself his virtual death. Thus, Adam because of his ignorance, or lack of mental stability, or both, denied to himself the state of being immortal. And for this reason, though he was the first man created by God, he did not become a prophet or a *guru.*

Avidyā (ignorance), as held by Vedāntins, is beginningless. In the place of *avidyā,* in Christianity, is original sin. It began with Adam, the first man created by God. That means it has always been part of human life ever since man came into being, and to that extent it also is beginningless. In short, any man, though created by God, if under the spell of *avidyā,* becomes mortal and thus a non-*guru.*

86. Jesus said, "[Foxes have] their dens and birds have their nests, but the child of humankind has no place to lay his head and rest."

5.33

Self-identity with the Body

> **87.** Jesus said, "How miserable is the body that depends on a body, and how miserable is the soul that depends on these two?"

MANY are the beings that live with concern for their own individual being, that consider the bodily existence alone as forming the entire being of themselves, and that live with their bodily existence alone in view. Such beings, ranked below the level of human life, also live happily in their own way as if with no worries in life. Still such animal life lacks perfection in the perception of humans when compared to theirs. Such animal life is treated to be of third in rank (*tṛtīyam sthānam*) in *Chāndogya Upaniṣad* (5.10.8), the first two ranks going to the enlightened men and ignorant men, respectively.

Although considered a higher life form, most humans live guided by the central notion "I am this body," just as animals do. In Vedānta this identification with the body is termed *deho 'ham buddhi.* They too consider the meaning of life, but it always remains confined to the domain of the bodily life and its pleasures and pains. Being ignorant, they live amidst many enigmas in life. The most frightful of all such enigmas is the phenomenon of death, and they live in worry and agitation about the so-called life-after-death. Such are to be ranked as the ignorant (*ajñānin*s).

As the ignorant face problems concerning life and death, certain answers that appeal to their ignorant mind are also forthcoming. One such is the concept of *pitṛ-yāna* (path of the manes), very popular in India, as against the *deva-yāna* (path of gods or path of the bright ones) that is known to the enlightened. The difference between these two paths is also made clear in *Chāndogya Upaniṣad* (5.10). Animals, on the other hand, live in the bliss of ignorance, as they have no doubts nor problems to be solved in life. Ignorant humans are not so; they live in the midst of a bunch of answerless questions.

Thus, in one sense, the life of the ignorant is worse than that of animals. The words of Jesus "How miserable is the soul that depends on these two" are to be appreciated as signifying the state of the ignorant.

In short, a perfectly happy and meaningful life is led by a *jñānin* alone. What he constantly experiences in life is immortality (*amṛtatva*). *Chāndogya Upaniṣad* calls it the life in *brahma-loka* (world of *Brahman*). Though the case of the *jñānin*s is not mentioned here by Jesus, *Chāndogya Upaniṣad* does so by referring to the *deva-yāna* (path of the bright ones) that leads one to *brahma-loka*.

5.34

Rewarding a Guru

> **88.** Jesus said, "The messengers and prophets will come to you and give you what is yours. You, in turn, give them what you have, and say to yourselves, 'When will they come and take what is theirs?' "

A MESSENGER may carry the word of God. But a messenger need not necessarily be a person who knows the real content of the message he conveys. For example, the followers of Jesus were often, and even now are often, messengers of his teaching; they are not necessarily prophets. Now a prophet is a messenger of God, meaning he knows the real meaning of the message he carries, either as revealed to him directly by God or as attained through a self-effort with the grace of God. He takes upon himself the responsibility of carrying the message to the general public. A *guru* is a messenger who knows the message he carries or the wisdom he teaches, but it is conveyed only to real seekers who earnestly approach him. Such is the difference among messenger, prophet and *guru*. The characteristics of both a prophet and a *guru* of this kind could be seen blended in Jesus.

A *guru* gives to the ignorant only one thing — he shows them who they really are. It, in essence, means giving them to themselves. It is when they really come into possession of themselves that they realize, until then they were not living as themselves. That means, the ignorant live as though lost to themselves. Jesus therefore tells the ignorant, "The messengers and the prophets will come to you and give you what is yours."

A *guru* apparently has done something for them. Don't they have to remunerate him for it? Jesus himself says in another context, "The worker is worthy of his food" (Matthew 10.10). Though a *guru* does not desire or ask to get any remuneration, all his needs are looked after by those who benefit by his teaching. The normal life of a wandering *saṁnyāsin* of India is of such a nature. The life of Jesus was similar as can be deduced from the Gospels. His words "You, in turn, give them what you have" are to be understood in relation to this context.

These words could be seen to have a more profound philosophical significance also. One who attains wisdom as taught by a *guru* ultimately gains oneself. One's most valuable wealth, then, is oneself. Hence the most appropriate reward the disciple can give to the *guru* is to offer oneself to the *guru.* That means, one dedicates oneself for the cause of the wisdom which the *guru* intends the people should attain.

Though the disciples may be so good natured as to be willing to offer all such in return, the *guru* never expects anything from anyone. The *guru* just lives as freely as a bird flying in the sky, fully absorbed in the joy of the Self. A disciple bent on rewarding the *guru* may think, "When will the *guru* come and take what is his?" Nothing really is there that a *jñānin* owns, or else, the entire world is owned by such a one. Thus, nothing is there for the *guru* to come and take.

5.35

Inside and Outside

> **89.** Jesus said, "Why do you wash the outside of the cup? Do you not understand that the one who made the inside is also the one who made the outside?"

THESE words possibly were addressed to the Pharisees. This saying reminds us also of Jesus's reference in another Gospel to the white-washed sepulchres.

Seen from the point of view of morality and decency, many are bent on keeping only their external behaviour and way of life looking tidy. But this tidiness is mostly absent in their ethical understanding. Many forget also that their inner life is just as important as their outer life. Therefore, external cleanliness and internal purity both have a place in life. In addition, one has to complement and compensate the other. So then, mental purity is as important as bodily or outward cleanliness.

The potter who made the cup did not create either its inside or outside; he simply made the cup. The differentiation of inside and outside arose out of its apparent being. Here, in the place of the cup we have to see ourselves. Our coming into being resulted in the arising of the inside–outside duality in us. Really, it is one and the same self-being that gave rise to the dual aspects of inside and outside. This duality vanishes on knowing ourselves properly, as if a cup were knowing itself.

As far as the world of knowledge is concerned, attempts to gain more and more clarity and specificity about the outside is ongoing throughout the world. Studies about the world of the mind and attempts to purify it scarcely are undertaken, and its necessity is felt only by a few. Really, knowing the inner world is as important as knowing the outer world. To use the analogy of the cup, we could very well say, it is neither the outer world nor the inner world that really exist; it is the world that exists; it is ourselves that exist. As we know ourselves properly, the nature of what is outside and what is inside naturally shines clearly.

5.36

An Easy and Gentle Yoke

> **90.** Jesus said, "Come to me, for my yoke is easy and my mastery is gentle, and you will find rest for yourselves."

HAPPINESS and peace are what everyone seeks in life. Most people think, this is ensured by possessing objects of enjoyment, and thus they yoke themselves to such objects, as though binding themselves to an odinary yoke. But this eventually results in making their life more unhappy and unpeaceful. They may then begin to feel their life is being harshly mastered by something else. Really lasting peace is gained when you live as yourself, by knowing yourself, and this knowledge is what in India is known as *ātma-jñāna* (self-knowledge). To gain this knowledge you should yoke yourself to a *guru* who is already enlightened about the Self, and who is willing to share that enlightenment with you. Yoking yourself to enjoyable objects is not at all an easy job; but yoking or rather uniting yourself with a *guru* is very easy, and the mastery of the *guru* is very gentle. Yoking yourself to pleasurable objects binds you, whereas doing so to a *guru* liberates you.

> **91.** They said to him, "Tell us who you are so that we may believe in you."
>
> He said to them, "You examine the face of heaven and earth, but you have not come to know the one who is in your presence, and you do not know how to examine the moment."
>
> **92.** Jesus said, "Seek and you will find. In the past, however, I did not tell you the things about which you asked me then. Now I am willing to tell them, but you are not seeking them."

The process in which a *guru* imparts his wisdom to a disciple becomes actualized only when the yearning on the part of the latter and the graceful willingness on the part of the former meet together. This happens very rarely, as though willed by God.

> **93.** Do not give what is holy to dogs, or they might throw them upon the manure pile. Do not throw pearls [to] swine, or they might . . . it [. . .].

94. Jesus [said], "One who seeks will find; for [one who knocks] it will be opened."

95. [Jesus said], "If you have money, do not lend it at interest. Rather, give [it] to someone from whom you will not get it back."

96. Jesus [said], "The father's kingdom is like [a] woman. She took a little yeast, [hid] it in dough, and made it into large loaves of bread. Whoever has ears should hear."

5.37

The Lapsing of Wisdom

> **97.** Jesus said, "The [father's] kingdom is like a woman who was carrying a [jar] full of meal. While she was walking along [a] distant road, the handle of the jar broke and the meal spilled behind her [along] the road. She did not know it; she had not noticed a problem. When she reached her house, she put the jar down and discovered that it was empty."

THE Father's kingdom or the wisdom secret is meaningful by itself, in itself. Discovering it makes our life fully meaningful as well. This is signified by the jar full of meal.

This secret has to become available to the future by handing it down from generation to generation. In the parable, this handing down process is represented by the woman walking along a distant road carrying the jar.

Often it so happens that the richness and purity of the wisdom gradually lapses during this process of transmission. A jar needs a strong handle firmly fixed to it to enable an easy handling of it. If it breaks and makes a hole by the lower part of the jar's side, the meal in it spills behind while carried on a long walk, leaving the jar empty once its carrier reaches home. The jar of wisdom secret also has a strong handle of its own, enabling easy handling when it is carried on to the future. We have tried to make this secret, known in the West as "dialectics" and in India as *yoga-rahasya,* stand out in our comments on various occasions in this study. If handled by those who are not at home with this secret aspect of the wisdom teaching, it is equal to a jar having lost its handle by breaking, leaving a hole in the jar. This hole causes a spilling loss of the originality, richness and purity of that wisdom secret. What remains finally is only some hard outer shell, now comprised of some fanatic belief patterns and customary behaviours. This deplorable state is indicated by the empty jar with which the woman reached home. The most glaring example of such a decay of wisdom is the religion taught by the Pharisees and scribes, who were the religious masters in Judea at the time of Jesus. But this plight could happen to wisdom in any cultural background. For example, *Bhagavad-Gītā* (IV.2) says:

> Thus handed down in line, this *yoga* was known to the sagely kings. With the long lapse of time, O Scorcher of Enemies, it came to be lost to the world.

Should such a tragic eventuality be avoided, those who become responsible for handling the wisdom down to the next generation must be at home with the dialectical, intuitive vision the original *guru* had when he revealed the wisdom secret.

5.38

Lift Yourself Up

> **98.** Jesus said, "The father's kingdom is like a person who wanted to put someone powerful to death. While at home he drew his sword and thrust it into the wall to find out whether his hand would go in. Then he killed the powerful one."

THE enemies a man who intends to enter the kingdom of God has to face are the formidable obstructions on the path of wisdom. These are termed *ṣaḍ-ūrmi*s in Vedānta, meaning six forceful currents, namely, *kāma* (desire), *krodha* (anger), *lobha* (avarice), *moha* (delusion), *mada* (ego), *mātsarya* (competitiveness). *Bhagavad-Gītā,* dealing with such obstructions, says:

> It is desire, it is anger, born of *rajo-guṇa* (the active, affective modality of nature), the all-consuming and the most evil, that causes it. Know it to be your real enemy here. — III.37

Gītā says also:

> To begin with, . . . master your senses, O Best of the Bharatas (Arjuna), and slay this sinful one, the annihilator of *jñāna* and *vijñāna.*
> — III.41

The enemy is within oneself; the means to kill him has also to come from within. This means comes in the form of an unfailing sense of detachment (*asaṅga*) that one develops within, as the *Gītā* again underscores (XV.3). If strong enough, the sword thrusted into a wall passes through it, letting the hand holding it also go in. Otherwise, the sword becomes bent and goes out of use. Likewise, if the sense of detachment in one is strong enough, the above-said enemies are defeated with ease. One of the peculiarities about this battle with the foe is that no one outside of oneself can help, as indicated in the parable.

> **99.** The followers said to him, "Your brothers and your mother are standing outside,"
>
> He said to them, "Those here who do the will of my father are my brothers and my mother. They are the ones who will enter my father's kingdom."

100. They showed Jesus a gold coin and said to him, "Caesar's people demand taxes from us."

He said to them, "Give Caesar the things that are Caesar's, give God the things that are God's, and give me what is mine."

101. "Whoever does not hate [father] and mother as I do cannot be a [follower] of Me, and whoever does [not] love [father and] mother as I do cannot be a [follower of] Me. For my mother [. . .], but my true [mother] gave my life."

An intimacy and sense of attachment among those of blood relations is normal in ordinary life. Without renouncing this closeness to relatives, no attainment of the ultimate spiritual goal is possible in life. A seeker's intimacy has to be and should be with those who lead him to eternal life or final liberation (*mukti*), and to co-seekers among spiritual relatives, the one with whom the intimacy should be at its peak is the *guru* himself.

The biological mother gives birth only to the bodily existence of the child. So also all the blood relations have meaning only in the realm of bodily existence. They care for only the bodily well-being. This bodily aspect of one's being is a fleeting one, has no real existence of its own. For this reason, it is unreal. It is to this unreality that the biological mother gives birth. What exists on its own is one birthless and deathless Reality alone. The appearance of this world is the never-ending self-unfoldment of that Reality, which the seeker forms a part of. Living in the state of perfect identity with that Reality is what is known as eternal life. A mother is there who gives birth to this eternal life. That mother is the real mother in the spiritual context.

102. Jesus said, "Damn the Pharisees, for they are like a dog sleeping in the cattle manger, for it does not eat or [let] the cattle eat."

103. Jesus said, "Fortunate is the person who knows where the robbers are going to enter, so that [he] may arise, bring together his estate, and arm himself before they enter."

104. They said to Jesus, "Come, let us pray today and let us fast."

Jesus said, "What sin have I committed or how have I been undone? Rather, when the bridegroom leaves the wedding chamber, then let people fast and pray."

105. Jesus said, "Whoever knows the father and the mother will be called the child of a whore."

This saying (105) could be seen from two opposite perspectives. He who understands that the one ultimate Reality alone is one's real father and mother is despised by the worldly-minded, and so they call him the son of a whore. On the other hand, he who treats his biological parents as his real father and mother, and who lives as their obedient child, is considered the child of a whore by the spiritually-minded.

> **106.** Jesus said, "When you make the two into one, you will become children of humanity and when you say, 'Mountain, move from here', it will move."
>
> **107.** Jesus said, "The kingdom is like a shepherd who had a hundred sheep. One of them, the largest, went away. He left the ninety-nine and sought the one until he found it. After he had gone to this trouble, he said to the sheep, 'I love you more than the ninety-nine'."
>
> **108.** Jesus said, "Whoever drinks from my mouth will become like me; I myself shall become that person, and the hidden things will be revealed to that person."

To drink from a *guru*'s mouth means, to fully understand the implications of the words of wisdom that come from his mouth. When those words are understood properly, even the differentiation between the *guru* and the disciple becomes meaningless, because for the enlightened, the two become equals. As far as a disciple who has reached such a state of equality with the *guru,* the entire secret concerning life and the world is felt to have become fully revealed and all veils are removed.

> **109.** Jesus said, "The kingdom is like a person who had a treasure hidden in his field but he did not know it. And [when] he died, he left it to his [son]. The son [did] not know (about it). He took over the field and sold it. The buyer went ploughing, (discovered) the treasure, and began to lend money at interest to whomever he wished."

The invaluable Reality within each of us and its wisdom are like a treasure hidden in a farmland whose owner does not know of it. Such a state continues sometimes for generations, as signified by the son taking over and selling the field. During this long process, it is by chance that someone in the line, through intense effort, denoted by the ploughing of the field by the new buyer, happens to discover the treasure within oneself, very rarely on one's own, but mostly with the guidance of a *guru.* What a person who thus discovers it can do is only one thing: share it with others. This sharing has a peculiarity of its own. Just as the money lent on interest increases, wisdom also gains more clarity as it is shared with more.

> **110.** Jesus said, "Let someone who has found the world and has become wealthy renounce the world."

The purport of this saying also could be perceived from two sides. The first is as an instruction given to the people who live guided by the notion that accumulating worldly wealth is what makes their lives rich. They are asked to renounce not only the worldly wealth but the world itself. The other meaning is related to those who live by finding the wealth of life in the wisdom they gain. They naturally become uninterested in the world and its kind of wealth, and they give them up.

5.39

Eternal Life

> **111.** Jesus said, "The heavens and the earth will roll up in your presence, and whoever is living from the living one will not see death."

An enlightened person perceives the heavens and the earth and all the worlds as different manifest forms of the one Reality or the Father. Those who see that Father alone as Real, intuitively perceive themselves and all the worlds as abiding within that one Reality. Hence the words, "The heavens and the earth will roll up in your presence."

That Father is a living Reality, was never born, and will never die. He has only life. In the perception of one who lives by seeing oneself as that Father in essential content, one is oneself the birthless and deathless Father. This state of realization is eternal life. It is said in this sense, "Whoever is living from the living one will not see death."

> **112.** Jesus said, "Damn the flesh that depends on the soul. Damn the soul that depends on the flesh."

Modern science as well as the philosophies that rely solely on logical reasoning, conceive a human being as comprised of a body and a soul. Then they ask the question, "Which abides in which?" They really become perplexed on finding themselves unable to answer the question they themselves have created by wrongly imagining the body to be separate from the soul. But an enlightened one perceives body and soul merely as the gross and subtle manifest aspects of one and the same non-dual Reality, called *Ātmā* and *Brahman* in Vedānta, and Father in the Gospels.

> **113.** His followers said to him, "When will the kingdom come?"
>
> "It will not come by watching for it. It will not be said, 'Look, here it is,' or 'Look, there it is.'
>
> Rather, the father's kingdom is spread out upon the earth, and people do not see it."

> **114.** Simon Peter said to them, "Mary should leave us, for females are not worthy of life."
>
> Jesus said, "Look, I shall guide her to make her male, so that she too may become a living spirit resembling you males. For every female who makes herself male will enter heaven's kingdom."

The mind of Simon Peter who asks the present question apparently, has become hardened with the idea that women have no right to attain wisdom and thus eternal life. There is really no such place for making a man–woman discrimination in the context of attaining eternal life (*mukti*). The reply Jesus gives here is a little bit humorous. He, in effect, says: If you think Mary has no right for liberartion (*mukti*) just because she is a woman, then I shall lift her up to the masculine right for liberation. Then she will find herself in a state of the malehood of enlightenment that transcends the bounds of the bodily differentiation between males and females. Just as you people think you have the right for eternal life on the count of being males, she will also have the same right because of being a male in terms of wisdom. In other words, it is not being male or female that makes one competent for attaining eternal life. What counts is whether one is enlightened or not.

The Gospel of Thomas thus concludes with the emphasis that both men and women equally have the right to be benefitted by the wisdom revealed herein, and to attain eternal life (*mukti*).

Glossary

abhinna-nimitto-pādāna-kāraṇa	The efficient cause (*nimitta-kāraṇa*) and material cause (*upādāna-kāraṇa*) undifferentiated. *Brahman* is considered by Vedāntins as such a cause of the world. In Biblical terms, that cause is the Father in heaven.
ācāryadevo bhava	Be one for whom the Master is equal to God. One of the moral teachings famous in India, quoted from *Taittirīya Upaniṣad.*
adharma	That which is not righteous. The opposite of *dharma* (see).
adhikāra	Competence to learn a particular branch of knowledge. In the Vedāntic content, competence for wisdom.
adhikārin	One who is competent for wisdom.
ādi-guru	The original *guru*. The first *guru* who had a clear vision of Truth and who initiated an easy way of teaching it that is understandable to the people who were around. Jesus is the *ādi-guru* in the context of Christianity.
advaita	Non-duality, non-dualism. The doctrine traditionally held as taught by all the Upaniṣads, *Bhagavad-Gītā* and the *Brahma-Sūtras,* the three basic textbooks of Vedānta. The doctrine that one Reality alone is what underlies the being of everything that appears to be manifold or as having dual aspects like mind and matter, cause and effect.
agrāsana	The seat of honour offered to the most respectable person in a gathering.
ahantā	The I-sense each person has.
ajñāna	Ignorance. In the Vedāntic context, the lack of proper understanding about oneself and the world.
ajñānin	An ignorant person; one who has *ajñāna.*
amr̥tatva	Immortality. On attaining wisdom, one realizes oneself to be the immortal Reality, and not the apparent mortal form assumed by the Reality. Equivalent to eternal life.
ānanda	Happiness; value experience. *Ātmā,* the ultimate Reality experientially is *sat-cit-ānanda* (see) in essence. Happiness and suffering in our actual life are perceived as two

	manifest forms, opposite in nature, of the one *ānanda*-content of *Ātmā* or oneself.
antaḥkaraṇas	Internal organs. The four stages of mental functions involved in every act of knowing, namely *manas* (mind) that asks a question, *buddhi* (intellect) that reasons, *cittam* (store-house of memories) that releases them as and when needed, *ahaṁkāra* (I-sense) that relates the knowledge arrived at with the value-sense of each.
aṇu	The atom; the smallest fragment of anything; literally, that which is indivisibly small.
anya	The other. According to Narayana Guru, the kind of knowledge which perceives the apparent many as real. See *sama*.
arati	The state of being uninterested in anything.
ārta	One who suffers. One of the four types of people, according to *Bhagavad-Gītā*, who seek the ultimate Reality or the Father in heaven.
arthavāda	Vedic exegesis. Stating the good arising from the proper observance of an injunction or teaching, and the evil arising from its omission, and also adducing historical instances in its support.
asat	That which is non-existent in the ultimate sense. In the appearance of a wave, what really exists is water alone, and therefore wave is *asat* (see *sat*). Similarly, the world-appearance is also *asat*.
āsurī-sampat	Demonic qualities in man marked by pretentiousness, arrogance, sense of self-importance, anger, harshness, ignorance, insatiable desire for wealth and the like.
atithidevo-bhava	Become one who treats a guest as a god. One of the moral instructions given in *Taittirīya Upaniṣad*.
Ātmā (*Ātmān*)	The Self; oneself. Literally, that which pervades the being of something and assumes the form of something, like water in waves. The substance, that assumes the form of both the body and mind of an individual, is his *ātmā*. Likewise the substance that assumes the form of the world, is *ātmā* in the universal context. In this latter sense, it often is called *paramātmā*. The prefix *parama* means "Supreme." In the neutral absolutist sense the word is written with a capital 'Ā.'
ātma-jñāna	Wisdom of the Self. The enlightenment one attains that oneself is nothing but the *Ātmā*. Equivalent to attaining the kingdom of God.

ātma-vidyā — The science of the Self. The science that enables you to attain *ātma-jñāna*.

ātma-sākṣātkāra — Self-realization. *Sākṣātkāra* literally means, "rendering as if perceived with your own eyes." The experiential aspect of *ātma-jñāna*. Equivalent to, be in the kingdom of heaven of the Gospels.

avidyā — Ignorance; nescience. The opposite of *vidyā* (see). The knowing function by which the unreal *anātmā* (non-self) is understood as the real, and the real *Ātmā* as the unreal. Almost equivalent to the original sin of the Christian Theology.

bhūmā — Literally, abundance; plenty. Used in *Chāndogya Upaniṣad* to denote the greatness, both existence-wise and value-wise, of *Ātmā* or *Brahman* in a realized state.

brahmacārin — From *Brahman,* the Absolute, and *cārin,* he who moves on. One who moves on the path of *Brahman* as a seeker. Name of one who is in the first stage of life as a student in a *gurukula* in the ancient educational system of India. Continence, as a helpful discipline in his search for Reality, is only one of the implied considerations in *brahmacarya*. Equivalent to a novice in the Christian context.

brahma-jñāna — *Brahman*-wisdom. Knowing oneself to be *Brahman* in essential context.

brahma-jñānin — One who has attained *brahma-jñāna*.

brahma-loka — In the context of mythology, the world of Brahmā, the Creator. In the wisdom context, Brahman-world, or the state in which *Brahman* is experienced as one's world.

Brahman — The Absolute. Derived from the verb root *bṛh,* "to grow constantly." Literally, "that which grows constantly." The one ultimate Reality that ceaselessly grows as everything in all the worlds. Also called *Ātman*. Equivalent to God or the Father in the biblical context.

brahma-sākṣātkāra — Realizing oneself as *Brahman* (see). The experiential state of self-identity with *Brahman*. The same as *ātma-sākṣātkāra* (see).

brahmavarcas — The splendour of wisdom seen in the person of the individual who has attained *brahma-jñāna* (see).

brahma-vidyā — The science of the Absolute, the science of *Brahman*. The science that helps the seeker to attain *brahma-jñāna*.

brahmavit — The knower of *Brahman*. Equivalent to *brahma-jñānin* (see) and the one who has attained the kingdom of God, according to the Gospels.

buddhi — Intellect, reasoning mind; understanding.

cit — Consciousness. The essential content of what is ultimately Real (see *sat-cit-ānanda*).

daivī-sampat — The divine qualities in humans marked by fearlessness, a transparent vision of the Real, stability in attuning oneself to wisdom, self-restraint, studying scriptures, straightforwardness, non-hurting, honesty, calmness, renunciation, aversion for slander and the like.

darśana — Literally, "vision." The Sanskrit equivalent to the English word "philosophy." Every school of thought is called a *darśana*. Christian Theology also, is, in this sense, a *darśana.* As a philosophical vision, according to the Advaita Darśana, the experience in which the perceiver, the perceived, and the perception merge in the being of pure *cit* (see).

deho 'ham buddhi — One's self-identity with the body.

deva-yāna — The path of god or the path of brightness. The way the enlightened perceive the phenomena of birth and death. Beings originate from *Brahman* that is brightness in essence and merge back with the same *Brahman.*

dharma — Righteousness. Literally that which supports the world order. Also the Sanskrit word for religion.

dharma-roṣa — Moral indignation.

dvija — Literally, "twice-born." A man of the first three castes of the caste system of India. Philosophically, the enlightened one in the sense he had a second birth in realizing himself to be *Ātmā.* Equivalent to the one who finds himself in the kingdom of God in the biblical context.

dvijatva — The state of being a *dvija* (see).

eṣaṇā — Intense cravings that become obstructive to spiritual attainment. These mainly are three: *putraiṣaṇā* (craving for one's own children), *vittaiṣaṇā* (craving for wealth), and *dāraiṣaṇā* (craving for wife).

guru — A master or teacher. Literally, the dispeller of darkness. The syllable *gu* stands for darkness or ignorance, and *ru* for dispelling it.

gurukula — The family of *guru, kula* meaning "family." This family is comprised of *guru* and his disciples. The ancient educational system of India was known as *gurukula sampradāya; sampradāya* meaning "system."

guru–śiṣya-pārasparya — Mutual rapport between a *guru* and his disciples. Considered essential in the context of education, especially in imparting wisdom.

*iṣṭāpūrta karma*s	Two kinds of meritorious actions according to Vedism: *iṣṭa-karma*s (perfoming burnt sacrifices). and *pūrta-karma*s (doing things beneficial to the public).
jaḍa	That which is inert. The Sanskrit equivalent for matter.
jñāna	Wisdom.
jñāna-kāṇḍa	The section of the Vedas that deals with wisdom comprised of the Upaniṣads.
jñāna-mārga	Resorting to the path of wisdom for spiritual happiness.
jñāna-yoga	The *yoga* state or the state of union with the Absolute or the Father in heaven through wisdom.
jñāna-mudrā	Wisdom-gesture. The hand-gesture shown with the raised open palm and with the thumb and the little finger joined together.
jñānin	The one who possesses *jñāna;* the enlightened one. The one who finds himself in the kingdom of heaven that is within oneself.
jyotiḥ	Effulgence.
kāraṇa	Cause. Indian philosophers think of only two causes: *upādāna-kāraṇa* (material cause) and *nimitta-kāraṇa* (efficient cause), whereas the Western philosophers differentiate material cause, efficient cause, formal cause and final cause.
karma	All actions in general. Philosophically, the creative urge inherent in the Imperishable Reality, causing the emergence of all manifest forms from Itself. In the Vedic context, the ritual of burnt-sacrifice enjoined by the Vedas. As a religious belief of the Hindus, the incipient memory factors clinging to the souls as a residue of their past deeds. All are bound to enjoy or suffer the fruits of their deeds, and will have to reincarnate for this purpose. One might be accumulating more *karma*s in the new birth. This vicious chain of actions and rebirths goes on till one attains final release. Such *karma*s are divided into three categories — *sañcita karma*s (actions accumulated in all the previous births), *āgāmī karma*s (fresh actions done in the present lifetime) and *prārabdha karma*s (action already initiated but eating of its fruits is not finished with).
karma-bandha	The bondage caused by *karma.* The attachment a doer of *karma*s has towards the *karma*s he does like "This is my *karma,* its fruits are also mine."
karma-kāṇḍa	The section of the Vedas that deals with ritual.
karma-mārga	Resorting to the path of rituals for spiritual happiness.

karma-yoga	Attaining union with the Absolute by means of *karmas*. This involves perceiving the individual's actions and the actions going on in the total nature as essentially forming one *karma.*
kūṭastha	The topmost one; perpetually the same. Signifies *Brahman,* or the one who finds oneself in *Brahman.*
Lakṣmī	The goddess of wealth, equivalent to Mammon of the biblical context.
lokānuvartana	The tendency in humans to be influenced by worldly considerations and the opinion of the world.
lokasaṁgraha	Usually translated as the well-being of the world. Literally means "the upkeep of the entire world."
loka-vāsanā:	Worldly traits in humans.
madhyama-adhikārī	One who is in the middle range of competence for wisdom.
mahā-samādhi	The great *samādhi*. The final attainment of finding one's Real abode and remaining one with It. Used also in reference to the death of great *yogīs* or *jñānins*.
mahat	That which is great; eniment; noble.
manana	Intense cogitation on the word of wisdom heard (*śravaṇa*) from a *guru.*
manda-adhikārī	One who is in the lowest range in competence for wisdom.
matam	Religion, one's confirmed belief, doctrine, creed. The conclusion arrived at after proper cogitation.
mātṛdevo bhava	Become one who treats mother as a goddess. One of the moral instructions given in *Taittirīya Upaniṣad.*
māyā	The mysterious urge inherent in the Absolute or God to become unfolded as all the worlds and the phenomenon of life. The very appearance of the world caused thus ends up in becoming a sort of veil that hides the Absolute or God from our view, and makes the illusory vision that the apparent world is the real. The mysterious power of God that makes Himself hidden from the view of His own creations.
māyin	The weilder of *māyā*. Refers to God.
mokṣa	Final liberation attained through wisdom. Realizing one's oneness with *Brahman* means, *Brahman*'s liberatedness becoming one's also. Equivalent to Eterual Life of the biblical context.
mukti	Another word for *mokṣa* (see).

nididhyāsana	The final stage in a seeker's search for Reality preceded by *śravaṇa* and *manana* (see). It consists of meditating on the conclusion arrived at through *manana* and finally realizing it experientially.
nimitta-kāraṇa	Incidental or efficient cause (see *kāraṇa*).
niṣedha	Prohibitions in respect of one's actions, as taught in the Smṛtis (see).
nivṛtti-mārga	The way of withdrawal from activities, preferred by those who are interested in wisdom.
pañca-bhūtas	The five basic constituent elements of physical nature, namely, *ākāśa* (space), *vāyu* (air), *agni* (fire), *ap* (water) and *pṛthvī* (earth). All are but part of the gross manifestation of the one absolute Reality or Father.
paramānanda	Supreme Happiness. Equivalent to the bliss of being in the kingdom of God.
parama-puruṣārtha	The fourth and the highest of all human values. It is attaining *mokṣa* or *mukti* (see). The other *puruṣārthas* are *dharma* (righteousness), *artha* (wealth) and *kāma* (desire or sex). Equivalent to attaining the kingdom of God.
pāramārthika	That which is related to *paramārtha,* the ultimate Reality. Śaṅkara classified the realms of reality as *pāramārthika, vyāvahārika* (transactional) and *prātibhāsika* (illusory).
paramātmā	The Supreme Self. *Ātmā* conceived as the universal ultimate Reality.
parivrājaka	A *saṁnyāsin* who wanders and teaches.
pitṛdevo-bhava	Become one who treats father as God, one of the moral teachings of *Taittirīya Upaniṣad.*
pitṛ-yāna	The path of the manes. The belief that the departed souls, after passing through many stages and reaching the *pitṛloka* (world of the departed souls) come back to this world to be reborn. A concept concerning life as held by the ignorant.
prakṛti	Nature. Literally "that which is always in an active state." God or *Brahman* in the active state is called *prakṛti.*
pramāṇa	Valid means of certainty.
prāṇa	The vital breath. The functions of vital breath are identified as five, namely, *prāṇa* (going upward), *apāna* (going downward), *vyāna* (that which takes vitality to every part of the body), *samāna* (that which keeps the balance of the body) and *udāna* (that which leaves the body at death).
pratyakṣa	Sense-perception.

pratiṣṭhita	One who has become well founded in life. This state is attained only through wisdom.
pravṛtti-mārga	Resorting to the path of activities in life as against the way of withdrawal (*nivṛtti-mārga* — see).
preyas	Worldly values in general.
pūrva-pakṣa	The anterior critique. The position that is proved to be unsound in an argument. In a wisdom dialogue, a disciple who asks questions to a *guru*.
rāga	Attachment felt towards pleasurable objects.
rājā	A king; literally, "the one who keeps everyone pleased."
rajoguṇa	The active modality of nature (see *triguṇa*s).
ṛṣi	A seer. Any of the ancient seers who composed the Vedic hymns and the Upaniṣads.
sacchiṣya (*sat+śiṣya*)	A true disciple.
sadguru (*sat+guru*)	A true *guru*.
*ṣaḍ-ūrmi*s	Six human infirmities, namely *kāma* (desire), *krodha* (anger), *lobha* (covetousness), *moha* (delusion), *mada* (arrogance) and *mātsarya* (competitiveness).
śama	Ability to restrain one's own mental activities; restraining the mind from becoming indulged in sense-pleasures. One of the disciplines to be undergone by a true seeker.
sama	Literally "equality." According to Narayana Guru's categorization of the knowing function of consciousness, that knowledge which perceives everything to be one in essential content.
samādhāna	Always orienting one's thinking mind to *Brahman*.
samādhi (*sam+ādhi*)	*Sam* stands for "proper," and *ādhi* means "abode." The word word means, finding one's own proper abode, and becoming stabilized in it.
śamādi-ṣaḍka	The six disciplines beginning with (*śama*). These are *śama* (mental self-restraint), *dama* (restraining the sense-organs), *uparati* (self-withdrawal), *titikṣā* (endurance), *śraddhā* (faith) and *samādhāna* (steadiness of attention to the one goal).
saṁsāra	The world of becoming. Literally, "that which always is in a changeful state." A synonym for worldly life considered full of sufferings.
saṁsāra-sāgara	The ocean of *saṁsāra* (see). The ocean of becoming.

saṁvit-sāgara	The ocean of Consciousness. On becoming enlightened one realizes that what was thought of as the *saṁsāra-sāgara* is really the ceaseless flow of self-unfoldment of the one Reality, pure Consciousness (*saṁvit*) in essence.
saṁśayātmā	He who doubts the veracity of the teaching of a true *guru.*
saṁnyāsin	One who has renounced everything worldly.
Sarasvatī	The goddess of wisdom.
śarīra:	The body. Literally "that which perishes."
sarvam khalvidam brahman:	"Everything here indeed is *Brahman.*" One of the cryptic dicta in *Chāndogya Upaniṣad.*
sat	Existence. That which has ultimate existence unaffected by temporal, spatial or substantial conditionings.
saccidānanda (*sat* + *cit* + *ānanda*)	The way the experiential content of *Ātmā, Brahman* or God is defined.
sattva-guṇa	The pure and clear modality of nature. One of the *triguṇa*s (see) of nature (*prakṛti*) (see).
sāttvika	A person endowed with *sattva-guṇa.*
satya	Reality, Truth.
satya-darśin	A person who has experientially visualized the ultimate Reality or the kingdom of God within himself.
satya-dharman	A person in whom the visualization of Reality (*satya*) finds expression in life as righteousness (*dharma*); the two thus mutually validating.
satya-saṅkalpa	A person with whom, whatever is pictured in his imaginations comes true. Refers to God.
siddha	A person of spiritual attainments.
siddhānta-pakṣa	In an argument, the side that establishes the final conclusion.
siddhi	Any spiritual attainment.
śikṣā	Education; in Vedism, the discipline that teaches how to pronounce the Vedic hymns with proper intonations.
śiṣya	Disciple. Literally, the one who is taught.
Smṛti	The general name for the set of Indian scriptures that teach moral codes.
śraddhā	One of the prerequisites on the part of a genuine seeker. His willingness to have full faith in the truthfulness of the teachings imparted by the *guru* and recorded in the scriptures. A necessary stepping stone to *manana* (see).
śraddhāvān	The one who is endowed with *śraddhā.*
śravaṇa	Literally, "to hear." Hearing with full attention and faith, the words of wisdom of one's own *guru,* or learning with

	the same attitude, the words of the *gurus* of the past, recorded in the basic scriptures.
Śruti	Literally, "that which is heard." Basic scriptures in general.
svarājya:	Literally, "one's own kingdom." One finding oneself in the kingdom of the Self or God.
svayam dhīra	A self-styled scholar.
tapas	Austere self-discipline. Literally, "heating up."
tat-paraḥ	One whose sole interest is in *tat* (That), denoting *Brahman* or the Father in heaven.
titikṣā	Endurance.
triguṇas	The three modalities of nature (*prakṛti*) (see). These are *sattva-guṇa* (pure and clear modality), *rajo-guṇa* (active modality), *tamo-guṇa* (dark and inert modality).
trimūrti	The three chief deities of the Indian pantheon — Brahmā (the Creator), Viṣṇu (the Sustainer) and Maheśvara or Śiva (the Destroyer). Resembling the theological concepts, Father, Son and the Holy Spirit.
tṛtīyam sthānam	The third place. Referring to the animal life, where thinking about the meaning of life is totally absent, as distinguished from the *deva-yāna* and *pitṛ-yāna* of the enlightened and the ignorant humans.
turīya	Literally, "the fourth." The transcendental state of consciousness, other than the waking, dreaming and sleeping states.
tyāgī	A renunciate.
ubhaya-bhraṣṭa	Thrown out of both the worldly life and the spiritual life, because of one's lack of stability in either.
udgītha	The ritual of singing the *sāman* chants, as part of the *soma yāga*.
Upaniṣad	(*upa* + *ni* + *ṣad* — just below, very near, to sit). Literally, "to sit closely and just below." The context in which a *guru* and disciple sit together, the former imparting wisdom to the latter.
uttama-adhikarī	The best among those who are competent for wisdom.
vairāgya	The sense of detachment towards everything of momentary pleasure.
vāsanā	The innate traits in every individual.
Vedānta	Literally, "the end of the Vedas" or "the end of knowledge." The wisdom texts appended to the four Vedas. These teach pure wisdom as against ritualism in the former parts of

	the Vedas, and this wisdom marks the end of all the quest for knowledge.
vidhi	The injunctions given in the Smṛti (see) category of Indian scriptures.
vidyā	Knowledge. That function of consciousness by which *Ātmā* is understood as the real and *anātmā* (non-self) as unreal.
vijñāna	In the ordinary sense, any branch of science. In the context of Vedānta, perceiving one Reality alone in every specific and minute element of experience.
viveka	The power to discriminate, particularly between the eternal and the transient.
vyāvahārika	The reality that has transactional value alone.
yakṣa	A mysterious being.
yoga	(From the root *yuj*). Each finding one's inseparable oneness with the one causal Reality, just as an ornament finds its oneness with gold.
	As a contemplative method of self- enquiry, the way of expressing an inexpressible reality by showing its two opposite sides and leaving the unitive meaning to be intuitively pereceived by the reader or seeker on his own. For example, attaining immortality and crossing over death are two expressions meaning the same. But these two expressions are opposite in nature. They have in between them a meaning that cannot be expressed as it is.
	Different systems of *yoga* have been developed in India, each giving emphasis to some particular pair joined together. Patañjali's system is known also as *Rāja-Yoga*. The names such as *Haṭha-Yoga, Karma-Yoga, Jñāna-Yoga, Bhakti-Yoga* are popular. Each of the eighteen chapters of *Bhagavad-Gītā* is also named a *yoga*. *Bhagavad-Gītā* itself claims to be a Yoga-Śāstra (textbook on the science of *yoga*).
yoga-buddhi	The awareness attained by the method of *yoga* (see).
yoga-rahasya	The secret of *yoga;* the dialectical secret.
yoga-śāstra	The science of *yoga;* the science of dialectics.
yogī	One who is adept in *yoga.*

Index